# Psychology of the Self
# and the Treatment
# of Narcissism

## About the Author

Richard D. Chessick, M.D., Ph.D., is Professor of Psychiatry at Northwestern University and Senior Attending Psychiatrist at Evanston Hospital. Dr. Chessick is the 1989 recipient of the American Society of Psychoanalytic Physicians' Sigmund Freud Award for outstanding contributions to psychiatry and psychoanalysis. He is a Fellow and a Trustee of the American Academy of Psychoanalysis, Life Fellow of the American Psychiatric Association and the American Orthopsychiatric Association, a Fellow of the Academy of Psychosomatic Medicine and the American Society for Adolescent Psychiatry, a corresponding member of the German Psychoanalytic Society, and a member of eighteen other professional societies. Dr. Chessick is on the editorial board of three major journals and has published more than 200 papers since 1953 in the fields of neurology, psychiatry, philosophy, and psychoanalysis. He is the author of *How Psychotherapy Heals, Why Psychotherapists Fail, Technique and Practice of Intensive Psychotherapy, Agonie: Diary of a Twentieth Century Man, Great Ideas in Psychotherapy, Intensive Psychotherapy of the Borderline Patient, Freud Teaches Psychotherapy, A Brief Introduction to the Genius of Nietzsche, Technique and Practice of Listening in Intensive Psychotherapy, What Constitutes the Patient in Psychotherapy,* and *A Dictionary for Psychotherapists: Dynamic Concepts in Psychotherapy.* Dr. Chessick is in the private practice of psychiatry in Evanston, Illinois.

# Psychology of the Self and the Treatment of Narcissism

*Richard D. Chessick, M.D., Ph.D.*

JASON ARONSON, INC.
*Northvale, New Jersey*
*London*

The author gratefully acknowledges permission to reprint excerpts from the following sources:

Basch, Michael Franz. *From Doing Psychotherapy.* Copyright © 1981 by Basic Books, Inc. Reprinted by permission of the publisher.

Goldberg, A. *The Psychology of the Self: A Casebook.* Reprinted by permission of International Universities Press, Inc. Copyright © 1978 by International Universities Press, Inc.

Goldberg, A. *Advances in Self Psychology.* Reprinted by permission of International Universities Press, Inc. Copyright © 1980 by International Universities Press, Inc.

Kohut, H. *The Analysis of the Self.* Reprinted by permission of International Universities Press, Inc. Copyright © 1971 by International Universities Press, Inc.

Kohut, H. *The Restoration of the Self.* Reprinted by permission of International Universities Press, Inc. Copyright © 1977 by International Universities Press, Inc.

Kohut, H. *The Search for the Self.* Reprinted by permission of International Universities Press, Inc. Copyright © 1978 by International Universities Press, Inc.

Kohut, H. *How Does Analysis Cure?* Copyright © 1984 by The University of Chicago Press, Inc. Reprinted by permission of the publisher.

Lichtenberg, J., and Kaplan, S. *Reflections on Self Psychology.* Copyright © 1983 by The Analytic Press. Reprinted by permission of the authors.

**Library of Congress Cataloging-in-Publication Data**

Chessick, Richard D., 1931-
  Psychology of the self and the treatment of narcissism.

  Includes bibliographies and index.
    1. Narcissism—Treatment.   2. Self.   3. Kohut, Heinz.   4. Psychoanalysis.   I. Title.
[DNLM: 1. Kohut, Heinz.   2. Ego.   3. Narcissism.   4. Psychoanalysis.   5. Psychotherapy.
WM 460.5.E3 C524p]
RC553.N36C48   1986      616.85′82      85-15621
ISBN 0-87668-745-1 (hardcover)
ISBN 0-87668-171-2 (softcover)

Manufactured in the United States of America. Jason Aronson Inc. offers books and cassettes. For information and catalog write to Jason Aronson Inc., 230 Livingston Street, Northvale, New Jersey 07647.

*To my colleagues
engaged in the practice of psychoanalytic psychotherapy
and to my friends everywhere
who work for the causes of empathy and peace*

# Contents

___

# Preface

This book presents and discusses the emerging "psychology of the self" and focuses on the clinical problem of narcissism. Kohut's orientation is placed into historical perspective and compared and contrasted with other views, the clinical problems it is meant to help understand are described, and the evolution of the psychology of the self as contained in the work of Kohut and his followers is explained. Two psychology of the self systems were developed; the earlier is to some degree compatible with standard psychoanalytic theory, while the later is at best complementary to Freud's psychoanalysis. Clinical application of these theories in psychoanalysis and psychoanalytic psychotherapy are reviewed, criticisms of the psychology of the self described, and unresolved issues indicated.

In breaking new ground, Kohut sometimes (especially in his earlier work) writes with an obscurity worthy of Heidegger, but once the therapist follows Kohut's reasonable request to withhold judgment and try to become immersed in the psychology of the self, neither the therapist nor the therapist's approach to patients will ever be the same. This is true regardless of one's acceptance or rejection of the theoretical conceptions offered to explain the experience-near phenomena highlighted by the psychology of the self. Any psychotherapist who studies this new approach carefully will gain important new ideas which aid in understanding clinical material, and insights that will influence his or her personal attitudes toward patients, and perhaps toward all human beings, as Kohut hoped. Even the therapist's orientation to other disciplines and their practitioners and the therapist's considerations about world social problems may be deepened and altered. Above all, the importance and powerful impact of the psychology of the self carries renewed hope and excitement about the continued clinical application of psychoanalytic psychotherapy to patients previously baffling and discouraging, and hope for the resolution of situations that previously would have resulted in stalemate or failure.

I am not a "disciple" of Kohut and this is not an "official" explication of self psychology. My approach to the subject has been in the spirit, as Kohut would describe it, of *sine ira et studio*. Those readers who are not familiar with the philosophical and psychological concepts that form the basis of psychoanalysis are advised to turn first to my books on Nietzsche (1983) and Freud (1980).

# Acknowledgments

The kindness, support, and contribution of many individuals made this book possible. My patients in psychoanalytic psychotherapy taught me the most and brought me back repeatedly to the clinical material, causing me to pause, reflect, and mature as a therapist and an individual. My colleagues in the German Psychoanalytic Society, Hebrew University of Jerusalem, Hawaii Psychiatric Society, University of Hawaii, Indiana Psychiatric Society, and the Illinois Psychiatric Society offered numerous helpful comments during my public presentations of some of this material. The same was true of my colleagues during two three-day presentations to the Seattle Chapter of the American Psychiatric Association and Seattle Psychoanalytic Institute, which were made possible by the vigor of Dr. Bryce McMurry. I also greatly benefited from discussions with colleagues during numerous presentations to various groups and institutions in the Chicago area.

I learned much from teaching courses on the subject of this book to residents and other mental health professionals in the Department of Psychiatry at Northwestern University at the Evanston Hospital branch of that department. Dr. Harold Visotsky, Chairman of the Department of Psychiatry at Northwestern University, and the late

Dr. Donald Greaves, Chairman of the Department of Psychiatry at Evanston Hospital, always supported my teaching and presentations, as did Dr. Leon Diamond and Dr. Ira Sloan, Directors of Residency Training at these two institutions during that time.

I also learned a great deal from my philosophy major and graduate students in philosophy, as well as from the philosophy faculty at the Loyola University of Chicago, where my teaching and presentations of some sections of this book were made possible by the Chairman of the Department of Philosophy at that time, Fr. Robert Harvanek. He showed infinite patience in putting up with the many irritating changes in scheduling necessitated by national and international trips and by concurrent presentations at two universities. I am deeply grateful to all of these prominent individuals for their kindness, as well as to the late Dr. Joel Handler, my teacher and friend for 30 years, who made many thoughtful and helpful comments.

I appreciate the encouragement received from Dr. Jason Aronson and the editorial review of my manuscript by Ms. Joan Langs, Ms. Melinda Wirkus, and Ms. Nancy Palubniak. Ms. Wanda Sauerman worked diligently on transcribing and typing the many versions of the manuscript. The book could not have been written without the long hours of devoted work and dedicated effort of my administrative assistant, Ms. Elizabeth Grudzien, to whom I owe a special expression of gratitude. And behind all the effort and turmoil was the always steadying presence of my ever tolerant and loving wife, Marcia. Thank you.

*Richard D. Chessick, M.D., Ph.D.*
*Evanston, Illinois*

*Classical theory cannot illuminate the essence of fractured, enfeebled, discontinuous human existence: it cannot explain the essence of the schizophrenic's fragmentation, the struggle of the patient who suffers from a narcissistic personality disorder to reassemble himself, the despair — the guiltless despair, I stress — of those who in late middle age discover that the basic patterns of their self as laid down in their nuclear ambitions and ideals have not been realized. Dynamic-structural metapsychology does not do justice to these problems of man, cannot encompass the problems of Tragic Man.*

Heinz Kohut, *The Restoration of the Self*

*Accustom yourself to give careful attention to what others are saying, and try your best to enter into the mind of the speaker.*

Marcus Aurelius, *Meditations*

# Section I

# NARCISSISM

# Chapter 1

─═══

# Narcissistic and Borderline Personality Disorders

Narcissus was a Thespian, the son of the nymph Leiriope, whom the River God Cephisus had once encircled with the windings of his streams and ravished. The famous seer Teiresias told Leiriope, "Narcissus will live to a ripe old age provided that he never knows himself."

Narcissus had a stubborn pride in his own beauty. By the time he reached the age of 16, so the myth goes, his path was strewn with heartlessly rejected lovers of both sexes. Among these lovers was the nymph Echo who could no longer use her voice except in foolish repetition of another's shout, her punishment for having kept Hera entertained with long stories while Zeus's concubines evaded her jealous eye and escaped.

One day when Narcissus went out to the woods, Echo stealthily followed him, longing to address him, but unable to speak first. At last Narcissus, finding that he had strayed away from his friends shouted, "Is anyone here?" "Here," Echo answered, and soon she joyfully rushed from her hiding place to embrace Narcissus but he shook her off roughly and ran away; "I will die before you ever lie with me," he cried. "Lie with me!" Echo pleaded. But Narcissus had gone and she spent the rest of her life pining away for love of him until only her voice remained. This story is reported by Ovid in the *Metamorphoses*.

Several classical authors also tell the story of how Ameineus, the most insistent suitor of Narcissus, was sent a sword by Narcissus. Ameineus took this and killed himself on Narcissus' threshold, calling on the gods to avenge his death. Artemis heard the plea and made Narcissus fall in love though denying him love's consummation. In Thespia he came upon a spring, clear as silver, and casting himself down near it, exhausted, to drink, he fell in love with his reflection. At first he tried to embrace and kiss the beautiful boy who confronted him but presently recognized himself and lay gazing enraptured into the pool, hour after hour.

The myth continues significantly: Although grief was destroying him as he longed to possess, *yet he rejoiced in his torments knowing that his other self would remain true to him, whatever happened.* Echo grieved with him and sympathetically responded, "Alas, alas," as he plunged a dagger in his breast and expired. His blood soaked the earth and up sprang the white narcissus flower from which came the well-known classical narcotic, Narcissus oil.

In this timeless Greek myth as paraphrased by Graves (1955, pp. 286–288) we see the manifestation of Narcissus' stubborn pride in his own beauty, the unempathic hostile and arrogant behavior toward others, the primary preoccupation of Narcissus that his other self, his mirroring selfobject,* always remain true to him whatever happens, and the condensing of death, sleep, narcosis, and peace.

## Narcissism

Ellis (1898) first used this myth to illustrate a psychological state in reporting a case of male autoeroticism; the term "narcissistic" was first used by Freud in a 1910 footnote to *Three Essays on the Theory of Sexuality* (Freud 1905). Freud's essay introduced the concept of narcissism into the psychiatric literature; the history of the development of this concept into the nosological entity called "narcissistic personality disorder" is carefully presented by Akhtar and Thomson

---

*Following Kohut's (1984) later writing, I will use the unhyphenated term selfobject throughout, but only when it is employed in his special sense of the term, as will be explained in Part II.

(1982). These authors remind us that Rank wrote the first psycho-analytic paper on narcissism in 1911 and that Freud's paper on narcissism was published in 1914. In 1925, Waelder presented the description of a "narcissistic personality" and, since that time, the term narcissism was used with an astonishing variety of meanings, ranging from a sexual perversion to a concentration of psychological interest upon the self (Moore and Fine 1967).

Just as the term narcissism has been used in many ways, the phrase narcissistic pathology has been used by various authors to shade over certain neuroses, psychoses, borderline conditions, and personality disorders. Freud stamped these disorders with an implication of poor prognosis for psychoanalytic psychotherapy when he distinguished them from the transference neuroses.

A more precise definition of the problem was offered in a classical paper by Reich (1960, also see Chapter 3 of this book), who conceived of narcissism as being founded on a pathological form of the regulation of self-esteem, a problem that may be found in both neurotic and psychotic individuals who "have exaggerated, unrealistic — i.e., infantile — inner yardsticks" and constantly seek to be the object of admiring attention "as a means to undo feelings of inferiority."

It is fascinating to study the evolution of the concept of narcissism and narcissistic pathology from the phenomenological and experience-near mythological descriptions of the Greeks to the psychodynamic and experience-distant conflict interpretations used to explain the condition by Freudian and post-Freudian psychoanalysts. Built into this situation is the eventual divergence of Kohut's contributions and his psychology of the self from the mainstream of Freudian conflict interpretation.

Freudian psychoanalysis and the subsequent North American ego psychology school, founded on the work of Hartmann, Erikson, Rappaport and others after the Second World War and developed well into the 1960's, take as their basis an empirical scientific orientation founded on a positivist philosophy that was considered the hope of the world at the turn of the twentieth century. Human mentation and behavior are visualized as the outcome of conflicting vector forces much in the manner of classical physics, and are amenable to empirical dissection in the consulting room by the properly trained psychoanalyst-observer who takes a neutral and equidistant position with respect to the id, ego, and superego of the patient.

Kohut's psychology of the self, regardless of its later evolution, was first envisioned as built on data gathered by what he calls the method of empathy or vicarious introspection. Its experience-near emphasis focuses on the patient's sense of self, utilizing wholistic concepts at least closer to the continental philosophical movements of phenomenology and hermeneutics than concepts such as Freud's hydrodynamic model (Peterfreund 1971), based on the usual positivistic naive nineteenth century approach to the "human sciences." It is not unreasonable to argue at this point, as some psychoanalysts do, that Kohut's psychology of the self, when contrasted with Freud's psychoanalysis and the subsequent North American ego psychology school of psychoanalysis, presents a system fundamentally different in its philosophical presuppositions, moral assumptions, experience-distant hypotheses, and theoretical constructs, and, most recently (Kohut 1984), in its theory of cure, although the extent of this difference remains an unresolved issue.

Kohut (1984), on the other hand, clearly asserts that his work is "squarely in the center of the analytic tradition" [and] "in the mainstream of the development of psychoanalytic thought" (p. 95), and that there is a "palpable" continuity between ego psychology and self-psychology. The differences from traditional psychoanalysis, he says are in the explanations provided for the process of cure and "the theories that, at least in some instances, inform the analyst's interpretations" (p. 104). He concludes, "self psychology does not advocate a change in the essence of psychoanalytic technique" (p. 208) and it does not introduce "parameters" (Eissler 1953).

Kernberg (1975, 1976, 1980) presents another popular and comprehensive theoretical system opposed to the psychology of the self in attempting to explain the phenomena subsumed under narcissism. Kernberg's system has significantly modified the theories of Melanie Klein into a form more acceptable to American scientific thinking. The "object relations theory" of Kernberg has become in the United States the principal alternative to self psychology in the area of the understanding, explanation, and treatment of narcissistic and borderline personality disorders (see Chapter 5, this volume).

Although Kernberg claims there is no fundamental difference between his object relations theory and the American ego psychology school, there is much disagreement on this subject which is not pertinent to the focus of the present book; *in nunce* the disagreement on premises between Kernberg and the ego psychology school and much of the resulting controversy are, in essence, outgrowths of the earlier disagreement in principles between the theories of Melanie Klein and Anna Freud.

However, it is possible, as the British school of psychoanalysis has demonstrated, for the followers of Melanie Klein and Anna Freud to remain within the same psychoanalytic school although they may differ on the nature of the conflicts involved and on the origin of the drives with which they feel every individual must contend. Both Anna Freud and Klein agreed that, fundamentally, the eventual cure of the patient would come about by the psychoanalytic working through of unconscious conflicts that remain from the various unsatisfactorily traversed eras of psychosexual development in childhood. At the center of this set of conflicts lies the Oedipus complex, believed by Freud to be the nucleus of all psychoneuroses; without the successful working through of the increased outpouring of sexual and aggressive drives that are postulated by Freud to emerge between the ages of, approximately, 4–6 in every human being, mental health, the Kleinians and Freudians agree, would be unattainable. This is true even though the Kleinians place the origin of the Oedipus complex in infancy and view its resolution somewhat differently.

## Narcissistic Personality Disorder

Let us take a general look at the phenomena subsumed under the label narcissism and at some of the agreements and disagreements on a phenomenological and explanatory level among these various theoretical orientations. A brief description of the narcissistic personality is presented in DSM-III (Spitzer 1980, pp. 315–317) which simply represents the commonsensible characterization of people whom we usually label as narcissistic, people who manifest a sense of self-importance with an exhibitionistic need for attention and admiration, feelings of entitlement, lack of empathy for others, and interpersonal exploitativeness.

Although there is nothing wrong with this description, it emphasizes the disorder aspect so that the individual described in DSM-III would clearly be somebody that no one could like, an individual who is obviously maladapted and headed for serious trouble in life. This is a reflection of the philosophy of DSM-III, which tries to describe psychiatric disorders as diseases in order to justify their need for medical attention and, in contrast to DSM-II, backs away from the concept of a continuum between normal behavior and mental disorders in order to avoid the common accusation that psychiatrists simply treat difficulties in living and minor exaggerations in people's personalities.

Both Kernberg and Kohut agree that patients with narcissistic personalities may not appear disturbed in their surface behavior and may function well socially and show good impulse control. Their great need to be loved and admired by others, their inflated concept of themselves, their shallow emotional life, and their minimal or lack of empathy for the feelings of others may only manifest itself on careful examination. These individuals may attain high offices and even be elected President of the United States, thus raising the issue of "the culture of narcissism" and the putative increased prevalence of narcissism and narcissistic disorders at the end of the twentieth century. Both of these issues will be discussed in the next chapter.

A more careful study of narcissistic individuals shows that, when they are not getting the tribute of other people or immersing themselves either in grandiose fantasies or the pursuit of the actualization of these fantasies, they do not enjoy life. They are bored and restless. They represent the ideal American consumer, always attempting to acquire something that simultaneously will exhibit their wealth, power, or sexual prowess in order to pass the time.

These people may overtly or covertly manifest exploitative and parasitic relations with other people and a chronic intense envy of others whom they imagine have what they want and enjoy in life. At worst, they are haughty, grandiose, and controlling, any of which they may show only privately in their relations with others or – to the common misfortune – only when they reach positions of power.

Narcissistic individuals cannot come to terms with old age and cannot accept the inevitable changes of aging as they watch the younger generation exhibit beauty and vigor. Their middle years are therefore often characterized by a so-called crisis filled with rage, depression, and sometimes strange impulsive behavior. Their selection of a hero to admire or depend upon, often is simply an extension of themselves or of their ideal, and they may suddenly transfer their feelings from one hero to the other.

This constitutes a clinical warning to psychotherapists, for at any time the idealized therapist may suddenly be dropped for even a slight frustration, regardless of how much praise the patient may have heaped upon the therapist up to that point. All authors agree that narcissists cannot experience a therapist as an independent person or relate to the therapist realistically, although therapists disagree as to the reasons for this. They also agree that the treatment of these individuals is a long one, and stressful for the therapist (Abraham 1919).

As in the myth of Narcissus, narcissistic individuals often have talents in childhood that arouse admiration; they are frequently considered to be children who have great promise. Often they were pivotal in their families — the only child, the brilliant child, "the genius" — and thus carried the burden of fulfilling family expectations. Yet these individuals often show surprisingly banal accomplishments as adults except for that rare individual, the successful narcissist. This sort of person, by dint of superior talents and luck, is enabled to realize grandiose expectations but then gets in trouble in attempting to actualize ever-increasing levels of grandiosity. The classical example of this is Lyndon Johnson getting up in the middle of the night to decide on bombing sites in Viet Nam. Johnson, 9,000 miles away from the war, was unable to accept the shattering of his hopes to be a great president (Tuchman 1984).

For Kernberg (1975, p. 248), psychoanalysis is the treatment of choice for narcissistic personality disorders except for those narcissistic patients that he characterizes as functioning on a borderline level. He defines the latter group as showing multiple symptoms, nonspecific manifestations of ego weakness (poor impulse control, lack of anxiety tolerance, impaired reality testing, and lack of sublimation), regression to primary process thinking, and constant relentless rage and depreciation of the therapist, especially if rage is early and open. "A more supportive treatment approach seems best for this group" (p. 249). Kohut would not define such patients as narcissistic personality disorders at all, as we shall see, whereas Giovacchini (1979) is inclined to recommend formal psychoanalysis for all such patients.

A few variants of the narcissistic personality disorder might illustrate the numerous ways in which this situation has been described. For example, Finlay-Jones (1983) discussed a syndrome called *acedia*, known since the fourth century A.D. Sloth, or acedia, was labelled as one of the "seven deadly sins" (Fairlie 1977) and meant a state of dejection giving rise to torpor of mind and spirit, sluggishness of will, despair, and desirelessness. This is not a DSM-III clinical depression and represents rather a disgust with life in general, as Finlay-Jones calls it, manifested by a mood of sadness, an inability to do anything useful, and an anhedonia, or insensitivity to pain and pleasure. He blames this condition on the lack of meaningful work and would thus be inclined to rename it a "suburban neurosis."

Solberg (1984) describes "lassitude" as a similar problem of growing proportions and "its synonyms (fatigue, weariness, tiredness, or listlessness) represent some of the most common complaints in primary care" (p. 3272). However, Solberg relates the psychological causes of lassitude more to "depression" without distinguishing the characteristic "empty" depression of the narcissistic middle-aged patients among, for example, the "1,050 forty-year old Danes" in a sample that showed a very high prevalence (41 percent of the women and 25 percent of the men) who felt "tired at present."

Tartakoff (1966) described the "Nobel Prize complex" involving people who are intellectually gifted and preoccupied with the pursuit of applause, wealth, power, or social prestige and recognition. She begins with a discussion of relatively successful middle-aged individuals with characterological problems rather than crippling neuroses who have applied for psychoanalytic treatment. These individuals, for the most part, appear "healthy" from the sociological point of view. Except for one subgroup, their unifying outlook on life was manifested by "an optimistic anticipation that their virtues, their talents, or their achievements would be rewarded by success if they took appropriate steps to work toward this goal" (p. 225), in this case the goal of completing psychoanalysis successfully. This expectation of recognition for achievement constitutes an initial resistance in these cases.

The subgroup of middle-aged professionals Tartakoff isolates are those who were motivated to seek psychoanalytic treatment by an intense feeling of disillusionment with life based on their conviction that they had neither fulfilled their "promise" nor received the objective acclaim to which they aspired. In this group, depressions, anxiety attacks under stress, and psychosomatic symptoms were not uncommon.

Related especially to this subgroup are intellectually or artistically gifted patients who have often achieved a great deal but for whom "objective achievement becomes overshadowed and, often, inhibited by a preoccupation with acclaim" (p. 237). In her study of these achievers, who are also marked by hypersensitivity to minor disappointments in later life, "in particular to lack of recognition" (p. 237), Tartakoff introduces a new nosological entity, the Nobel Prize Complex. "All or nothing" is its goal and it rests on the fantasy of being powerful and special with the childhood described above for the typical narcissistic personality. Tartakoff points out that these patients are neither borderline nor psychotic. On the whole, they are well integrated and they try to express the American dream which Tartakoff describes as "a narcissistic fantasy which has become institutionalized" (p. 238). She concludes:

> Our social structure continues to reinforce narcissistically oriented attitudes throughout adolescence and into adulthood. It does so without adequate consideration for the limited institutional means of fulfilling such wishes. Moreover, preoccupation with admiration and acclaim may lead to an inhibition of the individual's capacity to function. As a consequence, dissatisfaction and disillusionment may ensue when life does not fulfill the infantile "promise." (p. 249).

Murphy (1973) focuses on the narcissistic therapist, whom he describes in terms that might be included in DSM-III. Therapists such as these look for fast results, are hypersensitive to statements made about themselves but insensitive to the feelings of their patients, and need admiration and love. Consequently, they mishandle transference and countertransference. They cannot deal with idealization, punish negative transference by techniques such as scolding, sarcasm, or premature termination, ward off anxiety over their own passivity by constant activity and overaggressiveness with patients, misuse patients, considerably overcharge them, and finally, are seduceable and manipulable.

## Relation of the Narcissistic and Borderline Personality Disorders

The existence of a continuum between narcissistic personality disorders and borderline patients remains hotly debated. Adler (1981) tries to establish such a continuum which runs from the patient with a stable narcissistic personality disorder to the borderline patient capable of a serious regression, using "lines" that Adler describes as cohesiveness of the self, self-object transference stability, and the achievement of mature aloneness. Kernberg (1975) delineates "higher" and "lower" levels of ego functioning on which he attempts to differentiate between borderline and narcissistic personality disorders, but there is nothing in his descriptions that would theoretically preclude placing patients on a continuum based on the extent to which they use the higher and lower levels. Kernberg characterizes the borderline personality organization as marked by identity diffusion based on pathology of internalized object relations and reflected in lack of integration of the self-concept and of the concept of significant others. The borderline personality is typified by the predominance of primitive defensive operations centering around the mechanism of splitting, which occurs, however, in the presence of relatively well-maintained reality testing. This borderline personality organization, according to Kernberg, includes a spectrum of severe types of personality disorders among which are the borderline personality disorder described in DSM-III, the narcissistic personality disorder of DSM-III, and to some extent the schizoid, paranoid, and hypomanic personalities.

The problem of reaching agreement and definition about the borderline patient or borderline personality disorder is much greater than the situation involving narcissistic personalities (see Chessick 1966–1984b). A neurosis implies that the patient has traversed the pregenital stages of personality development fairly well and has formed a relatively well-functioning ego with a solid repression barrier and a strong superego. The assessment of the strength of the ego and its functioning has been given (Chessick 1974, 1977), described in greater detail by DeWald (1964) and in complete metapsychological detail by Kernberg (1976). The diagnosis of a neurosis implies that the therapist has assessed the ego functioning of the patient and finds it to be relatively strong and solid, employing for the most part so-called classical higher defenses of repression with related mechanisms that presume and require consolidation of the tripartite intrapsychic structure or, in Kohut's terminology, a cohesive sense of self.

Authorities disagree as to whether a sharp distinction ought to be made between the borderline patient and many character disorders. DSM-III (Spitzer 1980) recognizes this disagreement and places borderline patients under personality disorders, noting the presence of a "cluster" of "dramatic, emotional or erratic" personality disorders: histrionic, narcissistic, antisocial, and borderline. DSM-III continues, "Frequently this disorder is accompanied by many features of other Personality Disorders such as Schizotypal" [and here I would add the Paranoid and Schizoid from their 'odd or eccentric' cluster] "Histrionic, Narcissistic, and Antisocial Personality Disorders" (p. 322).

## *Diagnosis of Borderline Personality Disorder*

In this confusion one may try to make a diagnostic distinction again by reference to the ego as it manifests itself in the kind of acting out and reality testing employed by the patient. I prefer to maintain the diagnostic difference between borderline patient and character disorder on the descriptive criterion that, in character disorder, one set of well-known characterologic features consistently predominates the clinical picture in a relatively rigid and all-pervasive way; thus, we have the obsessive-compulsive character, the narcissistic character, the hysterical character, and so forth. The more extreme forms of these disorders, as adaptation becomes increasingly hampered, shade off into the disorders of the borderline patients, but there are certain typical descriptive clinical features of the borderline patient that in my opinion (1974b, 1983a), when they are present, greatly aid in the diagnosis.

Any variety of neurotic or quasi-psychotic, psychosomatic or sociopathic symptoms, in any combination or degree of severity, may be part of the initial presenting complaint. A bizarre combination of such symptoms may cut across the standard nosology, or the relative preponderance of any symptom group changes or shifts frequently. Vagueness of complaint or even a bland, amazingly smooth or occasionally socially successful personality may be encountered. Careful investigation reveals a poverty of genuine emotional relationships well hidden behind even an attractive and personable social facade. The borderline patient may present either a chaotic or stormy series of relationships with a variety of people or a bland and superficial, but relatively stable, set of relationships. In both cases a lack of deep emotional investment in any other person may be carefully — consciously or unconsciously — concealed.

The capacity for reality testing and ability to function in work and social situations are not as catastrophically impaired in borderline patients as in schizophrenics although the degree of functioning may vary periodically and may be quite poor. On the whole, these patients are able to maintain themselves, sometimes raise families, and otherwise fit more or less into society. They do not present as isolated drifters, chronic hospital or long-term person cases, totally antisocial personalities, or chronic addicts. They have, however, often tried everything and may present a variety of sexual deviations, but they are not functionally paralyzed for very long periods of time by these deviations or by their various symptoms or anxieties. Border-line patients suffer from a relatively stable and enduring condition. They may experience what appear to be transient psychotic episodes either for no apparent reason or as a result of stress, alcohol, drugs, or improper psychotherapy, but they do not remain psychotic for long. They quickly reintegrate, often learning what will help them to do so and administering a self-remedy.

This description is meant to supplement, not to replace, the DSM-III delineation (with which I agree) in order to further sharpen the diagnostic criteria. Any practicing psychotherapist can attest that these patients are commonly found and pose extremely difficult ther-apeutic problems because of the unpredictable fluctuations in their ego state and the intensity of the emotional impact they have on the therapist. Thus the debate in the literature does not address the real issue. The question ought not to be whether there are borderline pa-tients – which there certainly are – but rather whether there exists a pure metapsychological formulation that identifies the borderline patient as a distinct, different metapsychological entity from other patients. I believe, however, that "borderline patient" is primarily a clinical and practical diagnosis (Grinker and Werbel 1977) rather than an identification of an autonomous disorder. My views are closer to those of Kohut (see Chapter 11) and the Kris study group (Abend et al. 1983). The latter (pp. 19–20) presents the conclusion that "the borderline diagnosis is no more than a broad loose category of char-acter pathology and not a clear diagnostic entity with specific con-flicts, defenses, and developmental problems" (p. 237).

Meissner (1978) points out that the continuum concept that I have employed is "adhered to by analytic thinkers with a basically ego-psy-chological orientation." Criticizing Kernberg's insistence that "split-ting" is the characteristic defensive mechanism of the borderline per-sonality, Meissner states:

> It is not at all clear that the splitting mechanism adequately distinguishes the borderline from more primitive schizophrenic entities, nor is his [Kernberg's] argument that the borderline condition is satisfactorily dis-tinguished from the neuroses on this same basis beyond question. It may be that splitting can be found in many neurotics just as repression may be found in many borderline cases. (p. 304)

Meissner (1978a) agrees with my main objection to Kernberg's theory, seriously questioning "the extent to which [adult] defensive defects can be read back from a more differentiated and evolved state of intrapsychic organization to early primitive developmental levels." He concludes that it is "too simplistic or 'neat' to be able to ascribe the multiple impairments found in borderline pathology to a single type of ego defect." He continues:

> We need to think of multiple deviations in many areas of ego function-ing as possibly operating on a different level of disturbance in each area. Such ego functions, which may be subject to a series of gradation of im-pairments or levels of functioning, may also be subject to a partial re-versibility in their level of integration of functioning which is particularly labile in borderline pathology. (p. 578)

Following Sadow (1969), we can devise a scheme using the central role of the ego as the axis of a continuum along which are located the psychoses, borderline states, transference neuroses, and conflict-free capacities. Movement along this axis is a regressive or a progres-sive shift that could take place, for example, due to successful psy-chotherapy, the vicissitudes of life, and organic states. Borderline patients have an amazing and tremendous range and flexibility of movement along the ego axis. Therefore, we must study the ego's levels of defenses for "higher" or "lower," as Kernberg (1975) sug-gests, and also evaluate the ego's capacity for motility along the ego axis in making the diagnosis of borderline patient. Many therapists have been tricked into a pessimistic or hopeless prognosis for treat-ment of borderline patients because they observed these patients dur-ing a period when they were temporarily residing in the regressed area of the ego axis.

For example, after the therapist's two-week vacation, a male pa-tient reports the following dream:

> I'm looking over a beautiful pond, sun, trees. A girl there is fly-casting but gets the line knotted up and asks me to help; I am the hero in this dream.
>
> I'm at your office, but [contrary to the patient's actual complaint that it is too small] in the dream it is impressive, extensive, with a con-ference room and a secretary. However, there is a hole in the floor and workmen are there fixing or installing something. I am impressed with all the cables and electric wires hidden in the floor, walls, and ceiling. These are just for the ordinary purposes, not dangerous, not recording devices, etc., just awe-inspiring apparatus.

As part of a project, I am to describe three kinds of men who need love.

Self psychologists might view this dream as an example of incipient fragmentation along with some grandiosity, and as a reaction to loss of the therapist due to a vacation. If it progressed further, I would expect an influencing-machine type of delusion, in which case the fragmented patient would show a paranoid psychotic core. The dream illustrates the apparent gradation or continuum between the borderline and the paranoid psychotic. Note the incipient idealizing transference in making my office more godlike. Traditional psychoanalysts might stress the ending of the dream and view the paranoid elements as defensive against homosexual yearnings.

This same patient, a minister, in associating to the dream remembers lying on the floor of the living room as a child in his sombre, gloomy, religious home in the position of Christ on the cross and wondering how it was to be crucified and to ascend to God. As an adult, the patient felt many times "as if" he were being crucified but always used this metaphorically. Also, he often wished he were Jesus or God. But he never actually thought that he *was* God or Jesus. Thus, under pressure, the yearning to fuse with the idealized parent imago (Kohut 1971) shows itself but fragmentation never becomes so complete that delusion formation becomes necessary; therefore, the patient can function successfully as a minister.

Since this book is not primarily about the borderline personality disorder, I will discuss further contributions to the understanding of that disorder at length only when they emanate from the psychology of the self. For a more extensive discussion of the borderline personality disorder, see *Intensive Psychotherapy of the Borderline Patient* (Chessick 1977) and my subsequent papers (1978, 1979, 1982, 1983a) on the subject. Also valuable is Meissner's (1984) *The Borderline Spectrum*, Chapters 1–6.

## Aspects of Narcissistic Style

Akhtar and Thomson (1982) have reviewed a number of authors who have contributed ideas about the narcissistic personality disorder. Bach (1975, 1977, 1977a) has made many phenomenologic contributions, describing what he calls "the narcissistic state of consciousness."

He emphasizes the way in which narcissistic individuals use language in an autocentric manner rather than for communication, their typical fruitless pseudoactivity and, above all, the extreme dependence of their mood regulation on external circumstances. In his description of the depression following a narcissistic loss, Bach points out that this depression has apathy and shame as its primary qualities rather than guilt and, thus, focuses on a matter that is discussed at length by Kohut in his distinction between Tragic Man and Guilty Man.

Modell (1976) described what he called the initial cocoon phase in the psychoanalytic treatment of narcissistic individuals who live by themselves in a glorious but lonely way. This formulation follows from the work of Winnicott (1953), who stressed the trauma that narcissistic individuals experienced as children when their sense of self was developing. Winnicott stated that deficient maternal empathy during childhood necessitated the establishment of a precocious and vulnerable sense of autonomy supported by fantasies of omnipotence and around which the grandiose self develops (Chessick 1977a). For this and other reasons Kohut is said to have been strongly influenced by the work of Winnicott.

Our preliminary discussion of narcissism would not be complete unless we pointed out the intimate relationships that are known to exist (since the writing of Freud at least) among falling in love, romance, creativity, and narcissism. For example, some authors such as Gediman (1975) call attention to the distinction between loving— conceived as a rational, more durable, mature, genital object relationship—and being in love—a transitory state often experienced as an irrational, stormy, grand passion. These two states, Gediman points out, can be understood according to Kohut's position of a separate developmental line for narcissism which is never outgrown but rather transformed. Kohut (1966) tells us that, for the average individual, intense idealization, a transitional point in the development of narcissistic libido, survives only in the state of being in love, although he adds that gifted individuals idealize and despair about their work as well.

Thus any discussion of narcissism will have to carry with it some insights on states of being in love and states of creativity. Furthermore, Bak (1973) points out that "being in love" is often preceded by separation or by an important object loss—real, imaginary, or threatened—"or by one of the numerous losses of object representations that lead to melancholia." He adds:

To these precipitating causes I might add damage to the self-image and lack of fulfillment of strivings of the ideal-ego which indirectly lead to the threat of object loss. But whereas in melancholia the lost object is regained by identification, or, as Freud put it, "love escapes extinction" by regressing to narcissism, the person who suffers from "being in love" finds a substitute object; the loss is undone and the object is replaced or resurrected. (p. 1)

Bak states that sometimes when another love object cannot be substituted, there may be a turning towards severe depression and suicide, as perhaps most dramatically illustrated in Goethe's (1774) *The Sufferings of Young Werther*. We shall turn again shortly to the subject of love when we review the contributions of Freud to the study of narcissism.

# Chapter 2

## Narcissism in Our Culture

Cooper (Lichtenberg and Kaplan 1983) points out that psychoanalysts, beginning perhaps with Glover, who discussed narcissism as early as the 1930s, have claimed that there has been a
change in the human condition:

> They say that the classical neurotic patient seen by Freud has gradual-
> ly disappeared, to be replaced by types of severe character pathology,
> especially the narcissistic character, with a consequent diminution of
> analytic effectiveness and a lengthening of the analyses. . . . In recent
> years everyone from Spiro Agnew to Christopher Lasch has argued that
> we are living in an age of narcissism, surrounded by the characterologic
> fallout of postindustrial society and the cultural decline of the West. (pp.
> 28–29)

Cooper reports that "much of our literature since that time has
concerned our need to understand that change, to reconcile it with
our analytic theories, and to devise effective psychoanalytic treatment techniques in response to it" (p. 29). There is by no means
general agreement on any of these statements. Since there have been
no controlled or careful empirical studies of the matter, we do not
have good evidence either for or against the idea that there has been

a predominant change in the actual type of patient appearing in the consulting room of psychoanalytically oriented psychotherapists and psychoanalysts. But we do have considerable indication that the diagnosis being placed on these patients has shifted substantially from terms denoting the classical neurotic disorders to terms describing DSM-III character or personality disorders.

## "The Culture Of Narcissism"

A persuasive proponent of the notion that a new narcissistic personality is becoming predominant in our culture is Christopher Lasch, author of *The Culture of Narcissism* (1978). This book contains misunderstandings and misappropriations of some of the concepts of Kohut and Kernberg. However, Lasch's work aids in understanding the kind of problems that the psychology of the self is able to address and for which it especially claims to be a better explanatory paradigm than classical Freudian conflict or drive psychology.

Lasch emphasizes the current international malaise, which he connects with loss of the capacity and the will to confront the difficulties currently threatening to overwhelm current bourgeois society. He considers the sciences to be of no help with this problem and states that academic psychology in the face of it "retreats from the challenge of Freud into the measurement of trivia." He describes the new narcissist, similar to what Kohut has described as Tragic Man. In Lasch's terms, the narcissist is haunted not by guilt but by anxiety and seeks not to inflict his own certainties on others but to find a meaning in life: "He lives in a state of restless, perpetually unsatisfied desire" (p. xvi).

Lasch defines a narcissistic society as one that gives increasing prominence and encouragement to narcissistic traits with a corresponding cultural devaluation of the past. It is Lasch's general thesis that a narcissistic society produces narcissistic personalities which, in turn, produce more of a narcissistic society, with an implication that the past was "better" although it is hopeless to believe it can be regained. Lasch's Marxist-style interpretation of history leads him to see the development of our narcissistic society as the inevitable end stage of capitalism.

Lasch describes the narcissistic individual in current American "narcissistic" society as a person who lives for the moment, has a loss of historical continuity, needs others to validate self-esteem, and experiences the world as a mirror. He describes twentieth century peoples as "consumed with rage" (p. 11). There are, however, no empirical data offered to support these generalizations.

In a narcissistic society "therapy" establishes itself as the successor both to rugged individualism and to religion. Lasch describes the post-Freudian therapies, their converts and popularizers particularly, as aiming "to liberate humanity from such outmoded ideas of love and duty" (p. 13). Lasch states that the new therapies "intensify the disease they pretend to cure" (p. 30), and deplores the social invasion of the self and its accelerating disintegration in our culture, but no careful definition of "self" is put forward.

Further, Lasch attacks Erich Fromm's Marxism, offered as a solution to the problems set forth by Freud (1930) in *Civilization and its Discontents*. In describing the narcissistic personality of our time, Kernberg's works are quoted without recognition that they are based on premises incompatible with the writing of Kohut, who is also quoted. Lasch also misunderstands Kohut. For example, he confuses Kohut's theory of the "psychology of the self in the broader sense," which is meant to be applicable to everybody, with Kohut's discussions of pathological narcissism. Lasch's description is not convincing for presenting an individual different, for example, from the *fin de siècle* patient in Breuer and Freud's (1893–1895) *Studies on Hysteria*. He describes the new-style executive, who takes no pleasure in his achievements once he begins to lose the adolescent charm on which they rest: "Middle age hits him with the force of a disaster" (p. 45).

Lasch relies on the studies of Maccoby (1976) and others to argue that it is the increasing overorganization of our society with the predomination of large bureaucracies that encourage a survival mentality, destruction of the family, and narcissism which, to Lasch, "appears realistically to represent the best way of coping with the tensions and anxieties of modern life" (p. 50). This does not imply that narcissism is caused by our culture but that the prevailing social conditions tend to bring out narcissistic traits that are present in varying degrees in everyone.

Lasch also attacks advertising and its effect on the modern Western individual, with consumption presented as the treatment for the disease that it creates. It manufactures the perpetually unsatisfied, restless, anxious, and bored consumer and institutionalizes envy. Truth becomes irrelevant as long as things sound true and, as Kohut

repeatedly pointed out, the theater in our society, especially the so-
called theater of the absurd involving dramatists like Albee, Beckett,
Ionesco, and Genet, centers on emptiness, isolation, loneliness, and
despair. Lasch describes this drama as portraying the world of the
borderline; however, Kohut states that the theater of the absurd expresses the forces in our society that produce a vulnerable or fragmented self, not only borderline patients.

Lasch concludes by describing the new managerial class and their
children as identified with an "ethics of hedonism," and producing
a society in which narcissists achieve prominence and set the tone
while the culture itself reinforces everybody's narcissistic traits. Although there is further confusion manifested about Kohut's point of
view when it is applied to borderline conditions and even schizophrenia, capitalism and industrial production are seen as the basic
culprits, transforming the family and producing as well as encouraging the narcissistic personality.

The great difficulty that presents itself in the study of culture from
the point of view of narcissism and the narcissistic personality, as well
as in understanding the various descriptions of narcissism is in the
confusion about the meaning of narcissism itself.

Kohut's discussion of the psychology of the self begins with an attempt to understand the developmental transformations of narcissism
in the individual. On the basis of what is discovered, Kohut then offers more insightful suggestions on how our culture might be improved and how we can find a more worthwhile existence. The
psychology of the self supersedes Lasch's vague socialist solutions and
points more precisely to the area of human existence — the empathic
matrix in which we must all live — that must be cultivated if our
culture is to survive and improve.

## Other Views of Narcissism in Our Culture

Kohut's emphasis on the importance of early parenting is supported by Williamson's (1984) study of "the poetry of narcissism" in
contemporary American poetry. He documents how a whole generation of sensitive poets who came of age between the rise of Hitler and
the fall of Joe McCarthy — a time of greatly increased influence "of
irrational hatreds, fears, and identifications" in political life — show
a preoccupation in their poetry with their subjective experience of

a sterile empty self from which there is no escape, except perhaps by suicide. He stresses their gravitation towards "low-key anomie and depression" in terms similar to Finlay-Jones (1983) and Solberg (1984) (quoted in Chapter 1) and their introspective poetic reports about a self that is "unknowable, fragmentary, perhaps ultimately not there" (pp. 2–4).

Modell (Goldberg 1983) offers original comments on the rise of narcissism in our culture. He calls our attention to two books preliminary to a study of our culture, Trilling's (1971) *Sincerity and Authenticity* and *The Lonely Crowd* (Riesman, Glazer, and Denney 1950). The latter describes a change in the American character as a shift from an "inner directed" to an "other directed" individual, which is another way of describing a shift in self-esteem regulation from dependence on inner values to dependence on external mirroring.

Modell briefly describes the two phases of, as he calls it, the shaping of character. The earlier phase, when it leads to narcissism, is "a miscarriage in the process of mirroring" (p. 114). He delineates mirroring as authentic affective communication between the mother and the child and continues, "the child's cohesive sense of self is forged through the affective bond that is formed when the mother gazes at the child's face, reflecting the child's affects" (p. 114). This is connected to Trilling's definition of sincerity as a congruence between feelings and the truthful avowal of these feelings; to say there is breakdown of sincerity in our time would be another way of describing states of nonrelatedness and noncommunication that will reflect themselves in failures in the early mother–infant (and slightly later in the father–infant) relationship.

Modell delineates a second phase of character shaping that occurs during adolescence when the individual begins to interact with and perceive directly the culture of which the infant will become a full member. He concludes, "Our contemporary world confronts the adolescent with failures in the protective environment analogous to those experienced earlier in relationship to the parental environment, and this second disillusionment involves similar coping strategies" (p. 117).

We will return to this crucial problem of narcissism in our contemporary culture many times, because Kohut places emphasis on the quality of the mothering received by the infant as it influences the infant's formation of self. Kohut's views stand in sharp contrast especially to Kleinian concepts in which the intrapsychic processes in the infant are thought to proceed more independently of the external input.

Even though a number of critics such as Crews (1980) mount a vigorous attack on the application of clinical notions of psychoanalysis (whether taken from Freud or Kohut) to historical or cultural issues, the subject cannot be avoided as long as the reader keeps in mind the fierce opposition to this kind of approach. Clements (1982) criticizes both Lasch and Kohut for confusing "the macro-level of social system structures and the micro-level of individual structures, as if they were one homogeneous level" which leads to substantial methodological problems such as "a significant reductionist error" (p. 284). She also warns against other serious methodological dangers in the application of concepts from psychoanalysis on a social system level. Her caveat is important if we are to avoid the superficial and bland oversimplifications of "popular psychology" which pervade the media in our culture. Indeed, as Lasch points out, the media abounds with so-called "self-appointed, unlicensed experts" who, for narcissistic purposes and financial gain, prey on the insecure and offer fast and simple solutions to every personal and social problem.

# Chapter 3

## Freud and His Followers

*auteroticism → narcissism → mature + genital object relationships*

We turn now to some of the attempts made by psychoanalysts to understand the phenomena of narcissism in depth. Freud (1914) began the in-depth study of the subject in "On Narcissism" (see Giovacchini 1982, Chessick 1980). By the time he wrote this work, Freud had already outlined the importance of narcissism in the formulation of the psychodynamics of paranoid psychoses (Freud 1911). In 1909, Freud told Ernest Jones that he considered narcissism to be a normal stage of development between autoerotism and object relationships (Giovacchini 1982). This notion of a single line of libidinal development from autoerotism to narcissism to more or less mature and genital object relationships was assumed to be almost self-evident by earlier Freudian psychoanalysts and ego psychologists; it was challenged, however, by the so-called British school of clinicians, especially Michael Balint and others, but remained the prevailing view in American psychoanalysis until Kohut. Although Freud's view seems to be consonant with common sense, it leads to certain problems since Freud was never clear about his distinction between the state of autoerotism and primary narcissism (Abend et al. 1983, p. 102).

His paper on narcissism is of great importance in the evolution of Freud's views. It sums up his ideas on the subject of narcissism and

introduces the concepts of the ego ideal and the self-observing agency
related to it. The paper also occupies a transitional point in the development of the structural theory; Strachey (in Freud 1914) points
out that the meaning which Freud attached to *das Ich* — which
Strachey translates by the word "ego" — underwent a gradual modification: "At first he used the term without any great precision as we
might speak of the 'self'; but in his latest writings he gave it a very
much more definite and narrow meaning" (p. 71). Bettelheim (1982)
devotes a controversial book to a discussion of problems inherent in
the translation and mistranslation of Freud's words such as *das Ich*;
for example, he claims that to translate this word as "ego," or *das
Es* as "id," is to misrepresent Freud's language in an effort to make
it sound more "scientific." Ornston (1985) also examines this problem
in detail.

There is an inherent confusion in Freud's vocabulary. *Das Ich*
could be thought of either a) as a technical structure with certain
assigned functions in the mental apparatus or b) as more loosely representing the self. Freud thought of the ego in an increasingly technical structural sense as his work continued; he tended to anthro-
pomorphize it as a "little man within the man" as he grew older.

The year 1913 was one of the low points in Freud's professional
life. This period marked the breakup, due to the defection of Jung
and Adler, of the growing international psychoanalytic movement.
The debates which led to this defection forced Freud's attention to
the inexactitude of certain prior statements and definitions he had
introduced and motivated him to define them precisely in order to
demarcate his psychoanalysis from that of Jung and Adler. Admittedly "fuming with rage" (Jones 1955, p. 304), he wrote the polemical
"On the History of the Psychoanalytic Movement" (1914a) and "On
Narcissism" (1914). The latter work, which is condensed, complicated, and one of the most famous of Freud's writings, had a revolu-
tionary impact on his followers because it revised old ideas and introduced some new concepts. At the same time, it also introduced
some serious new confusions and difficulties.

## Freud's "On Narcissism"

Freud's main goal in this paper was to restrict the meaning of the
term libido to sexual energy; Adler regarded it as a force or striving
for power and Jung widened it to mean the energy behind all life

processes. In order to keep his original conception of libido, Freud had to make important theoretical revisions, the most fundamental of which was a change in his theory of instincts.

Freud's famous U-tube analogy of the flow of libido is presented in "On Narcissism." At first, all libido is developmentally collected in (cathected to) the ego, a situation Freud called primary narcissism. He defines its outward flow as representing the situation of object love — love for objects other than the self (or ego), a capacity that developmentally appears in the second year of life after an autoerotic phase (where no ego has yet formed) in the first two or three months of life, and then a primary narcissistic phase where, as stated, most of the libido is attached to the ego (self). However, the libido can flow back again or be withdrawn into the ego (not differentiated from self here) under various situations such as mental or physical disease, life threatening traumata or accidents, or old age, where this tendency toward self-preoccupation and self-love is especially obvious.

Whenever libido is mostly attached to the ego, we have the phenomenological situation defined as narcissism. In the early phase of life, this situation is normal, according to Freud, and is called a state of primary narcissism; in later stages of life when the libido is withdrawn again to the ego, the state is defined as secondary narcissism.

Jones finds the "disagreeable" aspect of this theory in the fact that it was difficult for Freud to demonstrate nonnarcissistic components of the ego. To say there is reason to suppose the ego is strongly invested with libido is not the same as saying it is composed of nothing else, writes Jones (1955, p. 303). "Something else" is difficult to pin down and opens Freud's theory to the criticism of being a monistic libidinal conception of the mind. Freud's metapsychological conception of narcissism is still not adequately clarified and resolved.

Current controversy is due to the ambiguity of Freud's position. For example Kohut (1977) refers to Freud's (1911) "most profound contributions to the area of archaic narcissism" in which Freud "shifted confusingly between the recognition of the importance of the regressive narcissistic position, on the one hand, and conflict issues on much higher developmental levels, namely, conflict concerning homosexuality, on the other" (p. 296).

At this point in "On Narcissism," Freud conceived of two kinds of ego drives, the libidinal and nonlibidinal. This theory was meant to precede a complete restructuring of psychoanalytic theory which was intended originally to be a book consisting of 12 essays entitled

"Introduction to Metapsychology" that Freud proposed in 1915. Only five of these essays were published; Freud destroyed the rest.

"On Narcissism" merits careful study because it is so rich in clinical material, for example, discussion of narcissistic and anaclitic object choices and its introduction of the concept of "ego ideal." Furthermore, Freud's paper is the agreed-upon starting point for all psychodynamic studies of narcissistic personality disorders and borderline patients. The reader should note here that Freud's U-tube analogy implies that, at least after the developmental phase of primary narcissism, there is *always* some residual primary narcissism, some secondary narcissism, and some libido directed toward objects; only the quantitative amounts of libido cathexes fluctuate, accounting for the varying clinical or phenomenological picture over a person's life.

Freud begins by stating that narcissism is not a perversion but rather "the libidinal complement to the egoism of the instinct of self-preservation, a measure of which may justifiably be attributed to every living creature" (pp. 73–74). The U-tube theory is then introduced. Freud also offers the analogy of the body of an amoeba related to the pseudopodia which it puts out and withdraws. Thus, just as the pseudopodia are extended and withdrawn, libido can either flow out to objects or flow back to the ego. This phenomenon of ego-libido spoils the neat dualistic, early instinct theory of Freud that divides all drives into sexual or egoistic (self-preservative).

Freud immediately employs the concept of narcissism in understanding schizophrenic phenomena; the megalomanic aspect of schizophrenic patients is explained as a consequence of secondary narcissism. Most of the libido is withdrawn from objects and directed to the self, seen clinically and most dramatically in paranoid grandiosity. The converse phenomenon, where the most libido possible is directed to an object, appears as the state of being in love.

Freud goes on to postulate a phase of autoerotism at the very beginning of life, even before the nuclei of the ego have coalesced. Once the ego has begun to develop, the libido is invested in it; this is the phase of primary narcissism.

The second section of the paper begins with a discussion of hypochondria, in which the clinical phenomena of hypochondriasis are seen as the result of flooding the ego with libido that has been withdrawn from objects. Thus, the psychic expression of the flooding of the ego with libido appears in megalomania and an overflooding (or damming up) is felt as the disagreeable sensations of hypochondriacal anxiety. No explanation is available as to *why* the libido-flooded ego should feel these disagreeable sensations, but an analogy is drawn to the so-called "actual neuroses," where, Freud thought, dammed-up libido due to inadequate sexual discharge leads to the disagreeable sensations of neurasthenia. In the case of hypochondriasis the libido which floods the ego comes from outside objects to which it has previously been cathected and is now being withdrawn; in the case of the actual neuroses, the libido comes from inside the individual and has been inadequately discharged.

In concluding his subsequent discussion of schizophrenia, Freud distinguishes three groups of phenomena in the clinical picture: those representing what remains of the normal or neurotic state of the individual; those representing detachment of libido from its objects, leading to megalomania, hypochondriasis, and regression; and restitutive symptoms in which an effort is made once again to attach the libido to objects or at least to their verbal representations. These distinctions form the foundation of Freud's theory of schizophrenia.

Another clinical application of the concept of narcissism — the distinction between anaclitic and narcissistic choices of love objects — concludes the second section of this paper. The anaclitic object choice attempts to bring back the lost mother and precedes developmentally the narcissistic object choice. The latter is a form of secondary narcissism in which the person chosen to love resembles one's own self. For example, in certain forms of homosexuality, the object chosen is the child-self who is then treated the way the homosexual wishes his mother to treat him. To avoid confusion, it is important to understand that in early development primary narcissism comes first; then, due to inevitable frustration, anaclitic object-choice occurs with the mother as the first object. Therefore, narcissistic object choice, when it appears, represents a form of *secondary* narcissism in which the person loves what he himself is or was, what he would like to be, or someone thought of as a part of himself.

INSTINCT THEORIES

In the first instinct theory, the instincts were divided into the sexual instincts — easily modified and changed, relatively speaking — and the ego instincts, such as hunger and thirst, which are more fixed. In the second instinct theory, certain ego instincts are thought of as nonlibidinal or "ego interest," but some are thought of as ego-libido, that is, narcissism. In this theory the ego's integrity depends on how much ego-libido is available, and ego-libido represents the glue holding the ego together. Thus an anaclitic object relationship may be viewed as a combination of two elements: the libido is directed toward the object that has been responsible for survival, the nutritive object, the mother; but if all the libido goes toward this object, the ego becomes depleted and helpless and depends on the object. The concept of sexual energies flowing within the ego made it very difficult to separate the libidinal and nonlibidinal ego instincts because the "alibidinous"part is not well defined. Hunger and thirst do not quantitatively balance the libidinal instinct, and this theoretical revision is generally agreed to be unsatisfactory.

A tentative effort to improve this situation was made by postulating sexual instincts on the one hand and aggressive instincts on the other; the latter would then represent the nonlibidinal ego instincts. The notion of aggression as an ego instinct strengthened Freud's idea of dividing instincts between sexual instincts and nonlibidinal ego instincts and was determined through a discussion of sadism. Freud argued that if self-preservative instincts include aggressive instincts along with hunger and thirst, they must become dominant over sexual instincts so that the reality principle could prevail. Since sadism permeates every level of living and can ally itself to all instincts as shown in the impulses to assert and control and aggress upon, the aggressive or sadistic instincts are seen as distinct from libidinal impulses. This is not a valid argument since, if sadism is found at every level of sexual development, why should it not be considered a part of the sexual instincts? The attempt to find a place for the aggressive drives characterized all Freud's further attempts at instinct theory, including his final theory of the life and death instincts and still remains an important and metapsychologically unresolved aspect, especially of any consideration of narcissism and the borderline personality disorders.

The final section of the essay begins: "The disturbances to which a child's original narcissism is exposed, the reactions with which he seeks to protect himself from them and the paths into which he is forced in doing so — these are themes which I propose to leave on one side, as an important field of work which still awaits exploration" (p. 92). Kohut's work may be understood as emanating from this statement.

At this point, the aggressive instincts in Freud's formulation should not be considered purely as sadism since he conceived of them here primarily as the will to power, control, and dominance, which only in certain cases involve a secondary need to inflict pain. We may say, therefore, that when the ego instincts are flooded by a libidinal complement from the sexual instincts, we have the clinical state of narcissism; when the sexual instincts are infused by an aggressive component from the ego instincts, we have the clinical situation of sexual sadism.

Missing from this temporary revision is the structural theory involving the id, ego, and superego; a step in this direction is present in "On Narcissism," in the third part of which Freud introduces the notion of the ego ideal, which in the course of development becomes infused with the subject's primary narcissism. Thus "what he projects before him as his ideal is the substitute for the lost narcissism of his childhood in which he was his own ideal" (p. 94). This substitution is differentiated from sublimation, in which the aim of the instinct is changed with an accent upon deflection from sexuality.

It follows that the ego becomes impoverished by either object love or ego ideal formation and enriched by the gratification of object love or the fulfilling of the aims of its ego ideal. Self-esteem arises out of either of these enrichments and contains three components: the leftover residue of primary infantile narcissism; the sense of omnipotence corroborated by experiencing the fulfillment of the ego ideal; and satisfaction of object-libido by an input of love from the love object. Thus loving, insofar as it involves longing and deprivation, lowers self-regard, "whereas being loved, having one's love returned, and possessing the loved object, raises it once more" (p. 99).

Besides explaining a variety of easily observable, everyday phenomena, these conceptions have an important bearing on the practice of psychoanalytic psychotherapy. If an individual is unable to love, that is, if there is a repression of the libidinal drive, only one source of self-regard is left: idealization or "fulfilling the ego ideal." As Freud says, such persons tend to attach themselves to individuals who have achieved what the patient's ego ideal clamors for, persons who possess the excellences which the patient cannot attain. This represents a "cure by love" and is the kind of expectation that often directs patients into psychotherapy. Thus, an important unconscious motivation for seeking therapy is the development of an attachment to a "successful" person (the psychotherapist) who has achieved the aims of the patient's ego ideal. The patient is tempted to form a crippling and permanent dependence upon the psychotherapist; there is further danger that, when some capacity to love is developed through the psychotherapy, the patient will withdraw from the treatment and choose a love object still permeated by the patient's ego ideal. The crippling dependence is then transferred to this new love object, and we observe the clinical phenomena that Odier (1956) has called the neurosis of abandonment.

## NARCISSISTIC WOUNDING

A final important hint leading to the work of Kohut is presented at the end of "On Narcissism," in which it is noted that an injury to self-esteem or self-regard — what today we would call a narcissistic wound — is often found as the precipitating cause of paranoia. Any falling short of the ego ideal, or any disappointment or depletion in the libidinal complement of the ego, would cause a withdrawal of libido from objects, with the subsequent clinical phenomena of hypochondriasis and megalomania.

Davis (1976) has presented an approach to depression based on similar considerations. He sees the core of depression as a feeling of uneasy helplessness, caused by psychic emptiness, coupled with a pressure to accomplish. He writes, "When we observe the sequence of depressive phenomena, we see that depressive emptiness is brought on by an acute diminution in self-esteem, what Freud called 'a narcissistic wound," (p. 417). Chronically depressed persons may have suffered repeated narcissistic wounds due to psychodynamic factors; their disorder is not only due to biological or constitutional factors. In this view, the requirements for therapy of at least chronic characterological depression are the need for alteration and modification of the self-esteem system of the patient.

## OBSCURITIES IN FREUD'S THEORY

Freud points out, "A unity comparable to the ego cannot exist in the individual from the start" (p. 77). Thus, during the autoerotic stage Freud thinks of the psyche as having very little structure. From this amorphous psyche, as the formation of a rudimentary ego takes place, the component instincts become directed towards it; Freud defines the attachment or cathexis of the libido to this rudimentary ego as primary narcissism; he distinguishes it from the energy of the ego- (or self-preservative) instincts. This original libidinal cathexis of the ego, from which some is later given off to objects but which fundamentally persists, would imply that a certain amount of primary narcissism remains as what Freud calls a "reservoir" throughout life; in that sense, narcissism to a certain extent is seen as normal and has no pejorative connotation.

In addition to a certain unclarity as to whether Freud regarded the persistence of primary narcissism in adult life as pathological, there is an inherent confusion in this essay because the locus of repression and idealization are placed within the same psychic structure. The ego ideal becomes the focus of self-love and contains all the perfections of infantile narcissism, but it also contains prohibitions since it is the instigator of repression. Giovacchini (1982) writes that today the standard Freudian viewpoint separates these factors and thinks of violation of the prohibitions as causing fear and guilt, whereas shame results from not meeting the standards of the ego ideal. Thus, there are two ego substructures, with the superego responsible for repression and the ego responsible for regulating self-esteem. Later followers of Freud elaborate on this considerably.

Finally, the essay on narcissism contains some curious statements. For example, Freud insists that men are much more capable of complete object love than women, and implies that there is always a substantial narcissistic component in female love object choice. Here he reverts to the more pejorative use of narcissism as part of his well-known prejudice against women. Even his disclaimer (p. 89) that he has no "tendentious desire . . . to depreciate women" contains a backhanded slap implying the superiority of the masculine type of love. Parental love, Freud writes, "is nothing but" the parents' narcissism born again. The famous phrase "his majesty the baby" is introduced, referring to a picture showing two London policemen stopping heavy traffic to allow a nursery maid to wheel a perambulator across the street. Of course, the great problem with this is the assumption that the baby is aware of what is going on and has the capacity to appreciate the royal situation in which it has been placed. Giovacchini's (1982) greatest objection to the various theories of narcissism of Freud, Melanie Klein, and Kohut is that they are adultomorphizing, assuming the recognition of external objects and the capacity to

introject and identify as being present in the infant. Are these
capacities present, or are they far beyond the abilities of the embryonic
ego at the stage of primary narcissism? Kohut's answer to this will
be discussed later.

In addition, there are two obscure paragraphs (pp. 96–97) in
which Freud takes up self-observation. The "self-criticism of conscience" in "paranoics [sic]," says Freud, "coincides with the self-
observation on which it is based." He sees this as a form of internal
research "which furnishes philosophy with the material for its intellectual operations." Apparently, Freud had in mind such works as Kant's
*Critique of Pure Reason*. According to Freud, "This may have some
bearing on the characteristic tendency of paranoics [sic] to construct
speculative systems." There is a pejorative implication here concerning the speculative systems of philosophers, but Freud's view, of importance to both psychologists and philosophers, is that the activity
of the critically observing agency in the mind can become heightened into conscience or philosophical introspection. Freud then adds
an astonishing statement implying that he is not a person who is gifted
philosophically or accustomed to such introspection!

## "Mourning and Melancholia"

Written in 1915, "Mourning and Melancholia" is regarded by
Strachey (in Freud 1917, p. 240) as an extension of the essay on narcissism which Freud wrote a year earlier. Freud's concept of identification is presented here; it precedes object cathexis and is distinct from
it, often taking place on the model of cannibalistic incorporation or
introjection. Three terms — incorporation, introjection, and identification — are used very loosely by Freud (and will be discussed in
Chapter 5). It is most important to understand the process by which,
in melancholia, an object-cathexis is replaced by an identification.
These "identifications" are the basis of what we describe as a person's character, and the very earliest of these "identifications" form
the nucleus of the superego.

Freud (1917) begins with a caveat sometimes overlooked by his
critics: depression or melancholia "whose definition fluctuates even
in descriptive psychiatry, takes on various clinical forms the group-
ing together of which into a single unity does not seem to be established with certainty; and some of these forms suggest somatic rather

than psychogenic affections" (p. 243). He thus drops all claim to general validity for his statements about melancholia and acknowledges he may be speaking only of a small subgroup within what might be called the group of melancholias.

Freud offers a general clinical distinction between mourning and melancholia based on the fact that the features are the same, except for the profound disturbance of self-esteem which Freud says is characteristic of melancholia and is absent in mourning. Since mourning is a reaction to the loss of a loved person, Freud suspects that a similar kind of influence may be at work in the production of melancholia if there is a "pathological predisposition," and he sets out to investigate this "pathological predisposition."

The cornerstone of Freud's reasoning is his clinical impression that the various self-accusations of the melancholic usually fit someone whom the patient loves, or has loved, or should love. Thus, Freud considers the key to the clinical picture his perception that the self-reproaches are reproaches against a loved object, reproaches which have been shifted from the object onto the patient's own ego. He adds that in both obsessive compulsive disorders and melancholia such patients succeed by the circuitous path of self-punishment "in taking revenge on the original object and in tormenting their loved one through their illness, having resorted to it in order to avoid the need to express their hostility to him openly" (p. 251). He mentions that the person who precipitated the patient's emotional disorder is usually to be found in the patient's immediate environment.

This reasoning led to many later psychoanalytic investigations of the psychodynamics of depression and also led Freud to the issue of narcissistic object choice and narcissism. Goldberg (1975) reviews the history of psychoanalytic concepts of depression and points out that certain key concepts seem to occur over and over. These are the persistent connection of depression with the mother–child unit in the oral phase of development; narcissistic issues are always raised in the description of object relations of the depressed patient, centering upon identification and the regulation of self-esteem; and a regular association of depression with aggression or hostility, superego, and resultant guilt. Goldberg utilizes the definition of narcissism as psychologic investment in the self and points out:

The "regression of object cathexis to narcissism" indicates an increase of feeling or interest in the self: what we would call a heightened self-centeredness. This follows upon object loss and may result in the object being internalized. Therefore, the lost object can be replaced by another one or replaced through an identification. Depending on how such a loss is handled, one may experience depression or merely a shift in object interest. (p. 127)

Melancholia is a pathological state "involving narcissistic blows to the ego experienced as losses and involving more wholesale or traumatic internalization of the offending object" (Goldberg 1975, p. 128). As Freud (1917) reasons, the predisposition to fall ill of melancholia lies in the predominance of the narcissistic type of object choice in the patient's psychic functioning.

The fundamental process in which, due to a loss "the shadow of the object fell upon the ego" (p. 249), is Freud's metaphorical way of describing an identification of the ego with the abandoned object, vital in the formation of character and of the superego. This narcissistic identification with the object forms a regression from adult erotic object choice to narcissistic object choice, as it has been defined in Freud's paper on narcissism.

Freud carefully differentiates this from identification with the object in the transference neuroses. In narcissistic indentification the object cathexis is abandoned, but in hysterical identification it persists and manifests its influence. Freud suggests that also in melancholics the original object choice has been of a narcissistic type, or at least there is a tendency for the predominance of the narcissistic type of object choice required in the disposition to fall ill of melancholia.

Most importantly, he raises the issue of whether a purely narcissistic blow to the ego (p. 253) may not be sufficient to produce the picture of melancholia, regardless of any realistic object loss. He mentions that the complex of melancholia "behaves like an open wound, drawing to itself cathectic energies . . . from all directions, and emptying the ego until it is totally impoverished" (p. 253).

When the melancholic process is released there may be a rebound in which the liberated energy leads to a hypomanic state characterized by Freud as "seeking like a ravenously hungry man for new object-cathexes" (p. 255). Thus, Freud distinguishes between the slow and gradual work of normal mourning which, when it is finished, is not usually marked by any hypomanic phase, and the narcissistic disorder of melancholia, which may be interrupted by a sudden

liberation of energies in a hypomanic state. In the intensive psychotherapy of narcissistic and borderline disorders this fluctuation between melancholic states and hypomanic states can be observed, and
the dynamics as described by Freud are still as useful in understanding these phenomena today even though the more extreme fluctuations of manic-depressive disorder need to be treated with psycho-
pharmacologic agents and may have an important organic basis.

Freud's paper also contains a discussion of suicide, an ever-present
problem in narcissistic, borderline, and schizophrenic patients. Freud
explains that the ego kills itself, if, on regressing to narcissism, it gets
rid of the object and treats itself as identified with the object. The
ego then directs against itself the full fury of the hostility which was
originally directed to the object in the external world.

## "Group Psychology and the Analysis of the Ego"

In the monograph *Group Psychology and the Analysis of the Ego*
(1921), the separateness of the "conscience" and ego ideal from the
ego began more specifically to appear in Freud's thinking. Here he
conceives of the possibility of the ego ideal-conscience as coming into
conflict with the rest of the ego and even raging with a critical cruelty
against the ego. The extent of this cruelty, which can function unconsciously, was a major motivation for his development and final
presentation of the structural theory in *The Ego and the Id* (1923).

Freud considered the development of the superego primarily as
a consequence of the resolution of the Oedipus complex. He increasingly emphasized the punitive and cruel aspects of the superego rather
than its benign, loving aspect. In *Inhibitions, Symptoms and Anxiety*
(1926) he thought of the threat from the superego as an extension of
the castration threat and finally, in *New Introductory Lectures on
Psychoanalysis* (1933), he viewed the superego as an internalized
parental authority dominating the ego through punishment and
threats of withdrawal of love. The common paradox of the clinically observed contrast between the harshness of the superego's imita-
tion of the parents and the actual gentleness of the parents in real
life was explained through the borrowing by the superego of the
child's own hostility to the prohibiting parent. Thus, the superego
is always thought of as having a direct connection to the id and as
able to drain aggression from the id by turning it upon the ego.

*Group Psychology and the Analysis of the Ego* was inspired by the collapse of the Austro-Hungarian Empire at the end of 1918 and by the panic and distress that followed. It proposes the rudiments of a sociology that rejects the concept of an autonomous social instinct and is based instead on Freud's libido theory and his emerging notion of the ego ideal. In the latter sense it is a transitional work on the structural theory to be more completely realized in *The Ego and the Id* (1923).

Freud starts by accepting and recapitulating the theories of LeBon and McDougall on the group mind. The behavior of groups is like that of a primitive savage or child; emotions become extraordinarily labile and intensified, and intellect is reduced. Freud writes: "A group is impulsive, changeable and irritable. It is led almost exclusively by the unconscious. . . . Though it may desire things passionately, yet this is never so for long, for it is incapable of perseverance. It has a sense of omnipotence" (p. 77). He continues, "A group is extraordinarily credulous and open to influence. . . . It goes directly to extremes; if a suspicion is expressed, it is instantly changed into an incontrovertible certainty; a trace of antipathy is turned into furious hatred" (p. 78).

As far as leadership is concerned, exaggeration and repetition affect the group far more than logic, because the group respects force and demands strength or even violence from its heroes. LeBon believed that a group wants to be ruled and oppressed and to fear its masters, and Freud seems to be in agreement. They also believe that the group seeks a strong-willed leader who has a fanatical belief in his ideas.

Groups tend always and naturally to behave toward each other as children or primitive savages; there is a collective lowering of intellectual ability of the group just by virtue of its being a group. This "regressive tendency," as Freud calls it, is inherent in the psychological nature of all groups, and it cries out continuously for a particular type of leader.

In what Freud calls the primary group, each member has put the leader in the place of the individual ego-ideal and the member has consequently identified with the group. Group formation, argues Freud, is always a regressive phenomenon in itself, because it takes place through identification and thus is based on a more primitive level of human functioning than individual object-choice. Similarly, there is a tendency to pick the leader of the group not through intellectual or mature object-choice but through what would now be called a consensus process. The leader needs often to "only possess the typical qualities of the individuals in the group in a particularly clearly marked and pure form, and need only give an impression of greater force and of more freedom of libido; and in that case the need for a strong chief will often meet him half-way and invest in him a predominance to which he would otherwise have had no claim" (p. 129).

Notice again that in group formation Freud considers this substitution of identification for object choice to be a consequence of regression. The common emotional quality which stimulates identification in the case of group formation is due to having the leader as a common ego ideal: "Identification is the original form of emotional tie with an object; secondly, in a regressive way it becomes a substitute for a libidinal object-tie, as it were by means of introjection of the object into the ego" (p. 108). Thus here as in "Mourning and Melancholia" when he discusses the shadow of the object falling upon the ego, Freud uses the concept of introjection of the object. In the situation of being in love, hypnosis, and group formation, the object is put in place of the ego ideal and the narcissistic libido flows from the individual's ego ideal onto the object. This will be reconsidered when we turn to aspects of the work of Kohut.

## Ego Psychology

Many careful studies were made by subsequent authors of the substructures of the ego and the interrelationship between the ego, the id, and the superego. Direct communication is postulated between the id and the superego, based on Freud's (1923) contention that the ego forms the superego out of the id, and the relationship between the id and superego is further exemplified by the well-known paradoxical increase of superego harshness when the external discharge of id aggressive drives is inhibited. The function of the benign aspect of the superego was portrayed and considered to carry those internalizations originating from the mother's benign attitudes and certain internalizations originating in the relationship to the father. The maternal benign superego was thought of as adjacent to the ego ideal because of the similarity between its origins in the maternal symbiotic relationship and the development of early narcissism into the ego ideal.

A conflict-free sphere of the ego was organized hierarchically by subsequent "ego psychologists." Beginning at the interface with the id were placed the primary autonomous functions such as control of motility, perception, anticipation, thinking, reality testing, memory, object comprehension, and language. Also included were the synthetic function, integrating function, the functions of judgment, intent, will, the self-observing functions, and the representations of the self and object. Independent traits of character were thought to form due to "change of function" among the secondary autonomous functions (which originally developed to deal with infantile drives), and ego interests such as social status, influence, power, professional status, and wealth arise from these. Inborn ego apparatuses were thought to exist, and the structural theory was elaborated at great length.

Hartmann (1950) distinguished from each other the libidinal cathexis to the ego, which represents a narcissistic ego cathexis; the libidinal cathexis to the self (or self-representation), which represents narcissism; and the libidinal cathexis to the soma, or body, which is clinically manifest as hypochrondriasis. Thus the focus in psychoanalytic theory shifted from the id (1897–1923), in which authoritative id interpretations were made to the patient, to the ego (1923 and thereafter), in which the emphasis was upon the interpretation of the ego as it functioned in defenses and resistances. A vast and detailed "ego psychology" literature arose on these topics, but it is beyond the scope of this book.

In this system, ambition was primarily conceived of in drive theory terminology. On the oral level, it was based on the wish to incorporate the world; on the anal level, to produce the biggest bowel movement — a productive orientation; and on the phallic level to have the biggest capacity and be the most outstanding. The ego ideal was approached by efforts to be magical and powerful in sublimated, socially acceptable ways and to get approval from one's self and others.

The ego contained defensive functions with which it had to mediate between its three harsh masters: the id, the superego, and external reality; it contained primary and secondary autonomous functions, and it was thought to contain intrapsychic self and object representations and identifications. We will deal at greater length with these representations in Chapter 5.

## Self-esteem Regulation in
## Traditional Psychoanalytic Theory

Reich (1960) described self-esteem regulation based on the use of classical conceptions. For her, self-esteem depends "on the nature of the inner image against which we measure our own self, as well as on the ways and means at our disposal to live up to it" (p. 217); and "growing up" means to realistically evaluate our potentialities and accept our limitations.

Aggression is stressed in both the infantile demand for magical absolute perfection and control and in the negative state of fear of complete destruction. Due to the warded-off feelings of catastrophic annihilation that occur as infantile grandiosity is collapsed, the rage is turned on the self with the production of hypochondriacal anxieties, depression, and self-consciousness. Thus, for Reich, self-consciousness is a step towards the paranoid pattern: "I am not the one who wants to exhibit himself aggressively, but other people aggressively observe and judge me" (p. 230). This fear of annihilation is followed by compensatory narcissistic self-inflation. In the narcissistic patient, "regressive abandonment of reality testing with respect to self-appreciation occurs frequently as an isolated lacuna in an otherwise well-coordinated personality" (p. 221).

Her paper represents an example of the effort to understand narcissistic pathology on the basis of classical psychoanalytic drive theory. She writes, "What we loosely describe as 'narcissists' are people whose libido is mainly concentrated on themselves at the expense of object love" (p. 217). Two basic implications are found in this paper that are characteristic of the Freudian and post-Freudian traditional psychoanalytic attitude. The first is a relatively pejorative use of the description of narcissism, and the second is that, unfortunately, significant help for patient treatment does not arise from the metapsychology employed. In general, beginning with Freud, there was a sense of discouragement about the psychoanalytic possibilities for the treatment of schizophrenic, borderline, and narcissistic (including depressed) patients. The metapsychology employed, based on the concept that the libido is concentrated on the ego of these patients themselves, implied the poor capacity of such individuals to form any object-related transference and therefore to be amenable to the method of psychoanalysis.

## THE CASE OF DANIEL

One of the cases that Reich describes is a classic for the diagnosis of narcissism, and indicates that she was describing the same kinds of cases that are discussed by Kohut. Daniel K. was an accomplished writer who wrote one book after another with marked success, but did not feel gratified by it. He would look at a bookshelf and see all the books he wrote and edited and say, "There are about two and a half feet of Mr. K. on the shelf." Reich emphasizes the phallic meaning of this statement and sees it to mean that Daniel was reassuring himself that his phallus was not only there, but of extraordinary size, a standard psychoanalytic interpretation.

Daniel was constantly preoccupied with attempts to feel great and important; he was a man of considerable talent, but his writing was careless and superficial — not up to the level of his capacities — because he was driven to produce too fast. He could not wait for results because he could not stand tension and unpleasure; he needed the immediate gratification of success. Reich explains:

> This need was so overwhelmingly strong that he had little control over it. He also was touchy, quick to take offense at the slightest provocation. He continually anticipated attack and danger, reacting with anger and fantasies of revenge when he felt frustrated in his need for constant admiration. (p. 218)

This is immediately followed by the dynamic interpretation that "his main aim was to increase his self-esteem and to ward off the underlying danger of passivity by incessant masculine activity" (p. 218).

Reich interprets what she calls "a bottomless need for grandiosity" as a compensatory striving under the impact of unbearable castration fears. In her view this is a narcissistic neurosis at the base of which is an Oedipus complex with castration anxiety. There is, however, the deeper conception that the castration threats contain the various fears from the pregenital phases of psychosexual development, so that the quest for phallic intactness also expresses the undoing of pregenital losses and injuries. In Freudian theory one would hope that there was enough libido available even after this secondary or compensatory narcissism formation had taken place for the development of a transference and a working through of the patient's Oedipus complex, at which point compensatory secondary narcissism would no longer be necessary. The patient's personality would then change in the direction away from infantile narcissism and toward the realistic evaluation of the patient's potentialities and the acceptance of limitations. Above all, the patient would manifest greater capacity for object love. A study of Reich's paper and the use of her case of Daniel K. as a paradigmatic example is an excellent place to begin a course on the study of Kohut because it illustrates the point of view of psychoanalytic ego psychology at the time of Kohut's contributions.

## SUMMARY OF TRADITIONAL PSYCHOANALYTIC THEORY

Teicholz (1978) presents a selective review of the psychoanalytic literature on theoretical conceptualizations of narcissism. She states that Freud's 1914 paper on narcissism held within it the seeds for almost all the subsequent theoretical developments of the concept. Freud's major contributions included a definition of secondary narcissism as a withdrawal of libido from the outer world and redirection of it onto the ego; the designation of the ego ideal as the adult version of infantile narcissism; the delineation of narcissistic object choice, in which the person chooses someone as much like one's self as possible or as what one's self was or would like to be; and a recognition of the important connection of self-regard and narcissistic libido.

Teicholz points out that the major subsequent changes in Freud's theory were Hartmann's delineation in 1950 of the object or target of the libido in narcissism as the self rather than the ego; an elaboration of the concept of "self" as a set of representations included in the structure of the ego; increasing emphasis on a distinction between internalized object relations as opposed to relations between the self and objects in the external world; and elaboration of the concept of self-esteem regulation as in the paper by Reich. Teicholz cites Jacobson's (1964) important work on the elaboration of the process by which self and object representations become differentiated and internalized as stable, enduring structures: "According to Jacobson, the normal regulation of self-esteem is dependent on the normal maturation and development of, and on the optimal interaction between several id, ego, and super-ego functions" (p. 847).

# Chapter 4

## Melanie Klein and Early Object Relations Theory

In *Civilization and Its Discontents* — better translated as "The Uneasiness Inherent in Culture" — Freud (1930, p. 122) wrote, "The evolution of civilization may therefore be simply described as the struggle for the life of the human species." He concludes:

> The fateful question for the human species seems to me to be whether and to what extent their cultural development will succeed in mastering the disturbance of their communal life by the human instinct of aggression and self-destruction. . . . Men have gained control over the forces of nature to such an extent that with their help they would have no difficulty in exterminating one another to the last man. (p. 145)

Forty-five years later Eissler (1975) wrote, "An anguished mood of desperation has settled over the whole world. . . . No remedy has obviously been found that could counteract the excess of aggression and narcissism that is a property of the species *Homo sapiens*." In this article entitled, "The Fall of Man," Eissler discusses the central Western image of Christ expiring on the cross and explains, "Possessed by a sentiment, perhaps amounting to a premonition, that something is basically wrong in human affairs, Christianity has, for almost two thousand years, been waiting for His coming." In an earlier paper, Eissler (1971) defends Freud's notion of the death instinct in a most enthusiastic fashion even though it is a notion rarely accepted by psychoanalysts today. Indeed, no better theory has been devised that fits so well with the rest of Freud's theories and discoveries (Kohut 1984, p. 35), and with the profound and detailed elaborations of these into a general psychology by the famous New York-based ego-psychology school headed by Hartmann, Kris, and Loewenstein (see Loewenstein, Newman, Schur, and Solnit 1966).

## FREUD'S VIEW OF HUMAN NATURE

In Freud's view, human beings are beset by lustful and aggressive drives, confined by the superego and the demands of reality, reluctantly attempting to tame the drives and arrive at a compromise that would preserve as much drive satisfaction as possible. Only after years of childhood struggle do people shift reluctantly (as little as possible) from the pleasure principle to the reality principle. This shift is forced on them by the need to survive in civilization, leaving guilt and neurosis in its wake. Innumerable theoretical revisions and rereadings of Freud have been offered in an attempt to get away from this basically pessimistic view of human beings, but the dismal course of human history keeps dragging us back to it. Even massive social experiments in the so-called Marxist countries have totally failed to eliminate the prevalence of lust and aggression as barely checked forces governing the relationship of one person to another.

In *Beyond the Pleasure Principle*, Freud (1920) views human beings as driven to their own death and destruction, somehow kept alive by the brief flicker of libidinal energies in the direction of life. He emphasizes the great primacy of the drive toward death and destruction, and sees the life instincts as fighting only a delaying or holding action while the individual, the species, and all organic matter speed on toward their own destruction. It is a remarkable fact that the most current cosmological theories in modern physics now view slow proton-decay as the ultimate process that will eventually result in the disappearance of all matter, leaving only light in empty space (Crease and Mann 1984). In later writing and without argument or explanation, Freud gave equal value to the life and death instincts, but this was a gratuitous change and is not supported by any clinical evidence.

In his basic formulation Freud made it clear that the dominant force in biological organisms must be the death instinct (Meissner 1980).

## Overview of Klein's Work

The controversial psychoanalyst Melanie Klein recognized the full consequences of Freud's theory. If Freud is correct, the human being's greatest and most serious problem lies in dealing with the "death instinct" that operates from the moment life is conceived. Klein recognized that, from birth, powerful innate aggressive drives posed fundamental obstacles to life. She understood and took seriously Freud's theory that, with the individual as with the species, there is a brief flicker of life and then ultimately extinction and destruction as the death instinct prevails and all organic matter returns to the inorganic form. She attempted to develop a metapsychology to explain that which Freud never made clear: how do the life instincts fight this delaying action? In Klein's view, this was accomplished by deflecting the death instincts outward in the form of aggression (as Freud said) and then attenuating this aggression through recurring cycles of projection and introjection of "good" and "bad" objects.

There is often a confusion in the literature between the views of Klein and those of Kohut on narcissism although Kohut takes great pains to distinguish his views from Klein (Kohut 1971, 1977, 1984). Klein's views — especially with modifications added later, for example, by Kernberg (see Chapter 5) — form an important alternative set of explanations for the phenomena of the narcissistic disorders. Furthermore, some critics of Kohut have insisted that his theoretical system is unnecessary because psychoanalytic ego psychology with the addition of object relations theory is a satisfactory explanation for all of the phenomena found in these narcissistic disorders; however even a brief review of Klein shows that there are just as many unresolved and controversial issues both in Kleinian theory and in later object relations theories (Greenberg and Mitchell 1983). I will concentrate mainly on what Freud thought of as the narcissistic disorders — psychoses, borderline cases, narcissistic personality disorders, some depressions, and some masochistic disorders — as they are explained by Klein.

There are five crucial concepts that form the basis of the system of Melanie Klein. First, she believed that stages of the Oedipus complex and superego formation exist in early infancy, which implies that the infant has the capacity for some very complex perceptions, emotions, and mental integrations. Second, she postulated that the early postnatal operation of introjection and projection build the infant's inner fantasy world; introjection and projection are based on dealing with the death instinct as the initial problem of life.

Third, Klein postulated two critical "positions," a difficult term which is thought of differently than Freud's developmental phases (such as oral, anal, genital). The paranoid-schizoid position deals with ambivalence by splitting and projection and occurs during the first three or four months of life; it is characterized by persecutory fears and anxiety over survival. During this position the good breast produces a feeling of love when the infant is satisfied which is projected and experienced as the good breast loving the infant, who then internalizes this sense of being loved as a protection against the death instinct. The infant's oral sadism springing from the death instinct and the bad breast imagined when the infant is frustrated, produces hate. This is projected and experienced as the bad breast hating the infant. This bad breast is also internalized in order to control it. The basic implication is that the infant can feel supported or attacked from within itself. Furthermore, the hate and love can be reprojected or reintrojected, so that if the hate is reprojected or reintrojected a vicious cycle of an increased sense of persecution from within or without is produced; if love is reprojected and reintrojected, it leads to a cycle of increased well being, "trust and gratitude."

Klein introduced confusion through the use of her term "part-object." Kernberg (1980a) points out that she used this term in two ways. First, Klein meant to represent a partial anatomical aspect of a real person, such as the breast, which the infant perceives as if it were the object to which the infant is relating. The second sense — predominantly used by Kleinian authors — is explained by Kernberg:

> As a result of splitting, part-objects constitute either part of persons or total persons perceived in a distorted, unrealistic way under the influence of the projection of pure libido or aggression, so that those objects are either all good or all bad. (p. 822)

The second half of the first year of life, according to Klein, is marked by the depressive position, emerging as self and object differentiation becomes possible in a cognitive sense. Splitting into part-objects is less present, and, as a consequence, anxiety occurs over the loss of good objects without and within, ushering in the depressive position. This is a consequence of the capacity for internalizing whole objects, which Klein says begins in the second quarter of the first year of life. The infant fears that its own destructive greedy impulses will destroy the good breast, which is later expressed as the child's fear that the parent may die. The destructive impulses can destroy the good breast by appropriating it; this is sometimes distinguished from the destruction of the breast due to envy, which we will discuss later. At any rate, a state of sadness is ushered in and becomes the key hurdle in ordinary development. If it is too painful, a regression to the paranoid-schizoid position or a defensive swing to the manic state occurs, and the psychological groundwork is laid for the psychoses — schizophrenia, or the manic-depressive disorders.

The good and bad breast in the paranoid-schizoid position are forerunners of the benign and harsh superego. For Klein, the oedipal triangle begins in the oral stage, and there is an inborn knowledge of the genitals of both sexes. Thus, there is a long and complex pre-history before Freud's oedipal stage, involving combinations of parents, splitting, projections, and internalizations. There may be a premature advance into oedipal material due to the use of genital love mobilized against pregenital aggression.

The fourth set of concepts are introjective identification and projective identification. Introjective identification results from the introjection of the object. Projective identification is a hybrid concept which is used differently by every subsequent author. Klein introduced it as having two aspects, one intrapsychic and the other interpersonal. In projective identification there is a forceful aggressive evacuation in fantasy consisting of a penetration into the object and a reinternalization of the object that was injured, which may lead to depression, or a reinternalization of the object that was rendered hostile, which may lead to persecutory hypochondria. It is also a very primitive means of communication, and leads to a "beyond the countertransference" distress in the therapist, an interpersonal interaction (Money-Kryle 1974).

The fifth basic concept was introduced by Klein in her seventies as a major addition, and produced new storms of protest against what she assumed was possible in the mind of the infant. She believed that there was an early infantile form of envy, also based on the death instinct, which was aimed at the destruction and possession of the envied good breast (or in treatment, the imagined serene analyst) and that there was a constitutional variation in the amount of envy and aggression present in each individual.

Thus, oral sadism is the first critical manifestation of the death instinct. Oral sadism varies with constitutional strength and is the key to understanding human development and pathology. It is first projected, resulting in persecutory fears and the fear of annihilation by the destructive devouring breast. Thus, the first source of anxiety arises when projected oral sadism threatens to destroy and invade the ego or self (again not carefully differentiated by Klein). Oral sadism also produces envy, which appears first; the breast is experienced as willfully withholding and there is a wish to scoop out, destroy, and possess it. Later derivations of envy are greed, which is a more sophisticated form of envy and arises from it, and jealousy, a later emotional development characteristic of triangular situations such as the oedipal conflicts. Here a third person is hated because that person preempts the desired love. It follows that constitutionally excessive aggression would foster a great deal of splitting and denial of reality in order to deal with these affects, and their associated fantasies, constituting envy, greed, and jealousy.

Conversely, the projection of "good" inner objects onto new objects forms the basis of trust in later life. Gratitude comes from good experiences, decreases greed, and leads to a healthy generosity in contrast to what Klein calls "reactive generosity," a defense against envy which eventually ends in feelings of being robbed.

## Klein on Narcissism

Klein defines narcissism as identification with the good object and the denial of any difference between one's self and the good object. There is no "primary" narcissism (Greenberg and Mitchell 1983). This definition is used to explain the clinical phenomena of narcissism and should be distinguished from narcissistic internal structures and narcissistic object relationships which are based on projective identification. Segal (1980, pp. 120–121) calls attention to Klein's differentiation between narcissistic states, which are states of identification with an internal ideal object and correspond to what Freud described as autoerotism, and the postulated complex narcissistic object relationships of the infant, which contain the internal fantasies of introjection and projection as described above. Each relationship is based primarily on an interaction between the individual and projected aspects of that same individual which the individual experiences as belonging to another person. In addition to splitting, idealization also preserves "all good" internal and external objects; when this breaks down there appears the fear of destruction from within as well as destruction from without.

Splitting originally occurs into good objects which are introjected and bad ones which are projected, but a secondary splitting can take place when aggression is strong and there is a related predominance of bad objects. These bad objects are then further split into fragments and when these fragments are projected we get the multiple persecutors or the so-called "bizarre objects" described dramatically by Klein's analysand and follower, Bion (1963, 1967).

Narcissistic internal structures and narcissistic object relationships arise in an effort to escape persecutory fears by an excessive dependence on an idealized object and by the use of others to confirm one's grandiosity. The idealization of external objects in the paranoid-schizoid position is marked by fantasies of unlimited gratification from these objects, which protects the individual against frustration, denies any need for aggression, and protects the individual against persecutory fears from the objects.

The idealization of internal objects in the depressive position protects the individual against unbearable reality. The denial of internal and external reality represents the denial of aggression and is a form of hallucinatory wish fulfillment at the cost of reality testing. The aggression of both the bad inner and outer objects is denied.

Stifling and artificiality of the emotions may protect one from aggression and persecutory anxiety, and represent a form of pathological consolidation in the paranoid-schizoid position. For Klein, projective identification is an acting-out of primitive sadism. Fear of internal aggression based on the death instinct is at the core of all of these mechanisms.

For example, sexual promiscuity or sexual conquests, seen commonly in the narcissistic disorders, may represent the turning from one idealized object to another in a desperate attempt to escape imagined inner and outer persecutors. Hypochondriasis is explained as the projection of persecutory bad objects to parts of one's own body; the fear of poisoning and of pathological control from the outside is based on a combination of persecutory paranoid and hypochondriacal fears.

## Klein on Depression and Idealization

In the depressive position the fear shifts from that of a persecutory fear to one of harming the good internal object, and idealization is used here to protect against aggression towards the good internal object. Depressive anxiety or guilt about the survival of good inner and outer objects are critical, so the object is idealized in the depressive position to protect against aggression to it and to remove guilt over this aggression. In contrast to Kohut, idealization is used in both of Klein's basic positions as a defense against sadism and destruction in fantasy (Segal 1974, 1980). Internalized bad objects are no longer projected in the depressive position nor are they reintrojected because now the total object is experienced and, therefore, the internal bad objects remain, forming the roots of the primitive superego which attacks the ego or self with guilt feelings. Good internal objects attenuate this attack.

The standards set by or the demands coming from the idealized good internal objects become, when combined with sadistic superego precursors, cruel demands for perfection leading to an unremitting harshness of the superego. This is complicated in cases where there is much sadism from the need to protect the good objects in the superego by excessive idealization so the standards of the superego become extremely high.

In Klein's theories mania represents a triumph in fantasy over the loss of the object, the basic fear of the depressive position. Mania is characterized by omnipotence, which represents a denial of need for the object and of any attacks on it; an identification with a sadistic superego in which external objects are depreciated with contempt or devaluation by projection of bad parts; object hunger—life is a feast so who cares if a few are eaten; triumph over a dead and dying universe of depression; or even an exaltation in which there is extreme idealization and identification with idealized internal and external objects leading to messianic states. In patients with manic and depressive symptoms no secure good internal object has been established. The various mechanisms described are all used to preserve the shaky, good internal object and protect it from destruction by aggression of bad internalized objects. There is a consequent failure to work through or resolve the depressive position.

When the depressive position is not worked through, there is a reprojection of the sadistic superego in order to deflect intolerable guilt outside, which in turn requires a regression to the paranoid-schizoid position. This, however, reinforces persecutory anxiety and leads to the greedy absorption of supplies as a protection against the dangers of threatening external attack.

All of this may be prematurely sexualized as an attempt to deny pregenital sadism through genital love. The longing for the good breast out of displaced oral dependency may be experienced as the longing for the father's penis and lead to homosexuality in males and hysteria in females. The bad breast out of displaced aggression may be experienced as the fear of the bad destructive penis. Similarly, the primal scene receives the projection of oral sadism characterized by the devouring phallic mother with the "vagina dentata," and the sadistic father. Due to this projection, an imagined sadistic father interferes with normal oedipal identification in males and the imagined devouring phallic mother interferes with normal oedipal identification in females, due to an increased fear of retaliation over oedipal aggressive competition. According to Klein, penis envy is derived from oral envy and is therefore not a critical feature of female sexuality. Conversely, sexual inhibition arises from defenses against sadistic impulses that are infiltrating sexual urges. Klein conceptualizes oral drives and oral conflicts as fueling and infiltrating oedipal developments everywhere.

## Criticism of Klein's Theories

There are some questionable assumptions in Klein's theory. First, she demands too much from the infantile psyche. Examples of this appear in her notion that envy is one of the earliest infantile expressions of the inborn death instinct, an expression requiring considerable cognitive skill on the part of the infant. Even more complex mentation would have to be postulated for her claim that the infant is born with an innate knowledge of the genitals of both sexes as well as postulated for her claim that the infant has the capacity to experience an oedipus complex in the first year of life. A similar objection has been raised to Kohut's postulation of the grandiose self and the idealized parent imago as intermediate narcissistic formations appearing before the age of 4. This, however, is a relatively minor assumption as compared to the extraordinary complex capacities assumed by Klein to be present in the mind of an infant.

Second, a powerful new movement in psychoanalysis actually arose from authors like Fairbairn and other neo-Kleinians, who pointed out the extraordinary neglect of environmental factors in her explanations of the development of psychopathology. Klein's baby, endowed with its constitutional share of aggression, reacts immediately to its early circumstances and then goes off in its own direction in fantasy with little further attention paid to environmental factors. Most of Klein's followers have recognized these deficiencies.

Third, there is a neglect of differences in adult clinical psychopathology in Klein's explanations. Interpretations involving primitive fantasies and defenses in the paranoid-schizoid and depressive position are used in treatments of all forms of pathology and are found in material from all levels of development. This has been criticized severely by a number of psychoanalytic authors (Kernberg 1980).

Most pertinent to a discussion of Kohut's work is the disagreement between Klein and her followers — who view adult narcissistic idealization and grandiosity as defenses against unconscious aggression — and Kohut, who views adult narcissistic idealization and grandiosity as based on developmental arrest and as originally representing, although not, as some critics misunderstand, identical with, a normal stage of development. Klein makes early oral sadism critical to an understanding of the appearance of idealization and grandiosity. Kohut views early oral sadism as a breakdown product of the self due to disappointment over failures in maternal empathy and not at all as the expression of any inborn death instinct, aggressive drive, or other "instinct." This is a profound and irreconcilable disagreement between the psychology of the self and all Kleinians and neo-Kleinians.

The role and origin of aggression and its transformations in both normal and pathological development remains an area of major controversy; furthermore, there is no reason to rule out the possibility that a new theory may at some future date provide an explanation of the vicissitudes and origins of aggression in a way more satisfactory and more acceptable to all psychoanalysts.

Melanie Klein postulated the existence of a functional ego from birth, and she insisted that the first phase of life was already based on a form of narcissistic object relationship with the mother, eliminating the autoerotic phase postulated by Freud. Thus, she acknowledged environmental influence but stressed the constitutional aspects of aggression. Klein disagreed with Freud, because she believed that even normal mourning always implied guilt since it reactivated the guilt of the depressive position. She also felt that normal mourning could reinforce the solution of the depressive position by causing a fresh working through and resolution of that position.

## Kleinians on Narcissism

Rosenfeld (1964, 1971) paid special attention to the subject of narcissism from a Kleinian standpoint. Segal (1983) points out that Klein gave us conceptual and technical tools to understand narcissism but says very little about it herself. Klein, as explained above, distinguished between temporary narcissistic states involving withdrawal to an identification with idealized internal objects and "narcissistic structures," a more long-standing organization involving projective identification to control objects and reintrojection of them in a way that affects the structure of the ego and the superego (Spillius 1983). She did not expand on this nor did she make an explicit connection between envy and narcissism although it is implicit in her book *Envy and Gratitude* (1975) that she thought of narcissism as a defense against envy. Segal (1983) stresses that narcissism is an expression of the death instinct as well as a defense against it, and proceeds to give clinical illustrations.

Rosenfeld (1971), like Segal, regards all but the most temporary states of narcissism as basically destructive and suffused with death instinct and not to be confused with self-respect and caring for one's self. He describes his concept of "destructive narcissism" as an organization based on idealization of the bad self, which triumphs in seducing the good self and defeating the analyst. Narcissism is experienced as the need to deny any dependency on an external object, because such dependency would imply the need for a loved and potentially frustrating object that is also intensely hated, with hatred taking the form of extreme idealization of the good object. Narcissistic object relations permit the avoidance of aggressive feelings caused by frustration and the awareness of envy. Rosenfeld says the narcissistic individual has introjected an "all good" primitive part-object or projected an idealized "all good" object into someone with the basic aim of denying any difference with or separation from the object; the individual with narcissistic object relations is allowed to avoid any recognition of separateness between self and object.

This should not be confused with Kohut's conception of the self-object. For the Kleinians, the lack of recognition of separateness between self and object is a powerful defense based on complicated introjective and projective mechanisms. If this defense is broken down, the separateness between self and object reappears with all the hatred and envy attached to the separate object of one's dependency strivings. In Kohut's theory, the notion of selfobject represents a primary experience and is normal at a certain phase of development. By the way of contrast, Rosenfeld (1964) says:

> The rigid preservation of the ideal self-image blocks any progress in the analysis of narcissistic patients, because it is felt to be endangered by any insight and contact with psychic reality. The ideal self-image of the narcissistic patient may be thought of as a highly pathological structure based on the patient's omnipotence and denial of reality. (p. 336)

This quotation is an excellent point against which to measure the theories of development and of treatment of Klein and the object-relations theorists on the one hand, and Kohut on the other. The development and function of the "ideal self-image," as Rosenfeld calls it, is viewed entirely differently by these two groups of theorists, in basically irreconcilable theoretical and clinical approaches.

One could conceive of a reaction to losses, whether wounds to one's self-esteem or the loss of objects upon whom one was dependent, in terms of Klein's basic premise that the depressive position is never worked through and therefore any loss will reawaken the problems of this position. If there is a relatively secure internalized good object, adult depression can lead to the working through of the depressive position with ego enrichment and creativity. If not, we see instead a regression to the paranoid-schizoid position with persecutory anxiety and dread. This would be a Kleinian type of explanation for the common phenomena in which narcissistic wounds are seen to produce at first a depressed state which then may be followed by an overcoming of that state in creativity and renewed efforts or a disintegration of the individual with the appearance of paranoid manifestations and hypochondriacal anxieties (Segal 1974).

Yet Segal's (1974, p. 119) postscript on technique, describing the relatively calm analyst as unaltered by the patient's projections and interpreting to the patient what is going on relatively free of counter-transference, has a certain similarity to Kohut's description of the calm, well-trained craftsman (Kohut 1968, 1971), explaining to the narcissistic patient the empathically perceived experience of the narcissistic wound involved when the session is over and the patient must leave the office. The nature of the explanations involved, however, and the concept of cure in the two theories are totally different (Kohut 1984).

According to Klein, at every phase of life the battle has to be waged anew, for with each loss the individual must avoid regression to the paranoid-schizoid position or the development of a manic defense; if the battle is waged successfully there will be further growth in the personality (Segal 1980). For Kohut the "battle" is not as vague. In an ambience of empathy and interpretation, the minor narcissistic wounds lead to new growth by transmuting internalizations; no early complex "positions" are postulated.

Spillius (1983) mentions the work of Bick who published some of her ideas in a brief paper on the skin as container (Bick 1968). According to Spillius, Bick presented the idea that the death instinct is experienced by the infant as falling apart, falling endlessly into space, or as the liquefying and pouring out uncontrollably of one's insides. Spillius writes:

> She thinks the response to this anxiety is a desperate use of all the senses to hold the self together — focusing on bright objects, on sounds, on being held, on the feeling of the nipple in the mouth; later on some form of activity and movement may serve this function of holding the self together. (p. 324)

There is a remarkable overlap here with Kohut in the language used to describe the fragmentation of the self and the attempt to prevent this catastrophe, but there is also a total difference in theoretical conceptualizations and in postulations regarding ego capacities in infants.

James (1973) insists that Kleinians have always been interested in the same kind of narcissistic phenomena that are studied by Kohut, but they have not acknowledged this interest. James cleverly spots what he calls the "nervousness" of Kohut at "seeming to subscribe to too many mental institutions in the first year" (p. 366), which would then leave Kohut open to the same criticisms leveled at Klein.

He emphasizes the similarities rather than the differences between the two theories. The views of Kohut and Klein are based on essentially conflicting and irreconcilable postulates and premises, and it would be even harder to reconcile them than it would be to reconcile the views of Melanie Klein and Anna Freud.

These three sets of explanations: the Kleinian, those of Freud and the ego psychologists, and the psychology of the self, represent alternative theoretical systems for the understanding of narcissistic phenomena. Whether they are "complementary" or irreconcilable has become today as much a political question within the psychoanalytic movement as a theoretical question.

In an effort to make Kleinian theory more consistent with the ego psychology school and more compatible with the tastes of North American psychoanalysts, Kerberg has produced an important revision of Kleinian theory which is still consistent with at least some of its principles. In so doing he has developed the major current popular alternative to the psychology of the self, known as modern object relations theory, which we turn to in the next chapter. Selecting from among Klein's major concepts and deciding which to accept requires further assumptions and postulates.

# Chapter 5

———

# Kernberg and Modern Object Relations Theory

## *Kernberg's Criticism of Klein*

Kernberg (1972, 1980) makes a number of critical comments about the work of Melanie Klein. He points out that Klein's technique, in which fantasies are collected from children aged 2 or 3, contains nothing to justify her assumptions about the fantasy life of the 1-year old. There is no evidence for assumed innate knowledge, for example of sexuality, genitals, or inborn oedipal strivings, or for the death instinct.

Kernberg maintains that higher levels of defenses are neglected by the Kleinians and that the distinction between the normal and the pathological in the infant is blurred. Klein's terminology, he explains, hopelessly confuses mechanisms, structures, and fantasies. For example, what is an "internal object"? Also, there is in Klein little distinction between diagnoses or in the treatment of various types of adult pathology.

Kernberg observes that the Kleinian emphasis on early object relations and projection leads in treatment to early deep magical transference interpretations, assumed to be critical for the cure but which he fears actually may set off further regression. The Kleinians, he says, neglect the therapeutic alliance and blur the distinction between the transference and the transference neurosis. They violate the well-known rule of interpreting resistance before content and of working in from the surface.

Kernberg, in an argument that he will later (1974, 1974a) apply to Kohut, believes that there is no evidence that fantasies emerging in the transference repeat actual fantasies occurring in the first year of life. He objects to the Kleinian equation of introjection and iden-tification, but he agrees with the Kleinians on the importance of early superego precursors. Still, the "mad language" of Kleinian analysts, quickly concentrating on breasts, milk, and so on, overemphasizes these confused concepts at the expense of everything else, says Kern-berg, and leads to an intellectual indoctrination with the same inter-pretations being made over and over again. This criticism was already made by Balint (1968).

As a case example, Kernberg (1972) refers to a treatment reported by the Kleinian analyst Segal of a candidate-analysand who started the first session "by saying that he was determined to be qualified in the minimum time and then spoke about his digestive troubles and, in another context, about cows." The analyst interpreted "that I was the cow, like the mother who breast-fed him, and that he felt that he was going to empty me greedily, as fast as possible, of all my analy-sis-milk; this interpretation immediately brought out material about his guilt in relation to exhausting and exploiting his mother" (p. 87). Kernberg wonders to what extent this eager patient-candidate would accept such a deep interpretation as part of his wish to learn a new magical language, and to what extent such learning would feed in-to defenses of intellectualization and rationalization. His main point is that "the patient's greediness might also reflect a narcissistic char-acter structure, and the extent to which such character defenses might later interfere with the deepening of the transference should be clar-ified by exploring that defensive structure further, rather than by gratifying the patient's eagerness with a direct interpretation of the possible ultimate source of the trait" (p. 87).

In further criticisms Kernberg states that stress on such concepts as "constitutional envy" and the "death instinct" represent a form of pseudobiology. There is no clarity in the Kleinian notion of "posi-tions" about how they are related to or different from the classical "defenses." These complaints, along with Gill's (1982) comment that "despite statements to the contrary, the Kleinians do seem to make inappropriately deep transference interpretations which fail to make adequate contact with the current reality of the actual analytic situation" (p. 136) are rejected by Sandler and Sandler, and by Steiner (Bornstein 1984, pp. 391–392, p. 446). These authors point out that Kleinians differ considerably in their acceptance of Melanie Klein's doctrines just as Freudians differ, and that many modern Kleinians — perhaps the majority — are sensitive and do not engage in premature deep interpretations.

Finally, Kernberg criticizes the Kleinian use of splitting, which is sometimes equated with repression and sometimes with a more primitive operation, and projective identification, which is a hybrid for the Kleinians of an internal psychic mechanism combined with an interpersonal attempt at control and communication.

Kernberg (1975, pp. 30–31) redefines projective identification as projection that has not succeeded entirely due to a weak ego, so that patients continue to experience their own aggression as well as fearing it from the external object. Patients, therefore, fear the external object and must control or even attack and destroy it before it destroys them. Abend et al. (1983) point out that every author defines this term differently and it just leads to confusion.

## Views of Modell

Many psychoanalysts feel that it is more realistic and practical in working with narcissistic and borderline patients to turn from the Kleinians to Modell's technique of allowing a transitional object transference to take place so that the development of the patient can resume; here we have a type of archaic transference (Gedo 1984). The notion of "transitional object" was first introduced by Winnicott and later referred to by Modell (1963, 1968). He defines a "transitional object phase" of the development of object love, during which there is a clinging dependent relationship to the external object, which is given magical powers to produce well being and protection. For Modell, this stands between primary narcissism, where there is no recognition of the object as separate, and true object love, where there is the capacity to relate to the object as separate, human, and having needs of its own.

Modell emphasizes that treatment should provide a good-enough holding environment that leads to a transitional object transference, "a primitive form of object relationship in the transference," which is "closer to schizophrenia than neuroses." In this transference mere contact with the therapist is expected to passively cure and afford magical protection; the patient does not expect to do any actual work in the treatment. By emphasizing the transitional object transference, Modell argues that he is distinguishing among the classical type of psychoneuroses where other typical transferences appear, the narcissistic patient — who attempts to maintain an illusion of self-sufficiency in a closed system and thus does not form a transitional object transference, and the borderline patient who shows this "intense object hunger." Such archaic transferences as described by Little (1981) and others are life-and-death types of transferences and therapist becomes an oxygen line to keep the patient alive.

This is a descriptive picture but is metapsychologically confused. It blurs the distinction between borderline personality disorders and schizophrenia and it ignores the difference between the "object" and the "aggregate of object representations." It does, however, call attention to the idea of healing as facilitated by the analytic setting serving as a holding environment. Winnicott (1958) called attention to the gratification implicit in the constancy and reliability of the analyst's judgment, the analyst's capacity to perceive the patient's unique identity, and the constancy and reliability of the person of the analyst.

Throughout the discussion and cutting across all the theories, there is a dilemma in that there are two basic psychoanalytic models of treatment and cure. The first stresses a neutral-interpretive stance of the analyst; the second stresses more the nurturing-reconstructive experience within the analytic interaction. Thus Kernberg and many "traditional" psychoanalysts in the United States are clinicians of the first approach, while Balint, Winnicott, and Kohut stress the allowing of regression to traumatic developmental phases and the resumption of growth via the analytic relationship.

The dilemma to which we will repeatedly return in this book is whether the neutral-interpretive stance when it is predominant generates overwhelming resistances due to the arid interpersonal ambience. Or, does the nurturing-reconstructive experience when it is emphasized at the expense of neutrality and interpretation really allow the patient to *experience* the beneficial aspects of the relationship without first analyzing the rigid stereotyped self and object images? Volkan

(1976) writes, "It is only when the therapist is differentiated from the archaic image that the patient's introjection of and identification with the therapist's function is seen as operating in the service of altering structures already formed and/or forming new ones" (p. 87).

## Problems in Object Relations Theory

The basic assumption of object relations theory is stated by Shapiro (1978):

> One can understand the relationships between people through an examination of the internal images they have of one another. In the healthiest people, these images correspond rather accurately to the reality of the other person and are continually reshaped and reworked as new information is perceived and integrated. In less psychologically healthy people, the images are stereotyped, rigid, and relatively unchanged by new information. (p. 1309)

Object relations theory is useful in understanding the puzzling lack of influence of the benevolent therapist, that is to say, why a corrective emotional experience, if it does occur in psychotherapy, occurs slowly at times, often to the agonizing countertransference frustration of the well-intentioned therapist. However, object relations theory tends to lend itself to medieval scholastics and obsessional disputes about postulated theoretical details, but it has also shown value in organizing direct observations of the preoedipal mother–child unit (Mahler et al. 1975).

There are many debatable problems inherent in object relations theory. No methodology has been developed to verify those reconstructions of object relations theory — which have been derived from adult treatment — of the various phases of development as described by Kernberg (Abend et al. 1983). Nor has an approach been devised that enables us to correlate these reconstructions with the data of direct observation of the preoedipal mother–child unit *without* the injection of preconceived notions of the observer.

Authors disagree about "primitive internalized object relations." Are these a source of motivation and the only or primary source or an additional explanation for behaviors insufficiently explained by drive theories? Neither of these views make clear what causes these internalizations to affect behavior; the relationship between "drives" and "internalizations" is not clear. Gedo (1979) points out that the rejection of the death instinct by most analysts "leaves that body of clinical data classifiable under the rubric of repetition compulsion without motivational underpinnings. In my judgment, the conception of early object relations as an additional source of human motivation was one major tendency to fill this metapsychological void" (p. 366).

In addition, the problem of "internalization" is complex. Schafer (1968) defines internalization as all those processes by which a subject transforms real or imagined regulatory interactions with the environment into inner regulations and characteristics. Perception is not the same thing as internalization and the cognitive creation of object representations is not the same as internalization. Internalization is structural; perception and cognitive creation are experiential. The relationship between the structural and the experiential remains unclear in these theories, and the path from the experiential to the structural represents a big problem and already assumes a certain ego capacity. Thus the intrapsychic movement from perceptions to object representations to introjects as internal foreign presences to psychic structure is characterized differently by different object relations theorists.

The authors in this group do not always distinguish between interpersonal relations, which Meissner (1978, 1980a) calls object relatedness, i.e., "real" observable interactions between people, and object relations, which are experiences of either party from within the interaction and their internal experiences of it.

Another confusion pertains to the relationship between "object representation" and "introject." According to Volkan (1976), Kernberg and Jacobson avoid the term "introject" entirely, whereas Giovacchini regards it as identical to an "object representation." Each author uses these terms differently.

Volkan offers a definition derived from his studies of the mourning process. He defines an introject as, "a special, already differentiated, object representation that strives for absorption into the self-representation in order to achieve identification" (p. 59). Introjects, in contrast to object representations, are "functional and may play a role in the formation and alteration of psychic structure" (p. 59). I will discuss and clarify this matter. For Volkan, an introject is experienced as an inner presence because it is *between* being an object representation and not yet having been absorbed into the psychic ego structure. Therapy for him, as for Giovacchini, leans heavily on absorbing the introject of the analyst into the psychic structure in order to alter or reform the psychic structure by, for example, replacement or attenuation of early malevolent introjects.

The mechanisms of internalization are very often confused in the literature. *Identification* is the most mature, less directly dependent on the drives, most adaptively selective, least ambivalent, more a modeling process, and originally a modeling on the parents. It is an automatic, usually unconscious mental process whereby an individual becomes like another person in one or several aspects. It is part of the learning process but also a means of adaptation to a feared or lost object. Identification is growth promoting and leads to better adaptation — a critical clinical point.

The word *introjection* was used by Freud in two ways. Originally (1917) he used it in "Morning and Melancholia" to mean a lost object taken in and retained as part of the psychic structure. Later (Freud 1933) it represented taking in the parents' demands as if they were one's own in the formation of the superego. Here one does not simply copy the object selectively, as in identification; a more encompassing process occurs. Freud's original definitions assumed a solid repression barrier with a cohesive sense of self and a relatively well functioning ego. Thus it has the flavor of a higher level in Freud's usage.

*Incorporation* is a form or model of introjection or taking into the mind the attributes of another person that involves the fantasy of oral ingestion and swallowing. Identification accomplished by incorporation implies change by fantasied cannibalism; "I am devouring your book like a hungry wolf," as a patient told me once. Incorporation is a primitive kind of interpersonal relations fantasy. It is primary process ideation, a form of fantasied "object-relatedness." At one time it was thought that this fantasy accompanies all introjection, but this is not now believed to be correct.

Schafer (1968) offers a modern review of introjection, which he defines as a process through which object representations are constituted as introjects or are changed into them. An introject is an inner presence with which one feels in continuous or intermittent dynamic relationship, says Schafer, and he lists certain characteristics of introjects which have great clinical value:

1. They may be conceived of as a personlike thing or creature.
2. They may be unconscious, preconscious, or conscious.
3. They may be experienced as exerting a pressure or influence on the subject's state or behavior independently of conscious efforts to control it.
4. They do not *copy* external objects since they are shaped by "fantasies, projections, symbolizations, misunderstandings, idealizations, depreciations, and selective biases originating in the subject's past history and present developmental phase and dynamic position" (p. 73).
5. Once formed, an introject diminishes the influence of the external object. This is a key point. An introject is formed due to severe ambivalence or more or less disappointment in an attempt to modify distressing relations with the external object.
6. Once formed, the introject alters a relationship with an external object in a way not correctable by further experiences with the external object since the influence of the external object is now diminished.
7. Introjection is an event, a change in psychic organization and in the psychic status of an object representation. Notice how this assumes an active role in the ego of the infant.

It is necessary to understand these descriptions of introjects and introjection in order to compare them with Kohut's notion of transmuting internalization that will be presented in Chapter 8. Introjection represents or expresses a regressive modification of the boundaries and the reality testing function of the ego. It perpetuates neediness and ambivalence, displacing it to the inside. In contrast to transmuting internalization, introjections are not growth promoting but represent a passive mode of mastery and are not adaptive per se.

Splitting is a term used differently by authors in object relations theory (Pruyser 1975). It generally represents a failure in the synthesizing function of the ego which Freud (1940) related to disavowal, but which has come to have many more preoedipal connotations. It is crucial to the turning away from reality in any condition, including dreams, perversions, neuroses, and psychoses, and it enables these processes to occur.

Projection is defined by the later object relations theorists as a process in which object representations and self representations charged with energy or influence (that is to say, made into introjects), are experienced as coming from outside the boundaries of the self, such as from the analyst, and ascribed to an independent object, creature, or thing (e.g., the influencing machine). It leads to a separation from the unacceptable in contrast to projective identification as defined above, which actively continues a relationship.

## *"Self" in Object Relations Theory*

Kernberg (1982) proposes eliminating the concept of "self" as opposed to "object" because he argues that used in this way it is a psychosocial description. For Kernberg the self as a psychic structure originates from both libidinally and aggressively invested self-representations: "It is, in short, an ego function and structure that evolves gradually from the integration of its component self-representations into a supraordinate structure that incorporates other ego functions" (p. 905). Thus, an aggregate of such self-representations exists in the psyche, with various degrees of internal contradiction and disjointedness or integration from the autistic to the realistic; the final set of self-representations is a function of how well integrated and developed these earlier representations have become. The same is true for object representations.

For any adaptively successful behavior there has to be a relatively well-organized, well-developed, and well-integrated set of self and object representations in the individual. Self and object representations are essentially subjective conceptualizations or experiential guideposts that lead to behavior for many modern object relations theorists, whereas an introject is thought of as exerting an influence on a person's thoughts or behavior whether the person likes it or not; unfortunately in the literature this distinction is often blurred. Greenberg and Mitchell (1983) claim that Kernberg, although he follows Hartmann in defining the self as a representation, switches to "referring to the self as a structure" (p. 335).

Before Kernberg, Jacobson (1964) reached the high point of complexity in the use of the vicissitudes of self- and object-representations to move toward understanding narcissism. She gave the definition of healthy narcissism as the libidinal investment of the self, but then described self-esteem as a more complex phenomenon (Teicholz 1978). Any factor disturbing self-esteem contributes to a disturbance of narcissism, such as split, unstable, or unrealistically worthless or grandiose self-representations, or:

> if the perceptual faculties or the judgment capacity of the ego is faulty, if the ego ideal retains too much of the primitive idealizations of self and object, if the critical powers of the superego are too harsh and unmitigated by a mature ego and if the superego is unable to regulate the libidinal and aggressive investment of the self, if the aggressive or the libidinal drives are insufficiently neutralized or if they are inadequately fused. (Teicholz 1978, p. 848)

A review of Jacobson's position by Teicholz (1978) demonstrates the scholastic complexity of Jacobson's object relations theory. As Greenberg and Mitchell (1983) put it, "Hairs are split and resplit until the flow of Jacobson's argument almost disappears" (p. 306).

Kernberg's theory — which admittedly rests heavily on the work of Jacobson — is a theory of normal and pathological internal object relations. His argument concerns itself little with object relatedness or relationships; instead it focuses on the internalized derivatives of experienced object relatedness or relationships, which Kernberg designates "internalized object relationships." Meissner (1978) points out that the latter "seem to come much closer to what has been described in other contexts as 'introjects'" (p. 587). Rather than a theory of object relatedness it is a theory of object representations, addressing itself to the vicissitudes and "metabolism" — yet see Kernberg's objections to Klein's pseudobiology mentioned above — of such internalized object relationships, or internalized objects, or introjects, with little attention to the relationships with objects as such. Meissner (1978) continues, "Consequently, its risk lies in its reductionistic tendency to read the development of later and more differentiated pathology in terms of the primitive vicissitudes of object relatedness" (p. 588).

## Kernberg's Developmental Stages

Kernberg (1976) now postulates five stages of the development of internalized object relations. His first or "primary undifferentiated" stage resembles the phase of "normal autism" of Mahler. Object relations theory lends itself well to the organization of direct observations of the initial preoedipal mother–infant dyad, during which there are no self- or object-representations, or images, as they are alternatively called by Kernberg. This stage lasts about a month or two and leads to the second stage, which corresponds to the symbiotic phase of Mahler between the age of 2 and 6 months, added to her first or "differentiation" subphase of separation–individuation from 6 to 8 or 9 months of age.

In this stage, there are representations, but these are roughly undifferentiated self-and-object constellations separated only into good and bad, and consequently there is in this stage no differentiation between self and object. Kernberg here postulates a "primary undifferentiated 'good' self-object representation" or "constellation" associated with pleasurable experiences ("pure pleasure ego") and invested with libido; and a "primary undifferentiated 'bad' self-object representation" associated with pain and frustration, and invested with aggression. Kernberg's conception of "self-object-affect unit" should not be confused with Kohut's "selfobject," which is an experience-near conception coming from an entirely different methodology and theory to be described in Section II.

The third stage, which follows the first rumblings of separation–individuation that occurred during the age of 6–9 months, begins when the self- and object-representations have been differentiated *within* the two primary constellations ("good" and "bad") that predominate in the second stage described above. It ends, as does the phase of separation–individuation of Mahler, somewhere in the third year of life, with the eventual integration of "good" and "bad" self-representations into an integrated self-concept and the integration of "good" and "bad" object-representations into "total" object-representations. The achievement of object constancy and the firm capacity to distinguish the inner from the outer world — stable ego boundaries — depends on this stage.

Kernberg (1976) postulates that "pathological fixation and/or regression to this stage of development of internalized object relations determines borderline personality organization" (p. 65). He explains that in this third stage, "the separation of libidinally invested and aggressively invested self- and object-representations becomes strengthened by active utilization of the mechanism of splitting, which is geared to protect the ideal, good relationship with the mother from 'contamination' by bad self-representations and bad representations of her" (p. 67). Normally this splitting decreases, but Kernberg continues with a statement meant to specifically delineate the intrapsychic pathology that predominates in the borderline personality: "The main objective of the defensive constellation centering on splitting in the borderline personality organization is to keep separate the aggressively determined and the libidinally determined intrapsychic structures stemming from early object relations" (p. 67). Although by the end of the third stage in normal development there is a firm self concept differentiated from object representations, within the self concept there is still some splitting of good and bad self-representations. Similarly, within the object representations "at first only representing mother, and then also father, siblings, etc." (pp. 66–67), good and bad object representations "coexist" by splitting which, however, is gradually diminishing.

The fourth stage, beginning in the latter part of the third year of life and lasting through the oedipal period "is characterized by the integration of libidinally invested and aggressively invested self-representations into the definite self-system, and of libidinally invested and aggressively invested object-images into 'total' object-representations" (p. 67). In this phase the ego and superego as intrapsychic structures are "consolidated." The typical pathology in this stage is represented by the neuroses and the organization of character pathology Kernberg calls "higher level," where "pathogenic conflicts typically occur between the ego and a relatively well-integrated but excessively strict and punitive superego" (p. 67).

One variant of character pathology forming at this stage is the narcissistic personality, which is, according to Kernberg, an abnormal consolidation, characterized by the formation of a pathological "grandiose self," embedded in a defensive organization "similar to that of the borderline personality organization" (p. 68), due to regression back to the third stage.

Thus, according to Kernberg, the coalescence of the "good" and "bad" self-representations into a definite, integrated, relatively realistic overall self-representation in the ego, and the coalescence of the "good" and "bad" object representations into definite, integrated, relatively realistic overall object representations in the ego, is the task of the fourth stage, and fails in the borderline patient. This failure may be due to congenital ego defect or excessive aggression fixing the patient in the third stage or causing regression back to it, and making the fourth stage, coalescence or integration, impossible. This coalescence is related to and based on Hartmann's concept of neutralization, freeing energy for ego functioning and the higher level exercise of repression, that is, setting up countercathexes; if it fails, the weakened ego must utilize splitting as its principal defense, setting in motion a downward spiral of further weakness and more splitting.

The fifth and final developmental stage, from age 5 to 7, is the resolution of the oedipal phase, the consolidation of the superego, a diminished sharp opposition between the ego and the superego leading to more internal harmony, and finally the formation and consolidation of "ego identity." Notice that in normal development, according to Kernberg, splitting begins around the third month, peaks several months later, and gradually disappears at the end of the second year and beginning of the third year of life, after which there is the development of repression and higher level defenses (p. 69).

## Kernberg on the Superego

In his conceptions of the superego and narcissism, Kernberg shifts from these more Kleinian concepts to a heavier reliance on the work of Jacobson. However, Jacobson avoided rigid stepwise descriptions and "considered parental interaction with the child of crucial importance rather than those conflicts which go on between 'primitive introjects'" (Abend et al. 1983, p. 163).

The main components of the superego are built up during the second to fifth year, earlier than Freud thought according to Kernberg. They are integrated in the fourth to the sixth years and toned down and consolidated (depersonified and abstracted) during the fifth through seventh years. The earliest superego structure is from "the internalization of fantastically hostile, highly unrealistic object-images reflecting 'expelled,' projected, and reintrojected 'bad' self-object representations" (p. 71). (Do not confuse this with Kohut's "selfobject.") The stronger the pregenital frustration and constitutional aggression, the more predominant are these sadistic superego forerunners; the sadistic superego peaks at the beginning of the fourth stage of development.

There is also a second primitive superego structure — the condensed, magical, ideal, "all good" self- and object-representations which form the kernel of the ego-ideal through "primitive idealization."

In the fourth stage of development these two aspects of the precursors of the superego are "integrated," leading to decreased defensive projection and permitting the internalization of more realistic demands and prohibitions of the parents during the oedipal period. Integration and internalization perform the function of "toning down" the superego from primitive and archaic to more modulated and reasonable functioning. In the fifth stage of development the toned-down superego becomes more integrated and harmonious with the ego, leading to consolidation of ego identity and the superego becomes more abstract and depersonified.

Thus in Kernberg's theory two types of superego failure can occur. In the first type there is a failure in the integration of the sadistic precursors of the superego with the benign or primitively idealized precursors which interferes with the internalization of more realistic oedipal parental images and so perpetuates the primitive sadistic superego forerunners and fosters excessive reprojection, leading to paranoia.

In the second type, as in the borderline personality, there is a similar type of failure of integration of these precursors due to a dangerous primitive idealization. External objects are seen as totally good in order to be sure they cannot be destroyed by projected bad objects. This phenomenon occurs too early and in too extreme a fashion due to the need to defend against so much aggression. Thus, again, idealization is seen as a defense against aggression. Furthermore, the internalization of primitively idealized early object-images creates impossible internalized demands, leading to an impasse in which "a catastrophic fusion" between these unrealistic ideal objects and the "external persecutors" or projected bad objects then forms. This leads to a sadistic superego nucleus which is perpetuated by reprojection and reintrojection. It leads to an interference with the toning down of the superego by the internalization of more realistic parental prohibitions, with the integration of the superego itself, and with the development of harmony between the superego and the ego. The latter causes interference with the formation of ego identity, leading to the lack of a consistent solid integrated self-concept, one of the important DSM-III characteristics of the borderline patient.

## Other Clinical Points

Kernberg distinguishes between the psychotic patient who presents fusion experiences with the therapist and the borderline patient who largely maintains reality testing. He claims (1980) that his object relations theory is an integral part of ego psychology but offers a theory of affects and motivation which is quite different from psychoanalytic drive psychology and which (Greenberg and Mitchell 1983) changes "from chapter to chapter" (p. 331).

For Kernberg, constitutionally determined pleasurable and unpleasurable subjective states that first arise in the undifferentiated psychophysiological self are integrated and differentiated in the context of internalized "good" and "bad" object relations and are critical in the differentiation of instinctual drives into libido and aggression. All three systems in the structural theory of Freud (id, ego, superego) originate from internalized object relations, according to Kernberg.

In this theory there is no such thing as primary narcissism (or primary masochism), and the earliest libidinal investment is in the undifferentiated self-object representation. (This should not be confused with Kohut's selfobject!) Kernberg (1980) states that "drives" are overall motivational systems that stem from the hierarchy of libidinal and aggressive constellations. We begin with "inborn affect dispositions" which are integrated as "good" and "bad" affect states into self- and object-relations and lead to "an overall hierarchical organization of drive systems, or libido and aggression in the broadest sense" (p. 108).

Kernberg (1980) separates a small group of what he calls schizoid borderlines who relate to the differentiation subphase of separation–individuation and require holding. The remainder of borderline patients are to be treated by the interpretation of their projection of "all bad" and "all good" self- and object-representations onto the therapist. He disagrees with Masterson (1976), whom he insists simplistically ignores the Oedipus complex and its distortions in borderline patients. Kernberg points out that condensations of oedipal and preoedipal issues must always be taken into consideration.

Kernberg emphasizes that supportive and interpretive techniques in intensive psychotherapy tend to cancel each other out, because two kinds of psychotherapy simultaneously presented to the patient activate splitting and projection. The basic assumption for the intensive psychotherapy of most borderline and narcissistic patients is that the interpretation of split off transference projections leads to better integration and the eventual development of normal transferences and more realistic object relations, which then allow the formal working through of the oedipal phase of development.

Kernberg hopes to combine the therapeutic effort to cognitively understand and make interpretations to these patients with a holding function or the "authentic concern" of the therapist. This authentic concern manifests itself by respecting the autonomy of the patient, surviving the patient's aggression, and being available for empathy and support but not abandoning neutrality; Kernberg feels that a certain balance is needed in managing the archaic transferences which tend to develop in borderline patients.

In contrast to Kohut, Kernberg believes that the defenses characteristic of the narcissistic personality disorder are similar to those of the borderline personality disorder. There is the same predominance of splitting, denial, projective identification, primitive idealization, and a sense of omnipotence, based on the same intense oral aggression as in borderline patients. However, the formation of the pathological grandiose self in the narcissistic personality by masking archaic aggression allows better superficial social and work functioning. Over a long period of time, says Kernberg (1975), we observe a lack of depth in such people that he calls "the emptiness behind the glitter" (p. 230). The basic divergence between the views of Kernberg and Kohut will be discussed in Chapter 11.

This grandiose self, for Kernberg (1976, 1980), is a defensive structure which is pathological and must be broken down, and represents the pathological fusion of the self-image with (a) the specialness in the reality of the child's early experiences; (b) the idealized self-image — which represents a compensatory glorious self-image; and (c) the idealized object-image, which is also compensatory and involves the fantasy of having the ever-loving and ever-giving parent. These fuse to form a pathological grandiose self that functions to avoid dependency, and to protect against anticipated attacks from external objects which have been devalued. External objects are invested with high and dangerous powers due to projection and so the world seems as hateful and revengeful as the patient. The patient must devalue these dangerous others, including the real parents, a devaluation which is then rationalized as disappointment in everybody.

## Criticism of Kernberg

Heimann (1966) argues that Kernberg's notion of splitting represents a regressive ego function and not a typical or normal infantile position. Holzman (1976) attacks Kernberg's gratuitous assumptions and his complex terminology and assertions, which unnecessarily complicate his ideas and are unclear. He concludes that the person of Kernberg's theory does not think — that person lives by introjects.

Calef and Weinshel (1979) argue that Kernberg's fundamental assumptions have not been made clear. They ask what criteria justify his selective borrowing from the work of Melanie Klein. These authors question the source of his clinical data, which comes from all sorts of treatment carried out by Kernberg and others. They claim that his material is presented without discussion of the contamination or influence by the differing forms of psychotherapy or psychoanalysis from which the data emerged, nor does the material refer to the stage of treatment (beginning, middle, or advanced) that may affect the material. Calef and Weinshel also criticize his difficult terminology; some of the terms Kernberg uses, they say, are defined and employed in an idiosyncratic sense. They question whether one single entity such as the borderline personality organization can be delineated in this precise systematization. They argue also that there are too many entities and pigeon holes resulting in "mental acrobatics."

As do other authors (Abend et al. 1983), they challenge the assumption that the interpretation of predominant primitive defensive operations such as the projection of "all-bad" self- and object-representations onto the therapist will strengthen the ego in these extremely disturbed patients, and they raise the possibility that such patients will actually be in danger of regression from such interpretations. They believe that Kernberg continually shifts and modifies his assertions so that he can maintain the discreteness of his concept of borderline personality organization. They question how, with all this tendency towards projection and projective identification going on, the borderline patient can maintain reality testing inside or outside of the therapy situation. They conclude that object-relations theory is *not* reconcilable with Freud's tripartite structural theory, which they also insist is explicitly replaced by the object-relations theory of Kernberg. They warn us not to view the patient through "a prism of prefabricated ideas" based on what is believed to be contained within a given diagnostic label — a regressive "harkening back to a sort of Kraepelinian taxonomy" (p. 489).

Calef and Weinshel raise certain issues that have been repeatedly suggested in criticism of the psychology of the self although that system certainly is different than Kernberg's approach. They sug-

gest that as a curious social phenomenon we are now in "the midst
of a flurry of such proposals" of revisions of psychoanalytic theory.
They do not feel it is yet possible to submit a specific formula that
encompasses all the elements of such revisions, but they warn that
"more often than not, however, they have enjoyed only a transient
significance and popularity" (p. 487). They worry about the retreat
from the centrality of the Oedipus complex and the emphasis on the
vicissitudes of sexuality to the role of aggression and pregenital factors in psychological life. They believe that there has not been sufficient attention to whether the material at hand represents a defensive regression or a "developmental *arrest* and/or defect" (p. 488).

Klein and Tribich (1981) state that Kernberg removes Freud's
drive theory and introduces a new metapsychology of his own. The
key to understanding Freud is the notion of the person driven by the
need to release something from within. These authors argue that
Kernberg confuses the object for attachment with Freud's object for
discharge of the drives. They point out that splitting, for Freud, related to the mechanisms of denial and disavowal, which Freud used
differently than Kernberg, and that Kernberg posits the need for human objects rather than drives as the basic human motivation. They
feel that this view is closer to Bowlby's "attachment" than Kernberg
admits and that it places psychopathology more in the area of interpersonal relations. They insist that Kernberg dodges and confuses the
issue of the origin of aggression, and changes the meaning of libido
and aggression from drives to affect states accumulating from environmental experiences (also see Goldberg 1985).

Klein and Tribich accuse Kernberg of misusing Hartmann's terms
of fusion and neutralization and argue that his criticisms of other
object relations theorists are defective. They conclude that Kernberg's
attempt at rapprochement and harmonious resolution between the
"constrasting and competing" Freudian instinct theory and object-
relations theory is "theoretically unwarranted" and leads only to "confusion, distortion and inconsistency" in which "Kernberg's synthesis
becomes Kernberg's theory" (p. 27). Their view is supported by the
detailed study of Greenberg and Mitchell (1983).

A general body of psychoanalytic knowledge of the narcissistic
and borderline disorders, and a generally agreed-upon set of psychoanalytic metapsychological formulations of psychopathology does not
exist. The psychology of the self does not represent some kind of sin-

gular heresy, as some authors have implied, nor does it constitute a "cult" or splinter group. The psychology of the self constitutes one of a number of current differing approaches to clinical phenomena, and provides some explanations of clinical material which hitherto seemed obscure or intransigent to traditional interpretations.

# Section II

## KOHUT'S PSYCHOLOGY OF THE SELF

# Chapter 6

━━

# Definitions of the Self

The first problem that confronts anyone who attempts to study the psychology of the self arises from the definition of "self." No two authors use this term in exactly the same way. Perhaps the most well-known use of the term "self" is that of George Herbert Mead (1962), a pragmatist who tried to eliminate the parallelism between the mind and the body by seeing the mind and the self as arising out of social interaction and having no innate separate existence. For Mead, the self was a social self that formed in two stages. At first, the individual's self is constituted simply by an organization of the attitudes of others toward both the individual and one another in the specific social acts in which the individual participates with them. Then, at the second stage, there is added "an organization of the social attitudes of the generalized other or the social group as a whole to which he belongs" (p. 158). Thus, for Mead, the mind or self is formed by "reflexiveness" from social experience, a view that probably influenced H. S. Sullivan (1953) in forming his "interpersonal school" of psychiatry (Chessick 1974, 1977a, Greenberg and Mitchell 1983). This view represents a "social behaviorism," an attempt to extend empiricism to the psychology of the mind or the self. McCall (Mischel

1977) calls it the "social looking-glass approach to the self," in which the self is essentially a social construction.

## Clinical Origin of Kohut's Definition of Self

Mead's approach is in direct contrast to the psychology of the self of Kohut, which focuses on the person's subjective experience, the inner sense of self. The therapist learns about this through empathy or vicarious introspection and attempts to understand the rising and falling of self-esteem in relation to the person's largely unconscious ambitions, on the one hand, and largely unconscious ideals, on the other. As Mischel (1977) explains:

> These in turn are seen as rooted in a sense of self that develops out of relations to others, beginning with the infant's relation to the nurturing mother, a development whose vicissitudes may lead to a self that is relatively cohesive . . . or a self that tends toward fragmentation, . . . as in hypochondria, or the experience of being driven to unusual sexual goals, or other behaviors which the person himself may experience as irrational. (p. 26)

Such apparent "irrationality" experienced by the patient, which is of great clinical importance, is emphasized by Wolf (Mischel 1977), who presents the case of Miss S., a graduate student whose boyfriend had to be away for six weeks on a trip. She not only missed him and felt sad but could not free herself of the recurrent thought that he would get involved with another woman and forget her, although rationally, in light of their excellent relationship, this was not an appropriate fear. Yet she could not stave off a sense of restlessness, depression, fatigue, mild insomnia, and impairment of work efficiency, and "she suddenly found herself staring at other women with fantasies of touching and sexual contact, became frightened about herself, wondering whether she was becoming a homosexual, and consulted an analyst" (pp. 205–206). From the point of view of the psychology of the self, this example illustrates the patient's subjective perception of a disturbed state of the self, the patient's own perception of apparently irrational thoughts and unwanted fantasies, and the patient's perception in the form of a feeling that something was going wrong with herself, which she characterized as perhaps being neurotic, or going crazy, or becoming a pervert. These feelings led her to consult a doctor.

Self-psychologists maintain that this is a fundamentally different approach from the framework of the natural sciences adopted by Freud. According to self-psychologists, the structural model of Freud — id, ego, and superego — is an attempt by the scientific observer stationed outside this psyche or "mental apparatus" to describe the inner psyche. Wolf explains:

> Kohut's self/self-object model, on the other hand, allows conceptualization of insights gained from psychoanalytic data in terms of a model that explicitly recognizes that these data are experienced from *inside* a psychic apparatus; it describes relationships from the point of view of an observer stationing himself *inside* the experiencing apparatus. (p. 209)

Wolf illustrates this difference using the case of Miss. S., described above. In classical psychoanalytic structural theory Miss S.'s relationship to her boyfriend is narcissistic, meaning that even a temporary loss of the invested object causes the narcissistic libido to be withdrawn — according to the U-tube theory — into the ego, which is modified to now contain an identification with the lost object. The ego becomes the target of the aggression originally directed at the lost object and suffers the experience of depression. The ego tries to remedy this by a new narcissistic form of object choice expressed by the fantasy of a homosexual relationship. We have to assume that the choice of Miss S.'s boyfriend also was a narcissistic choice; initially chosen because he was like Miss S. or like what Miss S. aspired to be. In Freud's theory this is contrasted to true object love, defined as the love of someone for their own and distinct qualities.

In Kohut's model analysts attempt to station themselves inside the patient's psyche and to conceptualize the patient's subjective experience. Miss S. was experiencing herself as a more or less well functioning "me" until the boyfriend left; she then began to experience tension, depression, and restlessness as if in a frantic search for something missing, "something with which to soothe herself to restore the previous feeling of calmness and well being" (p. 210). By means of empathy or vicarious introspection the therapist gains the experience-near conception of Miss S. not feeling like her old self or feeling that her cohesive self had suffered incipient or partial fragmentation. The cause of this is the absence of the boyfriend. He had performed a psychological function which became apparent only when he was no longer present; he "somehow" lent cohesion to Miss S.'s self, functioning as a sort of external glue. When the cohesion of self is lost, there is a restless search for a new selfobject to replace the missing part and restore cohesion.

With the loss of cohesion of the self, intense sexuality is often found among the disintegration products, "as if sexuality had lost its proper function within a harmoniously balanced matrix" (p. 211). It is a common clinical observation that perverse sexual behavior follows a self-fragmenting experience, almost as if the sexual excitement and gratification were warding off the feeling of deadness due to the lost cohesion of the self. Miss S. illustrates such pathological sexualization of her yearning for a new selfobject. Greenberg and Mitchell (1983) credit the psychoanalyst Erich Fromm with first describing "the use of sexuality and perversions in the service of maintaining a fragile sense of self" (p. 106).

This concept of the self as a cohesive configuration, experienced as a sense of self with a feeling of wholeness and well being as Kohut himself (1966) pointed out, is quite different than any social definition of the self. Again and again, Kohut's early work emphasizes the experience-near aspects, describing how fragmentation of the self (a loss of its cohesion) is experienced with extreme discomfort, such as feelings of depression or deadness together with possible anxiety and even panic. Even transient losses of cohesion are manifested by symptoms such as hypochondriasis and disturbances of self-esteem, painful subjective states which may drive the individual toward remedial actions like peeping and exhibitionism, that gain an addictionlike intensity. Thus, apparently irrational symptoms, fantasies, and behaviors that explode, for example, over the weekend while the patient and therapist are apart, point to an important function of the therapist in maintaining the cohesion of the self. A complete variety of hitherto confusing, and apparently irrational, clinical phenomena suddenly become intelligible!

The sense of self as originally used by Kohut refers to a subjective experience grasped by the therapist through vicarious introspection or empathy with the patient. As such, it was not directly incompatible with Freud's structural theory and could have been thought of as based on certain sets of ego functions. However, as Kohut's theories developed, anthropomorphic language began to creep into the psychology of the self in a way which is similar to the way that the "ego" was anthropomorphized as "the little man within the man" by Freud in his final writings.

## Kohut's Later "Bipolar Self"

In the later writing of Kohut (1977, 1984), the self as a supraordinate concept becomes elaborated in its bipolar nature, showing itself primarily when self cohesion is not firm. Metapsychological energic concepts are dropped, and the self is now seen to occupy "the central position" within the personality. This supraordinate self develops from a core self or nuclear self which does not begin (as Kohut thought earlier) as scattered nuclei that coalesce, but rather as a self which from the beginning of life constitutes a supraordinate configuration that is the basis "for our sense of being an independent center of initiative and perception, integrated with our most central ambitions and ideals and with our experience that our body and mind form a unit in space and a continuum in time" (Kohut 1977, p. 177). The self now resembles the center of our being "from which all initiative springs and where all experiences end" (Kohut 1978, p. 95). When Kohut moves to the bipolar self and its constituents, he apparently introduces a new paradigm. The self is no longer a depth-psychological concept that can be metapsychologically defined using classical terminology, nor is the self thought of as an entity within the mental apparatus or even as a fourth "agency" of the mind. "The area of the self and its vicissitudes," as Kohut (1978, p. 753) calls it, becomes separate from Freud's psychoanalysis; Kohut (1978) himself labels it "the science of the self" (p. 752n).

### PARALLEL TO KANT

Both Kant and Kohut use the concept of self differently in their earlier and later theories, as will be discussed more in Chapter 10. A remarkable parallel between Kant and Kohut appears in Kohut's (1977) discussion of free will. Choice, decision, and free will are explained by Kohut as "the positing of a psychic configuration — the self — that, *whatever the history of its formation*, has become a center of initiative: a unit that tries to follow its own course" (p. 245). This notion and the analogy that follows in the same paragraph regarding "the universe *in toto*" are two of the three classical "ideas of reason" as described by Kant (1781) and used in his moral philosophy to explain the possibility of choice and free will.

Although Kohut claims to maintain an experience-near definition of the self (just as Kant's philosophy points primarily to "the noumenal self in the negative sense"), he, like Kant, relies more and more as his theories evolve on the definition of the self as a supraordinate concept. Kohut's use of the supraordinate "bipolar self" resembles Kant's use of "the noumenal self in the positive sense" as an explanatory concept. We may trace the evolution of this in Kohut, beginning with his 1972 presentation (Chapter 31 in *The Search for the Self* [1978]), in which he offers the earlier definition. We then move toward his focus on the bipolar self in *The Restoration of the Self* (1977) as a supraordinate concept that solves the philosophical dilemma regarding the subjective phenomenon of free will. The turning point in this shift is labeled by Kohut (1978, p. 935) in his 1974 essay, "Remarks about the Formation of the Self" (Chapter 45 in *The Search for the Self* [1978]).

Kohut's original concept of the self was a simpler experience-near abstraction, marked in its fragmentation by certain clinical phenomena; it is certainly consistent with traditional psychoanalytic theory. His later use of the self, however, is not entirely consistent with this theory. Although he continues to derive his concepts from psychoanalytic experience, postulating the self as a center of initiative implies that a mysterious something besides the instinctual drives (either instead of them or in addition to them) is a main energic spring of human behavior and thought. And, indeed, Kohut regards manifestations of the drives already as "disintegration products" rather than fundamental to human nature. So Kohut and Wolf (1978) write, "Once the self has crystalized in the interplay of inherited and environmental factors, it aims toward the realization of its own specific program of action . . . " (p. 414). There will be much in this concept to interest certain Marxist thinkers, who view the very formation of the human self and its lifelong program, attitudes, and beliefs as largely a product of the predominant socioeconomic milieu in which it is formed (Wood 1981).

It is important not to confuse Kohut's "bipolar self" — which is a center of initiative and action — with certain other common uses of the term. The term "self" as used by followers of Kohut is entirely different than the "essential self" or, as Kohut (1977) calls it, "axiomatic self," of philosophers which is postulated as a center of free will and the basis of responsibility in human behavior. This "essential self" has a long philosophical history and is related to the metaphysical concept of "substance" and the theological notion of "soul." It has no unconscious or developmental aspects and the method of empathy and introspection is not applied in a clinical setting in order to unearth its nature. However, personal introspection expressed in the work of, for example, Kierkegaard or Augustine, sometimes illuminates what the authors consider to be a true, authentic, or philosophical self that is responsible for choices.

## Sartre's Definition of Self

The modern or existential version of this programmatic self assumes, again only using a conscious phenomenological psychology, that the self has no essence but is capable of forming itself in one way or another as the individual goes on in life. Sartre and other existial philosophers made no attempt to integrate their hypotheses or convictions with the empirical data of psychoanalysis. The British group of psychoanalytic authors discussed in the next chapter are clinicians who have also emphasized the world around the patient in an existential sense, but who have at the same time attempted to reconcile their theories with the views of Freud, or at least have tried to employ clinical psychoanalytic experience and the unconscious.

Murdoch's (1980) discussion of Sartre's (1964) *Nausea* sees it as a comment on the human condition. Sartre insists that our direct relationship to Being has a "gloomy" or "viscous" feel to it, although he offers no explanation of why this should be. This notion first arose, perhaps appropriately, in his *War Diaries* (1984). For Sartre, what does exist is brutal and nameless; this is basic Being-in-itself, which is absurd and given directly to us.

In the chapter "Quality as a Revelation of Being" in *Being and Nothingness*, Sartre (1973) discusses the "fascination of the viscous." It is an existential category, immediate and concrete. Sartre's "phenomenology" presents our direct experience of absurd or brutal Being-in-itself as a nauseating one.

The individual's Being shares the Being-in-itself with all else that is, but it also contains Being-for-itself that is an unavoidable consequence of human consciousness, and also a third form of Being that Sartre labels Being-for-others. This latter connects the individual inextricably with others as, for example, through the immediate shame experienced in certain situations precipitated by the look (*le regard*) of the other.

For Sartre, existence precedes essence and individuals make themselves whether they want to or not since they cannot avoid choices. There is no human nature from God, no essence to man, and no God. People make their own goals and ideals which are revealed retroactively in their actions. We are "condemned" to be free and our awareness of freedom is accompanied by anguish. To escape this anguish we can blame God, heredity, upbringing, circumstances, the unconscious, and so on, but all of these are what Sartre calls *mauvaise foi* (bad faith).

The individual's operative ideal or the ideal self and values are revealed in actions. They are first set by an original choice or basic project. We discover people's basic project through a review of their actions; the basic project unfolds itself as the individuals move toward their future.

All followers of Sartre stress the notion that the individual is *only* the sum of actions and conscious or preconscious purposes. All existentialists emphasize basic conscious choice as the key to our lives. They view Freud's unconscious and any other deterministic psychologies such as behaviorism as manifestations of *mauvaise foi* (bad faith). All existentialists would oppose breaking down an individual psyche into structural components such as id, ego, and superego (see Chessick 1984). The individual is seen not as an essence or entity but a process, for life is endowed with possibilities through the freedom possessed to make conscious choices and thus construct a self reflected in activities performed.

Brown and Hausman (1981) and Soll (1981) have presented powerful attempts to reconcile Sartre's attacks on Freud with the actual doctrines of Freud. Hanly (1979) has convincingly demonstrated that irreconcilable differences in attitude and approach persist between existentialist philosophers and psychotherapists, and Freudian psychoanalysts. Kohut's later (1977) "psychology of the self in the broader sense," although it retains the notion of the unconscious, is closer in philosophical orientation to Sartre than to Freud, as far as a holistic epistemological position is concerned.

Both Sartre and Freud agree that there exists something unknown to the person which may become known under certain conditions. For Freud, this implies repression and the unconscious; for Sartre, a unified psyche fooling itself — self-deception or bad faith, a concept closer to Freud's "disavowal" and Kohut's "vertical split."

Sartre believes that humans struggle to realize their freedom in an all-encompassing and alienating world. Material reality in Sartre's (1976) later writing is described as the "practico-inert," our total environment, which is in resistance to our projects, limits our knowledge, and is our only instrument for living. Man is a contingent being thrown into a universe allergic to man. Sartre gloomily describes man as a "useless passion" in the sense that the effort of human freedom or the Being-for-itself to achieve the basic project is doomed to fail since man dies.

The unresolved issue of individual human freedom forms one of the most fundamental and controversial problems in philosophy and psychology, and lurks behind Sartre's "basic project" and Kohut's "basic program of the nuclear self," to be described in later chapters. The irreconcilable differences between Sartre's various concepts of the "self" as reviewed by Barnes (1980–1981), and the "self" of Kohut in psychoanalysis are readily apparent. Kohut's work is *not*, as has sometimes been claimed, a version of existentialist philosophy.

Dryud (1984) states that Sartre treats preverbal developmental history much as H. S. Sullivan does: it is important but unanalyzable; later, Sartre speaks of that phase as "protohistory." Dryud points out that Kohut would not agree with Sartre that protohistory is unanalyzable. He continues that both Sartre and Sullivan viewed the self as a compromise, very similar to Winnicott's "false self" and much as Lacan (see Chapter 17) views the ego as the "enemy" (pp. 234–235). Sartre essentially uses a model of the self as an agent which makes choices and his so-called existential psychoanalysis is a methodology designed to bring to light "the subjective choices by which each living person makes himself a person" (Mitchell 1984, p. 258). For Freud however, the mind operates according to the principle of psychic determinism upon which a person can never generate his own causal impact; free will and free choice have no status in this theory. Freud depicts human experience as driven by forces largely unknown, a direct product of internal pressures and compromises.

## Kohut's Early Definition of Self

Kohut's "Forms and Transformations of Narcissism" (1966), the earliest definitive contribution to the founding of his psychology of the self, was generally accepted by the psychoanalytic establishment. Examination of Kohut's work shows the emergence of clear differences between Kohut, Freud, Sartre, and the various other views of philosophers and psychologists on the "self."

"Forms and Transformations of Narcissism" begins by stating that the antithesis to narcissism is not object relations but object love. Thus, a person may have many acquaintances but have no object love. Conversely a hermit can be, theoretically, past the stage of development of narcissism and capable of object love, although the hermit has no object relations. An individual may indeed have a profusion of object relations that make that person "popular" as we have seen unfortunately in certain American presidents or pathological media "personalities." Object love, on the other hand, represents a mature relationship with objects, based on a realistic intrapsychic representation of the object, shifting over continuing experiences with the object.

The archaic formations of the narcissistic self (later called the grandiose self) and the idealized parent imago are introduced in Kohut's work as the inevitable consequence of the disturbance of the infant's blissfully experienced balance of primary narcissism. At this point, Kohut says that the idealized parent imago is related predominantly to drive control while the narcissistic (grandiose) self is closely interwoven with drives and tensions. Speaking of the preconscious derivatives of these two structures, Kohut states that "man is *led* by his ideals but *pushed* by his ambitions" (p. 435).

In "Forms and Transformations of Narcissism," Kohut sees the narcissistic (grandiose) self and idealized parent imago as having to be gradually integrated into the web of our ego; as in Freud, the ego and the mature self are not carefully differentiated. Already in "Forms and Transformations," the term "ego" is used to represent organizations, functions, and structures that are remote from the conscious mind and more fixed, whereas the "self" is nearer to experiential consciousness and represents roughly the person the individual subjectively feels one's self to be. The concept of mastery of the narcissistic (grandiose) self is still presented somewhat vaguely as a function of the ego's capacity to harness narcissistic energies and transform narcissistic constellations into more highly differentiated new psychological configurations.

In Kohut's early work, the result of proper such mastery is described already as the development of creativity, the acceptance of transience, the capacity for empathy, a sense of humor, and "wisdom." But these are conceived of essentially as derivatives of successful ego functioning in the transformation of narcissism. We must ask eventually why Kohut did not stop with this important contribution, but instead began to diverge from the mainstream of traditional psychoanalytic theory in his first book, *The Analysis of the Self* (1971). The answer to this question is the key to the origin and continuing importance of the psychology of the self.

# Chapter 7

∼

# Self and Object:
# Fairbairn, Winnicott, Balint,
# and R. D. Laing

Three psychoanalytic theories that utilize the concept of the self have a resemblance to the work of Kohut and are often confused with his views. The theories of Fairbairn, Winnicott, and R. D. Laing use different conceptions of the self but all have in common with Kohut the assumption that the self is shaped and formed from its very beginning out of the interaction with the mother, or what Winnicott (1965) calls the facilitating environment. This is in sharp contrast especially to the views of Melanie Klein and other object relations theorists, who believe the psyche develops internally through cycles of introjection and projection. This development is seen to be relatively independent of environmental influences and more dependent on constitutional intensity or genetic unfolding of drive constellations.

## The Views of Fairbairn

W. R. D. Fairbairn (1889–1964) formed his theories in reaction to Melanie Klein's work because he felt that the so-called biological or "id" basis of her theories should be eliminated. For Fairbairn, the individual begins with a pristine ego that out of its inherent energy strives for self-development. His work gets into difficulty because he assumes that the ego becomes split in all development, normal as well as pathological. The precise metapsychological meaning of Fairbairn's split-up psychic self is not clear; for example, it employs the undefinable notion of "internalized object." Fairbairn uses "ego" in his theories to mean "the psychic self" (Guntrip 1974, p. 833). The struggle of this split-up psychic self to cope with the outer world is the problem, rather than the struggle of the ego with the id. In Fairbairn's view, there is no "id." Fairbairn thus differs fundamentally from Freud and presents an *entirely* different metapsychology, as discussed in detail by Rangell (1985, pp. 306–310).

Fairbairn, Winnicott, and Balint emphasize the primacy of the environment and the mother's influence. Unless "good enough mothering" (Winnicott 1958) occurs, the infant increasingly frequents the inner world of fantasy objects, but the ego always seeks and needs objects and always stands in some relationship to them. The ego is never regarded as an abstract set of functions or subsystems. Libido, for Fairbairn, in a totally non-Freudian definition, is always object-seeking rather than seeking discharge; "libido" is the energy of the search for good objects, which makes ego differentiation and growth possible.

As in the subsequent work of Kohut, Fairbairn views aggression not as an instinct, but as a reaction to the frustration of libidinal drive. Fairbairn rejects Freud's oral-anal-phallic phases and substitutes three phases of development: immature dependency of infancy, a transitional phase, and a final mature dependence among equal adults. This last phase has some superficial resemblance to the later work of Kohut, who emphasizes the "empathic matrix" needed by all adults.

Fairbairn (Guntrip 1974) presents a three-fold split in the psychic self and an internal struggle that he calls "internal ego-object relations." The infantile libidinal ego (analogous to Freud's id) in a state of dissatisfaction is related to an internal bad object that Fairbairn calls the "exciting object" which excites but never satisfies the child's needs. This "libidinal ego-exciting object" is illustrated clinically in the dream of a male patient who follows a woman who constantly retreats from him.*

---

*The use of manifest dream content to illustrate intrapsychic or self states by Fairbairn, Guntrip, and later allegedly by Kohut has been much criticized by traditional psychoanalysts. This is discussed in Chapters 11 and 19.

The next sector of the self is the infantile antilibidinal ego (the sadistic part of Freud's superego) which represents the identification with rejecting objects; it is turned against the individual's own libidinal needs. A clinical example of this aspect of the self, "the antilibidinal ego-rejecting object," is presented in the dream of a female patient: "I was a little girl who saw you and thought 'If I get to him I will be safe.' And I began to run to you . . . but another little girl smacked my face and drove me away."

The third aspect of the self or the central ego (Freud's ego) is the conscious self of everyday living attempting to deal with reality, and in so doing idealizing the parents (the ideal object, the moral aspect of Freud's superego). Thus "the central ego-ideal object" struggles to preserve good relationships with the parents for the purposes of strength and adaptation.

Guntrip, the analysand and pupil of Fairbairn,* added an ultimate split in schizoid patients postulated to be in Fairbairn's infantile libidinal ego itself. This aspect splits into a clamoring, orally active hysteric libidinal ego and a deeply withdrawn, passive schizoid libidinal ego. This latter "regressed ego" is experienced by the patient as a compulsive need to sleep, exhaustion, feelings of being a nonentity, a sense of having lost part of the self, of being out of touch — the commonly reported phenomena of schizoid states such as feeling that there is a sheet of plate glass between one's self and the world. Guntrip (1974) points out that the patient may protect against this sense of annihilation by remaining chronically angry and fighting in order to maintain one's energy level. This should be compared with Kohut's (1977) later theory in which the patient produces a pseudodramatization of everything in order to defend against the unbearable subjective sense of a depleted, empty self.

Fairbairn (1963) published a one-page summary of his complex views. Guntrip (1974) attempts to explain this theory, which rests on an apparently metapsychologically untenable notion of internalized objects. Kernberg (1980) offers some stimulating ideas on the use made by Guntrip of Fairbairn's theory, and he criticizes them both from his own point of view. Klein and Tribich (1981) denounce Kernberg's criticism of Fairbairn severely; they seem to prefer Fairbairn's object-relations theory over that of Kernberg. The psychology of the self, although it has some resemblances to Fairbairn's object

---

*The currently unresolved issue of to what extent and why Guntrip distorted the theories of Fairbairn is beyond the scope of this book.

relations theory, is not an object relations theory as defined by the British school and Kernberg. However, it shares with Fairbairn, Balint, and Winnicott their central emphasis on the mother-infant interaction ambience as crucial to the formation of the basic personality. In that sense it is a "modern" or neo-object relations theory.

Robbins (1980) reviews the current controversy in object relations theory, pointing out the striking resemblance between the views of Kohut and the ideas of Fairbairn. Robbins contrasts the views of Fairbairn and Kohut with those of Klein and Kernberg, which he feels are also closely related to each other.

According to Robbins, Fairbairn's terminology is confusing because Fairbairn uses the ego ambiguously to signify a primary self rather than simply an intrapsychic structure. Robbins criticizes Fairbairn because the latter's theory assumes capacities to differentiate among part-objects and affects, and to introject, segregate, and structure experience, all of which may be beyond the capacity of the infant. He adds:

> His core ideas are harbingers of Kohut, particularly his de-emphasis of libido, his conception of aggression as a disintegration product and his focus on the primary relationship between the self as a dynamic structure, and an empathic self-object. When such a relationship fails or disappoints, both Fairbairn and Kohut describe the expression of rage, the development of perverse, auto-erotic phenomena, and an overall picture of detachment and apathy. (p. 484)

## The Views of Winnicott

D. W. Winnicott (1896–1971) was a magnificent, intuitive clinician who used questionable and confusing terminology, for example, "ego-orgasm." He emphasized the difference between oedipal patients who require psychoanalysis and preoedipal cases requiring "management" or what he called an ego-adaptive environment of holding. Among his most important concepts are those of the true and false self associated with his notions of "the transitional object" and "the facilitating environment" (Winnicott 1953, 1958, 1965).

The false self develops in response to early nonempathic mothering and has to do with learning to be compliant, never exploring one's own authentic self and its needs. Kohut (1984) mentions repeatedly that continued compliance on the part of the patient in psychoanalysis is one of the most difficult resistances with which to deal. The false self produces a certain inherent rigidity and lack of autonomy or spontaneous feelings and it functions to keep the true self hidden. The patient is disengaged. For Winnicott this often has to be broken down through therapeutic regression, in order that the pathological false self-compliance can disappear and a real exchange of affect and feeling can emerge in the therapeutic situation. This is a time of regression to deep dependency when it occurs.

Winnicott (1958), before Kohut, writes that the patient makes use of the analyst's failures; these can be used therapeutically and treated as past failures about which the patient can be angry. This concept of the false and true self belongs to what Winnicott calls a schizoid subvariant rather than to borderline patients, who usually do not present compliance as a major problem in psychotherapy. But he describes patients who are split between a true self and a false self in terms very like Kohut's picture of certain narcissistic personality disorders. Winnicott (1965) writes: "Instead of cultural pursuits one observes in such persons extreme restlessness, an inability to concentrate, and a need to collect impingements from external reality so that the living-time of the individual can be filled by reactions to these impingements" (p. 150).

With emphasis on the management of preoedipally damaged patients and his concept of good-enough mothering, Winnicott believes that the setting becomes equally or more important than the interpretations used in psychotherapy (Greenberg and Mitchell 1983). For Winnicott, maturation requires and depends upon the quality of the facilitating environment. The infant in this environment creates and recreates the object. According to Winnicott (1965), the object is at first a subjective phenomenon which he labels "the subjective object." Later it becomes an object objectively perceived; this is a function of the formation of an "objective subject," that is to say, "the idea of a self, and the feeling of being real that springs from having an identity." Notice that the self is not the same as the ego for Winnicott, who (1971) defines the self as "the person who is me, who is only me, who has a totality based on the operation of the maturation process." The key point here is that the quality of maternal holding has the crucial role in the shaping and developing of the self.

Cassimatis (1984) writes that Kohut has "expanded Winnicott's epigrammatic ideas and made a major contribution in showing that analysis *of* (and respect *for*) the self needs to precede classical analytic approaches and interpretations" (p. 69). With this issue of the true and false self Winnicott (as does Kohut) introduces "existential" issues into clinical psychotherapy and psychoanalysis according to Cassimatis. He compares their work with that of Kierkegaard (1859) who writes of the desire to be a true self, by which Kierkegaard means an "authentic" individual, with theological overtones.

## Primary Narcissism and Secondary Narcissism: Balint

We can distinguish two basic opposing views about primary narcissism. M. Balint (1896–1970) insisted there is no such thing. Following Fairbairn, he maintained (1953) that the individual is born with "primary object love." Initially, the infant seeks an object that will gratify the person without the person needing to communicate the need to the object first. It is the primal wish for the intuitive, totally empathic, all-loving maternal object. There is no room in the theory of Balint for primary narcissism and he believes development progresses strictly along the line of object relations, moving from primary object relations to mature object love. Eagle (1984) reviews the experimental evidence from work with infants and children that seems to support this view.

Basch (Stepansky and Goldberg 1984) addresses this issue, crediting Ferenczi with founding an approach to human development that culminates in Kohut's crucial assumption of maturation as based not on instinctual frustration and conflict, but on "harmonious interplay between instinctually potentiated genetic patterns and the releasor mechanisms for that potential embodied in the caregiver's empathic response to the infant's affective communications" (p. 12). This concept of human development, argues Basch, is consistent with scientific findings since Freud. Self-psychology has, therefore, "restored psychoanalytic theory to scientific respectability" (p. 37). Note, however, that the self of an infant for Kohut (1977) is a *"virtual"* self (p. 101). It must be described in terms of increase or decrease in tension and *not*, as in Klein, in terms of fantasies that are at least potentially verbalizable. This is a common source of confusion, and Kohut to some extent avoids the pitfall of attributing complex ego functions to the infant.

On the other hand, Freud believed that the infant passed from an initial state of autoerotism, in which there are simply body states prior to the development of any ego nuclei, to a phase of primary narcissism, which begins with the formation of ego nuclei and represents an overwhelming cathexis of these ego nuclei with libido. Next, a gradual transition from the stage of primary narcissism to the state of object love occurs, as libido is divested from the ego (used interchangeably as self by Freud) and cathected to objects or object representations. Freud is not specific on this matter.

Secondary narcissism is also defined differently by different authors. Freud's secondary narcissism is a defensive withdrawal of libido from objects back to a cathexis of the ego or self, but all secondary narcissism is not just pathological. Some of this withdrawal is normal in terms of the vicissitudes of structure formation, which Mahler et al. (1975) call "sound secondary narcissism." On the other hand, Balint insists that *all* narcissism is secondary narcissism since there is no such thing as primary narcissism. Kohut argues that narcissism follows an independent line of development, entirely discarding the concept of secondary narcissism, and describing transformations of narcissism from primitive to mature forms.

According to Freud, the psychoanalytic treatment of narcissistic disorders is extremely difficult. Patients who have cathected most of their libido to the ego or self do not have libido available to cathect objects and therefore no transference can form. These patients are consequently unsuitable for Freud's psychoanalysis, which requires that a transference neurosis develop and be resolved by interpretation. A pejorative gloomy connotation to narcissism is implied.

THE VIEWS OF BALINT

According to Balint (1968), psychotherapists treating patients who are not classical neurotics, but whose disorders have begun before the consolidation of the repression barrier, must supply a "new beginning" to the patient in order to correct a "basic fault." The therapist attempts to provide an atmosphere that is an emotional experience corrective to the early nonempathic mothering given to the patient. Those who follow Balint emphasize the patient's absolute need for empathy from the therapist and stress the danger of inappropriate verbal interpretations; the empathic interactions described by Balint, rather than interpretations of transference, are essential for the successful treatment of such patients.

In the proper regression in psychoanalysis that Balint (1968) calls benign regression — to distinguish it from malignant regression for the sake of gratification, which has the unworkable qualities of despair and passion — the patient reaches what Balint calls the "arglos" state. In this state, the analyst must recognize the patient's needs and longings for satisfaction which are the essence of a "new beginning" and the patient's recovery from the basic fault. The arglos state, which Balint considers to be an absolutely necessary precondition for the new beginning, is explained by the patient's craving for primary love.

The special atmosphere provided during this state has much more to do with recognition than massive gratification. Only token satisfaction of need is provided, and there was a slow evolution of Balint's views so that the tokens of direct gratification were fewer; the recognition of the patient's need and the unobtrusiveness of the therapist are the essential ingredients. Even in this relatively crude precursor to the theories of Kohut, there is a move away from the more unsophisticated views of Balint's teacher Ferenczi, who (1955) advocated that an actual effort be made to gratify the needs of the patient on a massive basis, a procedure that always leads to chaos and destruction, often for the therapist as well as for the patient (Chessick 1974).

In his earliest cases, Balint allowed patients to jump rope or do somersaults before him, with Balint functioning as what Kohut would call a mirroring selfobject. He soon realized that even this sort of "corrective emotional experience" was futile except on a temporary basis. Yet, his intuitive recognition and interpretation of the patient's exhibitionistic need was an early step toward the concepts of the psychology of the self.

There are two clinically valuable ways in which the therapist can communicate recognition of the patient's needs and longings in order to enable the patient to make a new beginning. Balint communicates this recognition to the patient by, for example, an explanation or interpretation or perhaps by some token satisfaction of the need. Kohut's way is more subtle: the patient experiences the therapist's empathic recognition of his needs by the ambience of the therapy and the tone, phrasing, and timing of the interpretations. Both Balint and Kohut have been unreasonably criticized and accused of attempting to provide some kind of direct gratification to the patient on a massive basis. Therapists who attempt this are not psychoanalysts or psychoanalytic psychotherapists — such behavior is always an acting out on the part of an insufficiently analyzed therapist.

Balint and Winnicott introduced the concept of archaic transferences into the treatment of preoedipal disorders. The transference that forms in the regressions of patients with preoedipal disorders does not represent the crossing of a repression barrier of wishes for infantile libidinal need discharges. Instead, certain archaic transferencelike states develop, which respond not to interpretation at first — interpretations may even interfere — but to the quality of the therapist-patient relationship. The longings involved are more "archaic" and Modell, Little, Kohut, Gedo, and numerous others have attempted to describe these longings. It is difficult to discuss these archaic transferences in terms of classical psychoanalytic theory, and they require a sensitive therapist to understand and treat them. Prior to the work of Kohut, gifted clinicians usually responded to them intuitively.

Little (1981) presents an example of archaic transference in discussing "basic unity": a primary total undifferentiatedness, before symbiosis, before Klein's paranoid-schizoid position, occurring at birth. Premature disruption of basic unity is accompanied by annihilation anxiety; according to Little, basic unity becomes a crucial issue in borderline patients who cannot relegate it only to fantasy. They must regress to it with the therapist and rework repeatedly the separation from this basic unity in psychoanalytic psychotherapy. Needless to say, a heavy countertransference strain is placed on the therapist in dealing with this sort of archaic transference.

Unfortunately, theoretical formulations such as those of Balint or Little are based on adultomorphic errors and have a mystical aspect to them. Deliberate attempts to provide a special atmosphere for certain patients are manipulative, overly dramatic, and mystical. All patients (Stone 1961) should be presented with the physicianly vocation and the authentic self of the therapist. It is not clear what special techniques are involved in trying to provide the patient with empathic mothering. This vagueness about the notion of good enough holding pervades the therapeutic suggestions of intuitive clinicians such as Winnicott, Balint, and Little.

In the 1930s, Balint already noted an important theoretical change in the classical conception of psychotherapeutic technique. This change was determined by the increasing importance given to the actual experience or "education" (Freud called it "after-education") that the patient in a benign regression has with the therapist. Such a treatment is more crucial when dealing with preoedipal borderline or nar-

cissistic disorders than when dealing with the so-called classical neuroses. Balint attempted to divide types of treatment into those for
patients at the oedipal level and those for patients at the level of the
"basic fault." Whether this is psychoanalysis, intensive psychoanalytic
psychotherapy, or psychoanalysis with parameters remains highly
controversial even today. As Winnicott states (1965), "Analysts who
are not prepared to meet the heavy needs of patients who become
dependent in this way must be careful to choose their cases that they
do not include False Self types" (p. 151).

## Laing's "Divided Self"

To conclude this chapter I wish to review *The Divided Self* by
R. D. Laing (1960), in which Laing fuses the work of Winnicott, Fairbairn, and Balint of the so-called British school of psychoanalytic
clinicians with existentialist authors such as Sartre and Kierkegaard.
For my purposes here I will discuss only Laing's notion of "the divided
self" and not his later conceptions of schizophrenia, family and group
interaction, or his radical political and antipsychiatry views.

As in the work of Sartre, the individual's self as agent is at the
center of Laing's conceptions. However, Laing believes splitting of
the self is induced in childhood by forces outside the agent's control,
whereas Sartre recognizes only the self as a conscious agent with conscious intent and no preintentional causal origins (Hunter 1977).
Laing (1960) states that organic, biological, and genetic factors influence the formation and splitting of the self along with the politics
of the family or family pressures. In Laing's later work he drops this
aspect of his conception of schizophrenia, which I believe isolated
Laing from the mainstream of psychiatric thinking about schizophrenia.

Laing never explains why some patients develop schizophrenia from
a divided self and some do not. Later he does not see schizophrenia
as a clinical entity, and believes that "illness" is an unsatisfactory
model for mental disorders. Psychotic phenomena are intelligible,
says Laing, and he believes that there are no criteria for the term
schizophrenia and that it is a scientifically unsound concept. To
understand "madness," one must study the family and not only the
individual. People who are dissident members of a family or political
group are often incorrectly classified as mad, and statistical normality

is not necessarily preferable to madness. Thus, concepts of sanity and madness are socially relative, and he came to believe that madness can even be naturally curative (Collier 1977).

In his early work Laing presents what he calls the existential-phenomenological foundation of a science of persons. The schizoid individual has experiences split in two ways: with respect to the world, the individual is not at home in the world, is alone; and with respect to the self, the individual feels divided with only a tenuous link to the body, prompting the individual to speak of parts of the body in the third person. This leads to what Laing calls "human tragedy," which is not far removed from Kohut's concept of Tragic Man and is rooted in a double alienation of the person from the world, and from the false self and the body. This is the patient's way of being in the world, which we must understand by Laing's existential-phenomenological method; it resembles Kohut's effort through empathy or vicarious introspection to grasp what the other's world is and the other's way of being in it, although their methods rest on totally different epistemological foundations (Chessick 1980b). Laing, in contrast to Sartre, does not reject the unconscious, but uses it only in an adjectival sense and not as a realm with special laws of "primary process." Kohut's use of the unconscious is much closer to that of Freud.

Laing introduces the theoretically untenable term "ontological insecurity" to characterize an important clinical phenomenon, the individual who is unable to maintain a sense of continuity and cohesion of self. The patient with Kohut's cohesive self closely resembles the patient with Laing's ontological security. The patient with Kohut's fragmenting self resembles the patient with Laing's ontological insecurity. This coincidence continues in Laing's statement that patients with ontological security wish primarily for gratification of themselves. Thus, such patients are ready to enter libidinal and oedipal phases of development. In Kohut's terms (1978, p. 163) patients with a cohesive self seek satisfaction; those with self pathology seek reassurance.

The patient with ontological insecurity wishes to preserve the self and suffers from three forms of anxiety: *engulfment*, the fear of being overwhelmed, which requires strenuous desperate activity to preserve the self and uses isolation as the main defense; *implosion*, the fear that reality will crash in and obliterate the empty self (thus reality becomes the persecutor); and *petrifaction*, the fear of becoming an automaton or object, in Sartre's terms. The latter often is accompanied by *depersonalization*, which occurs when another individual becomes tiresome or disturbing, and the patient stops responding.

A coincidence of thought runs from Sartre in Part 3 of *Being and Nothingness* through Laing, through Kohut, in the concept that another individual can either enliven one's self or deaden an already impoverished self. When there is "ontological dependency" (Laing 1960) on the other person instead of genuine mutuality, there is an oscillation between isolation and merger with that other person. In normal mutuality, the oscillation is between separation and relatedness. In pre-Kohutian terms, Laing points out that if there is no mirroring there will be no "ontological autonomy" and the patient will not have a problem in the traditional sense of conflicts — Freud's unconscious pressing for expression and defended against by the ego — but the patient will need to seek ontological security. This disorder cannot be described by conflicts and drives in the Freudian sense but is "beyond the pleasure principle" as Laing puts it.

In the case of Mrs. R., described by Laing, the symptomatic difficulty was agoraphobia. Her parents were always too engrossed in each other for either of them to take notice of her; she longed to be important and significant to someone else.

In a manner similar to Kohut, Laing points out that Mrs. R.'s incestuous fantasies were a defense against the dread of being alone. He concludes, "Her sexual life and fantasies were efforts, not primarily to gain gratification, but to seek first ontological security. In lovemaking an illusion of this security was achieved, and on the basis of this illusion gratification was possible" (p. 61).

Laing distinguishes between the normal "embodied self" and cases manifesting the pathologically split off "unembodied self." In these pathological cases, a true unembodied self is split off from a defensively formed compliant false self which is attached to the body. Thus a detached, disembodied, inner true self looks on with tenderness, amusement, but usually hatred at the false self attached to the body. Laing explains how the unembodied self becomes hyperconscious, attempts to posit its own imagos, and develops a possibly complex relationship with itself and with the body.

Laing (1960, pp. 101–102) distinguishes between three false self systems:

1. In the normal false self system, some of our behavior is mechanical, but it does not encroach on spontaneity and has no subjective feel of an autonomous foreign body forcing itself on the individual, no sense of compulsivity; nor do we have a sense of being lived by something within us.

2. The hysteric false self system is a way of life aimed at gratification and characterized by pretending consciously or preconsciously — a form of disavowal related to Sartre's concept of bad faith.

3. The schizoid false self system is starved and ungratified, a system that aims at preservation, not gratification.

The compulsive compliance or "being good" of the schizoid patient involves hatred and a sense of persecution. The self-consciousness of the schizoid patient gives the assurance that the patient exists and represents an apprehensive awareness in the face of danger which is felt to be everywhere in the world.

Laing points out:

> The mother, however, is not simply a *thing* which the child can see, but a *person* who sees the child. Therefore, we suggest that a necessary component in the development of the self is the experience of oneself as a person under the loving eye of the mother. . . . It may be that a *failure of responsiveness* on the mother's part to one or other aspect of the infant's being will have important consequences. (p. 125)

Laing's theories are highly metaphorical, but his explanation of the schizoid personality is the first to attempt to employ the concept of the subjective sense of self that allows us to place ourselves empathically within the experiences of the individual that we diagnostically label schizoid. This method, even in Laing's poetic form, allows us to better understand the bizarre behavior of schizoid individuals, and the self-defeating nature of schizoid defenses.

Laing had an intuitive genius for understanding schizoid and schizophrenic communications. In a dramatic passage (pp. 29–31) he reviews Kraepelin's classic 1905 lecture describing a patient with catatonic excitement, in which Kraepelin finds the patient inaccessible and impossible to understand, thus diagnosing the patient as psychotic. Yet Laing's review of the patient's actual material demonstrates that the patient is presenting a dialogue between a parodied version of Kraepelin and the patient's defiant, rebelling self. The rise in popularity of the psychology of the self is based on its analogous potential to make behavior, symptoms, and communications, previously labeled as those of a "bad" patient, intelligible and amenable to the process of intensive psychotherapy or psychoanalysis.

## Chapter 8

---

# Kohut's First Version of the Psychology of the Self

Heinz Kohut was born in Vienna in 1913 and educated there, receiving his medical degree at the University of Vienna in 1938. He often described how he rushed to the train station and tipped his cap to wave goodbye to Sigmund Freud—whom he did not know personally—on the day Freud was forced by the Nazis to leave Vienna (Goldberg 1982).

Since Kohut's father was Jewish he, too, left Austria and eventually settled in 1940 at the University of Chicago; he joined the Chicago Institute for Psychoanalysis in 1953. His actual training was in neurology and his shift to psychoanalysis, he said, was a gradual one, bringing together his interests in neurology, literature, and the power of Freud's ideas (Montgomery 1981). He studied at the Chicago Institute for Psychoanalysis and became a central figure in American psychoanalysis, teaching psychoanalytic theory at the Institute for 15 years. He served as president of the American Psychoanalytic Association in 1964–1965 and was vice president of the International Psychoanalytic Association from 1965 to 1973. Kohut's publications on the "psychology of the self," marked by his first book in 1971, stirred up considerable hostility toward him. Montgomery (1981) quotes him as saying, "I was Mr. Psychoanalysis. In every room I entered there were smiles. Now everybody looks away. I've rocked the boat."

*Time* magazine on December 1, 1980, stated that he was "becoming such a cult figure that disciples compare him with Freud" (p. 76). From personal experience with his colleagues I can attest to the enthusiasm Kohut sometimes raised in senior psychoanalysts. For example, I remember one highly respected Chicago Institute training analyst declaring in a lecture to the Northwestern University Department of Psychiatry that Kohut's discoveries were the greatest advance in medicine since the discovery of penicillin.

Kohut had the reputation of being an excellent teacher. Physically diminutive, he was sometimes thought to have an ascetic charisma, but he claimed to enjoy the pleasures of life (Breu 1979). My impression of him in a brief interview and at the Chicago Conference on Self Psychology in 1978 (published by Goldberg 1980) was that he was brilliant, quite sure of himself, and an extraordinary extemporaneous speaker at the height of his profession. He was remarkably forbearing, complaining more of "the distortions which my work appears to be suffering through the unwelcome influence of some self-appointed disciples" (Kohut 1978, p. 884). On the other hand, Kohut challenged the entire field of organized psychoanalysis and did not hesitate to apply his self-psychological concepts when explaining the resistance to his work, a process which must have caused some extremely painful interactions with his colleagues.

## Kohut's Method

It is sensible to start with Kohut's method, which was presented in his 1959 paper, "Introspection, Empathy, and Psychoanalysis" (Kohut 1978). He writes, "Only a phenomenon that we can attempt to observe by introspection or by empathy with another's introspection may be called psychological. A phenomenon is 'somatic', 'behavioristic', or 'social' if our methods of observation do not predominantly include introspection and empathy" (pp. 208–209). Kohut leans heavily on the trained introspective skill which the analyst uses in the extension of introspection; he labels this extension of introspection vicarious introspection or empathy.

The often quoted example he gives is that of the unusually tall man: "Only when we think ourselves into his place, only when we, by vicarious introspection, begin to feel his unusual size as if it were our own and thus revive inner experiences in which we had been unusual or conspicuous, only then do we begin to appreciate the meaning that the unusual size may have for this person, and only then have we observed a psychological fact" (pp. 207–208). Thus, by empathy, we place ourselves into the shoes of the other person and by vicarious introspection we attempt to discover how that other person is feeling.

The emphasis on vicarious introspection differentiates Freud's and Kohut's psychoanalysis from Sullivan's interpersonal theory. For Kohut, "the psychoanalytic meaning of the term interpersonal" connotes "an interpersonal experience open to introspective self-observation; it differs thus from the meaning of the terms interpersonal relationship, interaction, transaction, etc., which are used by social psychologists and others" (p. 217).

Furthermore, the limits of psychoanalysis are prescribed by the limits of potential introspection and empathy. For example, Kohut takes up the problem of free will and determinism. As early as 1959 in the paper mentioned above, Kohut points out that the I-experience and a core of activities emanating from it cannot at present be divided into further components by the introspective method. Thus our sense of freedom of will is beyond the law of psychic determinism and cannot be resolved by the method of introspection. Kohut points out that Freud was not resolute on this issue, for in *The Ego and the Id* (Freud 1923) the latter states that psychoanalysis sets out to give the patient's ego freedom to choose one way or the other. Yet, Freud's earlier formulations were oriented toward absolute psychic determinism; there is little room in his earlier theoretical system for the freedom of the ego to decide. We will see in later chapters how Kohut's early mention of the I-experience became elaborated into his fundamental concept of the bipolar self.

TRANSFERENCE

Another important concept in this 1959 paper was Kohut's proclamation that in narcissistic and borderline patients:

The analyst is not the screen for the projection of internal structure (transference) but the direct continuation of an early reality that was too distant, too rejecting, or too unreliable to be transformed into solid psychological structures . . . He *is* the old object with which the analysand tries to maintain contact, from which he tries to separate his own identity, or from which he attempts to derive a modicum of internal structure. (pp. 218–219)

Here Kohut makes one of his crucial distinctions between transference which involves infantile object libidinal strivings crossing the repression barrier and aimed at the analyst as if the analyst were a significant person in the patient's childhood, and strivings towards objects that, although emerging from the psychic depth, do not cross Freud's repression barrier and represent attempts to derive a modicum of internal structure. Because of this distinction the well-known narcissistic or selfobject transferences of Kohut (mirror, idealizing, alter-ego) are not transferences in the original metapsychological sense of the word; especially in his earlier works Kohut refers to them as transferencelike phenomena, but this distinction is not always followed in the literature.

EMPATHY

In his 1966 paper, "Forms and Transformations of Narcissism," Kohut defines empathy as "the mode by which one gathers psychological data about other people and, when they say what they think or feel, imagines their inner experience even though it is not open to direct observation" (reprinted in Kohut 1978, p. 450). He makes several additional points about empathy:

1. Empathy is an essential constituent of psychological observation and is crucial in providing the data for psychoanalytic therapy.
2. The capacity for empathy belongs to the innate equipment of the human psyche, but the original empathic mode of reality perception — the primary empathy of the infant with the mother — soon becomes layered over by nonempathic forms of cognition which become dominant in the adult.
3. The aim of the analyst is "exhaustive empathic comprehension" (p. 452), which requires the ability to use the analyst's empathic capacity for prolonged periods. The attitude of evenly suspended attention, avoidance of note taking, curtailment of realistic interac-

tions, and concentration on the purpose of achieving understanding rather than on the wish to cure and to help, are for the purpose of encouraging empathic comprehension "through the perception of experiential identities" (p. 452).

The most important obstacles interfering with the use of empathy, especially for prolonged periods, are the narcissistic difficulties in the therapist and therefore "the loosening of narcissistic positions constitutes a specific task of the training analysis" (pp. 452–453). Kohut considered the highly developed capacity for empathic observation over a prolonged period to be critical to the analyst's skill, based on a certain inborn talent, childhood experiences, and the analyst's training analysis. Without this capacity for prolonged empathic observation or vicarious introspection it is impossible to properly practice psychoanalysis or intensive psychoanalytic psychotherapy.

The difficult subject of empathy has received extensive attention in the literature (Lichtenberg et al. 1984, 1984a). Basch (1983) reviews the subject and points out:

> Whether affective resonance is established fairly quickly or is delayed, empathic perception is never a matter of somehow getting a direct look at what goes on inside another mind; rather, it is a considered judgment that there is a correspondence between what we are feeling and what, in the case of the analytic situation, the analysand is experiencing, consciously or unconsciously. (p. 114)

Over a period of time the analyst develops an empathic understanding of the patient which permits an extension of vicarious introspection that is testable and correctable. This vicarious introspection is neither projection nor identification; we respond affectively to the patient's verbal and nonverbal communications and in the process learn something about the patient. Therefore, empathy is a process of coming to know. Although it has tended to be used to ascribe to the empathizer the intention of being helpful, this is not necessarily true. The knowledge obtained by the process of empathy or vicarious introspection can be used for good or for evil. The therapist will employ empathic understanding in the service of making appropriate and well-timed interventions and interpretations.

Kohut's emphasis on empathy has led to a considerable controversy in the literature, fueled partly by a shift in the thinking of Kohut himself. This controversy is brought into its final form in Kohut's last book (1984), in which Kohut insists that the very experience of being empathically understood has an important (although relatively "ephemeral") curative function, leaving Kohut open to the charge that his theory resembles Alexander's "corrective emotional experience" and separating him from certain analytic purists who insist that only the interpretation itself cures the patient in psychoanalysis. Already in 1977 Kohut writes, "It is not the interpretation that cures the patient" (p. 31), and with this, in his second book, he takes a decisive step away from traditional American psychoanalysis. We will take up this controversy in Chapter 10; however no author from the psychology of the self group advocates the deliberate effort to provide some kind of "empathy" defined as loving or special sympathetic caring to the patient; the psychology of the self definitely does not offer the patient a love cure. It is a serious psychoanalytic therapeutic system.

## "Narcissistic" Transferences

The 1966 paper on "Forms and Transformations of Narcissism" and the subsequent 1968 paper on "The Psychoanalytic Treatment of Narcissistic Personality Disorders" (Kohut 1978) surprised some of those in the psychoanalytic movement but did not lead to any great personal difficulty for Kohut. He retained Hartmann's definition of narcissism strictly defined as the libidinal cathexis of the self, using self here as intrapsychic self-representations, essentially as substructures of the ego. This is more or less consistent with the mainstream psychoanalytic authors' views described already.

The 1968 paper on "The Psychoanalytic Treatment of Narcissistic Personality Disorders" is an excellent place to begin a study of the psychology of the self, although it was later amended and modified by Kohut in a number of important ways. It is a clear description of what actually happens in the working through of Kohut's narcissistic transferences (later labeled selfobject* transferences). The paper outlines much of the more detailed and more difficult material presented in Kohut's (1971) first book, *The Analysis of the Self*.

*In his earlier work it was written "self-object," but later the hyphen was omitted for a more explicit denotation of how archaic objects are experienced.

The child's original narcissistic bliss is disturbed by the unavoidable shortcomings of maternal care, and the child attempts to save this experience of bliss by assigning to it (a) a grandiose and exhibitionistic image (the narcissistic self); and (b) an idealized parent imago — an imagined, completely devoted, all-powerful parent. Under optimal developmental conditions the exhibitionism and grandiosity of the archaic grandiose self are gradually tamed and the whole structure becomes integrated into the adult personality and supplies our ego-syntonic ambitions and purposes; under similarly favorable circumstances the idealized parent imago becomes integrated into the adult personality as our guiding values and ideals. The crucial point is that if the child suffers severe narcissistic traumata (later described as the failure of archaic selfobjects), the grandiose self does not merge or integrate but "is retained in its unaltered form and strives for the fulfillment of its archaic aims" (p. 478). Similarly, if the child experiences traumatic phase-inappropriate disappointments in the admired caretaking adult, the idealized parent imago is also retained in its unaltered form, and the individual requires a continual search for an archaic transitional object to cling to for tension regulation and for maintenance of his or her self-esteem.

These loose and metapsychologically vague concepts in the 1968 paper are used to describe the idealizing and the mirroring transference. The idealizing transference is "the therapeutic revival of the early state in which the psyche saves a part of the lost experience of global narcissistic perfection by assigning it to an archaic (transitional) object, the idealized parent imago" (p. 479). The patient ascribes all bliss and power to the idealized analyst and feels empty and powerless when separated from the analyst. The analyst, or any idealized parent imago transference object, is not loved for its own attributes, but needed only to replace the functions of a segment of the mental apparatus not established in childhood, which Kohut labels a structural defect.

As a clinical example — and this entire theory is closely based on clinical experience — Kohut gives us the case of Mr. A., who complains of homosexual preoccupations as his reason for entering analysis. Kohut emphasizes Mr. A.'s need to be forever in search of approval from various men in authoritative positions. As long as Mr. A. felt approved of by various authorities, he experienced himself as whole, acceptable, and capable, and did good work; at the slightest signs of disapproval he became depressed and angry, then cold, haughty, and isolated.

This introduces us to an issue that remains controversial in assessment of the psychology of the self: there is a tendency to interpret patients' complaints of "perverse" sexual activities and fantasies in terms of primarily nonsexual narcissistic and structural deficit difficulties. Some authors are afraid that the self-psychologist offers the patient inexact interpretations couched in terms of these structural deficit difficulties which help to defend the patient against repressed incestuous and oedipal conflicts. The self-psychologist would probably answer that proper empathy or vicarious introspection would enable the therapist to determine whether the patient's primary disorder resided in defects in the self or in the repressed oedipal problems in the presence of a cohesive self. But Kohut's views changed, as will be discussed later.

Kohut emphasizes repeatedly that the idealizing transference must be allowed to develop undisturbed. Once it has been established, the patient feels powerful, good, and capable. Then, due to the various vicissitudes of the treatment, the patient is deprived of the idealized analyst, e.g., on vacations or meetings. As a result there is a disturbed self-esteem and the patient feels powerless and worthless, turning perhaps to "archaic idealizations": vague, impersonal, trancelike religious feelings, hypercathexis of the grandiose self with emotional coldness, a tendency toward affectation in speech and behavior, shame propensity, and hypochondria. The alert therapist watches for this and, in an atmosphere of correct empathy for the patient's feelings, repeatedly explains and interprets what has happened.

Kohut claims that if properly done, there will gradually emerge a host of meaningful memories concerning the dynamic prototypes of the present experience:

> The patient will recall lonely hours during his childhood in which he attempted to overcome a feeling of fragmentation, hypochondria, and deadness, which was due to the separation from the idealized parent. And he will remember, and gratefully understand, how he tried to substitute for the idealized parent imago and its functions by creating erotized replacements and through frantic hypercathexis of the grandiose self. (p. 488)

Examples mentioned by Kohut of frantic childhood activities that commonly emerge in clinical experience are the child's rubbing his face against a rough surface, looking at mother's photograph, or rummaging through her drawers and smelling her underwear. Memories of reassuring flying or superman fantasies experienced in that situation may emerge. In the adult patient, during similar separations from the selfobject (see below) analyst, analogous activities occur, such as voyeurism, shoplifting, and reckless driving.

As this explanation is repeated with each "optimal frustration" and childhood memories are brought up (consistent with the classical method of psychoanalysis), the ego acquires increasing tolerance for the analyst's absences and occasional failures to be empathic. The patient's psychic organization acquires the capacity to perform some functions previously performed by the idealized object, leading, as we shall see, to Kohut's concept of transmuting internalization.

Analogous to the idealizing transference, Kohut describes the mirror transferences which in this early stage of the theory represent a therapeutic revival of the grandiose self. In the archaic form there is a merger through the extension of the grandiose self; an intermediate form occurs — later described as a separate type of transference (Kohut 1984) — in which the patient assumes that the analyst is just like the patient and is called the alter-ego or twinship transference. In the least archaic form of mirror transference the analyst is experienced as a separate person but who has significance only for the purpose of mirroring the patient's accomplishments. This latter "mirror transference in the narrow sense"

> is the reinstatement of the phase in which the gleam in the mother's eye, which mirrors the child's exhibitionistic display, and other forms of maternal participation in the child's narcissistic enjoyment confirm the child's self-esteem and by a gradually increasing selectivity of these responses begin to channel it into realistic directions. (p. 489)

Kohut gives several cases illustrating the great difficulty of getting through resistances in order to raise to the consciousness the patient's infantile fantasies of exhibitionistic grandeur. Not only are they often accompanied by shame and hypochondria, but often they are very frightening because of the danger of "dedifferentiating intrusions of the grandiose self and the narcissistic-exhibitionistic libido into the ego" (p. 491).

A similar process occurs in the working through of these mirror transferences when, as a consequence of the disturbance of a mirror transference, psychological and behavioral difficulties and impulses develop; the example that Kohut here presents is also that of voyeurism on the weekend separation from the analyst. The purpose of the voyeurism, typical of a male patient in a public toilet, is to achieve a feeling of merger with the man at whom he gazes in the absence of the analyst. These kinds of disturbances of the mirror transferences are explained and interpreted in the proper empathic ambience as with the idealizing transferences. This leads to an integration of the grandiose self "with a realistic conception of the self and to the realization that life offers only limited possibilities for the gratification of the narcissistic-exhibitionistic wishes" (p. 492), so that an integration and formation of more reasonable ambitions is permitted.


### ERRORS IN DEALING WITH NARCISSISTIC
### TRANSFERENCES

Even in this early paper we are specifically warned by Kohut not to actively encourage idealization in analytic psychotherapy but to allow it to occur spontaneously without interference. The two other major pitfalls often found with the narcissistic (selfobject) transferences are the analyst's readiness to moralize about the patient's narcissism, and the tendency to theorize instead of interpreting and explaining with direct reference to the patient's specific experiences.

Kohut states that the tendency to moralize and to become the patient's leader and teacher are most likely to occur "when the psychopathology under scrutiny is not understood metapsychologically" (p. 496); the tendency then is to supplement interpretations with suggestive pressure, and the weight of the therapist's personality becomes of greater importance. Kohut introduces the concept of the well trained, calm craftsman in contrast to the charismatically gifted individual who performs great feats of therapeutic heroism, and he seeks to provide an understanding of narcissistic personalities that will enable the therapist to take a craftsmanlike approach. This also requires some understanding of the reactions of the analyst to idealizing and mirror transferences. The idealizing transference tends to be rejected because it stimulates the therapist's own repressed grandiosity and the mirror transferences lead to boredom and even intolerance of a situation in which the therapist is reduced to the role of a mirror for the patient's infantile narcissism.

Somewhat analogous to Anna O., the patient of Breuer and Freud

(1893) who discovered the "chimney sweeping" method of free association, Miss F. is quoted at the end of Kohut's 1978 paper as the first patient who made him aware of her never-ending demand for mirroring. She wanted him only to summarize or repeat what she had already said, but whenever he went beyond this and offered an interpretation, the patient furiously accused him in a tense, high-pitched voice, of undermining her. No interpretations based on an oedipal level made any difference whatsoever and ultimately the high-pitched tone of her voice, which expressed in the tone of a very young child such utter conviction of being right, led Kohut to recognize that he was being used for mirroring purposes in the patient's effort to replace missing psychic structure.

Here he introduces another of the most controversial aspects of the psychology of the self, *"reluctant compliance with the childhood wish"* (reprinted in Kohut 1978, p. 507), which he feels might in some instances have to be provided temporarily only to form the beginning of an ultimate working through process of the grandiose self. The offering of the mirroring that the patient missed from the mother is a corrective emotional experience. However, Kohut is *not* advocating it as a curative factor but only as at times unavoidable in setting the stage for the ultimate working through and interpretation of the mirror transferences by traditional means.

## The First Definitive Psychology of the Self

The publication of *The Analysis of the Self* (1971) marked the first major divergence of the psychology of the self from traditional psychoanalytic theory. In the first place, it offers a new definition of the self as a comparatively low-level, comparatively experience-near, psychoanalytic abstraction, which is not an agency of the mind but is a psychic structure that can exist within each of the agencies of the mind. Kohut goes beyond the traditional structural theory (id, ego, and superego). He sees the definition of self as existing in a sort of side-by-side state within the mind but not as a traditional agency of the mental apparatus. This definition of the self changes as Kohut's theories develop and remains a highly controversial and difficult aspect of the psychology of the self; Kohut's notion of the self as it originates is an experience-near psychoanalytic abstraction. It is based on our observations through the method of empathy or vicarious introspection of the patient's sense of cohesion or disintegration (fragmentation) of the sense of self at any given time. This is the "psychology of the self in the narrow sense," an extension of the metapsychology of Freud. It eventually foundered on Kohut's metapsychological effort to extract a narcissistic form of libido which follows its own separate line of development.

In a good holding environment, minor failures in the mother's or the therapist's empathy are unavoidable, and lead the baby or the patient to absorb gradually and silently that which the mother or therapist used to do for the baby or patient. This process forms structures of drive regulation and drive channeling which contribute to the fabric of the self, and constitutes Kohut's notion of transmuting internalization. It is a microinternalization in contrast to introjection, in which, due to inappropriate disappointment, there is massive incorporation and the object is set up within the psyche so that a relationship between the self and the object, as introject, continues. Optimal psychic structure is not formed by introjection, and it usually only perpetuates an unsatisfactory relationship and removes dependency on the external object.

The concept of selfobject was introduced by Kohut to help distinguish between object relations and object love. The small child has object relations but not object love. The child relates to others as selfobjects, in which the object is experienced as part of the self and having no life of its own. There are two kinds of selfobjects: those who respond to, confirm, and mirror the child's sense of greatness and perfection, and those to whom the child can look up and with whom the child can merge. Selfobjects of the second category provide an image of calmness and omnipotence which can be borrowed to provide narcissistic equilibrium.

The selfobject is an object predominantly used either in the service of the self or experienced as part of the self. It is important to distinguish (Kohut 1971, pp. 50–51) among the narcissistically experienced archaic selfobject; psychological structures built up by "gradual decathexis of the narcissistically experienced archaic object" which continue to perform "drive-regulating, integrating, and adaptive functions" previously performed by the external object; and "true objects (in the psychoanalytic sense) which are cathected with object-instinctual investments, i.e., objects loved and hated by a psyche that has separated itself from the archaic objects" (p. 51).

Kohut's concepts are exciting and important because they appear in the archaic "transferences" of many patients, and they help us to understand certain aspects of behavior in psychotherapy that ordinarily will cause irritation and rejection on the part of the therapist. If one understands a clinging dependent transference in terms of the patient's phase of narcissistic object relations, or if one understands the rage of a patient upon separating from the therapist as representative of the total inability of the patient to conceive of the needs of the therapist or to tolerate any lack of control over the therapist, then a more appropriate empathic response and interpretation can be presented to the patient.

Kohut presents his concept of the vertical and the horizontal split. In this unfortunate use of geometry Kohut relates the vertical split to what Freud (in a different context) thought of as disavowal. The vertically split-off sector or the disavowed part of the personality is manifested in narcissistic personality disorders by openly displayed infantile grandiosity which alternates with the patient's usual personality. Indeed, the patient may show most of the time a low self-esteem, shame propensity, and hypochondria. Psychotherapy begins by dealing with the vertical split because it is usually possible to help the patient get examples of the vertically split-off sector from conscious everyday thinking and behavior. This terminates the openly displayed infantile grandiosity and increases the pressure from the repressed material hidden by the horizontal split.

The low self-esteem, shame propensity, and hypochondria represent a reaction formation to what is hidden by the horizontal split, which seems analogous to the repression barrier. Under the horizontal split are repressed unfulfilled, archaic narcissistic demands, representing the emerging true self of the child which should have been acknowledged by the gleam in the mother's eye. By blocking the disavowed expression of infantile narcissism, the pressure of this archaic narcissistic demand is increased and the archaic grandiosity begins to appear.

## Clinical Material and Comments

The following vignette provides an idea of the difference in approach to patient material between the psychology of the self and traditional intensive psychotherapy or psychoanalysis. A patient who had been in intensive psychotherapy for two years dreamed, "Mother was there and I impulsively wanted to fuck her; in the next scene she dies." This patient, who had a severe narcissistic personality disorder, had just received a wounding report from a superior in his corporation. He has a very sharp-tongued wife and a sharp-tongued mother. His associations led to "fucking" as a means of control, and the sense of how gratified he is in extramarital relations: "these women call me incredible as a lover, but my wife never acts that way. She just says, 'O.K., if you want to'." The purpose of "fucking" then, for this patient, has no primary sexual value. It is to be admired and called wonderful and incredible by these women who substitute for the mother that he needs — the women with whom he sleeps are mirroring selfobjects whose assignment is to praise his sexual performance. If his mother will not call him wonderful, she, his wife, and the boss should drop dead!

Compare this with the traditional oedipal interpretation of this material. Notice how it deemphasizes the hidden incestuous wishes and how an incestuous dream with manifest oedipal content is reinterpreted as hiding the desperate need to restore narcissistic equilibrium by a mirroring selfobject and the need to express narcissistic rage.

I wish to make a number of clinical comments to help bring Kohut's early theories into the experience-near data on which they are based. The observer watching the patient with a grandiose self thinks that the patient is arrogant, and the observer watching the patient with an idealizing transference is shocked to see that the patient believes the therapist knows everything and can always be relied upon for advice and strength. Formerly, the therapist was supposed to correct the reality testing in each of these situations, but Kohut insists that the "selfobject transferences" must be allowed to develop without interference. The therapist, on the basis of empathy or vicarious introspection, must decide whether the developing transference is object-related or narcissistic, and this will help with the decision regarding the interpretation of the transference. For example, if there is an object-related idealizing transference that is hiding oedipal hostility, it must be interpreted. If there is an emerging mirror transference in a patient who has primarily narcissistic personality problems, a statement such as "we look alike" is left alone by the therapist rather than being corrected, for such a correction is experienced as a "straight arm," a narcissistic wound, that keeps the patient from developing the required selfobject transference. The patient will abandon it later when it is no longer necessary. The "correction" causes the patient to withdraw, become arrogant, and fosters a retreat to the grandiose self in splendid isolation.

A mood of acceptance must be offered to these selfobject transferences rather than confronting the patient with "reality." It is sometimes difficult to distinguish between an idealizing and a merger transference; when the patient idealizes the therapist, the patient also wants to merge with the therapist. In a merger type of mirror transference, the patient treats the analyst as if the analyst were part of the patient, but in an idealizing transference, the patient first imparts all kinds of wisdom and power to the therapist. Again, Kohut argues that this idealization should be accepted and not corrected, as it will drop away by itself when it is no longer needed by the patient.

Narcissistic injury and consequent narcissistic rage are inevitable in the working through of these transferences. Narcissistic injury occurs when the environment does not react in an expected way; it may occur due to empathic lapses on the part of the therapist or apart from the therapy when the patient has done good work and received no reward. Raging even at minor narcissistic injuries should not be met with condescension and rage by the therapist, but rather by an attempt to explain what has happened, which often must be repeated. The explanation gradually makes more and more sense to the patient, who, it is hoped, adopts the therapist's rational way of looking at things. Taking on the therapist's way of looking at things, with a more benign view of patients toward themselves, is part of transmuting internalization. For example, the patient's self-hatred and rage if something is created without the expected acclaim, can eventually be replaced by the feeling that it is possible to do the best one can to get admiration even though the results are limited.

Self-psychologists feel that this approach causes the therapist to participate more, producing a more human quality and ambience to the treatment. It is very important to always add that deliberate attempts to provide mirroring or encourage idealization are never advocated by Kohut or his followers, and simply represent a narcissistic countertransference acting out on the part of the therapist. The selfobject transferences are mobilized by tolerating them and not straight-arming the patient or impatiently correcting them when they appear, or interfering with them by making premature interpretations to display one's own brilliance.

The idealizing transference can "telescope" from archaic to more mature forms and it is sometimes hard to determine the pathognomic period of trauma. What is perhaps more important are the clinically experienced aspects in an idealizing transference of a swing from disappointment to the grandiose self in the course of the treatment. This is manifested by coldness to the formerly idealized analyst, a tendency to primitivization of thought and speech — from stilted speech to the gross use of neologisms — attitudes of superiority, an increased tendency to self-consciousness and shame, and hypochondriacal preoccupations; patients become withdrawn and silent.

In the first phase of therapy, if the selfobject transferences are not hampered, we may see certain characteristic anxiety dreams due to a resistance to regression and the consequent remobilization of these transferences. Kohut (1971, p. 87) tells us to look for dreams of falling if a mirror transference is coming, and dreams of climbing high majestic mountains if an idealizing transference is coming. After the transferences have formed, when the idealizing transference is disturbed there tends to be more despondency, and when the mirror transference is disturbed there is a greater tendency towards rage. These clues may help to decide what kind of transference is predominant at a given time. Once the selfobject transferences have formed, the process of transmuting internalization, which had been traumatically interrupted in childhood, is now ready to be resumed in the treatment.

Developmentally the fabric of the ego is formed by numerous microexperiences that help tell the person what to do or not to do in any given situation. All of us have such a library of experiences to call upon. Interpersonal competence has to do with this internal library. In terms of tension reduction and narcissistic equilibrium, a reasonable empathic ambience between the mother and the child will enable the child, when realizing that the mother is not perfect, to learn in little ways to do things for itself which were once done by the mother. This is the notion of transmuting internalization, in which the fabric of the ego is built slowly by the child taking into itself the mirroring function and the object for idealization in the formation of internalized goals and values.

A similar process occurs in successful psychoanalysis, according to Kohut (1977), who explains that once the selfobject transferences have formed:

Little by little, as a result of innumerable processes of microinternaliza-tion, the anxiety-assuaging, delay-tolerating, and other realistic aspects of the analyst's image become part of the analysand's psychological equipment, *pari passu* with the "micro"-frustration of the analysand's need for the analyst's permanent presence and perfect functioning in this respect. In brief: through the process of transmuting internalization, new psychological structure is built. (p. 32)

For Kohut, cure is best described in terms of changes in psychological "microstructures" (p. 31), and in the psychoanalysis of any patient the essential structural transformations occur as a consequence of these gradual internalizations (p. 30).

## Details of Clinical Work Utilizing Self Psychology

The middle portion of Kohut's first book is rather difficult. In a full-scale analysis Kohut hopes to see the genetic sequence of child-hood unfold in the shifts in the selfobject transferences. If there had been in childhood first an attempted idealization, then a failure in it, and then a falling-back upon the grandiose self, one may see the development in the treatment of, first, a brief idealizing transference as an intermediate step backward in regression and then a more stable mirror transference. One should not interfere with the development of these transferences so they can evolve naturally and give a clue to the childhood of the patient.

The entire nosology of Kohut is based on the empathically ob-served cohesion of the self when the patient is in treatment. Those with narcissistic personality disorders, when disappointed in the mir-ror and idealizing transferences, may form a rapid hypercathexis of an archaic grandiose self-image defended by hostility, coldness, ar-rogance, and silence or even go further into hypochondriasis, but the situation is reversible in a relatively short period of time and under the influence of explanation from the therapist. The borderline pa-tient and the psychotic patient develop an irreversible fragmentation when they are disappointed in the selfobject therapist and therefore, according to Kohut, are not amenable to the method of psychoanal-ysis. They do not form any kind of stable narcissistic transference but soon fragment irreversibly. This leads to a gloomy prognosis for

borderline and psychotic patients by the method of intensive psychotherapy or psychoanalysis, and also generates a warning to eschew
such methods with schizoid patients who have developed protection
against further narcissistic wounding by withdrawal from human relationships; Kohut warns us not to be a "bull in a china shop" with
these individuals. Brandschaft and Stolorow (Lichtenberg et al.
1984a) have revised this gloomy prognosis for borderline patients
within the framework of self psychology which they claim (p. 344)
Kohut told them is compatible with his view. I will discuss this in
detail in Chapter 13.

A validation of the correct interpretation of a shift from the
idealizing transference to the grandiose self occurs when there emerges
a group of memories about similar situations in childhood. As an example, take the patient who on weekends must watch pornographic
movies in order to combat the sense of deadness and loss of the therapist with the excitement stirred up by the movies. (In Kohut's case
the patient went to the men's room and in fantasy merged with another man's imagined powerful alive penis.) Explanations of this to
the patient, validated by memories from childhood in which the patient attempted to deal with narcissistic disappointments by voyeuristic excitement, will gradually permit internalization of the reasonable, stable, calm, and soothing attitude of the therapist so that,
for example, the patient can sublimate and become a photographer
who takes many pictures on the weekend. This is validated clinically many times where, under severe stress or narcissistic blows, the
patient regresses back to the more archaic magical voyeuristic activities.

A gifted ego can often realize the archaic expectations of the grandiose self and achieve amazing successes at least in the early part of
life. But characteristically such successes are never enough; and there
is an endless demand for performance so that middle-aged depression in "successful" people is a typical result. Their lives become a
treadmill where success brings no release; there is always a wish for
acclaim, success, and endless satisfaction. Such people are driven by
a split-off grandiose self with its bizarre demands, and psychotherapy
from the standpoint of the psychology of the self offers much to
understand what has happened.

More subtle clinical examples of a hidden archaic grandiose self
include the patient who is ashamed to ask directions in a strange city
because the patient cannot tolerate not knowing everything, or the

student patient who will not say a word in class because the student is afraid that the comments will not be reacted to with excitement and awe. Similarly, lying, bragging, and name dropping often appear as an attempt to live up to the expectations from the grandiose self, and are often incorrectly handled in psychotherapy by lectures and correction of "reality testing."

The dangerous mobilization of infantile fantasies of exhibitionistic grandeur is a common clinical situation. The anxiety is not that of castration but of what Kohut (1971, p. 152) has called "dedifferentiating intrusion of narcissistic structures and their energies into the ego." The symptoms of such impending intrusions are vague and may involve:

1. A "fear of the loss of the reality self" (p. 153) through an ecstatic merger with the idealized parent imago, or in "quasi-religious regressions" with God and the universe.

2. A fear of the loss of contact with reality due to breakout of intense unrealistic grandiosity or megalomania.

3. Shame and self-consciousness due to the conscious intrusion of exhibitionistic wishes.

4. Hypochondriasis, which for Kohut represents the expression of fragmentation of the self through the use of the body as a place for the attribution of the discomfort that the patient is feeling, an elaboration by the ego of "the intrusion of archaic images of the fragmented body-self" (p. 152).

It is possible to differentiate the anxiety over the explosion of narcissistic structures into the conscious, from oedipal castration anxiety. In castration anxiety the clinical material contains a hint of the oedipal triangle, more details and elaborations, and usually the concept of an adversary as a dangerous person.

Another danger is that of acting out of the grandiose self. This occurs when it threatens to be hypercathected in treatment, and may place the patient in dangerous situations. It must be closely monitored by the therapist and blocked by interpretation.

The mirror and idealizing transferences of Kohut represent regressions to normal developmental positions. This is in contrast to the Kleinian descriptions of the appearance of projective identification — which parallels the idealizing transference — and introjective identification, which parallels the mirror transference. Projective and introjective identification appearing in the psychotherapy of adult patients are pathological and imply a higher cognitive infantile capacity for self and object differentiation in Klein's theories. They are not experienced primarily by vicarious introspection or empathy although some authors have insisted that they are clinically similar to Kohut's selfobject transferences.

Even in the early work of Kohut the ambience indicated is a greater participation by the therapist, especially in dealing with the responses to separation and in staying closer to the patient's experiences in the present rather than in producing interpretations of the past. The therapist is well advised to stay experience-near rather than attempting to unearth remote material. In fact, interpretations of the past may be experienced by the patient as a frustrating wound, because the patient cannot do much about the past. (Narcissistic patients are extremely sensitive about what they cannot control.) The whole ambience of the treatment is more benign say the self psychologists, and fosters the further development of a selfobject transference. Traditional psychoanalysts claim that there is nothing new in this advice.

This ambience is in contrast to the usual relationship that narcissistic (and borderline) patients experience with people, in which their grandiosity usually produces angry rejection and their idealization often produces irritation. In general, exhortation, suggestion, and sermonizing are reduced in the relationship and more effort is made to produce explanations about what happened and why the patients behave and feel as they do.

Certain rewards accrue to the therapist who is working with these difficult patients, patients that characteristically mobilize negative countertransference. These rewards are the enjoyment of progress in a difficult therapeutic task and the intellectual pleasure of comprehending how it is being achieved. The therapist must be able to do a lot of benign explaining to the patient, and sometimes a great effort is required to accept the narcissistic rage and narcissistic transferences. At the same time the therapist must guard against overempathy characterized by saccharine interpretations and an inability to retreat from the temporary merger with the patient in the therapeutic hour. Kohut's basic notion is that interpretation should be like reading an electrocardiogram: the readings are observed and reported objectively. One always addresses the explanations or interpretations to the adult ego of the patient.

## EARLY CRITICISM

These complex metapsychological formulations led to many criticisms of Kohut's early work. Authors like Giovacchini (1977) argued that Kohut's basic concepts are merely a rewording of Freud's terminology, using geometry. He attacks especially the "horizontal split," which is analogous to repression, described by Kohut to occur before the oedipal period. How can there be "repression" of a psychic imago in an immature preoedipal psyche? The term splitting is usually used for this, which would make the horizontal and vertical splits both splitting. Yet, Kohut is implying two different mechanisms.

The alteration of Freud's metapsychology by postulating two kinds of libido, narcissistic and sexual, undergoing separate lines of development, is sometimes called Kohut's "double axis theory." This has caused much confusion and argument (Loewald 1973), reviewed in Chapter 19.

Does the infant have sufficient self and object cognitive discrimination to form an idealized parent imago, which some argue would require an awareness of the parent and the external world? A similar problem exists with the notion of the grandiose self. Further objections attack Kohut's theory as being simplistic at this point, because there cannot be represented clinically a fixation at a normal stage of development since trauma at any stage leaves scars and leads to pathological formations and distortions in all the following stages. Thus, the appearance of the grandiose self in the adult cannot simply be an unaltered version of the childhood formation. Many other detailed criticisms were offered by Lichtenberg (1973) and by Loewald (1973).

Kohut increasingly recognized these objections, as we shall see in the next two chapters, and moved farther and farther away from traditional Freudian metapsychology as he developed the "psychology of the self in the broader sense."

# Chapter 9

## Kohut in Transition

### Review of Early Self Psychology

To summarize the psychology of the self in its first or "narrow" version, our self-assessment becomes closer to the assessment of us by others as our narcissism transforms and matures through a series of characteristic developmental pathways. In response to stimuli from the environment and due to an epigenetic preprogramming, these developmental pathways lead from autoerotism to primary narcissism — in which the infant blissfully experiences the world as being itself — and then, due to inevitable disappointment in such narcissistic omnipotence, the formation of the grandiose self and the idealized parent imago. The grandiose self carries the conviction of being very powerful, even omnipotent, with a demand for mirroring confirmation by the selfobject; the idealized parent imago attributes all omnipotence to a magical figure which is then viewed as a selfobject to be controlled and with which to be fused.

By a series of transmuting microinternalizations in an appropriate environment, the grandiose self becomes incorporated into the ego or self as ambition (in the later theory it becomes a pole of the self), a drive or push which can be realistically sublimated and is itself

drive-channeling (Kohut 1971, p. 187), resulting in motivated enthusiastic activity. The idealized parent imago becomes infused into
the ego ideal (or, in the later theory, becomes the other pole of the
self), which attracts the individual toward certain goals and performs
a drive-curbing function (Kohut 1971, p. 186). The proper integration of these narcissistic formations leads ultimately by further transformations to a sense of humor, empathy, wisdom, acceptance of the
transience of life, and even to creativity within the limitations of the
individual.

If the grandiose self is not integrated gradually into the realistic
purposes of the ego, derivatives of it are disavowed (vertical split)
or it is repressed (horizontal split) and persists unaltered in archaic
form; the individual then consciously oscillates between irrational
overestimation of himself and feelings of inferiority with narcissistic
mortification due to the thwarting of ambition. If the idealized parent
imago is not integrated into the ego ideal, it is then repressed as an
archaic structure, and the patient becomes unconsciously fixed on
a yearning, out of the need to resume narcissistic peace, for an external idealized selfobject, forever searching for an omnipotent powerful person to merge with and from whose support and approval
the individual may gain magical strength and protection.

As a consequence of this developmental arrest and failure to properly integrate these archaic structures, characteristic "selfobject transferences" (Kohut 1977), previously called "narcissistic transferences"
(Kohut 1971), occur. These "selfobject transferences" are the result
of the amalgamation of the unconscious archaic narcissistic structures
(grandiose self and idealized parent imago) with the psychic representation of the analyst, under the pressure of the need to relieve the
unfulfilled narcissistic needs of childhood. It remains questionable
whether they are to be called transferences in the strict sense. They
are not motivated by the need to discharge instinctual tensions nor
are they produced by cathecting the analyst with object libido. One
may wish to think of them as transferencelike phenomena, but I will
refer to them here as selfobject transferences, following Kohut's later
writing.

The goal of the idealizing selfobject transference is to share magically, via a merger, in the power and omnipotence of the therapist.
Occurring as the result of therapeutic mobilization of the idealized
parent imago are two basic types of such transferences, with a variety
of gradations in between. The most obvious type is a later forma-

tion, usually based on a failure of idealization of the father, which stresses the search for an idealized parent to which the patient must be attached in order to feel approved and protected. A more archaic type of selfobject transference may appear or be hidden under the other type; this transference is usually related to a failure with the mother, in which the stress is on ecstatic merger and mystical union with the godlike, idealized parent.

Once such a transference has been formed, clinical signs of its disturbance are a cold, aloof, angry, raging withdrawal which represents a swing to the grandiose self; feelings of fragmentation and hypochondria due to the separation; and the creation of eroticized replacements by frantic activities and fantasies, especially those involving voyeurism, with many variations.

The typical countertransference to the idealizing selfobject transferences (Kohut 1971) occurs through the mobilization of the archaic grandiose self in whatever unanalyzed residue is present in the therapist. This leads to an embarrassed and defensive "straightarming" of the patient by denying the patient's idealization, joking about it, or trying vigorously to interpret it away. Such countertransference produces in the patient the typical signs of disturbance and retreat to the grandiose self mentioned above.

Three forms of mirror selfobject transferences are seen as a result of the therapeutic mobilization of the repressed and unintegrated archaic grandiose self. The purpose of these transferences is to share with the therapist the patient's exhibitionistic grandiosity, either by participating with the therapist in the imagined greatness of the patient or by having the therapist reflect and confirm the greatness of the patient. In the archaic-merger type of mirror transference, the patient experiences the therapist as part of the patient, expects the therapist to know what is in the patient's mind, and demands total control of the type one demands from one's own arm or leg.

In the alter-ego or twinship type of mirror transference, the patient insists that the therapist is like or similar to the patient psychologically or that the therapist and the patient look alike. In his final writing, Kohut (1984) gives this a separate status as a third category of selfobject transference.

In the third type of mirror transference, or "mirror transference proper," the patient recognizes that the therapist looks and is different, but insists on assigning to the therapist the sole task of praising, echoing, and mirroring the patient's performance and greatness.

Kohut relates this to "the gleam in the mother's eye" as she watches her baby. It becomes very difficult at times to tell which type of selfobject transference has formed, especially in the less primitive transferences where it is hard to distinguish between the grandiose demand for mirroring and the demand for approval by the idealized parent.

Disturbance of mirror transferences leads to a sense of crumbling self, hypochondria, and hypercathexis of isolated parts of either the body, various mental functions, or activities. Compulsive sexuality, characterized by exhibitionism and other sexual varieties and perversions, often appears in order to combat the sense of deadness and an empty self; its purpose is to magically restitute the sense of self and the sense of being psychologically "alive." An excellent literary example of a prolonged desperate effort to restore a crumbling self is depicted in the novel *Money: A Suicide Note* (Amis 1985).

Typical countertransference reactions to mirror transferences (Kohut 1971) are boredom, lack of involvement with the patient, inattention, annoyance, sarcasm, and a tendency to lecture the patient out of the therapist's counterexhibitionism, or to obtain control by exhortation and persuasion.

It follows that in clinical work we can pick up certain early signs of selfobject transferences. We note that the patient reacts to our empathic lapses, cancellations and vacations, or even to the gap of time between sessions, with perverse or other sexual acting-out, hypochondriasis, irritable and arrogant behavior, painfully depressive moods, and a sense of emptiness and depletion. These signs may be understood as manifestations of partial fragmentation of the self due to the disruption of the selfobject transferences and as attempts to restitute and discharge the painful tensions involved.

The purpose of the selfobject transferences is to relieve the unfulfilled narcissistic needs of childhood for the selfobject to joyfully accept and confirm the child's grandiosity and for "an omnipotent surrounding," which Kohut and Wolf (1978) regard as "healthy needs that had not been responded to in early life" (p. 424). When these responses are forthcoming, a sense of narcissistic peace and equilibrium results.

Phase-inappropriate disappointment in the idealized parent imago that occurs very early in experiences with the mother leads to a need for optimal soothing from the idealized parent and a search for drugs, with a malfunctioning stimulus barrier. Such patients tend to become addicted to psychotherapy for just this reason. In the late preoedipal period, phase-inappropriate disappointment in the idealized parent imago attached to significant selfobjects causes a resexualization of pregenital drives and derivatives with a high incidence of perversions in fantasy or acts.

In early latency the severe disappointment in the idealized oedipal object undoes the recently established, precarious idealized superego. This leads to the search for an external object of perfection, an intense search for and dependency on idealized selfobjects which are conceived as missing segments of the psychic structure. For such patients each success can give only transient good feelings but does not add to the patient's self-esteem because the patient is fixed on finding an idealized parent imago outside of the patient and requires a continuing outside source of approval at this developmental stage.

## IDEALIZATIONS

Idealizations can also appear in the transference neuroses and are related to the state of being in love in the transference. In the transference neuroses idealization does not lose touch entirely with the realistic features and limitations of the object. In typical neurotic situations, idealization can represent a projection of the analysand's idealized superego onto the analyst and form a part of the positive transference, or defensive idealizations can form against transference hostility.

In the narcissistic disorders, however, the unconscious is fixated on an idealized selfobject for which it continues to yearn. Such persons are forever searching for external omnipotent powers from whose support and approval they attempt to derive strength. Thus, in the narcissistic transferences there is a sense of an eerie, vague idealization which becomes central to the material even to such an extreme delusion that the therapist is divine. One does not get the feeling of relating to the patient as one human being to another, but rather of an eerie quality of unreasonable exaltation to which the therapist reacts with embarrassment and negativism if the therapist does not understand the material conceptually. The intensity of the distortion gives the therapist an idea of how desperate the patient is. The greater the desperation, the greater the requirement for soothing from the therapist by presenting a consistent therapeutic structure, repeated explanations, and focusing on the current reality.

## WORKING THROUGH

In working with these developmental disorders, the therapist must participate by dealing specifically with responses to separation and disappointments in the transferences and by staying nearer to everyday experiences rather than offering deep interpretations of the past. In fact, interpretations of the past may come as a narcissistic injury because the patient cannot do much about the past and feels weak and impotent. Rage at such interpretations is the consequence of narcissistic injury and not, as it is often misinterpreted, part of the transference. The therapist takes a benign approach and fosters the development of the selfobject transferences by patient, craftsmanlike work.

The selfobject transferences represent a new edition of the relationship between the self and the selfobject from early life; infantile ambitions and idealizations are remobilized by the general ambience of the therapy and empathy with the patient's experience of the patient's needs. Small disappointments are recognized and interpretations are made with respect to the present and the past. Then, through transmuting internalizations, patients alter their inner world and self-regulation develops, paralleling the development of the child. Archaic grandiose demands are transformed into self-regulation, and workable standards are set by the child in this process and later in a similar fashion by the patient in psychotherapy. How closely this parallels childhood development remains an uncertain and controversial issue.

## TRANSMUTING INTERNALIZATIONS AND CREATIVITY

Transmuting internalization differs from other internalization processes. Gross identification due to the unconscious need for the power and skill of the therapist is magical and impermanent. Kohut argues that it is a favorable sign in the treatment if such gross identification does not occur. Identification with the aggressor tends to occur when the analyst is experienced as an aggressor, either realistically, or out of a projection from the patient's unconscious. The process of transmuting internalization in childhood, and perhaps later in adult psychotherapy, is related to autonomous factors with inherent endowment balanced by the significance of the kind of external care the child received. The notion of transmuting internalization focuses on the spirit and appropriateness of the response of significant selfobjects.

Self psychologists beginning with Kohut (1977, p. 287) often quote the plays of Eugene O'Neill, for example *The Great God Brown*, which portrays a lifelong struggle of the protagonist against fragmentation of the self. The cold unrelatedness with the father and the joyless pathological merger with the mother lead to a never-ending search for "glue" to hold the self together.

Sometimes highly creative individuals are able to find this "glue" within their own creative activities. For example, the biographer Leon Edel (1969) describes the profound narcissistic wounding of Henry James when his efforts at writing plays produced repeated failures. In spite of the assaults and misfortunes, a self-recreation took place, in which James turned to short story writing. Although he had no affectionately secure interpersonal relations in mid-life, he was able to accept his middle-aged loneliness by turning to the discipline of his craft. This indirect soothing of his psyche enlarged his vision of the world and produced a warmth to his personality and a sense of an invigorated self.

It seems to be a unique gift of certain human beings to soothe themselves through creating illusions and then internalizing their own created idealizations, providing narcissistic equilibrium. This may give a key to the formation of religions and artistic productions that would produce a view of these phenomena quite different from Freud's pejorative psychoanalytic interpretations of them.

In addition to an entirely different view regarding art and religion, the psychology of the self greatly influences the technique of psychoanalysis and intensive psychotherapy. For example, Kohut (1978) describes the aggressive image of the therapist created by Wilhelm Reich in his exhortations to attack the narcissistic "armor" of the patient: "Reich created an aggressive image implying hostility, fight, quarrel between patient and physician. The physician who wants to overcome the resistance turns into an attacker who undertakes breaking to pieces the armor of the analysand" (pp. 548–549). Another example given by Kohut is that of the analyst leaping on a parapraxis of the patient in the early stages of analysis: "All this must be interpreted carefully and with true empathy" (p. 552). Again, there is continuing emphasis on the proper tact, timing, and understanding on the part of the analyst of how an interpretation is *experienced* by the patient.

## *Narcissistic Rage*

After Kohut's (1971) *The Analysis of the Self* appeared, one of the main complaints about the book was that it did not deal with the subject of narcissistic rage, since it represents the hardest aspect with which to contend in treating narcissistic patients. Perhaps in response to this difficulty, Kohut (1978) wrote one of his most important papers, "Thoughts on Narcissism and Narcissistic Rage" in 1972 which led him in the direction of applying the psychology of the self to major world historical problems as well as to the difficulties of the individual.

"Thoughts on Narcissism" begins by describing the great story *Michael Kohlhaas* (Kleist 1976) by Heinrich von Kleist (1777–1811), who ended his short life by suicide and whose stature in German literature is only now becoming recognized in the West as surpassed only by that of Goethe (Maass 1983). More familiar is *Moby Dick* by Melville which, like Kleist's story, describes the fate of a man obsessed by interminable narcissistic rage. The outbreak of group narcissistic rage when the aspirations of the grandiose self are blocked, leading to a yearning for merger with the idealized selfobject, is next applied to an understanding of the rise of Hitler and the ruthless warfare of Nazi Germany.

Kohut flatly disagrees with the hypothesis that there is an inherent human aggressive drive which is only thinly protected by the veneer of civilization and accounts for the outbreak of war. In his view, human aggression arises in its most dangerous form out of narcissistic rage, which in turn is a disintegration or byproduct as a consequence of the profound disappointment in selfobjects. The narcissistically vulnerable individual responds to actual or anticipated narcissistic injury either with shamefaced withdrawal or with narcissistic rage, and Kohut's essay offers a splendid clinical description of the various forms of such rage.

The whole problem of "preventive attack" and the boundless wish for revenge in which every aspect of ego functioning is drawn into the service of narcissistic rage — as so well illustrated by our current insanity of a nuclear arms race with the Soviet Union — becomes understandable as a situation in which narcissistic rage actually enslaves the ego. Even the smallest narcissistic wounds can produce the most astonishing demonstrations of narcissistic rage in individuals who are narcissistically vulnerable. The rage becomes aimed at the "enemy" (or "evil empire") who is experienced as a flaw in the patient's narcissistically perceived reality. The patient expects total and full control, so that the independence or balky behavior of the selfobject is a personal offense.

When the selfobject fails to live up to absolute obedience expectations, narcissistic rage appears, characterized by no empathy whatever for the offender. The ego functions only as a tool and rationalizer for the attainment of revenge. Chronic narcissistic rage is even more dangerous, as secondary process thinking gets pulled into the archaic aggression and the ego attributes all failures to the malevolence of the uncooperative selfobject.

Such rage may also be directed at the self as an object, which leads to depression, or at the body-self, leading to psychosomatic disorders. Again this is applied to group processes when, through the blocking of acceptable outlets for national prestige or the destruction of group or religious values, the "flavor of narcissistic rage" (p. 658) appears, carrying an ominous threat to the peace of the world.

This also gives us an important clinical indicator of progress in treatment. As the patient matures, narcissistic rage begins to be transformed into realistic adult assertiveness in the service of worthwhile goals, and away from the many primitive explosions that characterize the early phase of intensive psychotherapy of narcissistic and borderline patients.

## The Increasing Importance of Empathy

With the passage of time Kohut shifted his emphasis over the mid-1970s away from the accurate interpretation of structural defects involving primitive grandiosity or idealization and focused on empathy. He gradually decided that the truth value of analytic interventions was less important than their effect on the therapeutic relationship; he began to stress the actual healing power of the analyst's "empathic" ambience. In practice this meant adherence to a therapeutic stance stressing the legitimacy of the patient's claim on the caretakers.

With this step Kohut's system crossed gradually into the realm of the nurture psychologies, and Kohut began stating that the basic point of difference between himself and analytic traditionalists was one of values. He insisted that psychoanalysis must become the pacesetter of a major shift in values, from emphasis on a truth-and-reality morality toward the idealization of empathy; from pride in clear vision and uncompromising rationality toward pride in the scientifically controlled expansion of the self. The world of yesterday, as he calls it, is the world of the independent mind, of the proud scientist standing tall and clearsighted. The world of today and of tomorrow is the world of Kafka's "Gregor Samsa" in "The Metamorphosis," of his "K" in *The Trial* and *The Castle*—the world of a family and a society indifferent to "K," who wanders through the world empty, flat, yearning for something he cannot understand. In such a world it is human empathy that forms an enclave of human meaning within a universe of senseless spaces and crazily racing stars, and prevents pairing finiteness and death with meaninglessness and despair.

The series of papers making up Volume 2 of *The Search for the Self* (Kohut 1978) traces Kohut's expansion of his psychology of the self into many other fields of human interest. The concept of the self remains an experience-near notion stemming from a nuclear self, but Kohut gradually revises his early notion that the self forms from the coalescence of a set of primordial nuclei; he now believes there is in rudimentary form a self present soon after birth. The introduction by Paul Ornstein (Kohut 1978) to this series traces in greater detail than possible here the development of Kohut's concepts.

Empathy becomes a central issue, expanding beyond the status of a mode of observation to the "positively toned atmosphere" and emotional climate in which interactions between humans take place; empathy as a psychological bond and nutriment can produce "wholesome social effects" (p. 707). Thus empathic observation becomes increasingly redesigned into the provision of an empathic milieu. The importance of this empathic milieu in the psychotherapeutic situation, in the situation of every human being, and as a necessity for world peace, becomes increasingly central to Kohut's thought.

## Psychoanalysis as a Vital Cultural Force

One of the most remarkable aspects of the psychology of the self is how readily it lends itself to an understanding of a great variety of human phenomena; this may explain why it has eagerly been taken up by workers in numerous scholarly disciplines, as various publications of conferences on the psychology of the self (Goldberg 1980, Lichtenberg and Kaplan 1983) demonstrate. Proponents of the psychology of the self have argued that Kohut and his work have revitalized the entire field of psychoanalysis and contradicted the common complaint that everything possible to be discovered by Freud's techniques has been discovered.

Let us look briefly at this important series of transition papers (Kohut 1978, Vol. 2) that roughly extend from around the time of Kohut's (1971) *The Analysis of the Self* to the appearance of Kohut's second book in 1977, *The Restoration of the Self*. In 1970 Kohut lectured at the Free University in Berlin on the 50th anniversary of the Berlin Psychoanalytic Institute. He said, "Everywhere are dying the Zhivagos who are incapable of adapting to the new conditions without the loss of the core of their life-sustaining traditions and ideals" (p. 513). This is a moral presentation in which Kohut argues for psychoanalysis as an important civilizing force in contrast to "my colleagues who, in quiet restraint, want to focus their whole attention on the concrete problems of their therapeutic activity without spending sleepless nights over the course that mankind is taking" (p. 517).

Psychoanalysis can become a powerful potential cultural force which may help us with the terrible problem of unfettered aggression that is rampant in the modern world. Man seems unable to control his cruelty toward his fellow man: "He appears to be forced to respond to differences of opinion or conflicts of interest in one mode only: through the mobilization of his readiness to fight and to destroy" (p. 526). Kohut's solution here is the intensification, elaboration, and expansion of humanity's inner life, perhaps illustrated by the work of the creative artist and performer and the psychological activities of those who are able to obtain pleasure from the arts. This inward shift toward the exercise of self-contained mental functions can be a fulfilling activity for those who are adequately endowed intellectually and emotionally, allowing them to enjoy life and satisfactorily employ their energies, according to Kohut.

## RELATIONSHIP OF THE SELF AND THE EGO

In a talk on the self first published in 1970, Kohut shifts from a view reminiscent of Nietzsche in which it is an "abstraction" to a view reminiscent of Bergson in which it is "enduring." He states, "The self, however, emerges in the psychoanalytic situation and is conceptualized in the mode of a comparatively low-level — i.e., comparatively experience-near — psychoanalytic abstraction, as a content of the mental apparatus. While it is thus not an agency of the mind, it is yet a structure within the mind since it is cathected with instinctual energy and it has continuity in time, i.e., it is enduring" (pp. 584–585). Kohut is having a struggle in this transitional paper between structural theory and the psychology of the self, while the two theories are rapidly diverging.

The mutually enhancing relationship between the cohesive self and a strong cathexis of ego functions is an important clinical aspect of Kohut's work, and in my opinion remains one of the principal arguments for differentiating the concept of the self from the concept of the ego with its substructures. Clinically, a person must have a secure feeling of who he is as a precondition for the ego's reliable ability to perform its functions. If the self is poorly cathected, ego functions are performed without zest, disconnected from one another, and lacking in firmness of purpose. Conversely, everyday phenomena of the activation of ego functions to provide an enhancement of the sense of cohesive self are also common. For example, Kohut lists recovery from a blow to one's self-esteem through physical exercise (which brings about a heightened cathexis of the body-self) or through the performance of intensive mental activities, which leads to self-confirmation.

An important clinical example is offered from the study of schizophrenia. During the prepsychotic phase the patient is aware of the fragmentation of the self; the patient feels "different," less "real." The patient may try to counteract this fragmentation through the frantic hypercathexis of ego functions of "forced thinking, talking, writing; forced physical and mental work" (p. 588). This "overwork" is then often incorrectly assessed by the patient and by his family not as an attempt at self-healing, but as a cause or precipitant of the disease; actually, it is an attempt to consolidate the crumbling self and prevent the schizophrenic fragmentation.

Kohut continues his struggle to conceptualize the "self" in a brief discussion in 1972, where he defines the nuclear self as the one that is experienced as most basic and is most resistant to change. This nuclear self firms up in adolescence through the help of peer relationships that act as confirming reflections for the maintenance of empathic contact.

In this discussion Kohut gives us a glimpse of himself, mentioning that he was in his own adolescence a member of a secret society from which he feels he derived as an adult a "characteristic idealism" (p. 661). He attributes to himself the capacity to be enthusiastic and also the ability to inspire enthusiasm in others for the causes in which he believes, a fact borne out by the energy of his followers. He admits, however, that the influence of aging produces a shift even in the nuclear self: "There is less enthusiasm in me now (and less Pollyanna) and more concern for the continuity (i.e., for the survival) of the values for which I have lived" (p. 661).

He ends with a remarkable statement about the movie *The Last Picture Show*, which has an extraordinary resemblance to Nietzsche's description of the last man: "There is parental disinterest in the younger generation, and the whole dying town, the dying society of the town, is a symbol for the unresponsiveness, the unempathic self-absorption of the parents" (p. 662).

KOHUT'S "REVALUATION OF VALUES"

Kohut's paper on "The Future of Psychoanalysis" presented in 1973 could be subtitled "Revaluation of Values," and again has a Nietzschean ring about it. He begins, perhaps because this is on the anniversary of his 60th birthday, by telling us about the father that he set up in himself:

> That internal ally who helps me maintain the integrity of myself under psychologically trying circumstances, has taught me, from way back in my life, to turn to reflection, to the search for meanings and explanations. And I have learned that the enjoyment of these mental activities must often take the place of the direct gratifications that are hard to keep in bounds. (p. 665)

Kohut argues that psychoanalysts must replace their archaic object (Freud) by a strong set of ideals and values that will lead to a new surge of independent initiative, for Freud was wrong on such subjects as religion and the psychoses. He quotes what he calls Freud's "touching admission" regarding the insane: "I do not care for these patients, that they annoy me, and that I find them alien to me and to everything human" (p. 672). Elsewhere (1980) I have summarized Freud's views on religion.

Kohut calls for a shift of emphasis from "a truth-and-reality morality toward the idealization of empathy, from pride in clear vision and uncompromising rationality to pride in the scientifically controlled expansion of the self" (p. 676). His next call is for an end to "tool-and-method pride" which leads to the wasteful isolation from one another of various branches of science. He argues that the scientist standing alone was a suitable ideal for the world of yesterday, but for the world of tomorrow a new, expanded inner self will be necessary as an avenue of escape. In addition to this solution, he offers a second way of coping with the world of tomorrow: "The expansion of the self, its increasing capacity to embrace a greater number and a greater variety of others through a consciously renewed and cultivated deepened empathy" (p. 682).

This essay ends with little to suggest how all this is to come about, and leads directly to the next essay, "The Psychoanalyst in the Community of Scholars," delivered in 1973. Here again Kohut gives some personal information, suggesting that if he had another life to live he would try to become a historian—his son is a historian. The essay deals with some of the thorniest problems in epistemology and the philosophy of science, after again reviewing the problem of tool-and-method snobbishness that separates each discipline in the university and leads to internal rigidity and lessened vitality.

Kohut also tries to explain the nonacceptance of psychoanalysis in the community of scholars not on the basis of any primary defect in the epistemological foundations of psychoanalysis as stressed by Grünbaum (1983, 1984), but on the basis of resistance "out of fear that the acceptance of its methodology will undermine the constructed edifice of scientific thought" (p. 696). The mind of modern man, which has worked so hard to achieve objective scientific investigation, has had to rid its thought processes of certain archaic or infantile qualities such as subjectivity, the animistic conception of nature, and immediate sensory impressions that lead to *post hoc propter hoc* hypotheses. Returning to the study of the inner life of man threatens the breakthrough of modern man's "unacknowledged still persisting temptation to return to animistic thought and to anthropomorphic concepts" (p. 696).

Kohut comes down firmly on the side of psychoanalysis as a science and not an art; empathy or vicarious introspection are the unique psychoanalytic tools of observation and gathering data, data which are then treated by the usual rigorous method of the empirical sciences. This is an important and frequently misunderstood point about Kohut, who writes, "I must object when psychoanalysis is welcomed among the fashions of the day on the basis of the erroneous notion that it is no more than a specific, sophisticated art — an art of understanding people via the resonance of empathy" (p. 701).

Kohut would also disagree with those who insist that psychoanalysis will be eventually superseded by traditional methods of scientific observation, for example, empirical studies of the development of children and statistical studies of therapeutic interaction (Eagle 1984). This position disregards what Kohut claims to be the decisive step that psychoanalysis has taken in the development of Western thought. It has combined empathy and traditional scientific method; the data of psychoanalysis are defined and limited by the method of empathy or vicarious introspection. In this argument, there is a curious parallel to that of Ricoeur (1970, outlined by Chessick 1985) who also feels that psychoanalysis took a decisive new step epistemologically in combining hermeneutics and energetics into a new process of gathering knowledge.

Kohut hopes that psychoanalysis can also introduce empathy into other sciences as an observational tool and as a matrix, if we are not to isolate science from humanity and allow science to become our inhuman master. Thus for Kohut the importance of empathy in human life is three-fold: by the recognition of the self in the other, it is an indispensable tool of observation; by the expansion of the self to include the other it constitutes a powerful psychological bond between individuals; and "the accepting, confirming, and understanding human echo evoked by the self" (p. 705) is a psychological nutriment at all stages of human life. Empathy in the first sense is a tool which can be wrongly used; it is "value neutral." In the second sense it can diminish rage and destructiveness by increasing the empathic bridge between disparate peoples; again Kohut emphasizes that the psychology of the self is not proposing "the nonscientific methods of a cure through love which characterize so many therapeutic cults" (p. 707).

Using empathy in the third sense, Kohut attempts to explain the widespread existential malaise of our times, not on a philosophical basis but on a concrete experiential basis. He states that "our propensity for it is due to the insufficient or faulty empathic responsiveness we encountered during the crucial period when the nucleus of our self was formed" (p. 713) in a view which seems consistent with Lasch (1978) in *The Culture of Narcissism*.

The remainder of this essay, which should be studied in basic philosophy courses because it throws psychoanalytic light on some important and urgent contemporary philosophical problems, describes "divinity schools and . . . departments of philosophy where, all too often, lines of thought are being pursued uneasily, whose irrelevance the best of the faculty have themselves long recognized within the silence of their souls" (p. 716). He hopes to revitalize these departments and remobilize the university as a genuine community of scholars by introducing a new kind of humanitarianism based on the notion that man "cannot fulfill his essential self in any better way than by giving emotionally nourishing support to man, i.e., to himself and to his like" (p. 715). There is a striking similarity of this view to the basic stance shown in the later work of Sartre, despite the different terminology. Sartre argues that the individual cannot be free unless all men are free, and engagement is an act, not a word (de Beauvoir 1984).

Finally, he suggests that we study the university hospital, a splendid testing ground for the investigation of the dehumanizing effect of the large institution, which any patient in a large hospital certainly has painfully experienced. Following the same orientation as Nietzsche, he concludes, "It is man's ultimate purpose to support the survival of man" (p. 722), even in our new mass society. To put the matter in a nutshell, Kohut writes, "The university's failure has been to carry on its traditional labors in the pursuit of specialized endeavors while closing its eyes to the tragedy of man, who suffocates in an increasingly inhuman environment that he himself continues to create" (p. 724). To my knowledge, little serious attention has been paid to Kohut's views on these matters by the academic hierarchy.

## Emergence of the Psychology of the Self
## in the Broader Sense

A letter regarding the formation of the self written in 1974 may be regarded as the turning point in Kohut's transition from the "psychology of the self in the narrow sense" to the "psychology of the self in the broader sense." It begins with his clinical observation that the self reacts three ways to selfobject failure. First, there may be temporary fragmentation marked by symptoms of hypochondriasis, disorganization, a disheveled appearance, and strange talk and gestures. Second, there may be regression to the archaic forms of the grandiose self and the idealized parent imago with their intrusive and disruptive demands. Third, there may appear empty depression and a drop in self-esteem. He reiterates that psychoanalysis is an empirical science and not art, and that the self does not form through the coalescence of parts. The child's self-experience arises separately from the body part experiences, and the fate of the self, which has a separate developmental line, is "beyond the pleasure principle" (p. 753).

Our understanding of the human condition is now approached by two roads: the traditional psychoanalytic approach conceives of the individual in conflict over the pleasure-seeking drives as "Guilty Man," and the approach of the psychology of the self defines "Tragic Man" as the individual blocked in the attempt to achieve self-realization. Freud's Guilty Man is pleasure seeking and struggling against guilt and anxiety, but this refers to the realm of parental responses that the individual receives as a child to single parts of his body and single bodily and mental functions. However, there is another realm of parental responses "attuned to his beginning experience of himself as a larger, coherent and enduring organization, i.e., to him as a self" (pp. 755–756).

Certain basic ambitions and ideals are laid down early in life; Kohut labels this the nuclear self. The self, whether in the sector of its ambitions or in the sector of its ideals, does not seek pleasure through stimulation and tension-discharge but strives for fulfillment through the realization of these nuclear ambitions and ideals. Its fulfillment, says Kohut, does not bring pleasure, as does the satisfaction of a drive, but, beyond the pleasure principle, it brings triumph and a glow of joy. Similarly, its blocking does not evoke the signal of anxiety but instead evokes shame and empty depression, "anticipatory despair about the crushing of the self and of the ultimate defeat of its aspirations" (p. 757). Thus Tragic Man fears a premature death which prevents the realization of the aims of the nuclear self, in a view reminiscent of Sartre's description of humanity as a useless passion.

Kohut worries that these considerations may appear speculative, philosophical, and unscientific, just as Freud (1920) worried in *Beyond the Pleasure Principle*. Kohut insists that this duality of the individual's major goals accounts for important clinical phenomena since the two major human tendencies — searching for pleasure and striving to realize the pattern of the self — can either work together harmoniously or can be in conflict with each other.

The remainder of this difficult letter-essay deals with the possibility of creativity arising from disharmony between these strivings. Kohut suggests a third type of basic parental attitude, besides those responding to the child's body parts or the child's nuclear self, which acknowledges the child as a new separate individual or new independent creative self in the next generation. This may lead to a separate line of development of the individual's capacity to enjoy a self-contained, creative aloneness. Here Kohut seriously attempts to apply his psychology of the self to an understanding of creativity.

Two brief subsequent essays, "The Self in History" and "A Note on Female Sexuality," deal with narcissistic injury and so-called "penis envy" from the point of view of self psychology. I have discussed this topic at length in two previous publications (Chessick 1983b, 1984a). The final transitional essay is entitled "Creativeness, Charisma, Group Psychology" and presents Kohut's reflections on the self-analysis of Freud. By 1976, when this essay was written, Kohut had moved a great distance from traditional psychoanalytic theory and considerations, and, one might suspect from this essay, was subject to increasing criticism and perhaps to some social ostracism from organized psychoanalysis.

## KOHUT'S STUDY OF FREUD

Kohut begins by remarking how difficult it is to be objective about Freud, whom he calls "a transference figure par excellence" (p. 793), because we are prone either to establish an idealizing transference toward Freud or defend ourselves against it by reaction formation. Analysts usually get acquainted with Freud during the crucial early years in which the formation of their professional selves takes place. Kohut believes that this idealization of Freud produces cohesion among the psychoanalytic group, borrowing from Freud's (1921) own statements in *Group Psychology and the Analysis of the Ego*. Sterba (1982) provides some personal recollections of the "glorious admiration" of Freud among the early Viennese psychoanalysts.

Psychoanalysts' idealization of Freud leads to conformity and over-caution in the putting forward of new ideas. Idealization also creates psychological conditions unfavorable to creativity because too many of the potentially creative narcissistic strivings of the individual psychoanalyst are committed to too large a proportion of the idealized goals of the group. The assumption is that original creativity is energized predominantly from the grandiose self, while the work of more tradition-bound scientific and artistic activities "is performed with idealizing cathexes" (p. 801). Kohut maintains that the idealization of Freud protects the psychoanalyst against shame propensity, envy, jealousy, rage, and disturbances of self-esteem; therefore any attempted deidealization of Freud would create tremendous resistances against taking an objective, realistic attitude toward Freud.

Turning directly to Freud's self-analysis, Kohut describes Freud's relationship with Fleiss as a transference of creativity; Fleiss was used as a transference figure, but the transference was not dissolved by insight. According to Kohut, people during periods of intense creativity have a need for another person that they may idealize, similar to the idealizing transference that establishes itself during the psychoanalytic treatment of narcissistic personality disorders. This is not to suggest that creative people have personality disorders that drive them to seek archaic merger experiences, but rather that the psychic organization of certain creative people is characterized by a "fluidity" of basic narcissistic configurations.

Periods of narcissistic equilibrium with stable self-esteem and secure idealized internal values are accompanied by steady persevering work characterized by attention to details. This is followed by a pre-creative period of emptiness and restlessness, in which there is a decathexis of values and low self-esteem as well as either addictive or perverse yearnings and difficulty in working. Finally, there is a creative period in which "unattached narcissistic cathexes which had been withdrawn from the ideals and from the self are now employed in the service of the creative activity: original thought; intense, passionate work" (p. 816).

This has been described in the psychological literature, for example by Ellenberger (1970) as a creative illness, but Kohut's explanation is the first detailed metapsychological discussion based on the psychology of the self. The transferences established by creative minds during periods of intense creativity represent the striving of a self, which feels enfeebled during a period of creativity, to retain its cohesion by a mirror transference or by the need to obtain strength from an idealized object, resembling an idealizing selfobject transference, not primarily involving the revival of a figure from the oedipal past.

This is followed by an example of the aging artist who regresses to homosexuality as a delaying action during the disintegration of his artistic sublimation, described in Thomas Mann's famous story, *Death in Venice*. We have now come full circle, as demonstrated by Kohut's first paper, written in 1948 (reprinted in Kohut 1978), which deals with the same story.

Kohut concludes that the resolution of Freud's transference to Fliess did not take place by any form of interpretation, but because the idealizing transference of creativity which Freud had formed to Fliess became superfluous and naturally dropped away after Freud's first creative work was finished. Freud was able to dispense with the illusory sense of Fliess's greatness, in contradiction to resolution of a transference by insight, after he finished his creative task at that point. A careful study of the recently published *Complete Letters of Sigmund Freud to Wilhelm Fliess* (Masson 1985) strongly supports Kohut's conclusion.


KOHUT ON GROUP PSYCHOLOGY

The remainder of this long 1976 essay may be considered Kohut's addendum to Freud's (1921) *Group Psychology and the Analysis of the Ego*. The characteristics of an individual suitable for group idealization are an unshakeable self-confidence and a voicing of opinions with absolute certainty. Kohut describes the charismatic individual who identifies with his grandiose self and the messianic individual who identifies with his idealized parent imago and becomes the "natural" leader. Such people have no elasticity and come in all shades and degrees from the narcissistic personality to the psychotic.

Kohut draws a parallel between normal times and crisis times in the history of a group, with group crises producing a situation similar to the temporary need of the creative person, for example, the need for a charismatic individual like Churchill during the Battle of Britain. The discussion includes the childhood of these charismatic and messianic individuals with examples such as Schreber's father, Hitler, and perhaps Fliess who

> seem to combine an absolute certainty concerning the power of their selves and an absolute conviction concerning the validity of their ideals with an equally absolute lack of empathic understanding for large segments of feelings, needs, and rights of other human beings and for the values cherished by them. They understand the environment in which they live only as an extension of their own narcissistic universe. (p. 834)

The essay ends with the suggestion of a parallel between the nuclear individual self and the nuclear group self. Therefore, we may apply to group phenomena what we learn from a study of the individual self. In a footnote (p. 837), Kohut tells us that a person who does not achieve the pattern of the unconscious self — the central unconscious ambitions of the grandiose self and the central unconscious values of the internalized idealized parent imago — will feel an overriding sense of failure in his life regardless of the presence or absence of neurotic conflict, suffering, symptoms, or inhibitions. Kohut suggests that group phenomena can be studied in a similar fashion. By the time he wrote an essay in which he stated that "group processes are largely activated by narcissistic motives," Kohut had formulated an elaborate psychology of the self which had been criticized as betraying some of the basic discoveries and theories of Freud. His answer is: "I am certain that decisive progress in the area of depth psychology is tied to personal acts of courage by the investigator who not only suffers anxiety but tends to be maligned and ostracized" (p. 843).

# Chapter 10

## Kohut's Second Version of the Psychology of the Self

Quinn (1980) quotes Kohut: "I've led two totally different, perhaps unbridgeable lives." Kohut's mother was a practicing Roman Catholic. His father, though an agnostic, was of Jewish descent; therefore, under Nazi racial laws, Kohut was in danger. Although he was passionately involved with German and Austrian culture he had to leave Vienna a year after Freud; the departure of Freud from Vienna symbolized for him the loss of "everything that I had lived for." Kohut is quoted as stating that this disruption of his life alerted him to the problems of the fragmented self and how the self tries to effect a cure, but he has repeatedly reported (Goldberg 1980) that the drift of the psychology of the self from traditional Freudian psychoanalysis has been a slow process based on the gradual accretion of clinical material.

Breu (1979) reports that Kohut's father was in the Austrian army five of the first six years of Kohut's life; he is quoted as saying, "I was deprived of a young, vigorous father . . . he was replaced by an old man, a grandfather, and that was not the same. So my male teachers had a tremendous role in my formation" (p. 63). Such a person would insist that what really counts in the formation of the child's self is not what parents do but what they really are. So Kohut concludes

(Breu 1979), "We need maternal and paternal responsiveness to know we are in the world. We need it from our first breath to our last" (p. 63).

## The Bipolar Self

Kohut's books, *The Restoration of the Self* (1977) and *How Does Analysis Cure?* (1984) contain his final views or what is generally called "the psychology of the self in the broader sense." We have come a long way from the essay, "Forms and Transformations of Narcissism" in 1966, and we have left classical metapsychology altogether in now stressing the two "poles" of the supraordinate concept: bipolar self.

These two poles are *self-esteem*, derived from the grandiose self and its strivings for exhibitionistic ambitious acclaim and mirroring, and *guiding ideals* and the pursuit of them, derived from internalization of the idealized parent imago. In psychotherapy one pole may be strengthened to compensate for defects in the other, a process known as functional rehabilitation of the self. Defensive structures (such as common fantasies of sadistically enforced control and acclaim) may develop to mask defects, and more hopeful compensatory structures (such as the more constructive pursuits of goals and accomplishments) may make up for weakness at one pole by strengthening the other. Thus, curative process for Kohut is now thought of *either* as filling a defect in the self by transmuting internalizations in the transference, *or* as strengthening the compensatory structures by making them functionally reliable, realistic, and autonomous, which would not constitute a cure in classical psychoanalysis. So Slap and Levine (1978) state, "Although Kohut refers to it as psychoanalysis, his therapeutic method depends on suggestion and learning, but not insight, conflict resolution, or making the unconscious conscious" (p. 507).

Another clinical example of a defensive structure would be a pseudovitality, in which the patient attempts to counteract by frantic mental or physical activity an inner feeling of deadness, the depleted empty self, through self-stimulation. Elsewhere (Lichtenberg and Kaplan 1983, p. 138) Kohut mentions gross identifications or gross macrointernalizations as defensive structures.

Kohut, as we have seen, contrasts "Guilty Man" of Freud's psychoanalysis with "Tragic Man" of the narcissistic personality disorder. Tragic Man has failed to realize nuclear ambitions and ideals, and middle age becomes the crucial test; at this point, life for Tragic Man becomes meaningless. Kohut speaks of an action-promoting "tension arc" or "gradient" between the two poles of the self (in the narrow sense theory he leans to geometry, in the broader sense theory he leans to physics), in which there is an "intermediate area" consisting of the executive functions and skills needed to realize the patterns of both poles.

Therapy, by firming the sense of self, helps the patient to make the "right choices." These consist of harnessing the patient's talents in the service of realistic long-term goals and relinquishing fantasies of sadistically enforced acclaim. These choices obviously must be in harmony with the person's true abilities, opportunities, and goals. They have occurred when the patient begins to experience a sense of joy in life based on meaningful creative effort, no matter how small that effort may be.

Thus we have a nuclear self which emerges in the second year of life and consists of pole one, self-esteem (ambition, exhibitionism, stemming from the grandiose self), connected by an intermediate area of executive functions and skills — a tension arc or gradient which forms an action-promoting condition — with pole two, guiding ideals (pursuit of these values after fusion with the idealized parent imago and containing a voyeuristic aspect). Eroticized exhibitionism sometimes represents a breakdown of the ambitions pole and eroticized voyeurism of the ideals pole.

A defect in the psychological structure of the self can manifest itself by certain reparative activities. These can be either defensive structures, which mask the defect (pseudovitality, pseudodrama, and sadistic fantasies of power to counteract a sense of deadness), or compensatory structures, which make up for weakness at one pole of the self by strengthening the other pole.

Treatment then can either fill the defect through the selfobject transferences and transmuting internalizations, offering the patient a third chance in life, or provide what Kohut calls "functional rehabilitation," a strengthening of compensatory structures in order to make them functionally reliable and autonomous. The successful utilization of skills and talents in the service of well-established ambitions and ideals creates a sense of contentment: the self is experienced as whole and complete. In contrast, an inability to use one's skills and talents in the service of ambitions and ideals results in the opposite phenomenon and the self is experienced as empty and worthless.

The selfobject transferences are seen as a form of belated maturation and development, with therapeutic stress on the completion through transmuting internalizations of the structure of the self, or on a strengthening of compensatory structures. The selfobject environment becomes critical in structure building for the self. Destructive aggression or narcissistic rage are not drives but consequences of self-pathology. Assertiveness is a healthy precursor of aggression and part of the healthy bipolar self, so that in one pole there is assertiveness and ambition, and in the other, inner values and goals with a capacity to regulate inner tensions.

As the child grows, subsequent mirroring or turning to the idealized parent imago may offer the strengthening of secondary or compensatory structures in the self, whereas excellent early mirroring and satisfactory idealization lead to a healthy primary structure of the nuclear self. Joyful creative activity is deeply rooted in the structure of the nuclear self, which in turn is based on wholesome empathic maternal responses to the child's needs. This includes responding to the child's mounting anxiety and rage by limiting them to a signal, so that the child experiences the mother's adequate and appropriate soothing before there is a disintegration of the primitive sense of self.

## The Status of "Drives" in Self Psychology

In this new theory narcissism is usually not thought of as a defense against the Oedipus complex. Indeed, there is a brief oedipal phase at the termination of treatment accompanied by a warm glow of joy and which arises *de novo* due to functional improvement of the self; it is not a remobilized Oedipus complex left over from infancy. For Kohut, the oedipal phase helps to firm the self and represents a positive aspect, a phase-appropriate opportunity, and requires an empathic selfobject environment. In the normal situation it does not lead to an Oedipus complex. In this theory, only if there is an enfeebled or fragmented self is there a pathological fixation on oedipal strivings so that, in the transference neuroses, an abnormal Oedipus complex is revived. The ubiquitous Oedipus complex conceived by Freud is not universally present. For Kohut interpretation of material in disorders of the self primarily as oedipal would be experienced as unempathic and represents an intolerance of the patient's forward movement when the patient attempts self-assertion.

In contrast to the traditional idea of psychoanalytic cure which represents conflict solution through the cognitive expansion of the conscious mind, Kohut's view emphasizes the attainment of cohesiveness of the self and restitution of the self through empathic closeness of responsive selfobjects. The capacity for achievement and enjoyment of life becomes important evidence that such a cure has taken place. In his last book Kohut (1984) emphasizes also the capacity to develop for one's self an empathic selfobject matrix to sustain one throughout life. Self-esteem becomes a function of a cohesive and well-functioning self with emphasis on self-soothing capacities and a built-in capacity for internal tension regulation that enables self-esteem to remain relatively stable.

A subtle shift in the meaning of transmuting internalization took place between 1971 and 1977. In 1971, the microstructures were thought to have been built into the fabric of the ego but now transmuting internalization is thought of as developing structure and functions within the bipolar self.

Sexual "drives" are considered to be disintegration products which may secondarily be employed to soothe or stimulate a narcissistically injured or damaged self. Gross maternal failures in empathy are seen as leading to direct damage in the structure of the self, in contrast to the complex formulations by object-relations theorists. This led to the severe criticism that self psychology, rather than moving toward more intense depth psychology, was moving toward the shallows of existentialism which, like the psychology of the self, tends to abrogate the importance of unconscious drives and conflicts. Remember that "acceptance of the idea of drives which set the activity of the psychic apparatus in motion . . . has become the litmus test for the 'orthodox' psychoanalyst" (Greenberg and Mitchell 1983, p. 304).

The psychology of the self in the broader sense represents a highly controversial theoretical system quite different than classical psychoanalysis. The student will have to do a great deal of self-scrutiny and return to patients in order to decide whether this represents a useful and valid contribution. It represents an important psychological and philosophical system with ramifications for philosophy and politics as well as for the practice of psychoanalysis and intensive psychotherapy.

## The Psychology of the Self in the Broader Sense

The psychotherapist working with narcissistic and borderline disorders must have a thorough grasp of the process of working through, in which minor disappointments in the narcissistic transferences, followed by characteristic reactions in the patient, must be explained calmly to the patient. Without this conceptual understanding, the temptation occurs to launch all kinds of extratherapeutic activities toward the patient. Some of these temptations are based on countertransference hostility, others on reaction formations to this hostility. The principle, however, remains that the therapist's temptation to step outside the role of the calm, benign craftsman is based on a misunderstanding of what is happening in the therapy and what is motivated by countertransference. There is no end to the rationalizations which the unanalyzed psychotherapist may present to justify the exploitation of and retaliation toward the patient.

In order to protect themselves against rejection and further narcissistic wounding, patients with an insufficient ego ideal tend to withdraw into grandiosity, which bothers and irritates people and produces further rejection leading to further withdrawal. In addition, such patients are much harsher on themselves because they can fall back only on the harsh critical superego, for internalization of the love of the idealized parent imago has not occurred.

Typically, narcissistic peace and clinical improvement can be established with concomitant better functioning when the idealizing transference occurs, but such transferences may also lead to a fear of loss of ego boundaries and fusion if the wish to merge with the idealized parent imago is quite strong. A negative therapeutic reaction results. The patient must resist the threatened merging for fear of becoming more like the therapist than is tolerable for maintaining ego boundaries.

A gifted individual can actually realize some of the boundless expectations of the grandiose self but whatever successes might be achieved are never enough, and the patient is plagued by an endless demand for superb performance. For example, we see the middle-age depression so common in successful people who have been on a treadmill and achieved money and power, yet whose success brings no relief. Such patients always need continuing acclaim and more success; they have the talent to realize many of their wishes but they never get satisfaction since they are driven by a split-off grandiose self with its bizarre demands. "Lying" and name-dropping in such patients can be understood as an attempt to live up to the expectations of the grandiose self and thus must be removed from the therapist's tacit moral condemnation. As Basch (Stepanksy and Goldberg 1984) explains, "An intellectual, superficial accommodation to the reality of his relative lack of power and significance, and his less than central position is made by the child while, as far as the self is concerned, the earlier sense of narcissistic urgency holds sway" (p. 28). The reader should turn back here to Reich's (1960) case described in Chapter 3 and compare her traditional psychoanalytic explanation of the pathology with this approach. Then, for a detailed self-psychological explanation of an analagous case of a writer, "Mr. M.," see Kohut (1977).

### DEVELOPMENT OF THE BIPOLAR SELF

For narcissistic patients therefore, the handling of their characteristic transferences becomes the essence of the treatment. These narcissistic "transferences" do not involve the investment of the therapist with object libido, as in the oedipal neuroses, although they do involve a crossing of the repression barrier of the mobilized grandiose self and idealized parent imago. It is therefore vital to have a clear and precise understanding of Kohut's final notion of the development and vicissitudes of these structures.

For children of 8 months to 3 years of age, Kohut postulates a normal, intermediate phase of powerful narcissistic cathexis of "the grandiose self" (a grandiose exhibitionistic image of the self) and the idealized parent imago (the image of an omnipotent selfobject with whom fusion is desired). These psychic formations are gradually internalized and integrated within the psychic structure. The grandiosity, as a result of appropriate minor disappointments, is consolidated at around 2 to 4 years of age (Kohut 1977, p. 178); it forms the nuclear ambitions pole of the self, driving the individual forward. It derives most from the relationship with the mother, and in the narrow theory is thought of as forming a part of the ego. In the broader theory, the "self" and ego are separated and thus the internalized grandiose self is thought to form the nuclear ambitions pole of the self.

At 4 to 6 years of age (Kohut 1977, p. 178) at the height of the oedipal phase, the idealized parent imago, which derives from both parents, is also internalized and integrated. In the narrow theory it was thought of as an infusion of both the superego and the ego with the love and admiration originally aimed at the idealized parent imago, which then serves as a vital internal source of self-esteem and the basis of the ego-ideal aspect of the superego. This ego-ideal forms a system toward which the person aspires; thus the individual is driven from below by nuclear ambitions, and pulled from above by the ego-ideal. In the psychology of the self in the broader sense, the consolidation of the idealized parent imago forms the other pole of the self, the nuclear ideals pole. This notion of the bipolar self is the crucial concept of the psychology of the self.

Later, Kohut (1984) adds a third "separate line of selfobject development" (p. 198) involving important twinship (alter-ego) experiences from about 4 to 10 years of age (known in drive-psychology as early latency [p. 194]), for example, the little girl kneading dough in the kitchen next to grandmother or the little boy "shaving" or "working" next to daddy with daddy's tools. This selfobject need corresponds to and confirms the intermediate area of skills and talents which, with the ambitions and ideals poles, forms the nuclear self.

When these three major consolidations have to some extent occurred, a vigorous cohesive sense of self is formed, and the person is ready to continue by resolving the oedipal phase. In drive-psychology terms, the superego can form, and moral anxiety (from within) replaces castration anxiety. The repression barrier is established and eventually consolidated in latency and adolescence, and anxiety becomes confined to function as signal anxiety (essentially Kernberg's "fifth stage"). But for Kohut, even after adolescence still further transformations of narcissism occur, resulting eventually in mature wisdom, a sense of humor, an acceptance of the transience of life, empathy, and creativity. These transformations involve an increased firming of the sense of self, making mature love possible.

In the narrow sense theory, the idealized parent imago, when internalized, performs in the pre-oedipal ego and superego a drive-curbing function. In the oedipal superego it forms an idealized superego, which now leads the person. The infantile grandiose self forms the nuclear ambitions, and crude infantile exhibitionism is channeled and transformed into socially meaningful activities and accomplishments. Thus, narcissism, when properly transformed, is both normal and absolutely vital to mature human personality functioning; it is no longer a pejorative term.

In the "psychology of the self in the broader sense," these internalizations as explained form into a cohesive bipolar self, and a complementary role in development beyond that described by Freud is given to the oedipal phase. Here the response of the parents to the child's libidinal and aggressive and exhibitionistic strivings — their pride and mirroring confirmation of its development — permits these internalizations to occur and integrate smoothly. In Freud's theory, for example, it is the boy's fear of castration by the father that causes him to identify with the aggressor and internalize the values of the father. For Kohut, it is *also* the father's pride in the boy's emerging assertiveness as it shows itself in the boy's oedipal strivings and imitative efforts, that softens the boy's disappointment about not possessing the mother and enables a firm internalization of the idealized parent imago as a nuclear pole of the self.

If, for example, the father or mother withdraw from the child as a response to their horror of the child's oedipal strivings, this internalization cannot occur, and the child remains fixed in development on finding some individual to which the child attaches the idealized parent imago. The child's internal self-esteem in this case remains very low, and its self-esteem and sense of self require continual and unending bolstering from the external object which has been invested with the idealized parent imago. When such bolstering is not forthcoming, profound disappointment, narcissistic rage, and even a sense of impending fragmentation of the self occur. Thus we have what self psychologists call a complementary theory, in which new explanatory concepts and the structural theory of Freud are employed in order to make sense of the common but puzzling aspects of the narcissistic personality.

The sense of continuity of the self emanates not only from the contents of the constituents of the nuclear self and from the activities they establish, but from the relationship of these constituents. This relationship provides "an action-promoting condition" or "tension gradient" between the two poles of the self, a person's ambitions and ideals, "even in the absence of any specific activity" (Kohut 1977, p. 180). Kohut emphasizes ceaselessly "the pervasive influence of the personalities of the parents and of the atmosphere in which the child grew up" to "account for the specific characteristics of the nuclear self and for its firmness, weakness, or vulnerability" (Kohut 1977, pp. 186–187). The basic difference between "the psychology of the self in the narrow sense of the term" and "the psychology of the self in the broader sense of the term" is that in the former the self is a content of the mental apparatus, whereas in the latter, the self occupies "a central position" (Kohut 1977, p. 207).

## THE BIPOLAR SELF IN PSYCHOPATHOLOGY AND MENTAL HEALTH

Kohut stresses two key consequences of the lack of integration of the grandiose self and idealized parent imago. First, adult functioning and personality are impoverished because the self is deprived of energy that is still invested in archaic structures. Second, adult activity is hampered by the breakthrough and intrusion of archaic structures with their archaic claims. These nonintegrated structures are either repressed (Kohut's "horizontal split") or disavowed (Kohut's "vertical split"), and they quickly show themselves in the psychotherapy situation of both narcissistic and borderline patients.

Patients want us to respond as if we belong one hundred percent to them; a benign view of this desire, rather than an angry retort or harsh criticism, detoxifies patients' attitudes toward themselves and prevents a withdrawal into arrogant grandiosity. Outside success for such patients gives only transient good feelings but does not add to the idealization of the superego, for these patients are arrested developmentally on finding an idealized parent imago outside of themselves—a stage where they still need continuing outside sources of approval. Narcissistic injury produces great rage, which also appears if the transference selfobject does not live up to the idealization. Thus narcissistic and borderline patients present a psychic apparatus ready to ignite at any time, and with their poor ego ideal they cannot neutralize the explosions and disintegrations when they occur.

Kernberg (1976) warns that in working with borderline patients "the therapist tends to experience, rather soon in the treatment, intensive emotional reactions having more to do with the patient's premature, intense and chaotic transference and with the therapist's capacity to withstand psychological stress and anxiety, than with any specific problem of the therapist's past" (p. 179). In fact, intense and premature emotional reactions on the part of the therapist indicate for Kernberg the presence of severe regression in the patient.

The repressed or split-off grandiose self with its bizarre demands may drive the patient relentlessly and, as previously mentioned, even force him into "lying," bragging, and name-dropping in order to live up to expectations of the grandiose self. Certain types of dangerous acting-out may also occur as part of the effort to feel alive and to establish a conviction of omnipotence and grandiosity; one female patient of mine often rides a motorcycle at high speed down the highway when visibility has been obscured by fog. In working with such patients the therapist must deal with responses to separation and disappointment and stay near current experiences and strivings for omnipotence and grandiosity. Benign acceptance, conceptual explanation, and education of the patient have a major role in the psychotherapy of narcissistic and borderline patients.

The vicissitudes of the transferences and the appearance of the rage provide the opportunity for the calm, nonanxious therapist, working as a careful craftsman, to help the patient understand and transform the archaic narcissism so that the aggression can be employed for realistic ambitions, goals, and ideals. The signs of successful resumption of the developmental process and appropriate transformations of narcissism can be found in two major areas of the patient's life. First, an increase and expansion of object love will take place, due primarily to an increased firming of the sense of self. Patients become more secure in their own identity and acceptability; they become more able to offer love. The second area is in greater drive control and drive channeling and a better idealized superego, as well as more realistic ambitions and the change of crude infantile exhibitionism into socially meaningful activities. We hope to end up with a sense of empathy, creativity, humor, and perhaps ultimately, wisdom.

From the point of view of the "psychology of the self in the broader sense," the self is critical to achieving joy in life and making the right choices that are in harmony with our abilities, opportunities, and goals. We establish an empathic matrix with others if we have a cohesive self. But a functioning self may be established by achieving success in the development of compensatory structures, such as compensating for weakness in "the area of exhibitionism and ambitions by the self-esteem provided by the pursuit of ideals" (Kohut 1977, p. 1). A functioning self is defined as "a psychological sector in which ambitions, skills, and ideals form an unbroken continuum that permits joyful creative activity" (p. 63). Activity which maintains self-esteem may even take on the character of an "addiction" since it is so powerful and rewarding in the joy it brings.

"Addiction" — used here by Kohut "half-jokingly and half-seri-ously" (Goldberg 1980, p. 497) — refers to the "reverberating bene-ficial cycle" (Kohut 1977, p. 135) which becomes established:

> The strengthened self becomes the organizing center of the skills and talents of the personality and thus improves the exercise of these func-tions; the successful exercise of skills and talents, moreover, in turn in-creases the cohesion, and thus the vigor, of the self. (1977, p. 135)

But we are warned (Kohut 1984, p. 161) that under such "addiction" to one's form of mental health lies a fear of the return of former in-securities and imbalances if this activity is given up or relaxed.

It is important to keep in mind that Kohut (pp. 179–180) sug-gests the sense of self-continuity emanates from the content of the constituents of the nuclear self, the activities established "as a result of their pressure and guidance," and the relationship among the con-stituents of the self, which produce an action-promoting condition. Continuous striving, or activities based on these creative tensions, are central in maintaining a sense of continuity and joyful living, in spite of the vicissitudes of life. As Freud (Schur 1972) wrote on his eightieth birthday, "Life at my age is not easy, but spring is beautiful and so is love" (p. 480).

## Problems in Definition of the Bipolar Self

Kohut stresses repeatedly the physicianly vocation of the psycho-therapist or analyst, not the model of the surgeon or the computer. This is because traditional neurotics were overstimulated as children, but patients with self-pathology need less distance, and, if this is not provided, one sees the appearance of narcissistic rage. This rage, says Kohut, is an empathy problem and not, as the Kleinians say, due to inborn infantile aggression and subsequent fear and guilt. When analysts focus on conflicts regarding drives, they tend to become either educational (such as by urging self-control) or unnecessarily pessimistic about the continuing narcissistic rage.

A continuing problem is Kohut's (1977) admission:

> We cannot, by introspection and empathy, penetrate to the self per se; only its introspectively or empathically perceived psychological mani-

festations are open to us. Demands for an exact definition of the nature of the self disregard the fact that "the self" is not a concept of an abstract science, but a generalization derived from empirical data. (p. 311)

Yet at times the self is used existentially, as if it were a choosing agent, which Kohut and his followers excuse as a method of shorthand or figure of speech (Kohut and Wolf 1978, pp. 415–416). This ambiguity in the use of the concept of the self appears in the developing thought of both Kant and Kohut (Chessick 1980a).

According to Kant (1781), we experience the mind through our "inner sense" or "empirical apperception," our consciousness of the flux of inner appearances of the state of the self. There is no permanent or abiding "self" in this, as both Hume and Kant agree. Thus the phenomenal self, the self studied in psychology, is known to us empirically as a succession of mental states in time, for time is the *a priori* form of our inner sense, says Kant (1781) in the *Critique of Pure Reason*.

This is distinguished from the noumenal or transcendental self, the self which knows, the self enduring and as it "really" is. Thus, for Kant, we can think about reality "out there" and about the "real" knowing self, but we cannot ever directly know either of them or make direct statements to describe them.

Both Kant and Freud assume that there is a reality "outside" of or "behind" the world of appearance and that there is a part of the mind behind the phenomenal self. For Freud, a concept analogous to Kant's noumenal self, which cannot be directly known but yet profoundly influences our experienced sense of self, was, in the topographic theory, the system unconscious. In the structural theory it becomes the id (and portions of the ego and superego). Freud (1940a) writes, "The core of our being, then, is formed by the obscure *id*, which has no direct communication with the external world and is accessible even to our own knowledge only through the medium of another agency" (p. 197).

The crucial argument of Kant's fundamental "transcendental deduction of the pure concepts of the understanding" rests on the premise of the transcendental unity of self-consciousness, the sense of "I am I," the cohesive sense of a single continuous self. This continuing core of self-consciousness is clearly required to distinguish one's self-boundaries and self-experiences from experiences coming from the external world. Kant points out that Hume erred fundamentally in overlooking the inextricable interdependence of self-awareness and awareness of perceptual objects. Conversely, Kant argues that, if the subjective unity of the consciousness begins to shatter for various reasons, the individual becomes confused about the distinction between one's self and self-experiences and experiences of the external world. Thus, even for Kant, fragmentation of the sense of self implies a diffusion of ego boundaries and a loss of reality testing.

When Kant is most consistent in his doctrine of noumenal self and phenomenal self, he would define these as follows: the phenomenal self consists solely of the empirically experienced self-states of classical psychology as revealed by introspective investigation of inner states or experiences; the noumenal self is a nonempirical "limiting concept" that reason leads us to from a study of our phenomenal self. The noumenal self, as a limiting concept, is experience-near, in the sense that it is directly suggested to reason by our experience; it is a regulative concept in Kant's terms, useful to reason in describing and classifying our phenomenal self experiences. Because it is only such a purely rational concept, nothing more can be said about it (Ewing 1967). When Kant uses the concept of noumenal self this way, he speaks of it as the noumenal self in the negative sense. This is the only nonempirical (Kant would call it transcendental) notion of self that is justifiably arrived at by the action of reason on our empirical data in its efforts to develop unifying and explanatory concepts.

In the rest of Kant's philosophy, he ignores his own arguments and uses the concept of noumenal self in quite a different sense. This unresolved contradiction in Kant's philosophy is lucidly discussed by Scruton (1982, Chapter 5). In his moral philosophy, noumenal self is employed as an independent agent, and a good deal is postulated about it. This shift is usually described as a movement on Kant's part — an incautious movement — from the noumenal self in the negative sense to the noumenal self in the positive sense. It is a shift from a notion of noumenal self suggested to reason from immediate empirical experience to a far more complex and experience-distant concept of noumenal self, a shift not justifiable by Kant's own philosophy in the *Critique of Pure Reason*.

This noumenal self to which Kant and others refer is used in a positive sense to justify matters of faith and approaches what Kohut (1978, pp. 659–660) refers to as an axiomatic self. When we use the notion of self in this manner, we have thus moved from the realm of science. This is the meaning of Kohut's (1977, p. 311) statement that the self "in its essence" cannot be defined; such a definition would postulate an "axiomatic" self, which Kohut rightly considers to be unscientific and abrogates the importance of the unconscious (see Ornstein's discussion in Kohut [1978], pp. 95–96).

For Kant, as Smith (1962) points out, the self is the sole source of all unity. But Broad (1978) concludes that "Kant's account of the nature of the human self and of its knowledge of itself is extremely complicated, and it is doubtful whether a single consistent doctrine can be extracted from his various utterances" (p. 234).

Kohut (1978) explains that the fundamental advance of psychoanalytic fact-finding is to take the further step into a new methodology by which the therapist vicariously introspects with the patient and experiences the inner self and the world around the patient in a manner congruent to that of the patient. This yields important data about the state of the patient at any given time which cannot be obtained by any other approach. Kohut's early notion of the sense of self is not "axiomatic" but comes from empathic identification with the patient's sense of self at any given time. It is in truly understanding by vicarious introspection how the patient's sense of self coheres and fragments that we gain an explanation of why and how the patient perceives the inner and outer world and behaves accordingly.

This is more experience-near than Freud's metapsychology, because additional apparatuses or structures are not postulated as homunculi within the head of the individual determining the outcome of behavior. For Kohut the patient's perception and behavior are directly attributable to the patient's sense of self at any given time. His approach avoids what Freud (1937, p. 225) called "the Witch Metapsychology" to a considerable extent, but understanding then depends fundamentally on the capacity of the therapist to empathize with the patient's inner state.

Yet Kohut at times, like Kant, slips into the concept of self in the positive sense, as when he speaks of it as empty and depleted or as "yearning" for mirroring or merger. The self in these situations is used as an "as if" concept and the anthropomorphic language has been criticized. In *The Analysis of the Self* Kohut (1971, p. 130) mentions that the cohesive experience of the self in time is the same as the experience of the self as a continuum, which seems to be the same as Kant's notion of inner states. Yet, in the same paragraph Kohut also mentions the "breadth and depth" of cohesiveness of the self, but without definition.

## Fragmentation and Cohesion of the Self

The concept of the fragmentation of the self is never made satisfactorily clear (Schwartz 1978). It seems to be equated with psychotic-like phenomena, at which time reality contact even with the therapist is in danger of being lost. It is characterized as a regressive phenomenon, predominantly autoerotic, a state of fragmented self-nuclei, in contrast to the state of the cohesive self which Kohut (1971) describes as "the growth of the self experience as a physical and mental unit which has cohesiveness in space and continuity in time" (p. 118). Here Kohut seems to disagree with Kant's contention that time is the sole form of our inner sense. Kohut speaks also of space, having in mind Jacobson's (1964) discussion of the "development of object and self constancy" (p. 55).

Kohut's (1971) original notion of the cohesiveness of the self has to do with a "firm cathexis with narcissistic libido" (p. 119), leading to a subjective feeling of well being and an improvement of the functioning of the ego. In later writings this metapsychological explanation is omitted; signs of fragmentation of the self have to do with a subjective feeling of self-state anxiety and objective and subjective signs of deteriorating ego function. As Kohut (1971) explains, this is accompanied by frantic activities of various kinds in the work and sexual areas, especially in an effort to "counteract the subjectively painful feeling of self fragmentation by a variety of forced actions, ranging from physical stimulation and athletic activities to excessive work in . . . profession and business" (p. 119). Thus fragmentation of the self that Kohut in his early work calls "the dissolution of the narcissistic unity of the self" (pp. 120–121) is manifested by certain characteristic subjective sensations such as hypochondria and frantic activities in order to stem the tide of regression.

Kohut (1971) sees a regression from the cohesiveness of the self to its fragmentation as parallel to a regression "from narcissism to autoerotism" (p. 253). A clinical description of this is based on the self as "an organizing center of the ego's activities" (pp. 296–298). When the self fragments, the personality which has not participated in the regression attempts to deal with the central fragmentation, but "the experience of the fragmented body-mind-self and self-object cannot be psychologically elaborated" (p. 30).

In *The Restoration of the Self* (1977) the self as a supraordinate concept in its bipolar nature becomes our clinical focus primarily when self-cohesion is not firm. Metapsychological energic concepts are omitted, and the self is now seen as occupying "the central position" within the personality. Thus, fragmentation of the self is defined by the experiences which it produces. In this later book the self is finally a "supraordinated configuration whose significance transcends that of the sum of its parts" (p. 97).

So Kohut first presents the self in the negative sense as an experience-near abstraction from psychoanalytic experience. As his work evolves, he focuses more and more on the self, finally placing the self in a central and transcendent position. This emphasis on the self resembles Kant's noumenal self used in the positive sense to explain free will — a center of our being from which all initiative springs and where all experiences end — which Kohut (1978, pp. 659–660) rejects.

## Is the Bipolar Self Complementary to Freud's Metapsychology?

When Kohut moves to the supraordinate bipolar self and its constituents, he introduces a new concept. The self is no longer a depth-psychological concept that can be metapsychologically defined using classical terminology, and the self is no longer thought of as either within the mental apparatus or even as a fourth "agency" of the mind. "The area of the self and its vicissitudes," as Kohut (1978, p. 753) calls it, is essentially a separate science from Freud's psychoanalysis, just as the study of the phenomenal world in the *Critique of Pure Reason* is a separate discipline from the study of the noumenal world in the *Critique of Practical Reason*. Kohut (1978) himself labels this "the science of the self" (p. 752n), and the implication is inevitable that he has attempted to found a new science.

Freud would not have accepted Kohut's theory of the psychology of the self in the broader sense as "complementary" but rather as a different although related theory which uses an alternative explanation of the treatment procedure from that of Freud's metapsychology in psychoanalysis. The new explanation is based by Kohut (1977) on the Zeigarnik effect (1927) (discussed below in Chapter 11), for which Kohut postulates some kind of inner motivation of undeveloped structures to resume their development when given the opportunity; the energy behind this motivation has nothing to do with Freud's instinctual drives, and the origin of it is not explained. I assume it is a sort of biological growth force. The basis of therapy in the psychology of the self postulates that proper development of "selfobject transferences," or transferencelike structures in the treatment, make it possible for this force to take over and thus for development of the self to resume via transmuting internalization; this is fundamentally different from the resolution of conflicts via interpretation of a transference neurosis.

This represents a different scientific paradigm. It is better for the progress of human knowledge to face this situation directly; otherwise, students of the subject will become hopelessly confused in attempting to somehow reconcile the early and the late Kohut, or to reconcile Freud's psychoanalysis and the "psychology of the self in the broader sense." Like Kant's noumenal self used in the positive sense, Kohut's self in the broader sense becomes crucial to joy in life and the making of right choices; there is no room for such an independent or supraordinate postulated entity in the *Critique of Pure Reason* or in the "psychology of the self in the narrow sense." As Kohut (1978) himself recognizes, this supraordinate self is beyond the laws of psychic determinism and outside the limits of traditional psychoanalysis. Just as Kant's ethical philosophy is developed for the moral use of placing faith on a firm foundation, so Kohut's "psychology of the self in the broader sense" addresses itself to the moral purpose of alleviating the tragedy of modern humans suffocating in an increasingly inhuman environment they themselves continue to create.

## COMPARISON OF DRIVE PSYCHOLOGY
## AND SELF PSYCHOLOGY

Many of these concepts are discussed at great length by a variety of authors in the two published proceedings of conferences on the psychology of the self (Goldberg 1980, Lichtenberg and Kaplan 1983). In psychoanalysis the status accorded to new ideas is a very personal decision reached after much study and often with much discomfort, writes Goldberg (1980) in his introduction to *Advances in Self Psychology*. Kohut himself repeatedly asks us for prolonged immersion in the psychology of the self and for much patience in making up our minds.

The basic objection of self psychologists to the traditional ego psychology school is in its Freudian notion that development proceeds to "independence." Kohut sees a fundamental value difference here; he insisted more and more as he reached the end of his life that the presence of an empathic selfobject matrix is a crucial requirement throughout life for a cohesive sense of self; the self always requires a milieu of empathically responding selfobjects in order to function effectively. The unrolling of its nuclear aims is critical and the attainment of "independence" from selfobjects at any point of life represents serious pathology — often paranoia or "Hitlerian pseudo-productivity."

We have here a collision of the views of Kohut and Kernberg. Kernberg stresses the primacy of hostility and the Kleinian defenses and values the move from merger to autonomy via the analysis of the Oedipus complex. Kohut is interested in the sequence of self–selfobject relations occurring throughout life and considers this interest to be based on a different moral system. Whenever a sustaining selfobject matrix is absent, creative-productive activities cease, ego functions deteriorate, and fragmentation threatens. How many cases of so-called pseudodementia in lonely elderly people could be explained in this fashion?

This implies a new definition of mental health. At least one sector must be established in which ambitions, skills, talents, and idealized goals form an unbroken continuum. Since the content of these differs from person to person, health is different for each different individual and the functional preponderance of ambitions, skills and talents, and idealized goals, differs with respect to the choice of the key constituents and the degree of dominance of each constituent, leading to behavioral differences that determine mental health for each individual.

For Kohut, a mentally healthy person lives out the design of the nuclear self. This leads to socially beneficial results and the continual creation of an empathic selfobject matrix; health is not merely adaptation. A person must mobilize adequate individual skills and talents in order to realize nuclear goals and must also find after protracted search a matrix of freely chosen empathic selfobjects.

This is greatly emphasized by Kohut in contrast to Freud's independent "love and work" or Hartmann's "adaptation" and is elaborated in Kohut's (1984) final book, *How Does Analysis Cure?* A section of this book is devoted to replies to numerous criticisms of the *Restoration of the Self*. Kohut suggests (pp. 61–63) that self psychology has been accepted by those who are more directly in touch with modern man's primary need of an empathic selfobject matrix. He feels that a wall of secondary, prideful disavowal protects those who reject self psychology from the narcissistic blow that a self cannot exist successfully outside of such a matrix.

He moves away from traditional psychoanalytic "conflict" explanations of all the clinical phenomena of psychiatry and diminishes the central and traditional importance of interpretation alone (the "pure gold" of psychoanalysis) as a curative factor in psychoanalysis. I will discuss this in detail in the next chapter. Kohut (1984, p. 78, p. 153) anticipates that he will be accused of advocating a form of Alexander's "corrective emotional experience" because he presses the crucial role of empathy or vicarious introspection again and again. The traditional notions of defense and resistance are also reinterpreted by Kohut in these terms. The therapist experiences through vicarious introspection or empathy that which the patient is experiencing rather than empirically experiencing the patient's feelings through observing the workings of a "mental apparatus."

Kohut's (1982) posthumous paper, "Introspection, Empathy, and the Semi-Circle of Mental Health," reviews his assertions about empathy and again emphasizes Kohut's proposal for a whole new value system upon which to base the understanding of the individual. By contrasting the parricide of Oedipus with the story he says is told by Homer* of how Odysseus protected his infant son, Kohut attempts to demonstrate that it is the primacy of parental support for the succeeding generation which is normal. Intergenerational strife and mutual wishes to kill and destroy are abnormal. He writes, "It is only when the self of the parent is not a normal, healthy self, cohesive, vigorous and harmonious, that it will react with competitiveness and seductiveness rather than with pride and affection when the child, at the age of 5, is making an exhilarating move toward a heretofore not achieved degree of assertiveness, generosity, and affection" (p. 404). Only in response to such a flawed parental self that cannot resonate with the child's experience does the self of the child disintegrate, and do the by-products of hostility and lust constituting the Oedipus complex make their appearance. This represents a basic

---

*This story is not found in Homer but is from *Fabulae* (Graves 1955), a collection of mythological legends from the works of Greek tragedians since lost. *Fabulae*, usually wrongly attributed to the Latin scholar Hyginus, was produced by an unknown author in the second century A.D.

challenge to Freud's emphasis on the Oedipus complex as the normal central source of conflict in every child's development and at the core of all psychoneuroses.

Kohut differentiates between an oedipal *stage*, referring to the normal state of experiences at that age, and the Oedipus *complex*, referring to the pathological distortion of the normal stage (Lichtenberg and Kaplan 1983, p. 211). In a much quoted passage Kohut continues:

> I first emphasize again that self psychology does not consider drives or conflicts as pathological. Nor does it consider even intense experiences of anxiety or guilt as pathological or pathogenic per se. Three cheers for drives! Three cheers for conflicts! They are the stuff of life, part and parcel of the experiential quintessence of the healthy self. (p. 388)

Kohut protests (p. 397) that he is still a drive psychologist in the sense that self psychology is only offering a complementarity of perspective but not attempting to replace drive psychology. However Greenberg and Mitchell (1983) claim that "Kohut uses complementarity to obscure the necessity for choice" (p. 363). Kohut (Lichtenberg and Kaplan 1983) continues:

> We must modify our perspective on the role of drive-related conflicts in such disorders to accommodate the realization that underlying self-object failures lead to the disintegration of the oedipal-stage self and thereby account for the expression of sexuality and aggression that typifies the Oedipus complex. (p. 399)

He claims only that there are no built-in primary conflicts in the psyche from birth, but he concedes that traumatic disruptions lead to defects or deficits in structure building, which, in turn, lead to secondary conflicts that can be studied by the usual methods of psychoanalysis as a drive psychology, provided one wishes to use that vantage point at that time. Kohut insists (Goldberg 1980) that "the reasons for my assertion that drives, psychologically conceived, occur secondary to the break-up of the self are empirical. . . . It fits the data of observation while the theory of drive primacy does not" (p. 489). Kohut (Goldberg 1980) concludes that:

An outlook that puts the drives in the center of the personality will use a model in which the quality of drive processing becomes the yardstick with which to measure therapeutic success; an outlook that puts the self in the center of the personality will use a model in which the degree of fulfillment of the basic program of the self (the nuclear self) becomes this yardstick. (p. 509)

# Section III

## CLINICAL APPLICATIONS

# Chapter 11

## Kohut's Special Clinical Observations and Classifications

### Special Clinical Phenomena

Let us first turn to certain specific special clinical phenomena identified by Kohut.

TRAUMATIC STATES

The new clinical concept of *traumatic states* (Kohut 1971, pp. 229–238) is explained as an intrapsychic flooding with narcissistic libido and sometimes oral sadistic rage due to the poorly internalized regulatory functions of the ego. Two clinical types are described. The first occurs as a nonspecific reaction to any variety of frustrations and narcissistic wounds, for example, a *faux pas* made at a party; the second paradoxically as a result of a correct interpretation which releases deep overwhelming yearnings for soothing and idealization.

Clinically, the patients feel uncomfortable, overburdened, and overtaxed. They may show a sexualization of everything, expressed by compulsive masturbation, sadistic controlling or masochistic or perverse fantasies to combat the sense of inner deadness, or by exhibitionistic and voyeuristic behavior. The patient may appear disheveled and even temporarily "insane," in the manner of Hamlet. Further reactions are great irritability to sensory stimuli, such as noises, lights, children's hi-fi or TV sets; sarcasm and punning, followed by the tendency to get into dangerous activity or arguments in traffic, or to race people to stop lights; and a general rage and lashing out at the whole world that is experienced as strange, unsupportive, unempathic, and persecuting (for example Rockefeller's giving his widely publicized finger sign after he did not receive the 1976 Republican nomination for President).

Every request or demand made on the patient at this point is experienced as unwelcome and produces rage. The patient restores equilibrium by reassuming control of selfobjects, by pseudo-obsessive compulsive behavior "to get all in order," or by various personal or religious rituals, an important function for religion.

*Disintegration anxiety* typically occurs due to the failure of a selfobject to live up to demands, severe narcissistic wounding, or to the danger of uncontrolled regression in intensive psychotherapy. It is clinically different in dreams and experienced phenomena from the classical signal anxiety in Freud's structural theory which is based on castration fears or fear of separation. It is not related to the fear of the loss of love, but rather to the fear of disintegration of the sense of self, which would essentially result in a psychosis "in consequence of the loss of an intense archaic enmeshment with the selfobject." It is vague, cannot be pinned down by clinical questioning, cannot be expressed in detail, and is not attached to one situation such as a phobic object.

SELF-STATE DREAMS

In dreams which Kohut (1977, p. 109) calls "self-state dreams" that announce such anxiety, associations lead nowhere. One should not challenge the patient's "explanations" of this anxiety — a different approach from the approach to oedipal anxiety — as the self-produced "explanations" of the patient provide a tension-reducing intellectual structure, just like the paranoid patient's "explanations" of what is happening. Instead of fault-finding or arguing with the patient's explanations, it is best to concentrate on finding the narcissistic wound that touched off the anxiety and then explaining the sequence to the patient.

This type of dream, characterized as a "self-state dream" has been the target of strong disapproval by some critics of self psychology. Kohut (Lichtenberg and Kaplan 1983) attempts to directly address this problem, which arose out of a misunderstanding of a short passage from *The Restoration of the Self* (Kohut 1977, pp. 109–110). It is not true that such dreams are interpreted only from the manifest contents. Associations are not ignored. Kohut points out that the clue to the self-state dream is that associations lead nowhere; "at best they provide us with further imagery that remains on the same level as the manifest content of the dream" (Lichtenberg and Kaplan 1983, p. 402). It is most critical that the analyst's understanding of the state of the patient's self as depicted in the imagery of self-state dreams be accurate because, "only when an analysand feels that the state of his self has been accurately understood by the selfobject analyst will he feel sufficiently secure to go further" (p. 406). To press the patient for further associations in order to emerge with dynamic-genetic conflict-based interpretations will be experienced by the patient as an empathic failure and will generate rage and "resistances." Kohut does admit that most dreams are *not* self-state dreams (p. 404) and must be pursued in the traditional way.

Awareness of these types of dreams is important to the proper conduct of psychotherapy. For example, a woman patient who suffered from transient psychotic episodes gradually improved in psychotherapy to the point where severe stress manifested itself more in psychosomatic symptoms, such as premature ventricular contractions and bouts of nervous colitis and "indigestion." With continued improvement and understanding of her states of temporary fragmentation, the danger of impending fragmentation in stress situations began to announce itself in self-state dreams. One week, when her husband was being particularly oblivious to her needs and the needs of her children, she had just started a new job and was under incredible pressure to manage everything alone. She dreamed, "I was coming to your office, walking up the stairs, and someone stopped me and asked me to run an errand. I don't know what happened — I lost track of three hours of time and arrived at your office in a state of confusion." She woke up from this dream with great anxiety, because it was "very unlike me" to lose track of time and not know where she was for three hours. She was a very well organized and careful person, and recognized with alarm that this represented an abnormal state of her self. Associations led repeatedly to the current overburdened situation which she was in and her disappointment in her unempathic preoccupied husband for whom she ran many "errands." She was convinced that the dream was a warning that unless she reduced the stress, her psychosomatic fragmentation symptoms would return. In clinical practice such dreams often herald some form of disintegration; associations are vague and do not lead to any depth understanding of conflicts.

## HYPOCHONDRIASIS

*Hypochondriasis* is more important in Kohut's theory and better explained than by Freud's structural theory, as the latter is used, for example, by Arlow and Brenner (1964) to explain the bizarre somatic complaints of psychotics: "The symptoms of hypochondriasis are the expression in body language of a fantasy which is itself a compromise between an instinctual wish . . . and the defense" (p. 173). This ignores the vagueness and fleeting nature of such hypochondriasis and its stubborn persistence despite interpretations in the treatment of narcissistic, borderline, and schizophrenic patients.

For Kohut, on the other hand, as disintegration anxiety appears, certain body parts become the carriers of the regressive development "from the patient's yearning for the absent selfobject to states of self-fragmentation." These body parts become crystallization points for hypochondriacal worry. Anxiety and complaints become attached to a fragment of the body, indicating a desperate attempt to reconstitute and to explain the fragmentation of the self.

In the schizophrenic, a part of the self may become split off and utterly divested of libido in order to permit a shallow reconstitution of the rest; this may be represented by a part of the body which is then viewed as useless, unwanted, and may even be literally cut off by the patient.

The usual clinical sequence in the development of hypochondriasis is as follows: a narcissistic wound by, for example, the empathic failure or absence of a selfobject; disintegration anxiety; hypochondriasis and traumatic states; insomnia; sexualization and an attempt to soothe the self in that fashion; deterioration of ego function, often accompanied by frantic compensatory increase of various physical and mental activities, e.g., "overwork," in an attempt to pull together by combating an inner deadness through self-stimulation.

At this point judgment becomes poor, memory impaired, and even a disheveled confusion state may occur. Note how narcissistic wounding and fragmentation of the self precede the deterioration of ego function in contrast to Arlow and Brenner's theory, and how "overwork" is a symptom rather than a cause of fragmentation. Also some hints of concrete thinking may appear. The patient may become confused by interpreting figures of speech or instructions literally. One highly sophisticated patient thought that a bank cash dispenser that read "cash available only in multiples of five" meant that only five dollar bills were available.

NARCISSISTIC RAGE

We are now in a position to offer a clinical classification of rage as it appears in our work with preoedipal disorders. Narcissistic rage, from mild annoyance to catatonic furor, is seen over the disappointment in one's expectations from the selfobject. It is typically accompanied by feelings of humiliation and may arise in an acute episode or with chronic unforgiving relentlessness and may or may not be expressed in acute or chronic somatic symptoms such as headaches or increased blood pressure. At worst it is projected and a fixed paranoid state may develop; such patients are sometimes very dangerous.

The sequence of depression followed by self-mutilation or even suicide is the world of the empty self; there is either a hopeless despair, where the individual is robbed of vigor and even muscle tone, or a state of unfocused agitation which is beyond the patient's control. This often also follows disappointment in the selfobject, revealing a crucial weakness in the nuclear self, which can only sustain itself by a relationship to external selfobjects for soothing or idealization. Patients who show this sequence are often labeled as borderline.

Sadomasochistic behavior combines the expression of rage with restitutive activity. In masochism there is self-soothing by repetitive activity and feeling alive through pain along with identification with the powerful, omnipotent torturer. In sadism the individual imagines or acts out reassuring fantasies of power and control which are very common in masturbation fantasies, usually central to pornographic movies, and acted out in rape. Because of the ever-present threat of fragmentation, these restitutive activities gain a compelling, repetitive, and all-pervasive quality.

In the normal individual a combination of selective assertiveness, achievement, and tolerance of disappointment must be balanced; there is not merely tension reduction. So assertiveness, says Kohut, also has a developmental line of its own which can be diverted into rage and aggression if there is sufficient narcissistic wounding or empathic failure from the selfobjects.

In therapy we focus not on the rage but on the state of the self that has produced the disintegration product: narcissistic rage. This is a critical difference in the psychotherapeutic approach of the psychology of the self from the more common conflict-based theories, and shifts our focus away from the sexual and aggressive "drives," a source of controversy.

A tantrum has no object. For Kohut, "drives" are secondary disintegration products due to empathic failures in the childhood selfobject matrix. Thus the perspective is on the whole person and his or her achievements, not on viewing all human creations and activity as produced by the collision of drives and defenses. Kohut maintains that Freud's famous pessimism was an unavoidable consequence of his drive theory and that it followed from his metapsychology. Other authors blame the disasters of World War I and the death of Freud's daughter for his dark views expressed in *Beyond the Pleasure Principle* (1920) and *Civilization and Its Discontents* (1930).

For Kohut aggression is the response of a self threatened with fragmentation, not an instinctual discharge. The release of aggression in war does not subsequently reduce aggression in the world but increases aggression because it diminishes the cultural situation where parental selfobjects have sufficient security and comfort to be empathic with their children and each other.

All activities with a rage component, including exhibitionism, voyeurism, and oral and anal sadistic strivings, are secondary consolation or breakdown products due to the failure of the selfobject matrix and represent for Kohut "a despair of the child in the depths of the adult." Thus the concept of the selfobject is the pivotal point of organizing clinical data by self psychologists.

PHOBIAS

Phobias are also understood differently by the psychology of the self. As an example, a case of agoraphobia is brought up by Kohut (Goldberg 1980, pp. 521–522). In this case, a female patient can only go out on the street if accompanied by someone, usually an older female. In contrast to Freud's explanation of this as representing a defense against an oedipal-based wish on the part of the woman to prostitute herself, Kohut asks, "What is it in the selfobject matrix, not acquired yet, that requires the patient to have the company of an older woman when she goes out?" Notice the great change of focus and interest here as well as the way in which Freud's and Kohut's explanations of agoraphobia contrast with R. D. Laing's. The latter interprets agoraphobia in the Freudian fashion, but the sexual wish itself is seen as a manifestation of ontological insecurity and not primarily of an oedipal drive. For both Kohut and Laing the emerging person is not essentially a bundle of untamed or barely tamed drives always striving for gratification.

Another example from work with preoedipally damaged patients is the spider phobia, in which the individual is terrified by spiders, feels helpless, and needs another person, a magical protector, to kill the spider. Again, a variety of interpretations are possible, for example Sullivan's (1953) use of the spider to symbolize the "not-me" or the anxious raging mother. In the psychology of the self, the patient is seen to be searching for a missing part of the self, for an omnipotent selfobject; the idealized parent imago has not been integrated into the self.

For the psychology of the self, some depression is based on the inadequate idealization of the self and not on a predisposition to ambivalence due to fixation in the oral phase or the inability to neutralize aggression for various reasons.

## Classification of Disorders of the Self

Kohut and Wolf (1978) present a nosology of the disorders of the self. I will borrow heavily from their important paper and from Kohut (1977, pp. 191–193) in the discussion which follows. Disorders of the self can be divided into secondary disturbances and primary disturbances. The secondary disturbances of the self are reactions of a structurally undamaged self to the natural vicissitudes of life and health. Here is a critical area of understanding for crisis intervention and adolescent adjustment problems. The psychotherapy of secondary disturbances provides a mirroring and idealizable selfobject so that the self automatically firms up. The patient's ego functions improve *pari passu* and the difficulties and vicissitudes can be handled in an optimal, relatively brief fashion, without much interpretation.

This approach is sometimes all that is possible in the psychotherapy of adolescents with profound disorders of the self that have temporarily undergone regressive fragmentation. I recall one famous case of an intuitively gifted psychoanalyst who successfully treated a transiently psychotic adolescent by debating the theological meaning of certain biblical passages. I had a similar case in which an adolescent made an excellent functional recovery after many hours of discussing motorcycles. No interpretations were offered; I could sense from his reactions that the patient was unwilling or unable to utilize them. Yet the patient was profoundly attached to the therapy.

Primary disturbances of the self may be divided into five categories. In *psychoses* there has been serious damage to the nuclear self and no substantial or reliable defensive structures to cover the defect, whether biological or not, have been formed.

In *borderline states*, there is the same defect as in psychoses, but it is masked by complex defenses with which it is unwise for the therapist to tamper except to improve their adaptability. This pessimistic outlook on borderline states has been challenged as stated above; I will discuss it in Chapter 13.

*Schizoid and paranoid personalities* wall off the self and keep themselves at an emotional distance from others in order to protect against "a permanent or protracted breakup, enfeeblement, or serious distortions of the self" (Kohut 1977, p. 192). Again, we are warned by Kohut (1971) not to be a "bull in a china shop" in trying to reach such patients. Here, too, I believe there is an excessive pessimism expressed. If the therapist is empathic and relatively patient, stable selfobject transferences are sometimes formed by these patients and much improvement can occur.

In *narcissistic behavior disorders* there are symptoms of perversions, addictions, and delinquency, but the self is only temporarily

distorted or enfeebled. These patients have a significantly more re-
silient self than patients in the first three categories and are more
amenable to treatment. However they are not *easier* to treat than
borderline or schizoid personality disorders.

In the *narcissistic personality disorders* the problem is the same
as the previous category with one exception. Instead of predominantly
behavior symptoms, there are symptoms of hypochondria, malaise,
boredom, depression, and hypersensitivity to slights. According to
Kohut, only narcissistic behavior and personality disorders are analyzable, as the self in the first three categories cannot withstand the
reactivation of narcissistic needs without fragmentation. This is a kind
of reverse definition and depends on whether or not stable narcissistic
transferences form.

Kohut and Wolf (1978) review certain clinical syndromes in iden-
tifying disorders of the self. The *understimulated self* is due to a
chronic lack of stimulating responsiveness from the selfobject of childhood and the individual shows a lack of vitality, boredom, and
apathy; such patients may have to use any excitement to ward off
painful feelings of deadness.

The *fragmenting self* occurs when the patient reacts to narcissistic
disappointments, such as the therapist's lack of empathy, by the loss
of a sense of cohesive self. Here we must watch for disheveled dress,
posture and gait disturbances, vague anxiety, time and space disorien-
tation, and hypochondriacal concerns. In a minor way this occurs
in all of us when our self-esteem has been taxed for long periods and
no replenishing sustenance has presented itself, or after a series of
failures which shake our self-esteem.

Kohut (1978, p. 738) points out that a narcissistic blow can lead
to regression of the self in which there are archaic but cohesive forms
and can lead also to empty depletion or "enfeeblement," or temporary
fragmentation. Such regression can manifest itself by a shift from normal assertiveness to narcissistic rage, voyeurism in the search for an
idealized parent imago, or gross exhibitionism in the search for mirroring confirmation of the grandiose self.

The *overstimulated self* is caused by unempathic excessive responses from the childhood selfobject, the intrusive overconcerned
narcissistic excitement of neurotic parents. If the grandiose-exhibi-
tionistic pole has been overstimulated, the patient is always in danger
of being flooded by archaic greatness fantasies, which produce anx-

iety and spoil the joy of normal successes. Frightened by their intense ambition, these patients avoid normal creativity and productivity and avoid situations where they would attract attention.

If the ideals pole is overstimulated by parents displaying themselves to get admiration from the child, internalization cannot occur and an intense merger need remains. Loss of healthy enthusiasm for normal goals and ideals results.

In the closely related *overburdened self* the childhood selfobject has not been calm. There has been neither merger with the calmness of an omnipotent selfobject nor development of an internalized, self-soothing capacity. A world that lacks soothing selfobjects is experienced as inimical and dangerous. When the therapist fails in empathy, the patient dreams of living in a poisoned atmosphere surrounded by snakes and other creatures and complains of the noises, odors, and temperature in the therapist's office.

Certain behavioral syndromes in the realm of the disorders of the self are also presented by Kohut and Wolf (1978). *Mirror-hungry personalities* thirst for selfobjects who will give them confirming and admiring responses. "They are impelled to display themselves and to evoke the attention of others, trying to counteract, however fleetingly, their inner sense of worthlessness and lack of self-esteem" (p. 421).

*Ideal-hungry personalities* are forever in search of others whom they can respect and admire for various idealized traits such as prestige, power, beauty, intelligence, or moral or philosophical stature. Such patients can only experience themselves as worthwhile when they are related in some way to these idealized selfobjects. Perhaps the most pathological example of this comes from the autobiography of Albert Speer (1970) containing his own description of his idealizing transference to Hitler, which he apparently shared with a good many others.

*Alter-ego personalities* want others to experience and confirm their feelings, appearance, opinions, and values, and are capable of being nourished longer than mirror-hungry personalities and even forming friendships of a sort. These three types of narcissistic personalities are not primarily pathological although, like Speer, they may be so if carried to an extreme.

Two other types of behavior represent psychopathology. These are the *merger-hungry personalities* who have a compelling need to control their selfobjects, are very intolerant of the independence of the selfobject, very sensitive to separations, and demand their continuous presence. A literary example of this is the relationship of Marcel to Albertine in Proust's (1981) *Remembrance of Things Past* in the section entitled, "The Captive" (see Chessick 1985a).

*Contact-shunning personalities* are the reverse of merger-hungry personalities in that they avoid social contact and become isolated. The intensity of their need is so great that they are excessively sensitive to the slightest sign of rejection, which they prevent by isolation and withdrawal from others.

## DIAGNOSIS OF NARCISSISTIC PERSONALITY DISORDER

The diagnosis of narcissistic personality disorder for Kohut (1971, p. 23) is suspect if certain presumptive symptoms are observed clinically: in the sexual realm, perverse fantasies or lack of interest in sex; in the social realm, work inhibitions, an inability to form and maintain significant relationships, and/or delinquent activities; in the realm of personality, a lack of humor, lack of empathy, distorted sense of proportion in life, and a tendency to attacks of rage, lying, and name-dropping; and in the psychosomatic realm, hypochondriasis and various autonomic nervous system function problems.

The diagnosis of narcissistic personality disorder is certain, says Kohut, if stable spontaneous selfobject transferences develop. These consist of the amalgamation of unconscious narcissistic structures (the grandiose self, the idealized parent imago) with the psychic representation of the analyst in the service of the need to resume interrupted development. They should be compared with the transferences as defined by Freud in classical neuroses, which are the amalgamation of object-directed repressed infantile wishes and the analysand's preconscious wishes and attitudes toward the analyst. Whether the selfobject transferences are true transferences is a "vexing question," but Kohut points out that the narcissistic or borderline ego seeks reassurance, not satisfaction, as in the neuroses.

## Comparison of Kohut's and Kernberg's Views

To clarify Kohut's clinical views on the narcissistic personality disorder, let us briefly compare them with those of Kernberg (1974, 1974a, 1975, 1975a, 1980; Schwartz 1973). For Kohut the central pathology of narcissism comes from a developmental arrest, whereas for Kernberg narcissism represents "a defense against paranoid traits related to projected oral rage" (1975, p. 228). Kernberg (Schwartz 1973, Kernberg 1974a) agrees with Kohut on the clinical characteristics displayed by these patients.

Such patients for Kernberg (1975, p. 229) cannot be depressed but experience rage, resentment, and massive devaluation of the other person with a wish for revenge when a loss occurs; Kohut recognizes this but sees the patient's early selfobject experience as the key explanation of the clinical phenomenon (Ornstein 1974).

For Kernberg (1974a, 1975), the defenses of the narcissistic patient are similar to borderlines. There is a predominance of splitting, denial, projective identification, and primitive idealization with a sense of omnipotence. Kernberg says (1975, p. 234) that narcissistic and borderline patients have the same intense oral aggression either constitutionally determined or due to frustration as infants and this is the key to the etiology. The grandiose self of narcissistic patients allows better superficial social and work functioning, but over a long period we observe the "emptiness beneath the glitter" (1975, p. 230).

For Kernberg (1974, 1974a), in psychotherapy we must focus on the positive and negative transferences since the patient has the need to devalue the therapy and the therapist, and to avoid dependency. Devaluation and treating of the analyst as an appendage gives a typical countertransference reaction of impotence, boredom, worthlessness of the therapy, and rage (1975, pp. 245–248). For the patient, the therapist as a source of envy and projected rage must be devalued, controlled, or destroyed. The grandiose self is a defensive pathological structure and must be broken down. Kohut's idealizing and mirror transferences are alternative activations of components of the fused pathological grandiose self (Schwartz 1973, p. 621; Kernberg 1974, p. 260; 1974a, p. 223), and an early idealizing transference in psychotherapy is a defense against envy and devaluation of the feared external object or therapist. Rage is at the core of the disorder.

For Kernberg, Kohut's reluctant compliance with idealization hides what is underneath and avoids facing the patient's hatred and envy. The idealizing transference gives less countertransference problems than the devaluation and it is therefore tempting to leave it alone. However, Kohut's acceptance of the transference allows the patient to make a better adaptive use of the grandiose self. It constitutes a reeducation but does not lead to basic structural change

(Kernberg 1974a) and so Kohut's method is by implication not psychoanalysis (which Kernberg recommends for these patients [Schwartz 1973, p. 622; Kernberg 1974, p. 265]), except for those functioning on a borderline level (Kernberg 1974, p. 257, 1974a, p. 217).

The "self" for Kernberg is part of the ego and contains multiple self-representations and affects. Unlike Kohut, for Kernberg (1974, 1974a) the grandiose self is formed from the pathological vicissitudes of structural development of the ego. For Kohut the grandiose self is a replication of an archaic normal primitive self-image and not a pathological structure. Kernberg (1974, 1974a) argues that the grandiose self of the adult differs significantly from that of the child: the adult grandiose self is more extreme and distorted in its demands; there is a warm quality to the child's self-centeredness; there is less abnormal destructiveness and ruthlessness in the normal child's self-centeredness. Kohut (1971, pp. 124–125), however, notes that the grandiose self is a "regressively altered edition" of the child's grandiose self mixed with sadistic drive elements that are fragmentation products, so this is not an irreconcilable difference.

For Kohut, narcissism follows a separate line of development, but for Kernberg (1974a) we cannot separate it from libido and aggression and the vicissitudes of internalized object relations. There is no separate line of development. Kernberg (1975a) argues that Kohut's method leads to better adaptive use of the grandiose self but is not accompanied by much change in pathological object relations because the grandiose self is not analyzed. Kernberg states the process of improvement does *not* occur simply because lines of development of narcissism and other libido are separate. These views are basically irreconcilable and cannot be synthesized.

## Kohut's Other Clinical Contributions

Another late clinical concept of Kohut (1984) is what he calls "the principle of the relativity of diagnostic classification and the specific prognosis" (p. 183). A clinical vignette is presented (p. 178) in which the critical task of the analyst was based on self-scrutiny in order to prevent the tendency to attack the analysand's transference distortions. Such an attack "only confirms the analysand's conviction that the analyst is as dogmatic, as utterly sure of himself, as walled off in the self-righteousness of a distorted view, as the pathogenic parents (or other selfobject) had been" (p. 182). Kohut recommends continuing sincere acceptance of the patient's reproaches as psychologically realistic, followed by a prolonged attempt to look at the analyst and remove barriers that stand in the way of the empathic grasp of the patient. If successful, this process may produce the reward of a borderline case becoming a narcissistic personality disorder; in Kohut's terms an unanalyzable patient becomes an analyzable patient. In a way, this could be considered the answer of Kohut to the approach of Kernberg in the treatment of narcissistic personality disorders.

For Kohut, there exist two types of dreams, those expressing latent contents that involve drives, conflicts, and attempted solutions, and those attempting "to bind the nonverbal tensions of traumatic states (the dread of overstimulation, or of the disintegration of the self [psychosis]). Dreams of this second type portray the dreamer's dread vis-à-vis some uncontrollable tension-increase or his dread of the dissolution of the self" (1977, p. 109). These are the self-state dreams discussed above. It follows from what has been said that the so-called bedrock beyond which analysis cannot penetrate is not the castration threat in the male or the lack of the penis in the female and is more serious than a threat to physical survival itself. Kohut (1977, p. 117) says it is the threat of the destruction of the nuclear self. Any price will be paid to prevent this.

Thus Kohut (1977, p. 121, p. 124) points out the failure of the Kleinian emphasis on the manifestations of rage as a bestial drive that has to be tamed: for Kohut, rage is a specific regressive phenomenon arising from a deficiency in empathy on the part of the selfobject. In hypochondriasis certain body parts become the carrier of the regressive development "from the patient's yearning for the absent self-object to states of self-fragmentation and will, therefore, especially lend themselves to becoming crystallization points for hypochondriacal worry" (Kohut 1977, p. 156).

Kohut (1977) introduces the clinical concept of "action-thought" which is not the same as acting out in the usual sense (Chessick 1974). It represents steps made by the patient who is healing a disorder of the self on the path to psychological equilibrium. It consists of action patterns, creatively initiated by the patient on the basis of actual talents, ambitions, and ideals but to be further modified and perfected in order to provide a reliable means of establishing the postanalytic maintenance of a stable psychoeconomic equilibrium in the narcissistic sector of the personality. Such activities should not be expected to dissolve as a consequence of correct interpretation and do not represent regressive steps but rather constitute a forward movement. Lack of recognition of the forward nature of this movement is experienced by the patient as an empathic lapse.

The sequence described in the case of Mr. M. (Kohut 1977) of movement from playing the violin, to befriending an adolescent boy, to opening a writing school, is an excellent description of action-thought as clinically observed. A similar form of action-thought has to take place as the patient gradually develops a more effective empathic matrix of selfobjects that reflects the improvement in the cohesion of the self and the integration of the archaic narcissistic structures internally.

Another important clinical psychiatric phenomenon examined by Kohut is his emphasis on middle age. Late middle age for Kohut is the pivotal point in the life curve of the self that forms the final crucial test of whether previous development failed or succeeded. Patients presenting with hopelessness, lethargy, empty depression, without predominant guilt, but with self-directed aggression are strong candidates for the diagnosis of a disorder of the self and are common in clinical practice.

Another important clinical contribution results from Kohut's reflections on patients who continually seem to make the wrong choices which result in suffering attributed to "unfortunate circumstances." Such patients often have pathology of the self which makes it difficult for them to make realistic choices, defined as "choices in complete harmony with the innate abilities he possesses and with the external opportunities open to him, choices that serve his principles or fully support the pursuit of obtainable goals" (Kohut 1977, p. 283). Another clinical marker of recovery from self-pathology is the patient's manifest improved capacity to find a productive and creative existence that is actually realistic in the sense defined above, as well as the gradual accretion of a consistent selfobject matrix.

This brings us again to the "Zeigarnik phenomenon," from which Kohut postulates that the selfobject transferences will develop as a result of the need to complete unfinished developmental tasks. These tasks, if completed in childhood, would have produced a cohesive self. The Ziegarnik (1927) effect in experimental psychology generated the theory that interruption of any task leads to tension, and that the tendency to resume that task at the earliest opportunity relieves the tension. Transference in the narcissistic disorders develops out of the need to complete the development and form structure, not as a result of striving for instinctual gratification via objects as in classical metapsychology (Kohut 1977, p. 217). This notion of the reactivation in the treatment situation of the "developmental potential of the defective self" is what Kohut (1984, p. 4) calls the "central hypothesis" of self psychology.

One of the biggest arguments against Kohut's theory involves the vagueness of this conception. How does an individual know that a part of the structure is missing? What are the nature and origin of the developmental forces that drive the patient to replace or form missing structures? The assumption is that the forces of development will resume, in a properly conducted treatment, in order to continue a development that was interrupted at the age of two. These spontaneously arising selfobject transferences lead to what Kohut (1984) calls a basic therapeutic unit common to both forms of patients: those with oedipal conflict neuroses and those with narcissistic personality disorders and narcissistic behavior disturbances.

The first phase of the treatment is understanding. This begins with the inevitable need activation in the treatment and its optimal frustration, nonfulfillment of the need or "abstinence." The therapeutic process provides the substitution for direct need fulfillment by reestablishing the bond of empathy between the self and selfobject, which is threatened by nonfulfillment of the need directly, through the communication of empathically based recognition that the patient is suffering. Sometimes this occurs even through a "wild interpretation," regardless of the psychoanalytic "school" from which it arises. This substitution provides limited structural accretion and might be thought of as a form of psychotherapy with ephemeral results, a form which is incomplete because it is not broad or deep and takes place in the presence of a weaker empathic bond.

The second phase of the therapy is explaining, which also depends on empathy. Here the dynamics are interpreted to the patient with respect to the transference experience. The genetic precursors of the patient's vulnerabilities and conflicts are discussed and explained. This leads to a more powerful empathic bond and a broadening and deepening of the patient's self-understanding and acceptance. Basically, however, the cure does not rest on an expansion of cognition but on an accretion of psychic structure. In this approach to psychotherapy the use of confrontations is discouraged (1984, p. 173) and should be replaced by consistent interpretation of selfobject transferences. Kohut concludes that the patient

> must be able to mobilize . . . the maturation-directed needs for struc-
> ture building via transmuting internalization of the revived selfobjects
> of childhood. As precursors of the child's psychological structure, these
> selfobjects perform the functions . . . which the psyche of the adult will
> later be able to perform with the aid of a selfobject milieu composed
> of his family, his friends, his work situation, and . . . the cultural re-
> sources of the group to which he belongs. (1984, p. 71)

## AMBIENCE OF THE TREATMENT

Contrary to many misconceptions about self psychology, Gold-berg (1978) states:

> The analyst does not actively soothe; he interprets the analysand's yearn-
> ing to be soothed. The analyst does not actively mirror; he interprets
> the need for confirming responses. The analyst does not actively admire
> or approve grandiose expectations; he explains their role in the psychic
> economy. The analyst does not fall into passive silence; he explains why
> his interventions are felt to be intrusive. (pp. 447–448)

The analytic ambience, based on the therapist's reasonable, humane, tactful, nonhumiliating attitude, facilitates the process of psychoanalysis and psychoanalytic psychotherapy and has a soothing effect that can also be interpreted. Interpretation rather than gratification is the rule. But at times a certain "reluctant compliance" is necessary to avoid a cold, critical, unaccepting ambience, which will certainly disrupt the treatment of, especially, preoedipal disorders.

An average expectable environment is necessary (Wolf 1976). If the patient in a hot room, "half rising off the couch, half turning back toward the analyst" (p. 108), asks if he may remove his suit jacket and the response of the analyst is an icy silence or poker-faced stare, there will result "transference artifacts" which often may be mistaken-ly interpreted as aggression arising from the transference. Why might the hypothetical "classical" analyst respond with an icy silence or poker-faced stare to such a request? The therapist may have thought he was following the "rule of abstinence" and did not want to gratify the patient's erotic or exhibitionistic wish, assumed to underlie the request. Although this may be technically correct, it loses sight of the narcissistic wounding involved when an average expectable environment is not provided, and the psychology of the self tends to help us keep our perspective on this important factor.

The patient must adjust to whatever ambience the therapist insists on providing, regardless of the theoretical grounds given by the therapist for this ambience. For example, Kohut (1984) mentions (without naming) the practice of Langs (1981) who criticizes (pp. 162ff) making available a box of tissues for the patient, out of the wish to avoid any "intervention" which would give gratification to the patient. Patients will adjust to such extreme aridity, but, according to the psychology of the self, a price will be paid for it in the development of an iatrogenic narcissistic withdrawal and a reactive grandiosity.

The importance of such iatrogenic regressions, which harden into "resistances" that are extremely difficult to resolve by interpretation, is discussed at length by Stone (1961, 1981). Both he and Lipton (1977, 1979) discuss this as an erroneous understanding and application of Freud's views. Leider (1983, 1984) reviews the controversial subject of "analytic neutrality" and the arguments for and against the role of empathy and non-interpretive interventions which basically arise "from differing views of the essential functions of the analyst in the psychoanalytic process" (1983, p. 673) in detail. Kohut's work has fueled much new controversy on this subject, as we shall explore in the clinical examples from self psychology to be reviewed in subsequent chapters. The argument is over whether the "classical" (or "neoclassical") analytic stance is or is not sometimes so nonresponsive as to interfere with the analytic process, or whether the "empathic" stance of Kohut and his followers does or does not contaminate the transference and interfere with analysis.

## Kohut's View of Psychoanalytic Cure

I will now turn to Kohut's final version of psychoanalytic treatment. As stated above, empathy does not require any sort of deliberate attempt to mirror or gratify the patient. At its base it requires that the therapist first accept the prevailing selfobject transference without interpretation. Empathy must always pervade both of the crucial steps that constitute the ultimately curative interventions of the analyst.

First, through empathy the analyst must understand what the patient is experiencing at any given time, and why; then the therapist must explain "over and over again" (Kohut 1984, p. 206) that which has led to temporary interruptions of the selfobject transferences by empathic failures and connect this historically with the childhood milieu provided by the significant selfobjects. This requires that the empathic therapist not interfere with the developing selfobject transferences by interpretation, for example, in an effort to reach a postulated underlying aggression that is thought to be hidden by an idealizing transference.

If the understanding and explaining of the therapist is experienced repeatedly by the patient, and if empathy generally pervades both of these interventions, structure building via transmuting internalizations will occur. This is how analysis cures disorders of the self, and Kohut (1984) describes some degree of such self disorders as universal in psychopathology. The "proof" of cure is not abstract but lies within the patient's capacity to develop a secure empathic matrix with others, a matrix that Kohut considers to be vital to self-cohesion throughout life (p. 77).

Kohut insists a psychoanalysis grounded in self psychology does not lead to any change in basic psychoanalytic technique. Psychoanalysis and intensive psychotherapy share the "understanding" step (or phase) of treatment, which entails a sequence of three substeps "of the therapeutic miniprocesses that lead to the laying down of psychic structure and thereby prepare the soil for the analytic cure" (p. 103). These three substeps are the reactivation of a need by the therapeutic situation, "abstinence" or nonresponse by the selfobject analyst, and the reestablishment of a bond of empathy between the self and selfobject by the analyst's communication to the patient of his more or less correct understanding of the patient's inner experience.

Despite the analyst's understanding of what the patient feels and the acknowledgment that the patient's upset is legitimate from the patient's experience in the selfobject transference, the analyst still does not directly act in accordance with the patient's archaic need. However, through the understanding and communication of it, an empathic bond is established or reestablished between the analyst and the patient. This substitutes for the fulfillment of the patient's need, allowing structure to be built by transmuting internalization. Whether these are new structures that fill in defects or compensatory structures is not the main point. Some patients will require long periods of understanding alone before the second step (or phase) of analytic cure can be usefully undertaken.

The second step (or phase) of analytic cure constitutes psychoanalytic explanation via well-designed interpretations. Not only does it increase the impact of the first or understanding step, but, by referring to the genetic precursors of the patient's vulnerabilities and conflicts, it broadens and deepens the sense of being understood for the patient. It also allows the patient to face experiences similar to those that have previously led to the interpretation of a transference disruption, such as the analysand's reaction to the analyst's canceling a session, which produce what Kohut (1984) calls "undulations" (p. 67) in the flow of empathy between analyst and analysand that has been established in the understanding step.

There are two substeps of this second or "explanatory" step or phase (Kohut 1984, p. 106). The first constitutes interpretations which explain the undulations in dynamic terms, and the second refers to exploring and explaining the genetic precursors of the patient's vulnerabilities and conflicts. Thus genetic reconstructions for their knowledge value alone are not as important as they are for deepening the patient's sense of being understood. Through these two substeps a truly psychoanalytic therapeutic effect can be achieved, an effect which is "qualitatively different from the effect that resulted from the understanding phase alone" (p. 105).

The critical point of methodological difference between Kohut and traditional psychoanalysis is in his (1984) statement that, "the basic therapeutic unit of the psychoanalytic cure does not rest on the expansion of cognition. (It does not rest, for example, on the analysand's becoming aware of the difference between his fantasy and reality, especially with reference to transference distortions involving projected drives)" (p. 108). The essence of the cure is the accretion of psychic structure based on an optimal frustration of the analysand's needs or wishes. The accretion of psychic structure is provided first by understanding and then by explanation and interpretation involving the genetic precursors of the patient's vulnerabilities, which establish a basic change in a sector of the self. This leads to cure of the disorder of the self by transmuting internalization.

This emphasis on the structure-building aspect of understanding, explanation, and interpretation, as well as on "the self and survival of its nuclear program" (Kohut 1984, p. 147), separates the psychology of the self from traditional psychoanalysis. To emphasize the difference, Kohut points out that he cannot accept the notion that psychoanalysts primarily are engaged in a battle to increase knowledge and that everything that impedes progress toward becoming conscious and sharing liberated cognitive content with the analyst is a "resistance." On the deepest level, the patient's motivations are "an expression of his enduring wish to complete his development and thereby realize the nuclear program of his self" (p. 148).

The difference between psychotherapy and psychoanalysis is as follows: the results of the analyst's more or less accurate empathic understanding of the condition of the patient's self, when communicated, promotes the movement toward health and leads to the laying down of new psychological structure, but the results of this tend to be "ephemeral" (p. 106). The second step (or phase) of dynamic genetic explanations or interpretations "not only broadens and deepens the patient's own empathic-accepting grasp of himself, but strengthens the patient's trust in the reality and reliability of the empathic bond that is being established between himself and his analyst by putting him in touch with the full depth and breadth of the analyst's understanding of him" (p. 105). For Kohut, a rise in self-esteem occurs as the direct consequence of optimal new self-structures acquired in treatment as well as from the firming of existing structures. The proof this has occurred is provided by the patient's increasing success in finding a stable empathic selfobject matrix and developing at least one area of joyful activity between the poles of the self that harnesses genuine preexisting talents in the service of realistic long-term goals.

# Chapter 12

## Kohut's Clinical Case Presentations

Kohut presented many case vignettes, which critics complained were too short and lacked the necessary clinical evidence to support Kohut's hypotheses. Perhaps to counter these criticisms, Kohut wrote one of his most important papers, "The Two Analyses of Mr. Z." (1979), which rapidly became a paradigmatic case for the study of self psychology and generated a mixed response in the literature.

Critics argued that the extensive case history of Mr. Z. provided insufficient evidence for Kohut's hypotheses since the case material could be interpreted in a variety of ways. For example, Edelson (1984) claimed that Kohut showed no understanding of "what is required to make convincing the argument that evidence he presents is related probatively to his hypothesis" (p. 61). To answer his critics Kohut wrote, "Case histories — not to speak of the brief case vignettes that I often use in my writings — can never be more than illustrative; they are a special means of communication within the professional community intended to clarify scientific information from a clinical researcher to his colleagues. Even if the professional colleagues can grasp the meaning of the message, it is still up to them to make use of it in their own work" (1984, p. 89).

With this debate in mind, let us turn primarily to the case of Mr. Z. First I shall summarize the case and then turn to the comments of Ferguson (1981) and Ornstein (1981), and others.

## Summary of the Case of Mr. Z.

Mr. Z. first consulted Kohut when Mr. Z. was a graduate student in his mid-twenties. He is described as handsome and muscular with a pale, sensitive face, "the face of a dreamer and thinker." He lived with his widowed mother in comfortable financial circumstances because father, a successful business executive, died four years earlier, leaving a considerable fortune. Mr. Z. was an only child.

His vague complaints involved mild somatic symptoms such as extrasystoles, sweaty palms, fullness in the stomach, and either constipation or diarrhea. He felt socially isolated and was unable to form relationships with girls; his grades were good but he felt he was functioning below his capacities. He was lonely and had only one friend, unmarried, who also had trouble in his relations with women. A few months before the patient consulted Kohut, this friend became attached to a woman and lost interest in seeing Mr. Z.

Masturbatory fantasies, in which he performed menial tasks submissively in the service of a domineering woman, were masochistic. Yet he insisted that he had an excellent relationship with his mother as far back as he could remember. When he was three and one-half, Mr. Z.'s father became seriously ill and was hospitalized for several months; during this time father fell in love with a nurse who took care of him. He did not return home but went instead to live with the nurse for about one and one-half years, rarely visiting the family. There was no divorce, and when the patient was five father returned home.

The opening transference was narcissistic, marked by an attempt to control the psychoanalytic situation and a demand to be admired and catered to by a doting mother. This was construed by Kohut as the wish for an oedipal victory but such interpretations were responded to by explosive rage.

An important turning point in the first analysis occurred when Kohut casually prefaced an interpretation by mentioning, "Of course it hurts when one is not given what one assumes to be one's due." The significance of this was not understood at the time by Kohut, who thought that the case was moving toward the central area of the patient's psychopathology: his Oedipus complex and castration anxiety.

Kohut interpreted the narcissism as protection against the painful awareness of the returned father, a powerful rival who possessed his mother sexually, and against a castration anxiety to which an awareness of his competitive and hostile impulses toward his father would have exposed him. Thus the axis of the case was a regression to pregenital drive aims out of fear of taking a competitive stance against the father. The masochism was explained as a sexualization of his guilt about the preoedipal possession of his mother and about his unconscious oedipal rivalry, using fairly standard traditional psychodynamic interpretations.

The patient revealed that at the age of 11 he was involved in a homosexual relationship with a 30-year-old teacher, the assistant director of his summer camp. The relationship was marked mostly by mutual caressing and lasted about two years. The relationship was a happy one for Mr. Z., who idealized his friend. It was destroyed by the appearance of pubertal changes of Mr. Z.'s body, at which time gross sexuality entered into the picture. Puberty just increased his sense of social isolation and tied him more to his mother; there were no heterosexual experiences.

The first analysis showed some apparently good results: the masochistic fantasies gradually disappeared and the patient moved from his mother's house to an apartment of his own. He began to date and had several sexually active relationships with girls of his age; during the last year of his analysis he seemed to have found a serious relationship with a woman and was considering marriage. All this occurred *pari passu* with Kohut's firm rejection of Mr. Z.'s narcissistic expectations and his insistence that they were resistances against deeper fears connected with masculine assertiveness and competition with men.

An important dream appeared about half a year before termination: "*He was in a house, at the inner side of a door which was a crack open. Outside was the father, loaded with gift-wrapped packages, wanting to enter. The patient was intensely frightened and attempted to close the door in order to keep the father out*" (p. 8). Kohut felt that this dream confirmed the ambivalent attitude toward the father and the basic interpretation of the patient's psychopathology involving his hostility toward the returning father, the castration fear of

the strong adult man, and the tendency to retreat from competitiveness and male assertiveness "either to the old preoedipal attachment
to his mother or to a defensively taken submissive and passive homosexual attitude toward the father" (p. 9).

In retrospect, Kohut felt that something was not quite right about
the termination phase of the first analysis because it seemed emotionally shallow and unexciting compared to the earlier part of the
analysis when the patient talked glowingly about the idealization of
the preoedipal mother and his admiration for the counselor. But the
analysis ended with a "warm handshake" and there was little contact with Mr. Z. for about four and one-half years, at which time
he contacted Kohut and mentioned that he was in trouble again.

On the first visit of the second analysis he reported that, although
he was living alone and doing reasonably well in his profession, he
did not enjoy his work. In a *non sequitur*, he quickly and somewhat
defensively added that his sexual masochism had not returned. Kohut
felt that his masochistic propensities had simply shifted to his work
and to his life in general. Indeed the patient had to call them up sexually during intercourse with girlfriends, using the fantasies (not explained how) as "an antidote to premature ejaculation" and to enhance the sexual experience. After breaking up with his most recent
girlfriend, he had become alarmed about his increasing sense of social
isolation and an internal pressure to go back to masturbation with
masochistic fantasies. This was akin to a former addict threatened
by the temptation to succumb again to an addiction.

After Mr. Z. moved away from his mother during the first analysis
five years before, she developed a set of circumscribed paranoid delusions and Kohut at first thought that her disintegration dragged Mr.
Z. back to his former illness, but this turned out to be incorrect.

The second analysis began while Kohut was writing "Forms and
Transformations of Narcissism" (1966) and ended while he was deeply
immersed in writing *The Analysis of the Self* (1971). The second
analysis coincided with the time that he was beginning to test the
hypotheses of self psychology. When Mr. Z. felt better soon after
beginning the second analysis, Kohut understood this to represent the
beginning of an idealizing transference similar to the time when he
had turned from his mother to the assistant camp director.

This idealizing transference lasted only a short time and was
replaced by a merger type of transference similar to that which had
appeared at the beginning of the first analysis. However this time

it was not seen by Kohut as defensive in the traditional interpretation but rather a reopening of a childhood situation. Kohut did not take a "stand against it" which in turn "rid the analysis of a burdensome iatrogenic artifact — his unproductive rage reactions against me and the ensuing clashes with me" (p. 12). Kohut describes giving up his therapeutic ambitions to get the patient to grow up and attempting instead to study the patient's early experiences involving his enmeshment with the pathological personality of the mother.

The true image of the mother emerged and filled many hours of the second analysis of Mr. Z. Many examples of her bizarre use of him as a selfobject are presented; she was not interested in him but only in certain aspects of his body such as his feces and bowel functions and later his skin, subjecting him to sadistic intrusions to which he had to submit without protest. It became clear from these descriptions of her behavior that she had been able to temporarily cover her psychosis by a rigidly maintained control over her son, and when he left home she eventually came apart.

Kohut argues that this material did not appear in the first analysis because his attention was on interpreting regression from the Oedipus complex rather than on the personality of the mother. So the improvement from the first analysis was a transference cure in which the patient complied with the convictions of Kohut, the traditional analyst, by presenting him with oedipal issues. Outside the analytic office, Mr. Z. met the analyst's expectations by suppressing his symptoms and changing his behavior to fit the appearance of normality as defined by the analyst's maturity morality, the move from narcissism to object love.

In the second analysis however, the awareness of the mother's psychopathology and understanding of its pathogenic influence on Mr. Z. was extremely emotional and dramatic, stirring up even disintegration anxiety. This was in sharp contrast to the emotionally shallow termination phase of the first analysis. As the depressed aspects of the patient's self, hopelessly caught in an archaic enmeshment within the psychic organization of the mother, were gradually worked through, a new assertive and vital set of interests arose, quite different than the submissive relinquishment of Mr. Z.'s independence to the maternal figure.

A new interpretation of the homosexual involvement was now presented; it represented not a regression to the phallic mother, but rather a yearning for the figure of a strong fatherly man, perhaps the admired older brother Mr. Z. never had. At the crucial moment in the treatment, it became clear that a powerful, positive, unrecognized relationship had formed to his selfobject father. This was frightening, because it required the separation from the archaic self connected with the selfobject mother, a self that Mr. Z. had always considered his only one. There was possible in the analysis the reactivation "of a hitherto unknown independent nuclear self (crystalized around an up-to-now unrecognized relationship to his selfobject father)" (p. 19).

The analysis took an entirely different turn than the first analysis, moving away from hopeless rivalry with the father to a feeling of pride in him; oedipal material and conflicts did not lie hiding underneath, says Kohut. The analyst-father was experienced as strong and masculine, an image of masculine strength with which to merge temporarily as a means of firming the structure of the self. The termination was marked by a spontaneous return to the dream quoted above from the termination of the first analysis which, according to new, surprising associations, explains Kohut, took on a different meaning. In contrast to the previous explanation that it involved the ambivalence of the child toward the oedipal rival,* this dream is now explained as the father's sudden return, exposing the patient to the massive potential satisfaction of a central psychological need. This endangered the patient with a traumatic state in being offered, with overwhelming suddenness, all the psychological gifts (the packages) for which he had secretly yearned. Kohut writes, "This dream deals in its essence with the psycho-economic imbalance of major proportions to which the boy's psyche was exposed by the deeply wished-for return of his father, not with homosexuality, especially not with an oedipally based reactive passive homosexuality" (p. 23).

Kohut explains that the most significant psychological achievement of Mr. Z. in analysis was "breaking the deep merger ties with his mother" (p. 25). All three constituents of his self were decisively changed during the analysis. The patient married, had a daughter, and was able to lead a reasonably satisfying and joyful life.

---

*Kohut felt it necessary to put a quotation from Virgil in this description, which parallels Freud's use of a quotation from Virgil that opens *The Interpretation of Dreams*. Kohut's quotation, "*Timeo Danaos et dona ferentes*" (*Aeneid*, Book II, l. 49) means, "I fear the Greeks even though they bring gifts."

## Comments on the Case of Mr. Z.

According to Ferguson (1981), it was not until ten years after the termination of Mr. Z.'s second analysis that the case was published by Kohut, who had to be "sure of the permanence of the beneficial effect it had on Mr. Z.'s life" (p. 141). Ferguson maintains that Kohut's new theoretical views offer greater conceptual clarity and increased explanatory power with greater therapeutic efficacy. In the case of Mr. Z., it also shows that psychoanalytic theory need not be circular; there is observable evidence independent of any given theoretical orientation which can provide evidence either for or against the theory. This case offers an unusual instance of progressive change in psychoanalysis, according to Ferguson. Although any therapist's scientific thinking is contaminated by theoretical preconceptions or personal biases, the fact that psychoanalysts are aware of this allows progressive successive paradigm choices. Observations in psychoanalysis are not determined by the theoretical orientation of the analyst, but certain observations relevant to evaluating a psychoanalytic hypothesis or interpretation can be independent of the theory in question. Ferguson's view, therefore, is essentially in agreement with Kohut's depiction of the two analyses of Mr. Z. as representing progressive and desirable important theory change in psychoanalysis.

Ornstein (1981) agrees, and claims that Kohut established a new paradigm based on the selfobject concept (p. 357). For Ornstein, this represents a decisive theoretical advance with many important consequences. He again points out that Kohut, by permitting the full unfolding of the mirror transference rather than seeing it as a defense against the remobilization of the Oedipus complex, allowed the discovery and mobilization of the profound depression and hopelessness that the mother's attitude evoked in Mr. Z. This permitted the working through of the archaic merger with the mother, and permitted successful analytic resolution of Mr. Z.'s massive adaptive compliance and his childhood masochistic masturbation fantasies. When worked through, the fantasies permitted the unfolding of the idealizing transference through the repressed yearnings for the strong and powerful father.

It became possible for Mr. Z. to set in motion "the long-ago traumatically derailed developmental sequence involving the idealized father" (p. 370). Interpreting the dream near termination as involving an oedipal rivalry shut off the resumption of this developmental step in the transference in the first analysis. The new interpretation was not that he wanted to close the door and keep his father out in order to retain the oedipal mother for himself, but he wished to open the door gradually in order to receive father's gifts one package at a time, "so that he would assimilate their contents and make them his own through the developmentally occurring transmuting internalizations" (p. 371). Thus, the acquisition of idealized male strength through transmuting internalizations, Ornstein says, "was the central event of the second phase of the second analysis" (p. 372).

Ornstein concludes that a comprehensive understanding of the mother's psychopathology and its impact on Mr. Z. became possible when the mode of listening shifted to empathy or vicarious introspection, in which the self psychology point of view focuses the analyst's attention and perception on how it feels to be the subject rather than the target of the patient's needs and demands (Schwaber 1979, Chessick 1985c). He adds that even if the traditional analyst had been able to perceive the mother's psychopathology and its impact on Mr. Z., the single-axis theory along which archaic narcissism tends to be seen as defensive would seriously limit the results of the analysis. Ornstein hails this case as a demonstration that the psychology of the self approach led to more accurate genetic reconstructions, a better grasp of the nature of the psychopathology of Mr. Z., and more profound therapeutic results.

In 1979, the same year Kohut's paper was published, a letter to the editor from the psychoanalyst Ostow (1979) appeared in a subsequent issue of the same journal. Ostow argued that Kohut's report shows merely that the first analysis was not conducted with proper classical technique, while the second procedure corrected some of its defects. Ostow claims that in the first analysis Kohut missed the contrast between the idyllic relation the patient described with his mother and the hostility exhibited in the transference. According to Ostow, the transference suggests repressed hostility to the mother, an interpretation which is confirmed by the masochistic masturbation fantasy of enslavement to a woman. This deeply repressed hostility was so strong, and generated so much anxiety and resistance, that it indicated the dominant need was to maintain the attachment to the mother at all costs.

When this material was not properly treated, the patient tried to please the analyst as he had also pleased his mother, by offering appropriate analytic material; "the analyst did not recognize this maneuver for what it was" (p. 531). Thus Kohut erred in his interpretation that the patient's preoccupation with pregenital material was defensive against oedipal and castration anxiety. Ostow calls this "imposing well-known formulations onto clinical data that really did not call for them" (p. 531). Missing the hidden hostility to the mother, imposing an interpretation which was not called for by the data, and finally suppressing material brought up by the patient simply because it does not accord with what the analyst expects or desires (as happened at the end of the first analysis) represents poor psychoanalytic technique. Therefore, the second analysis which worked through the pathological relationship with the mother only represents a correction of the omissions and defects of the first.

Goldberg's (1980a) response to Ostow points out that the problem of variant interpretations of case material leads to unproductive debate, and argues that the essential purpose of the case presentation was to illustrate the usefulness of self psychology in enabling Kohut to conduct a more successful analysis. Like Ornstein (1981), he stresses that self psychology also offers by far the best explanation of the overall psychopathology of Mr. Z.

Could a traditional psychoanalyst like Ostow have performed the first analysis correctly using the traditional theoretical stance? Rangell (1981) would say yes, and he writes, "The 'two analyses of Mr. Z.' reported by Kohut should have comprised one total classical analysis" (p. 133). A study of the psychoanalytic literature seems to indicate that traditional analysts basically view the second analysis of Mr. Z. as a corrective to the first, which need not have taken place had the first analysis been carried out properly. Notice that all authors agree that there needs to be no change in the analytic technique in the actual management of the transferences between these two analyses. The big difference as summed up by Kohut (Meyers 1981) is that self psychology considers as primary the psychological contents that had formerly been considered as secondary and defensive. Kohut claims that this leads to a subtle change in the analytic atmosphere, making it conform to the requirements of the narcissistically damaged patient.

Wallerstein (1981) attempts to bridge the gap between traditional analysis and self-psychology by suggesting that, in the flow and flux of clinical material, "we deal constantly, and in turn with both the oedipal where there is a coherent self and the preoedipal where there may not yet be, with defensive regressions and with developmental arrests, with defense transferences and defensive resistances, and with re-creations of earlier traumatic and traumatized psychic states" (p. 386). In a symposium on the bipolar self, the sharpest area of disagreement (Meyers 1981) questioned whether the self should be viewed as a supraordinate concept or as a content of the mental apparatus. This is a critical division and what is behind it is the question of whether the self-psychological approach requires a whole new metapsychology with the supraordinate self holistically developed. Wallerstein does not think so.

## FURTHER CRITICISM OF KOHUT'S CASE REPORT

The common criticism of Kohut as supplying a corrective emotional experience (Stein 1979) is countered by the incisive arguments of Basch (1981). But the lingering complaint about the effort to give a corrective emotional experience through Kohut's increasing emphasis on the power of empathy in the curative process has not disappeared from the critiques of self psychology. Wallerstein (1981) does not think that a new metapsychology is necessary and claims that what we are dealing with is the well-known principle of overdetermination and, in Waelder's (1930) terms, multiple function. Thus, all aspects of the analytic material involving conflict as well as deficit problems are appropriate in the overall understanding of the picture. It becomes a matter of tact and timing as well as clinical judgment as to when and with what emphasis interpretations and explanations should be given.

Another line of criticism of the case of Mr. Z. is illustrated by Mitchell (1981), who claims that Kohut's point of view has shifted to an interpersonal theory in which his formulations are couched in terms of narcissism and his clinical discussions reflect the relations between the child and parental figures. The report of Mr. Z. shows strikingly "the absence of the parents as real people in the first analysis," whereas in the second analysis "the patient is seen within a network of relationships" (pp. 320–321).

A similar view is presented by Kainer (1984), who argues that the shift from the traditional analytic attitude of evenly hovering attention to Kohut's vicarious introspection moves from conflict centered on one's internal instinctual environment to "conflict around satisfying or regulating one's 'external', i.e., empathic, object-related environment" (p. 110). Kainer's argument is based on Kohut's emphasis on the vertical split in the case of Mr. Z. (disavowal) in which Mr. Z. shifts between his arrogance (based on his mother's overvaluation of him as long as he remains merged with her) on the one hand, and his low self-esteem, depression, masochism, and defensive idealization of his mother on the other. Emphasis moves from the unconscious and the id and toward a study of disavowal rather than repression. Simultaneously, the etiological emphasis shifts from the intrapsychic to the interpersonal.

A more extreme complaint is entered by Robbins (1982), who concludes that self psychology is not linked with the body of psychoanalytic metapsychology: "The disjunction is so significant that one must almost choose between a self-psychologist and a more traditionally rooted psychoanalyst" (p. 459). Robbins argues that Kohut's case of Mr. Z. indicates that his conceptualization of Mr. Z.'s pathology is at variance with his own theory of developmental arrest. He attempts to reinterpret the data and Kohut's diagrams of the vertical and horizontal splits in the paper as better supporting a formulation of the narcissistic personality disturbance proposed by Robbins. This goes back to the constant difficulty inherent in interpreting and reinterpreting reported analytic case material.

The issue of the two analyses of Mr. Z. as constituting one analysis is broached again by Wallerstein (Lichtenberg and Kaplan 1983) in a discussion similar to his earlier paper. Wallerstein takes Rangell's (1981) claim quoted above in a constructive fashion but Ornstein (Lichtenberg and Kaplan 1983) finds this quotation "an inexplicable claim." He writes, "How the conception of the mobilization and working through of the selfobject transferences can be both Kohut's significant addition to classical analysis (Wallerstein) and simultaneously be considered an integral part of a total classical analysis (Rangell) is beyond my comprehension" (p. 380).

## Kohut's Reply to Critics

Kohut (Lichtenberg and Kaplan 1983, pp. 408–415) reiterates the discussion of Mr. Z. to support his claim that he was guided by a different theory during the second analysis, and that this different theory allowed him to see Mr. Z.'s personality disorder from a vantage point that was closer to the psychological truth. The clearest example of this is in the interpretation of Mr. Z.'s dream of his father's return, which occurred near the end of the first analysis and was spontaneously remembered by the patient and reanalyzed from a new point of view during a similar time in the second analysis.

Kohut does not like to view this shift in theory as the creation of a new paradigm and here he agrees with Ferguson's (1981) paper. The importance of the theory change that took place between the two analyses of Mr. Z. is best described as a change which carried greater explanatory power and scope. This is different than the well-known paradigm shifts described by Kuhn (1962). Kohut concludes, "In the first analysis my attention had been focused almost exclusively on the scrutiny of psychological macrostructures (i.e., on Mr. Z.'s conflicts), whereas in the second analysis the theory changes that had taken place during the interval between the analyses guided me toward the examination of microstructures (i.e., to the condition of Mr. Z.'s self)" (p. 415).

Kohut (1984) returns to the case of Mr. Z., emphasizing the change in the atmosphere that prevailed in the two analyses. He divides the comments of others on the case into two classes: the comments of an inimical group of colleagues who claim that the first analysis was conducted poorly or that Kohut was the victim of countertransference, and the comments of a friendly group of colleagues who are essentially made uncomfortable by the suggestion that self-psychologists have somehow a greater humaneness in their approach to patients, as allegedly demonstrated by comparing the two analyses of Mr. Z. Kohut rejects the poor technique criticism, the countertransference criticism, and the "propaganda" criticism.

Kohut believes that his technique in the first analysis was traditional and acceptable although he admits that perhaps some intuitively gifted analysts may have approached Mr. Z. more in the method of the second analysis. He claims that traditional analysts would not have recognized the correct interpretation of the self-state dream that arose in both analyses, and would have been more inclined to analyze the dream as Kohut did in the first analysis. A shift to the theory of the psychology of the self was first necessary. A shift from a focus on faulty psychic functioning to a focus on the faulty structures responsible for the faulty functioning was required before a shift in listening and interpretive technique was possible that enabled the eventual understanding of the patient's psychopathological merger with the mother.

Kohut admits to a certain irritability with Mr. Z. in the first analysis. He suggests that his irritability was based on his dim recognition that he was coming forward with a decisive shift in emphasis for the theory and practice of psychoanalysis. He writes:

> Can I really blame myself for not having overcome a countertransference to Mr. Z.? Or should I not rather affirm that the countertransference involved was directed at having to make a scientific step that, as I dimly realized, would arouse strong controversy among my colleagues and require the mobilization of all my intellectual and emotional resources for the rest of my life? (p. 89)

He adds that the clinical picture of Mr. Z.'s first analysis was consistent with what the traditional orientation would lead an analyst to expect from a neurosis in which the Oedipus complex forms the center of the illness, and that many other analysts would have reacted with the same firmness that characterized Kohut's stance toward Mr. Z. in the later phases of the first analysis.

He concludes the discussion of the case of Mr. Z. by insisting that self psychology results in an attitude and an atmosphere in the treatment that differs from the treatment situation that tends to prevail as long as the analyst sees narcissism as part of a defensive structure, and drive manifestations — especially the patient's rage — as primary rather than reactive phenomena to empathic failures. The most important lesson to be learned from the two analyses of Mr. Z. is how the analyst's apprehension of the selfobject transferences affects the handling of clinical material through expanded empathy.

## APPLICATION TO PSYCHOTHERAPY

The psychotherapist who is looking for case vignettes from Kohut that show how to practice *psychotherapy* will be disappointed. We sometimes forget that Kohut's writing is that of an experienced psychoanalyst and written for psychoanalysts. The case of Mr. Z. is intended as the presentation of two psychoanalyses; because of this, however, Basch (1981) points out that it can be used as a paradigmatic case to distinguish between psychoanalysis and psychotherapy in general, as well as to delineate psychotherapy derived from psychoanalytic insights. One is doing psychoanalysis if:

> The patient's cure or improvement depends primarily on his pathology being brought into the transference to the analyst, interpreted so as to enhance the patient's understanding of himself and worked through to the point where the formerly malfunctioning structures have been restored or the defective structures strengthened to such an extent that the patient is capable of leading a productive life. (p. 345)

From Basch's point of view, it is not necessary to add any parameters in the psychoanalytic treatment of narcissistic personality disorders, although surely some would argue that Kohut's "reluctant compliance" is a parameter. The old-fashioned intuitive attempt to get the patient to "grow up" through the use of pressure, persuasion, or other extra-analytic maneuvers — a hint of which is shown in the first analysis of Mr. Z. — is no longer necessary.

For Basch, Kohut's clinical discovery of the selfobject transferences allows us to conduct psychoanalytic treatment in the same fashion as the analysis of psychoneurotic patients: fostering the patient's associations, avoiding premature closure, depending on the unconscious to provide the material, proper and appropriate interpretations, and engaging the patient in the working through process until insight is demonstrably achieved. Attempts to mirror the narcissistic patient or offer oneself as a potential ideal are no more psychoanalytic than attempting to seduce a hysterical patient. This is consistent with Kohut's contention that the psychology of the self is firmly rooted in traditional psychoanalysis and is not meant to be a rival or competing paradigm. Kohut aphoristically explains (Meyers 1981) that classic analysis discovered the despair of the child in the depth of the adult, "while self psychology discovered the despair of the adult in the depth of the child" (p. 158), mourning a not-to-be lived, unfulfilled future consequent to a damaged nuclear self.

# Chapter 13

―

# Cases Presented by Kohut's Followers

During his lifetime Kohut's followers began making changes in Kohut's conceptions of certain psychiatric diagnoses and of psychoanalytic psychotherapy. In some instances these changes were an improvement, but in others they made the psychology of the self more ambiguous and difficult to understand.

## "The Casebook" – Gedo's Criticism

An important collection of case presentations by Kohut's followers — young analysts who worked under his supervision — comprises the *Psychology of the Self: A Casebook* (Goldberg 1978). This collection is examined by Gedo (1980), a psychoanalyst from the same institute as Kohut who differs from Kohut in several important respects. Gedo reports, "We have witnessed the formation of hostile ideological camps engaging in global condemnation of or cultish enthusiasm for Kohut's 'system'" (pp. 363–364). Gedo asks to what extent the case reports can be used to support or refute the hypotheses of the psychology of the self.

Gedo believes that the cases make possible an operational definition of fragmentation of the self in the broader sense of the term. The use of the self as a supraordinate psychological organization rather than as the representation of a concrete person appears prior to Kohut in other works cited by Gedo. He believes that the clinical material of the casebook is organized according to Kohut's hypotheses and is therefore unsuitable for testing them. However, Gedo underemphasizes the significance of a quotation from the casebook: "I was unable to 'hear' the significance of what the patient was saying until I had the conceptual assistance of a new analytic discovery" (p. 203). This acknowledgment from one of the analysts in the casebook is analogous to the point of Kohut's (1979) report on Mr. Z. and separates the psychoanalytic psychology of the self from numerous other theoretical orientations which are unlike those of Freud.

Kohut's followers contend that immersion in the psychology of the self enables the therapist to find significant themes in patient material that could not be noted without the assistance of Kohut's psychology of the self. The sudden coherence of hitherto apparently irrational material often causes the psychology of the self to have a dramatic impact even on an experienced psychotherapist. Gedo's argument that at least half of the case reports could be criticized as being "flawed as models for the natural unfolding of the analytic transference" (p. 371) is reasonable; he reminds us that only the cases of Mr. E. and Mrs. R. were essentially complete "and beyond reasonable criticism in terms of technique" (p. 371).

Gedo questions whether repair of a developmental deficit occurs through transmuting internalization. More seriously, he argues with Goldberg that the "Goldberg casebook does not confirm his claim that 'the activity of the analyst is *interpretation*' (p. 9)" (p. 379). Gedo and others have criticized the tendency of Kohut and his followers to explain perverse behavior as the eroticization of other psychological needs or wishes. For example, it is not clear to Gedo (p. 381) why a fantasy of incorporating masculine power through fellatio should be sexually exciting as in the case reported by Kohut (1977, p. 201).

The final criticism concerns Kohut's view of empathy, which the authors in the casebook now regard not only as a tool of observation but as an agent of healing. Gedo calls this an "idiosyncratic view of empathy as a quality of *behavior* that should characterize the conduct of the analyst" (pp. 381–382).

## *"The Casebook" Reviewed*

The casebook was written in response to a persistent request from many clinicians for more clinical data, and Kohut's followers have been energetic and dedicated to producing material for study. None of the six cases are thought to be borderline in Kohut's sense of the definition. The introduction states that a group of psychoanalysts met, discussed this material, and that "there was, rather, a general impression that each of the patients had benefited enormously and that the classical clinical theory of psychoanalysis had little to offer in understanding these changes" (p. 3). A general idea of the goal of treatment is given:

> Results of successful working-through are indicated by an accretion of drive-controlling and drive-channeling structures, by idealization of the superego through diminution of the idealizing transference, and by integration of the grandiose fantasies into reasonable ambitions and purposes. (p. 8)

Unfolding narcissistic transferences are not viewed as defenses against the unfolding of object-instinctual transferences, i.e., not as "defense-transferences" (p. 14), but as indications of the beginning mobilization of archaic narcissistic configurations, which must be allowed to move into and occupy the center stage of the analysis. For example (p. 115), Mr. I. attached himself to the analyst with an intense, addictionlike quality because he had serious difficulty in maintaining his own narcissistic equilibrium. Either there was too much inner tension with a feeling of overstimulation requiring immediate, frantic, and uncontrollable discharge or too little of it, reflected by a feeling of emptiness that required immediate and frantic self-stimulation. This is also a typical and instructive situation among cases in intensive psychotherapy.

The case of Mr. M. described by Kohut (1977) is given in detail in the casebook. Here, there seems to be an answer to Gedo's complaint that there is no explanation of the erotization in perversions if they are thought of as the expression of other needs:

> In childhood, as well as in later life, perverse fantasies and activities appear to serve the defensive function of turning a painful affect that was

passively endured in childhood through erotization into a sense of active mastery. While the sexual context affords the sense of mastery over the painful affect, it also provides a discharge channel for narcissistic tensions whether these were aroused from frustration or from overstimulation. (p. 136)

In the casebook there is little theoretical discussion of Kohut's idea that the sexual drives represent disintegration products of a fragmenting self after empathic failure. The casebook appeared not long after *The Restoration of the Self* and is written more along the lines of the "psychology of the self in the narrow sense."

A common clinical problem reported (p. 157) in the case of Mr. M. appears behind the disintegration of many marriages. Mr. M. was unable to be empathic with his wife who was an aspiring artist, and he could not give her the encouragement she needed. In a woman's attempt to achieve liberation, a career, and a healthy self of her own, the functioning of the husband as a reciprocal selfobject is vital. In the case of Mr. M., he was too needy to have known what she needed from him and from their marriage, and so, the marriage failed. Kohut's (1984) emphasis on the importance of reciprocal mutual selfobject functioning and empathy in a marriage is valuable in understanding the apparent tragic disintegration of many marriages as the needs of the partners change.

Chapter 4 of the casebook presents a difficult patient (Mrs. Apple) who might well be thought of as borderline from the standard DSM-III diagnostic point of view. Mrs. Apple had been treated by a dedicated woman analyst. The case almost stalemated with the patient in a tremendous rage, but the analyst approached Kohut in an informal discussion, and attended his seminar. She was able to examine the patient's material in a new way.

Mrs. Apple's analyst mentions three possibilities which could explain the painful analytic situation: the patient's insistence on direct cure does not represent "resistance" to the reexposure of childhood rage toward the oedipal and preoedipal mother but involves instead the analyst experienced as an archaic selfobject; when the selfobject analyst is uncertain about the nature of the original disorder and the transference, the analyst is experienced by the patient as the self-absorbed mother who spitefully refuses to respond to her, with all the rage and disappointment that entails in the patient; and the bombardment by the patient's narcissistic rage evokes an emotional withdrawal on the part of the analyst which further exacerbates the rage in a vicious cycle. Thus the return of childhood structural conflicts is not at the center of these disorders. The insistent demands are part of a mirror transference which, when misunderstood, represents another chronic exposure to an apparently unavailable and unwilling selfobject, with the expectable consequence of narcissistic rage in the patient. The analyst reports (p. 231) that, when reconstructions were made on the basis of this approach, there was a dramatic alteration of the patient's mood and state; this apparent "calming down" after an explanation of what is perceived by the patient as empathic failure is a common clinical finding.

The report on Mrs. R. in Chapter 6 is an example of how a small item in the treatment can be blown up into a major stumbling block because it condenses into one complaint the patient's disappointment in a number of minor empathic failures by the selfobject analyst. The patient could not accept the analyst's insistence on calling her Mrs. R. rather than by her first name. In his long discussion we can sense that this sensitive analyst struggled about what should have been done. At the time he decided not to call her by her first name, but now he apologizes, for it is possible that by doing so he might have avoided an iatrogenic regression.

This is an example of Kohut's "reluctant compliance," which the analyst tries to distinguish from a parameter in Eissler's (1953) sense of the term and from the traditional emphasis on the "barrier" (Tarachow 1963) that is presumably required between analyst and patient. The dispute is over whether "reluctant compliance" represents a "collusion" (Langs 1982) that avoids the rage or whether the lack of it represents an unempathic response to the patient. This is one of the more difficult clinical judgments every therapist has to make. The decision is affected by acceptance or rejection of self psychology and by the countertransference implications.

The problem of *mea culpa* also arises in this case and illustrates the danger of the possible misuse of self psychology to blame all the problems of the patient on failures in the therapist. The analyst did not telephone the patient from an international trip and display a hoped-for magical knowledge of when the patient's child was born. The analyst felt, however, that he should have made a "special effort" to contact the patient close to her expected delivery date, "not simply as a compliance to regressively distorted demands, but as a concrete, needed acknowledgment of, and the providing of, an ap-

propriate analytic atmosphere for her massively intensified needs"
(p. 341). This attitude can lead to dangerous acting out on the part
of the analyst and an infantilization of the patient; I (1983b) have
given an example of this problem in my discussion of Greenson's
psychoanalytic therapy with Marilyn Monroe. There is much room
to argue about what constitutes the proper analytic atmosphere. In
this instance the patient made substantial gains from serious pathology; it is also clear in all the cases presented that the analysts were
caring and dedicated.

The final case is probably the most controversial, to the point of
whether it constitutes an analysis. The therapist did some active mirroring in complying with the patient's request to view his new car
(a used jeep): "I admired it, and he was pleased" (p. 387). A great
deal of this sort of mirroring occurs in the privacy of the consulting
room and not much of it is reported in the literature. The author of
this case reports such incidents with great candor. She lends the
patient money (p. 399) twice, although she does so reluctantly the
second time (p. 404). In many ways this case history employs a psychoanalytic technique almost diametrically opposed to the recommendations of Langs (1981, 1982), which limit the activity of the
analyst strictly to interpretations.

This case report provides an opportunity to study whether self-
psychology offers the patient a "corrective emotional experience"or
a genuine analysis. At best the analysis was incomplete, but more
mature transference wishes and attitudes did appear, indicating a
significant gain in self-cohesion. However, this gain could have come
about by either an analysis or a corrective emotional experience. One
will have to decide whether the extent of the gain is best explained
by transmuting internalizations and the consequent formation of compensatory structures or whether the improvement in self-cohesion occurred primarily through a corrective emotional experience supplied
by the therapist.

An additional argument about the perversions is offered in the
conclusion to the casebook, where these eroticized behaviors were
found to be precipitated by the vicissitudes of relationships involving narcissistic transferences and disappointments in demanded selfobject experiences. These narcissistic transferences were not difficult
to discern and disruption of them most commonly appeared in the
psychoanalysis through disconcerting symptoms on weekends, which
would be much harder to detect in less frequent psychotherapy.

The cases were conducted under Kohut's supervision: "Now, having an enlarged schema for understanding what patients are saying, the analyst's potential for narcissistic injury is not stirred up nearly as readily" (pp. 444–445). Clinicians attempting to evaluate the psychology of the self should keep this in mind to see whether they have similar experiences in better understanding difficult or unreasonable patients. None of this clinical material demonstrates the scientific validity of the hypotheses of the psychology of the self.

## Borderline States Viewed by Self Psychologists

A more extreme use of the psychology of the self can be found in reports by the followers of Kohut who have attempted to modify his rather pessimistic view on the borderline states defined as "permanent or protracted breakup, enfeeblement, or serious distortion of the self, which is covered by more or less effective defensive structures" (Kohut 1977, p. 192). This seems to represent a long-term condition and to relate the borderline state to the paranoid and the schizoid personalities, who are attempting by defensive organizations employing distancing to prevent a similar permanent or protracted breakup, enfeeblement, or serious distortion of the self.

Tolpin (Goldberg 1980) discusses the "makeup and analyzability" of the borderline patient. According to Tolpin, Kohut maintains that, although borderline patients are able to establish varying degrees of rapport with the analyst, the core sector of the self does not enter into transference amalgamations with the image of the analyst. Therefore, no stable selfobject transferences can form. These archaic transferences are not allowed to develop because of the patient's fearful anticipation of a massive disruption. Without such in-depth transferences, proper transmuting internalizations cannot effect any basic change in the self.

For Kohut the borderline disturbance is always marked by a potential for protracted disturbance of the cohesiveness of the self, whereas the narcissistic personality disorder shows only a transient disturbance, a temporary breakup, enfeeblement, or distortion of the self at times of serious experienced selfobject failure. In the psychotic patient, there are not even the organized defensive capabilities of the borderline person. However, in some psychotic individuals, such as the paranoid patient, cohesively organized sectors of the personality may parallel the core psychotic organization. An apparently normal social facade can even be maintained. This explains the clinical confusion between patients with a manifestly psychotic core and patients with a borderline personality who have more effective defensive structures, but are more overtly disruptive.

The argument about the treatment of the final case in the casebook rests on the issue of whether a workable in-depth transference or series of transferences actually developed in the treatment. If so, one may say that the patient underwent at least a partial psychoanalysis. If not, the explanation of the patient's marked improvement would have to be explained by Tolpin's (Goldberg 1980) statement:

> Nonetheless, a meaningful rapport with the therapist may be fostered in relation to nonpsychotic personality sectors through the use of a variety of ingenious psychotherapeutic strategies, and these efforts will result in consequent strengthening and greater dominance of these nonpsychotic personality sectors. (p. 304)

## Tolpin's Classification

Tolpin makes an effort within the self-psychology framework to bridge the gap between "unanalyzable" borderline disorders and "analyzable" narcissistic disorders. He suggests that there is a group of borderline disorders which form "the 'border' of the true borderline personality" (p. 306) — the "border" borderline personalities. Somehow "despite the more blatant social maladjustments that may occur, the individual in this group has a self that is better organized than the self of the true borderline patient" (p. 307). Some members of this group develop massive, almost unmanageable, sometimes highly eroticized merger transferences (Chessick 1974b). As Tolpin says, such transferences "may severely tax the understanding, equanimity, and effectiveness of the therapist" (p. 307).

Tolpin suggests a spectrum concept based on the quality of the structure of the self, ranging from the healthy to the near-psychotic personality organization. The spectrum concept dictates that various disorders cannot be differentiated from a brief examination. Criteria for the diagnosis of disorders do not necessarily lie in behavior, symptoms, or the form of the disease — its manifest content or its social severity. Instead, diagnosis arises out of a prolonged evaluation or test of treatment which gives sufficient time for the development of adequate transference clues. In these cases the personality and empathic limitations of the therapist play a significant role in the assessment of the patient's primary core disturbance: "The assessment is at least in part based on the interaction of two participants in an extended diagnostic or treatment process. It is a process that operates within a two-party system and the therapist may be as important a variable as the patient" (p. 308).

Tolpin gives an important clue: "The essence of a core psychotic personality organization," whether defended against, as in the true borderline patient, or not, as in the psychotic patient, lies in the "extremely limited viability of positively toned primary selfobject experiences" (p. 311). For a nonpsychotic personality organization, including Tolpin's "border" borderline patients, there have to have been some viable, self-nourishing, attuned selfobject experiences from infancy and childhood to provide a beginning for therapeutic rehabilitation of these severe disorders of the self. This allows the formation of what Kohut (1984, p. 206) calls a "pivotal" selfobject transference, based on the least traumatic childhood selfobject experiences, that can lead in treatment to the strengthening of crucial compensatory areas of the self. In taking a history one searches for memories and patterns of experiences involving significant adults who were entrusted with the care of the infant and young child. Sometimes a maid or a grandparent has provided the crucial spark in the otherwise dark ambience of the patient's childhood.

However, we can be easily misled by taking a history; for this reason I (1974) suggest that all patients be given a trial of intensive uncovering psychotherapy when there is any possibility that they may benefit from it. This is preferable to flatly rejecting the use of this procedure on the basis of a DSM-III clinical diagnosis. Tolpin emphasizes the perseverance of the therapist and the empathy and sensitivity of the therapist; the less we understand a patient, the more we are prone to call the patient borderline. The talents and the empathy of the analyst are crucial. With such patients, vitality-producing empathic responses are desperately needed, sometimes for a very long time. Kohut (1984, pp. 182–184) makes the same point, referring to the concept of borderline pathology as relative, often depending on the analyst's ability to retain empathy despite repeated narcissistic wounding by the patient and to enable the patient, through the understanding of the patient's experiences, "to reassemble his or her self sufficiently with the aid of the selfobject transference to make possible the gradual exploration of the dynamic and genetic causes of the underlying vulnerability" (p. 184).

The unresolved theoretical and clinical questions revolve around whether borderline patients can be helped to develop a cohesive self — at least sufficiently cohesive to form relatively stable selfobject transferences — and to what extent this is a function of the personal style, empathic capacities, and sensitivities of the therapist. My own clinical experience supports Tolpin's approach. A point of view firmly based on self psychology, which is also corroborated by the clinical experience of intuitive investigators who practiced before the codification of self psychology, constitutes further evidence for the validity or clinical efficacy of the psychology of the self. Many clinicians, on first acquaintance with Kohut's views, may have an "a-ha!" experience when they are thus given some theoretical understanding for what intuitive therapists already have been doing for some time. Traditional psychoanalysts would retort that what is new in self psychology is not good and what is good is not new.

TOLPIN'S CASE REPORT

In a subsequent publication, Tolpin (1983) presents a detailed case of what might be called a pseudo-oedipal neurosis treated from the point of view of self psychology. The patient, a divorced woman in her early forties, sought treatment for recurrent depressive states, insomnia, overuse of sleeping medication, and occasional kleptomania. Her biggest problem, however, was a love affair with an older man who could not bring himself to marry her. On the surface the case appeared to be that of a histrionic personality disorder, but these symptoms, argues Tolpin, actually covered primary deficits in the patient's self and defended her against reexperiencing the effects of the disappointment in her early childhood selfobject needs. In the dream material and in the use of Beethoven's Quartet, Opus 130,*

---

*"She wore out two records of Opus 130. She put it on tape so it would always be available" (p. 471). I had a similar patient who used Wagner's entire *Ring of the Niebelung* (see Chessick 1983c for discussion of preoedipal elements of the *Ring*) for this purpose, playing it constantly and collecting every available recording — to the agonizing dismay of his roommates! For a related but failed experience, see the novel *An Evening of Brahms* (Sennett 1984).

the patient made a gradual substitution in which she internalized the idealized analyst. This resulted in an increased concept of her own self-worth and repaired a deficit in the self so that the patient no longer needed an outside idealized figure in order to maintain her self-esteem.

Self psychology enabled Tolpin to recognize the patient's primary needs and to define these to her so that the elaborate histrionic symptomatology which defended her — what Tolpin calls "a complex and overdetermined defensive facade" (p. 480) — could be reduced via "the development and transformation of an idealizing transference" (p. 480). The clinical material depicts this development and transformation which were dominant in the treatment, although a variety of mirror transferences also appeared.

## Brandchaft and Stolorow on Borderline States

Brandchaft and Stolorow (Lichtenberg, Bornstein, and Silver 1984a) carry this discussion of the borderline state further. They reject the idea that "borderline" refers to a discrete pathological character structure. DSM-III recognizes it as a diagnostic entity stressing impulsivity, intense unstable relationships, inappropriate anger, and mood swings, with additional reference to their physically self-damaging behavior, complaints of emptiness or boredom, and intolerance of being alone. Kernberg (1975) suggests that the borderline personality organization has a specific structure with splitting as the major defense. He carefully differentiates psychotic patients from borderline patients on the basis of their capacity for reality testing; in borderline patients, reality testing is seen as intact and only transiently blurred when the patient is under severe stress.

Utilizing the psychology of the self, Brandchaft and Stolorow have not suggested that the term "borderline" refers to an entirely iatrogenic illness, but rather that the patient's manifest psychopathology which leads to the diagnosis "is always *codetermined* by the patient's self disorder *and* the therapist's ability to understand it" (p. 367). They claim therefore (in direct opposition to Kernberg) that the concept of borderline personality organization is invalid and that borderline character structure is not rooted in any pathognomonic conflicts or defenses. To insist that "borderline personality organization" denotes a specific type of characterologic organization represents a misunderstanding on the part of therapists and "the difficulty therapists have in comprehending the archaic intersubjective contexts in which borderline pathology arises" (pp. 367–368).

Clinically, minor empathic failures of the selfobject therapist as they are subjectively experienced by the patient — *not* to be used as an objective index of the therapist's technical competence — are crucial to the production of borderline symptomatology. These empathic failures are experienced within the psychic reality of the patient from the archaic frame of reference created by the selfobject transference. When the patient's intrapsychic experiences and convictions come from a subjective point of view of the empathic failure of the therapist and are chronically unrecognized, DSM-III borderline phenomena displayed by the patient become chronic. The patient is then labeled a borderline personality disorder.

These authors also warn therapists against blaming themselves for psychopathological symptomatology that may appear in the treatment. In focusing on the empathic failures of the therapist as they are experienced by the patient, there is a tendency among followers of self psychology to ignore that this occurs in the context of an archaic selfobject transference which is bound to produce disappointments in the selfobject. Kohut (1984) maintained that, if there is a reasonableness in the ambience of the treatment and the therapist has the capacity to recognize that the therapist has been experienced as producing an empathic failure and communicates this recognition to the patient, a situation arises which produces "optimal frustration." By transmuting internalization patients can gradually learn to do for themselves what they want the therapist to do for them in the selfobject transference. A misunderstanding of this is a common beginner's mistake in the application of the psychology of the self and leads easily to much unnecessary self-castigation.

Brandchaft and Stolorow point out that when the needs of the "borderline" patient are not

> recognized, responded to, or interpreted empathically, violent negative reactions may ensue. If these angry reactions are presumed to represent a defensive dissociation of good and bad aspects of objects, this in effect constitutes a covert demand that the patient ignore his own subjective experiences and appreciate the "goodness" of the analyst and his interpretations. It precludes analysis of the patient's subjective experience in depth. (p. 335)

By reverting to concepts of projection and projective identification, the therapist deprives patients of a way of marking those instances where they feel the therapist is being cruel, distant, controlling, or demeaning. (Explanations utilizing projection and projective identification encourage the assumption of the analyst's goodness and correctness.) This can actually lead to a dangerous double-bind situation that resembles patients' experiences with parents.

Following Tolpin, these authors agree that at least in some borderline personalities it is possible for the patient to eventually form stable and analyzable selfobject transferences although it is true that these are more primitive and intense, more labile and vulnerable to disruption, and much harder on the therapist. But these patients do not, if properly understood, develop severe chronic protracted break-ups of the self, because patients often will leave treatment before allowing such a break-up to occur (Chessick 1977, 1983a).

The borderline symptomatology is increased when there is a misunderstanding of what has exacerbated it, but I think Brandchaft and Stolorow are too sanguine in their hope that many borderline patients could eventually be analyzed. Kohut is quoted (p. 344) as telling them that to whatever extent the therapist is able to build an empathic bridge to the patient, the patient is no longer a borderline case but is now one of a severe narcissistic personality disorder. Borderline personality organization is not seen by self-psychologists as representing a fixed entity with characteristic defenses such as splitting, but as a fluid situation within an intersubjective field. An example of this is the case of "Carolyn" presented by Brandchaft and Stolorow (in Lichtenberg et al. 1984a).

In another publication (Stepansky and Goldberg 1984), Brandchaft and Stolorow offer more clinical material from the standpoint of the psychology of the self. They argue that the selfobject theory of development "is a contemporary theory of object relations. It concerns the most archaic relationships to objects experienced as part of the self, merged with the self, or in the service of the self" (p. 108). This should be differentiated from the object-relations theories based on the work of Melanie Klein and carried forward by many other authors such as Kernberg. Here Brandchaft and Stolorow contend that the excessive pregenital aggression of borderline patients is "the inevitable, unwitting consequence of a therapeutic approach which insists that certain arrested archaic needs and the archaic states of mind associated with them are in their essence pathological defenses against dependency on or hostility toward the analyst" (p. 113). For them the appearance of such aggression in the treatment represents a reaction to further narcissistic wounding due to a misunderstanding or misconstruction by the analyst. These self-psychologists emphasize the importance of analyzing innumerable and inevitable episodes of frustration and disappointment experienced by the patient as a failure on the part of the selfobject analyst to fulfill a particular archaic wish or need.

As Kohut (1984) points out, a long period of simply understanding and communicating this understanding may be necessary before any form of deeper or genetic interpretation or explanation will have much of an effect. Patients with severe self-pathology must receive from the analyst the repeated experience of being understood many times over before they are able to remain sufficiently stable in the transference situation to utilize explanations and interpretations. In my experience (1982, 1983a) it *is* possible over long periods of time with some borderline patients for such a gradual improvement in self-cohesion to occur. Much depends on the dedication of the therapist to the individual patient and the therapist's empathic capacities and willingness to endure a very long and difficult treatment.

A factor that has not received sufficient explicit consideration in the literature, but which shows itself strikingly in the case material of the followers of Kohut, is the vigorous and persistently tenacious dedication to these disturbed patients that appears in all the case material. As the therapist in Chapter 6 of the casebook writes:

> She experienced me as someone who would vigorously persist in an emotional involvement with her despite her tendency to detachment and retreat to quiet, defensive grandiosity or affective isolation. And as someone who would honestly recognize and respond to her growing sense of important inner value. All this effected a firming of her sense of well-being. (Goldberg 1978, p. 327)

It is hard to ignore the implication that this powerful investment in the patient has an important corrective experience similar to the early cases treated by Freud, whose dedication to his patients and personal integrity form the model for us all (Chessick 1980).

# Chapter 14

Psychology of the Self in
Psychoanalytic Psychotherapy

In order to follow the psychology of the self we must keep in mind
one goal of treatment described by Kohut (1977): to help the patient strengthen compensatory psychological structures, enabling the
patient to become active and creative, and to work toward meaningful goals. Throughout his work Kohut places heavy stress on creativity. For some patients, creative life must take precedence even
over relationships. Evidence of success appears in the patient's report
of a sense of feeling alive, real, and worthwhile, so that "these attitudes and activities give me a sufficient amount of joy to make life
worth living; they prevent the feeling of emptiness and depression"
(p. 17).

Psychoanalytic psychotherapy and psychoanalysis can open an
avenue to productive activity that permits this joyful self-realization.
In Kohut's terms, "These activities could now be carried out effectively because the analysis had established a more firmly functioning structure of idealized goals, which served as organizers for the
archaic ambitions of the revitalized grandiose self. And the analysis
had also led to the strengthening and refinement of the already existing executive apparatus" (p. 53). These essential transformations,
according to the psychology of the self, do not result from intellec-

tual insights or cognitive understanding, but come through transmuting internalizations brought about "by the fact that the old experiences are repeatedly relived by the more mature psyche" (p. 30). In healing disorders of the self, the therapist as an empathic and modulating selfobject is the key to the patient's self-regulation despite optimal frustration and through transmuting internalizations.

## Psychoanalysis and Psychoanalytically Oriented Psychotherapy Compared

What it means for a patient to be "not suitable" for psychoanalysis takes on a new meaning in self psychology. In ordinary practice when a patient is called "not suitable for psychoanalysis," the recommendation for psychoanalytically oriented psychotherapy is often made. The treatment procedure is now shifted to a less understood process with more idiosyncratic variations from one clinician to another and requiring the introduction of "parameters." This is called by some authors intensive psychotherapy, by others psychoanalytic psychotherapy or (Kohut) psychoanalytically oriented psychotherapy. I shall use these terms interchangeably, depending on the authors under discussion.

An effort is made in psychoanalytically oriented psychotherapy to approach some of those goals that we might expect from a successful psychoanalysis, but these are selective, and therapeutic ambition is limited carefully. For various reasons, the patient may be seen less frequently. The therapist is more active and may even introduce questions and advice, thus "contaminating" the transference or diluting it, and leaving the procedure open to the charge that it relies more on suggestion or education.

Whether self psychology oriented psychoanalysis is a form of psychoanalytically oriented psychotherapy or is a genuine psychoanalysis remains unanswered and is dependent upon the definition of "psychoanalysis." The distinction between psychoanalytic psychotherapy and psychoanalysis is extremely controversial, as a recent International Psycho-Analytical Association monograph (Joseph and Wallerstein 1982) demonstrates. Wallerstein concludes, "We seem not one bit closer to consensus on this question today than we were exactly a decade ago" (p. 122).

In psychoanalytically oriented psychotherapy, if no transference neurosis has formed and been worked through, it would be difficult to call the procedure a psychoanalysis, regardless of the frequency of the sessions. The most conservative traditional psychoanalysts argue that psychoanalysis conducted from the standpoint of self psychology is not a genuine psychoanalysis. They find it offensive for self psychologists to imply that the ambience of traditional psychoanalysis is any less pleasant or empathic than what they have to offer. Self-psychology, they say, is essentially unnecessary and simply repeats knowledge gathered from clinical experience by traditional analysts. Some would add that psychoanalytic self-psychology and all psychoanalytically oriented psychotherapy is only psychoanalysis conducted by an untrained analyst.

Kohut is more charitable toward psychoanalytically oriented psychotherapy. He attempts to make a distinction between psychoanalysis proper and psychoanalytically oriented psychotherapy, using a crucial geometric metaphor. He (Goldberg 1980, p. 532) argues that psychoanalysis proper "aims at bringing about changes in a *sector* of the self" of patients who are suffering from self-pathology disorders, while psychoanalytically oriented psychotherapy "aims at bringing about changes in a *segment* of the self." He attempts to show that psychoanalysis affects the "depth of the psyche" while other forms of therapy only touch the surface. Thus he apparently means that a "sector" of the self reaches into the depth of the psyche, while a "segment" of the self is more superficial, or that sectorial changes in the self are attempted by psychoanalysis and are efforts to affect the depth of the psyche, whereas segmental changes are superficial and more likely produced by psychoanalytically oriented psychotherapy.

Like the "vertical" and "horizontal" splits (Kohut 1971), this is specious use of geometry.* A careful study of the meanings of "sector" and "segment" in the *Oxford English Dictionary* (1970) and the *Webster's New International Dictionary* (1961) does not support this differentiation either in the use of the terms in geometry or in other

---

*I am criticizing the terminology here, not the concepts expressed by these geometric metaphors. My interpretation of Kohut's metaphor given here is supported by his contrast in another place (Kohut 1977, p. 251) between a "sector" of the psyche and a "layer" of the psyche. Later (1984, p. 49), he refers to "sectorial" as "experience in depth."

areas of discourse. To understand his concepts it is important to remember that Kohut is defining "sector" as depth and "segment" as surface layer.

In the discussion from Goldberg (1980), Kohut concentrates on the working-through process following the selfobject transference. The process is more extended in psychoanalysis, and leads gradually to the relinquishment of the archaic selfobject with a consequent internal strengthening of the poles of the self, as well as the functions and skills on the gradient between them. In psychoanalytically oriented psychotherapy the transference interpretations are thought by Kohut to be less thorough and kept to a minimum, and they attempt to enable the patient to shift from the selfobject analyst to other selfobject figures "and to diminish his sensitivities sufficiently to enable him to make use of the selfobject support that he can obtain from appropriate people in his surroundings without immediate withdrawal from them when they disappoint him" (p. 535). This outside selfobject support can also be obtained from various societal institutions such as religions. The selfobject transference is not resolved and the patient, if necessary, feels free to return for a temporary reactivation of this transference when external circumstances have been especially taxing.

Psychoanalytically oriented psychotherapy emphasizes the genetic-*dynamic* while psychoanalysis emphasizes the dynamic-*genetic* in its ultimate aims, says Kohut (p. 536). He also concedes that "these differentiating lines cannot always be drawn sharply" (p. 535).

## A TENTATIVE CLASSIFICATION OF TREATMENT MODALITIES

For didactic purposes and as a rough sketch only, and leaning on Gedo and Goldberg (1973), we can establish a hierarchy of treatment modalities associated with developmental phases as conceived of in traditional psychoanalytic theory, correlated with self psychology. Phase one, from birth to six or eight months of age, represents the time from birth to cognitive self and object differentiation. Primary narcissism reigns supreme. "Primal repression" of Freud (Chessick 1980) is the crucial proto-mechanism of defense, and the primary anxiety is that of annihilation through overstimulation or flooding. Patients who have to regress to this phase experience overwhelming severe traumatic states or psychotic panics. The treatment of these cases is pacification, which represents the control of excitation, controlled catharsis, and, if necessary, the use of medications and hospitalization. The essence of pacification is that of tension reduction and mastery through partial discharge (Gedo and Goldberg 1973, p. 162).

A second phase of life, between eight months and three years, is the phase during which cognitive and affective self and object differentiation progress to allow essentially irreversible cohesion of the nuclear self if this phase is successfully completed. During this phase the grandiose self and the idealized parent imago are utilized to deal with inevitable phase-appropriate disappointments in selfobjects. Separation anxiety is the characteristic anxiety, magic is the kind of reality testing used, and massive projection and introjection are employed. The "bedrock" danger in this phase, from the point of view of self psychology, is the disruption of the newly forming nuclear self. Patients who regress to such a phase present borderline or psychotic disintegration, and the treatment is that of unification. Such patients require external help for a cohesion of the self; we must provide reliable and consistently available selfobjects and settings. An uninterrupted relationship with the therapist is crucial. As the therapist becomes a transitional object in the life of the patient, there occurs what Balint (1968) has called repair of a basic fault. The therapy is a real experience for the patient in which an uninterrupted relationship with a real object experienced as an archaic selfobject occurs. The therapist sometimes must gently intrude as a real object into the life of the patient, but rather than gratification and pacification, it is usually sufficient to establish an uninterrupted relationship.

The third phase of life, from three to six years, spans the time of the newly formed but incomplete cohesive self to the solid formation of the superego. For Freud, narcissism becomes more confined to the phallus, and castration anxiety is typical. Disavowal is at first the mechanism of defense as the repression barrier is still being formed, but the self and object are perceived as whole and different or separate and realistic most of the time. According to Kohut, the narcissistic personality disorders are developmentally fixed in this phase of life. Massive disruption of the self no longer occurs, but the archaic grandiose self and idealized parent imagos have not yet been properly integrated into the nuclear self so there is a tendency to retreat back to these upon narcissistic wounding, which produces the clinical features of the disorder. The treatment for them then is optimal disillusion, "confrontation with reality" (Gedo and Goldberg 1973, p. 164), or perhaps Kohut's kind of psychoanalysis in which stable narcissistic selfobject transferences are allowed to form and are accepted and eventually interpreted. The patient, through transmuting internalizations, is gradually able to give up the narcissistic sense of entitlement. The grandiose self and the idealized parent imago are properly integrated into the personality.

The final phase of childhood, between six to eight years of age and puberty, is the phase of consolidation of the ego and the solid formation of the repression barrier after the superego has been formed. The reality principle becomes prominent. The person, now with a firm sense of self, is guided by the ego ideal and pushed by ambitions. Moral or guilty anxiety is typical, repression occurs as the characteristic basic mechanism of defense, and we have the era of the formation of infantile neuroses of Freud. The treatment of disorders that are represented by regression to this phase is the classical psychoanalytic method. It is based on the structural theory using interpretation of the transference neurosis, in which there is strengthening of the ego, mitigation of the severity of the superego, and small quantities of dammed-up inner energies are discharged. Sublimation capacities are developed and become crucial to future success in adult functioning.

To illustrate the distinction between a therapy of disillusionment and a traditional psychoanalytic treatment, one patient who had collapsed in an earlier traditional psychoanalysis said, "In my previous treatment the child inside the adult was encouraged to diffusely come out but in treatment with you the adult inside the child is *determined* to come out."

Gedo and Goldberg (p. 107) add a fifth phase of life from completion of puberty through adulthood, called the "era of the fully differentiated psychic apparatus." Signal anxiety is typical at this time and narcissism has been transformed into wisdom, empathy, humor, and creativity. Difficulties during this time are hopefully resolved by careful introspection and even self analysis. An outstanding detailed example of this is offered by Calder (1980).

## Some Critical Comments

None of the theories of narcissism are wholly satisfactory, and the above delineation and integration of various points of view is easy to criticize; its value is only as a rule of thumb for clinical work. The first two sections of this book already include some objections to Freud, Fairbairn, Klein, and Balint. Kernberg assumes much capacity on the part of the infantile ego for splitting and the formation of self and object representations during a period Piaget has claimed to be without such capacities. I believe the tremendous rage that appears in therapy apparently attached to split-off self- and object-representations actually is a kind of psychic telescoping. When the id presents derivatives of itself, it presents itself via images or representations that have been produced by the ego. Malevolent projective representations, such as devils, influencing machines, or the evil psychotherapist, are utilized by the ego in the presentation of affect in the transference, but it is adultomorphic to assume that such specific self- and object-representations are already present in the psyche of the infant.

This issue is fundamental to such elaborate neo-Kleinian interpretations of the paranoid process as that of Meissner (1978b), who mentions Kohut's theories only in passing and without discussion of the fundamental opposition between drive psychology and self psychology. Compare Meissner's views with Kohut's (1971, Chapter 1 and pp. 255–256) quite different approach to paranoid delusions. For Kohut (p. 10), "their establishment follows the disintegration of the grandiose self and of the idealized parent imago." In psychoses, the destruction of these "structures" is followed by a secondary reorganization of their disconnected fragments into delusions, which are then rationalized by the remaining "integrative functions" of the psyche.

Positivists and empiricists would insist that our introspective notion of "self" is just a bundle of perceptions or representations that we habitually (according to Hume) put together as an unwarranted abstraction into an entity. Kohut wandered into the area of philosophy and moved to a higher level of abstraction in much of the more experience-distant and holistic concepts of self psychology, which will appeal more to the religious and philosophical-minded and perhaps less to the clinician. For example, Jaspers already in 1913 devotes a section of his *General Psychopathology* (1972) to a discussion of our awareness of the self, using a combined psychiatric and existential point of view.

Kohut's emphasis on middle-age empty depression based on the depleted self (1977, p. 243) — the world of unmirrored ambitions and devoid of ideals — has a long tradition in psychoanalysis (Jung 1933) and philosophy. Wollheim (1984), for example, borrowing heavily from Freud and Melanie Klein rather than Kohut, argues in his existential philosophy that a holistic notion of the self as a process with projects is central to a person's "finding life worthwhile," which in turn is "a matter of the opportunities it promises him for the satisfactions of those desires or plans of his which he thinks important" (p. 246). Like Kohut he distinguishes this from "finding life worth living" (p. 244), which has to do with the balance of pleasure and pain in life.

For Kohut, if one has successfully undergone a transformation of narcissism, a certain inner peace results in middle age. The same result is claimed even by Hegel (Taylor 1975), but based on the person's realization that the unfolding of the self in this transformation represents an emanation of universal *Geist*. At this point the person's longing for integrity will no longer be "doomed to frustration," the person suffering what Hegel calls the "unhappy consciousness," and the person will be able to accept the transience of life and feel empathy with other selves. In fact, Butler (1984) even claims that, "Hegel's dialectical method is a version of the method of empathic understanding" (p. 19).

Kohut has carried psychoanalysis away from nineteenth-century empirical natural sciences and — as he (1978, p. 751) admits — deeper into the realm of humanistic philosophical thought, a tendency that Freud constantly tried to restrain within himself. Each psychotherapist has to decide how far to go in this direction, which is represented by his or her reliance on empathy or vicarious introspection.

Kohut offers a more clinically useful approach to the preoedipal disorders, especially in psychotherapy, than the Kleinians. He carefully avoids the retrospective adultomorphic errors of attributing to the baby all sorts of formed cognitive representational concepts of self, object, superego, penis, breast, and so on. This remains controversial, but clinicians must make choices about their approach every day, and these choices will have a profound effect on how they practice psychotherapy. Rotenberg (1983) presents an overview of the treatment of personality disorders based on self psychology compared with that based on ego psychology; he emphasizes the differences in clinical technique contingent on one's choice of orientation.

We are forced by immediate exigencies with patients to make crucial decisions regarding our approach and we may utilize one or the other of controversial theories. The therapist should make these choices deliberately, based on a firm understanding of all the options available, and watch carefully for subsequent clinical material in an ongoing effort to validate interventions. Consultation with experienced colleagues is always desirable.

## Implications for Clinical Practice

A number of implications for the practice of intensive psychotherapy are represented by those didactic and tentative distinctions I have made. Some people use formal psychoanalysis for pacification and unification, and conversely, interpretation of a transference neurosis can occasionally occur in a less frequent psychotherapy if the conditions are appropriate. This implies a continuum theory of psychoanalysis and psychoanalytic psychotherapy which is opposed to the differentiation theory of some traditional psychoanalysts. Furthermore, the issue arises as to whether traditional psychoanalysis is suitable for developmental defects or structural disabilities in addition to neuroses which are based on repressed infantile conflicts; Anna Freud (1971) was dubious about such suitability. Self-psychologists argue that they have now developed a technique which makes psychoanalysis applicable to deficit disorders.

I am not referring here to what might be called repair of the self, which represents restoring it to the best it once was. This sort of therapy might be a three-month, short-term psychotherapy which does not focus on transference and reorganization or formation of a newly organized self. In fact, some analysts claim controversially that the only legitimate forms of psychotherapy are brief psychotherapy for repair and formal psychoanalysis. For a historical review of this unresolved dispute, see Sachs (1979).

The skill of the therapist is a major factor in determining whether intensive psychotherapy can be more than an interminable supportive selfobject relationship for a patient. There is a danger in pushing the differentiation theory; it is often presented in a way pejorative to psychoanalytic psychotherapy, suggesting psychotherapists believe that any practice is permissible. That which the patient wants and has the capacity to accomplish, together with that which the therapist is able to perform, determine whether the patient gets a full-scale psychoanalysis or psychotherapy. As Kohut indicates, a combination of the empathic capacities of the therapist and the degree of cohesiveness of the self (so that even the most minor empathic failures do not bring about total disruption of the treatment each time) determines whether the patient is capable of a "sectorial" or a "segmental" treatment.

Self psychology shifts our perspective to the inside of the patient — we ask ourselves what the patient is experiencing. We examine those feelings that the patient stirs up in the therapist. We ask ourselves what or whom the patient is asking us to be or how we are being utilized by the patient as a selfobject. In intensive psychotherapy we are careful to be consistently available, which allows the patient to make use of us for repair of the self. Whether we then go on to eventually interpret and work through these selfobject transferences distinguishes psychoanalysis from intensive psychotherapy. In psychotherapy, as Kohut explains, rather than concentrating on interpretation of these selfobject transferences, we encourage the patient to displace them to friends, family, and various social organizations, providing the patient with a much-needed empathic matrix that eventually can take the place of the therapist.

A common error in the misunderstanding of self psychology is the belief that patients will be satisfied and happy if only the therapist does not make gross empathic lapses. This ignores the fact that certain patients are frightened of forming a selfobject transference due to their fear of merger and loss of autonomy, and must continuously devalue the therapist even if they allow themselves to secretly form a merger transference. Thus, the unhappy complaining patient who is continuously devaluing the therapist and the therapy but who is coming regularly and showing favorable changes in external circumstances, should not necessarily bring about a lowering of the therapist's self-esteem or lead to therapeutic despair. Again therapists must ask themselves in what fashion they are being used and whether the patient's use of the therapy is showing evidence of an improved self-cohesion and consequent improvement in ego functioning.

If the therapist realizes what sort of selfobject transference has formed and can accept it, this will aid the patient in control and regulation, a channeling of excitation, and a setting of realistic goals through the idealizing transference, all of which produce a restored narcissistic equilibrium. The therapist will spot this restored equilibrium even if the patient does not report it, and it enables the patient to show functional improvement in psychotherapy even without interpretation of transferences.

## PSYCHOTHERAPY WITH ADOLESCENTS

The converse — that therapy will break up if the therapist is either unable to recognize the needs of the patient or tries to use the patient for personal selfobject needs — is also true. In the case of the adolescent Dora (Freud 1905a), Freud grossly missed the total subjective experience of Dora (Wolf 1980) when he interpreted her reported disgust during the time she was kissed by Herr K. as hysterical and resulting from sexual excitement. Freud was not thinking of or showing vicarious introspection with a young girl's experience here. Dora was 14 years old at the time Herr K., 40, surprised her with a kiss. A strong argument could be made by psychiatrists experienced with adolescent patients that her disgust was age-appropriate; it was Freud's countertransference arising out of his intense commitment to his sexual theory that Wolf believes probably caused him to lose empathic understanding of this adolescent girl. Or perhaps there were deeper reasons involving Freud's attitude toward women.

Self psychology (Kohut 1971, p. 119n) teaches that, in adolescence, sexual activity serves primarily narcissistic purposes by enhancing self-esteem and does not merely consist of the explosion of pubertal drives. Especially when self-pathology is present, it often represents an escape from unbearable feelings of self-depletion and deadness. August Aichhorn (1955), Kohut's (1978) analyst, facilitated the formation of an idealizing transference in his delinquent adolescent patients (Kohut 1971, pp. 161–164) through his unusual intuitive skills as a therapist and his charismatic personality.

Self psychology has many ideas to offer to those psychotherapists who work with adolescents. Their preoccupation with sexuality and the typical adolescent oscillation of moods are better understood in terms of the vicissitudes of disturbed narcissistic equilibrium that are apparently inevitable at this stage of life, at least in our culture. Adolescence represents an important transformational aspect of the unfolding life curve of the self; it begins with the dissonance of puberty and the recapitulation of oedipal conflicts and offers a period of potential freedom to become an authentic self, with postadolescent idealized ethics and values. For this reason Kohut (1971) calls it "a decisive final step" (p. 43) in the establishment of nuclear psychological structures.

The clinician must avoid confusing the frantic search of the individual with a fragile sense of self for soothing and self-consolidating activities, which may be quite dangerous, with the search of the late adolescent to find a philosophical or "authentic" self, a search that already requires a cohesive and relatively firm self in Kohut's sense (discussed in Chessick 1985a). The precipitation of an "identity" in adolescence in turn enables a final firming and cohesion of the patient's self — an important task of adolescence which is only beginning to be explored by self-psychologists such as Wolf, Gedo, and Terman (1972).

## "DIFFICULT" OR "RESISTIVE" PATIENTS

Basch (Stepansky and Goldberg 1984) tells us that when Kohut's (1971) *The Analysis of the Self* was first published, the verdict of the elder statesmen of psychoanalysis was "clever, but not psychoanalysis" (p. 25). According to Basch, Kohut's work became utilized in many ways although no "official" recognition of his achievement was forthcoming. Instead, the "establishment" stopped condemning Kohut as unanalytic but now claimed that he presented nothing new.

Kohut's work encourages us to deal with patients who previously would have been sent for supportive treatment by using instead more psychoanalytically oriented uncovering methods. (Some Kleinians and North American psychoanalysts have been advocating this for many years.) Patients with archaic selfobject transferences who are intense, labile, and highly vulnerable to disruption, can now be better tolerated and understood, in turn leading to the receding or disappearance of the more florid psychopathology in some cases and allowing some patients formerly labeled borderline or even psychotic to become analyzable.

Stolorow (Stepansky and Goldberg 1984) illustrates the typical self-psychology approach to the so-called negative therapeutic reactions, which are understood from this orientation to be based on "intersubjective situations in which the patient's selfobject transference needs are consistently misunderstood and thereby rejected" (p. 48).

Even "resistances" in intensive psychotherapy or psychoanalysis are understood differently by self psychologists, as discussed by Kohut (1984) and Wolf (Stepansky and Goldberg 1984). Self-psychologists interpret resistances as manifestations of the patient's fear of "humiliation or rejection or some other form of depreciation" and this fear makes them "sensitively cautious" against self-revelation (Wolf, in Stepansky and Goldberg 1984, p. 152). This caution does not represent defense against the drives but "against selfobject failures which may fragment the self." Wolf calls these "measures of obligatory self-protection." Actually Wolf feels that a patient should not be labeled borderline until there have been trials of analysis "by more than one or two analysts" (p. 153) because he believes the disruptions in the treatment of these patients can often be brought to an end "by interpretation and explanation" (p. 155), allowing a stable selfobject relationship to form eventually; again, the skill and empathic attunement of the analyst are very important. There are at least two potential traumas to which the self is exposed, "the loss of a needed selfobject response" and the "intrusion of the selfobject across its boundaries into its own core." Wolf explains that "the more fragile the self structure, the more vulnerable the self and the more distorted the self's defensive maneuvers against the potential danger" (p. 152). From the point of view of self psychology, the more the therapist learns about his or her patient-assigned function as a selfobject in the treatment, the better the therapist will be at practicing psychotherapy.

COUNTERTRANSFERENCE

Self psychology also has a great deal to say about transference and countertransference, as summarized by Wolf (1979). Gunther (1976) offers a new self-psychology-based view of the origin and meaning of countertransference: "Countertransference phenomena serve as compromise formations designed to restore disturbances in the analyst's own narcissistic equilibrium" (p. 206). This explains in a less moralizing or pejorative fashion various reports that have been presented of analysts acting out their narcissistic, sexual, or aggressive wishes with patients; the periodic violent denunciations of the field of psychoanalysis by previously traditional and now renegade analysts and their offering of what Gunther calls a "salvational ideology"; and the occasional news of the tragic, sudden depressive disintegration or suicide of a promising analyst or established psychotherapeutic clinician. Gunther's paper provides an unusually ample bibliography. He maintains that countertransference arises not from a moral failure but as the result of the "endangered position of the analyst" in being traumatically flooded by the patient's narcissistic needs. Any interference with the analyst's empathic function may lead to regression to earlier forms of narcissistic gratification and concomitant aggression, which produce countertransference phenomena in an effort to restore narcissistic equilibrium.

In Gunther's view countertransference behavior is already the result of a narcissistic wound in the analyst's professional self-expectation. Especially in preoedipal cases there are dangers to the core stability and self-esteem regulation of the analyst's cohesive adult self due to the continuing, relentless archaic demands of the patient for the selfobject analyst's perfection. Countertransference arises as the result of inevitable narcissistic humiliation or disappointment in the analyst's own professional self-expectations in a relationship involving regressive restimulation and archaic demands. Gunther concludes:

> The disequilibrium in the analyst's own narcissistic integrity . . . may now be acknowledged as a significant additional source of countertransference stimulation. The clinician's manifest symptomatic behavior may therefore constitute a compromise formation related to narcissistic regression and serving the function of *defense*, rather than necessarily constituting a primary *cause* of the disruption of his optimal analytic focus. (p. 222)

Thus, the psychology of the self offers a better understanding of the dangers in the long-term practice of psychotherapy or psychoanalysis for the therapist.

## Basch: "Doing Psychotherapy" from a Self-Psychological Perspective

Basch (1980) presents the optimal ambience of psychotherapy from the self-psychological point of view; the holding and comforting tone that is set with patients throughout when compared with other published case reports,* argues implicitly that psychotherapy or psychoanalysis informed by self psychology does indeed undergo a certain benign shift in ambience.

Basch's "how-to-do-it" book provides us with six extensive clinical illustrations, gives some alternative responses, and explains the value or disadvantages of each. The book has been criticized as utilizing the concepts of self psychology "to avoid exploration of the sexual conflicts of the patient" (Waldron 1983, p. 626). Basch's explanation of the clinical material, argues Waldron, "suffers from the imposition of preconceived concepts slanted toward problems of the self and toward preoedipal issues" (p. 627), and the patient's achievement of full genital object love as interrupted by powerful unresolved oedipal issues is neglected.

This again illustrates the continuing criticism by traditional psychoanalysts that self-psychologists may be leading psychotherapists and analysts into a collusion with patients to avoid confronting lust and aggression arising from unresolved Oedipus complexes. Basch implies that the cases he presents are primarily preoedipal disorders of the self and that their oedipal difficulties are secondary. Self psychologists believe that most patients seen in psychotherapy in clinics are such patients, and differ from the traditional cases in classical psychoanalysis who have an Oedipus complex at the core of a psychoneurosis. However, Kohut in his last work (1984) places pathology of the self underneath even the traditional Oedipus complex.

The reader must judge from studying the case histories reported by Basch whether Basch is justified in treating his patients as representing disorders of the self or whether their pathology represents regression from an unresolved Oedipus complex. It is a difficult judgment to make since we do not have the data of a full-scale psychoanalysis on which to base our thinking. I agree with Basch that the specific cases presented by him are typical of those which the average trainee confronts. Basch's cases are not well approached as neuroses based on an unresolved Oedipus complex.

Let us take for example the case criticized by Waldron (1983) of Ms. Banks, who presents herself to a therapist who is going into private practice in eight months. Her previous therapist worked with her for three years on her "unresolved Oedipus complex" until he

---

*But *not* those of Freud. See Lipton (1977, 1979) and Chessick (1980, 1982).

finished his training in psychotherapy and went into private practice. The patient could not afford to continue with him and presents
herself in an extremely injured and antagonistic state, which the
therapist handles with superb skill. This case illustrates how easily
such a patient could be labeled borderline if there were not a correct understanding of what she had experienced. Basch explains that
when patients with poor impulse control are called "borderline":

> Often this is simply a pejorative attesting to the fact that the therapist
> is angry at and unsatisfied by a patient who will not play the game by
> the rules and leaves the therapist at a loss as to what to do next to make
> therapy effective. If a patient is "borderline" the implication is that he
> is essentially a psychotic individual who manages to adapt marginally
> to the demands of life but is in ever-present danger of disintegrating if
> his brittle defenses become strained. (p. 60)

Basch feels that Ms. Banks is not a borderline case but represents a
narcissistic personality disorder, a developmental arrest. He explains
her tantrums in therapy as based on a child's unrealistic expectation
"that he will have a smooth passage through the world, and that if
such a passage is not forthcoming, there is someone to blame — and
that someone must then be forced to set matters right again" (p. 61).

In treating such patients, says Basch, rather than "working toward
getting the patient to like him, the therapist needs to work toward
being able to like himself as he is functioning with the particular patient in the particular session. . . . Failure to be satisfied with himself
is a clear signal that something is amiss" (p. 75).

As the case of Ms. Banks unfolds, the ambience and acceptance
offered by the therapist lead to the establishment of a vital selfobject transference, which was not essentially interpreted or resolved
in the therapy. As termination was being considered, Ms. Banks
decided to become a physician like her father and devote herself to
this goal; a year later she called the therapist to tell him she had been
accepted at a medical school and felt content with her life at that
point.

The point of contention about whether self psychology avoids
oedipal strivings of patients manifests itself in Basch's report:

> When for a brief time the patient sexualized the transference and became
> frightened by her thoughts, the therapist pointed out to her she was

mistakenly attributing genital motives to the love and affection she felt for him who was, through his work, giving her a chance to achieve satisfactions heretofore closed to her. She was helped to understand that her emotions were appropriate to the child who stands in awe of and wants to unite with the powerful, giving parent, and were not those of a sexually excited woman. (p. 86)

Basch insists that her decision to become a physician does not represent an unresolved transference — an identification with both her physician-father and the physician-therapist — or "an attempt to resolve a neurotic conflict through action rather than through psychological insight," because she proceeded with her plans in a thoughtful fashion, was not "driven," and achieved genuine satisfaction from the process.

Trying to understand what happened and whether or not Basch offered an "inexact interpretation" that led to the termination of the therapy is a controversial issue, fraught with the difficulty of varying interpretations of reported psychoanalytic data. I do not think such an argument can be resolved, and it tends to obscure Basch's point: if the patient is judged to be suffering from a disorder of the self or a narcissistic disorder, the therapeutic work ought to focus on threatened fragmentations, disruptions, and temper tantrums that occur upon disappointment in the selfobject, phenomena which restrain the patient from having any successful interpersonal experiences or ever being able to form an affective, empathic selfobject matrix.

The appearance of sexualization is muted in this approach and not interpreted as a representation of infantile lust or aggression; the focus is on the patient's need for mirroring or idealizing selfobjects. If the therapist has judged wrongly, or if the narcissistic phenomena are predominantly defensive regressions from an unresolved Oedipus complex, therapy according to the approach of self psychology will represent a collusion between patient and therapist to avoid the emergence of infantile aggressive and sexual issues (both homosexual and heterosexual). Clinical judgment is involved.

A similar dilemma is presented by Basch in his report of a patient with a depression. Basch "explains" in part to the patient that

The hallmark of depression is the sense or the attitude that life is meaningless — an indication that the perception of the self is no longer a unifying focus for ambitions and ideals . . . the myriad symptoms of depression are an attempt to circumvent helplessness and to enlist assistance in restoring some meaning to life — that is, to recapture a sense of direction for the self. (p. 136)

Again, this approach may be viewed as a collusion with the patient in order to avoid the issues of infantile lust, aggression, and oral ambivalence that are often postulated to lie behind depression. However, Kohut distinguishes the depression of Tragic Man, which is based on the depleted empty self that has failed to achieve its nuclear aims, from the problems of Guilty Man described by Freud (1917). Clearly Basch believes that the patient he refers to belongs in the "Tragic Man" category of Kohut, which explains his "explanation."

The assessment of Basch's book depends on an acceptance of the underlying premise in the cases presented: they represent primarily disorders of the self and not regressions from an unresolved Oedipus complex. These are presented as cases in psychotherapy, not traditional psychoanalytic treatment reports. Basch illustrates the activity of the therapist in explaining repeatedly to the patient in psychotherapy what has occurred in terms of the patient's expectations and disappointments. This increased activity of the therapist is also a consequence of the concept of cure presented by self psychology and again exposes the procedure to the accusation of representing suggestion, education, and persuasion.

But one might question whether the particular cases presented by Basch would have responded better to a silent, solely interpretive approach such as that of Langs (1982), or even a more moderate traditional approach such as that of Kernberg. Would the patients have exploded with rage and disappointment, which then might have been interpreted to them as manifestations of a projection of their all bad self- and object-representations onto the therapist? It is left to the reader to ponder which approach would be correct, and for what reasons.

# Chapter 15

---

# Some Tentative Clinical
# Applications

The application of self psychology seems to work consistently and helps us to understand certain clinical and group phenomena that were previously obscure or baffling. In this chapter and the next I will make some attempts to apply self-psychological concepts to some of my own clinical case material. I hope to stimulate therapist-readers to make self psychology part of their therapeutic working armamentarium and conceptual system, and to try to apply it to their own special interests in individual and group phenomena. This is an effort to motivate readers to immerse themselves in self psychology, as Kohut (1984) repeatedly asks us to do, "for protracted periods and with a variety of patients" (p. 90); then to see whether it actually produces a significant change in your examining and understanding various clinical phenomena.

Since I am now presenting my own material and ideas, self psychologists may object that I have misunderstood or misapplied their concepts, and traditional analysts may raise the same criticisms that were applied to Basch's book. My purpose, however, is to encourage the reader to think in self-psychological terms at the practical, everyday clinical level.

It would be a legitimate suspicion and expectable contention on the part of traditional analysts that psychotherapists or psychoanalysts who shift to employing the psychology of the self are revealing an insufficiently analyzed Oedipus complex. Traditional analysts might claim that self psychologists are attempting to defend themselves by adopting a psychological system which proclaims that the Oedipus complex is not at the nucleus of the various characterological disorders and narcissistic phenomena seen in our clinical work. Kohut's (1984) counterargument to this is that warm acceptance of self psychology is found in "those who are more directly in touch with modern man's primary need" (pp. 61–62), and those who reject it cannot face the narcissistic blow in Kohut's discovery that the self's autonomy is always relative: the self "can never exist outside of a matrix of self-objects" (p. 61).

## The Case of Dr. E. as an Introduction to Psychology of the Self

I usually introduce the psychology of the self to student therapists (who already have had a course in traditional psychoanalytic therapy) by the following case presentation: E. was a psychiatrist who was born in a small town. His father was a minor businessman who was married twice. The second marriage of the father, who was in his forties at the time, produced E., the first son of this marriage. The father also had two sons from his first marriage at age 17. Father was one of those people who was always expecting something good to turn up; he was unsuccessful as a businessman.

By the time of his second marriage, father was already a grandfather because a son from his first marriage had had a son, and so E. was born an uncle. E.'s nephew, the son of his half-brother, was one year older than E. As children, the nephew was a close friend of E., but also a hated rival who was stronger because he was a year older. Yet he was still close enough in age for a continuing contest to take place.

E.'s mother was an attractive 21-year-old woman when E. was born, a year after she married his father. Their second child was a boy, born when E. was 11 months old. The child died 8 months later when E. was 19 months old. A sister was then born when E. was 2½ years old; after that, four more girls were born, followed by a final child, another son, born when E. was 10 years old. E.'s mother was described as a much respected but emotional lady.

An important figure in E.'s earliest years was a family maid, who was a strict Catholic, preoccupied with issues of paradise and the fires of hell, and who was discharged for stealing from the family when E. was 2½ years old — at the same time his oldest sister was born.

E. was born in a caul, which was believed by the family to mean that he was destined for greatness, and there were several prophesies made in his childhood of his eventually becoming a great politician.

E. presented two early memories: at the age of 2½, when his sister was born and the maid was discharged, he saw his mother naked; and a memory at the age of 3 when he moved to a small city where the family lived for a year. (When E. was 4, the family moved again to a large city). The specific memory was during the move at the age of 3 to the small city; he saw gas jets from industrial plants which reminded him of souls burning in hell.

His early childhood was marked by the fact that he excelled in school and by an increasing disillusionment with his bumbling businessman father. He attached himself to older father figure teachers and formed an ambivalent relaionship to his friends, often ending the friendship with competition and a quarrel. He became a physician, with his main interest being scientific research in the laboratory.

At the age of 41 he had his first psychoanalysis due to depressive symptoms, a "cardiac neurosis" with palpitations and hypochondria, and anxiety which became severe after the death of his father one year earlier. This first psychoanalysis dealt extensively with his Oedipus complex and took about three years. It produced a satisfactory result but still left him with two symptoms that interfered with his work.

Following his first analysis, Dr. E. experienced a gradually deepening pessimism and cynicism about people and loss of hope for the future of humanity, symptoms which became worse and more pervasive as he got older. He also continued to experience a strong aversion to receiving any awards, honors, or adulations, especially in public. These situations made him irritable and uncomfortable, and he even avoided celebrations of his birthday. Even before his psychoanalysis, he once wrote to his fiancée, "I am sure you will agree to do without the presents, the congratulations, the being stared at and criticized; even the wedding dress that everyone gazes at and even the 'ah's' of admiration when you appear."

E. became a successful man despite his residual difficulties, but he continued to have unpleasant interpersonal experiences with his friends, especially those who wished to compete with him, and he sometimes showed what certain observers considered to be a disavowed autocratic tendency; certainly, his attitude toward women could at least at times be arrogant.

It is a case such as this — where the successful psychoanalysis, because it did not go more deeply into the self-pathology behind the Oedipus complex, left residual narcissistic pathology — which led Kohut to turn to a deeper study of narcissistic structures to be seen as separate in their development and transformations from the usual oral-anal-phallic (oedipal) phases of the libido. I am sketching here the history of Sigmund Freud, who, in spite of his great genius, remained unable (Kohut 1977, pp. 292–297, Chessick 1980) to appreciate music, philosophy, or modern art, all of which were developing rapidly in *fin de siècle* Vienna (Janik and Toulmin 1973).

I will not attempt to "analyze" Freud's alleged unresolved narcissistic transformations, both out of respect for the extraordinary genius of Freud and because Kohut has discussed the subject at length (1984). When Kohut was asked by students what to read in the field of psychotherapy and psychoanalysis, he is alleged to have said, "Read Freud." When asked what to read after that, Kohut allegedly replied, "Read Freud again."

A study of Freud's biography and his writings gives us a hint of what self psychologists are talking about when they argue that the psychoanalysis of certain psychoanalytic candidates has often floundered because insufficient attention was paid to disorders of the self. Kohut (1984, pp. 163–170) attempts to use this claimed common defect in training analyses to explain the remarkable history of the psychoanalytic movement, in which narcissistic injuries repeatedly produced serious inimical major schisms. Indeed, even a friendly observer of psychoanalysis would have to concede that, from its origins to the present day, it suffers from an extraordinary number of personally acrimonious disputes, beginning with those among Freud and his disciples (Roazen 1975). It does not follow from this, however, that Kohut's controversial explanation of this unfortunate historical trend is correct.

While attending psychoanalytic meetings, Kohut listened to the various manifestations of quarrels and injured sensitivities among his putatively well-analyzed colleagues:

> I was at that time president of our national association and had been puzzling about the dissensions within our group and particularly about the fact that now and then people who seemed to have been friends suddenly turned and became enemies. I learned to recognize that . . . one could always find some small but nevertheless important narcissistic injury at the pivotal moment that determined the later inimical attitude of such an individual. (Kohut 1978, p. 772)

## The Case of Ms. X.: A Classic Clinical Error Corrected by Self Psychology

Here is a case vignette illustrating a classic error in psychotherapy as corrected by self psychology. I erred in my focus on the patient's conflict over her eroticized longing experiences. This eroticized longing, however, in self psychology does not represent a sexual "drive." Addressing it as such interpretively was perceived by the patient as an unempathic wounding assault and led to further anger as a disintegration product. I also realized from this error that I must not miss the forward moves in psychotherapy and must consider confirming these! This is discussed by Kohut (1984, pp. 187–190) along with careful warnings that sometimes such confirmations can themselves represent empathic failure, for example, by not recognizing the anxiety that may accompany attempts at new achievements, and using the tone of a coach addressing his football team.

In supportive psychotherapy we naturally encourage and praise the patient. Even if the psychotherapy is primarily uncovering, the forward moves should be empathically acknowledged, unless there is good reason not to do so, because this confirming response increases the cohesion of the self and secondarily improves ego function. In contrast, focusing interpretations on conflicts and needs while essentially ignoring forward moves revives the memory of the parent who was always criticizing and never praising. Thus the tone of the way we do psychotherapy changes, as illustrated by Basch (1980) in the case of Ms. Banks, where he warmly congratulates her on a success in her work. Picking up and recognizing forward movement becomes more in the foreground of the therapist's interventions.

Ms. X. first presented herself in a way that DSM-III would immediately define as a borderline personality disorder; after considerable therapeutic work she now would be diagnosed as a narcissistic personality disorder. Following a session during intensive psychotherapy (twice weekly), when I had made an interpretation that she displaced certain erotic yearnings for me on to her new boy friend Dan, she dreamed: "Dr. Chessick was taking care of a deaf child." Her association was, "Nobody is more deaf than those who will not hear." The patient did not want to hear the prior interpretation of displacement because she did not wish to be flooded with unacceptable and frustrating yearnings for me. This was a patient who had such an intense need for merger that as a young child she remembered lying in bed with her sleeping older sister and attempting to literally synchronize her breathing to exactly that of her sister while she lay in close physical contact with her.

The next day Dan took in a male roommate. The patient reported being enraged at Dan because the new roommate invaded their privacy; she felt humiliated getting up in the morning after sleeping with Dan and finding his roommate there. Dan, on the other hand, argued that he needed the money. The patient reported the following dream:

> A biplane is landing. A flap falls and it crashes. It touches off a series of explosions and we must all run. I climb some hills trying to reach and cling to safety, but the scene is scattered with garbage and tin cans, and I must climb from one hill to the other, like Sisyphus. As I climb up, I note that if I slip the fall down will be very steep.
>
> In the next scene Dr. Chessick is driving a car and puts a hand on my breast. I say to myself, "What is this?" Then I realize it is part of a physical examination — after all he is a doctor. He feels my stomach and says it is bloated and I should not eat so much. Then in the next scene I find myself squeezed into a very small space, but this is not painful or frightening.

It should be noted that the narcissistic patient who dreams of climbing reminds us of Kohut's (1971, p. 87) comment that such dreams often are harbingers of the impending formation of an idealizing tranference and that the narcissistic patient who dreams of falling may be about to develop a merger transference.

The associations to this dream were as follows: "I am proud of myself because in contrast to previous episodes when Dan disappointed me I did not explode at him. This is the first dream in three years I have had where Dr. Chessick appears interested in me (in contrast to many dreams where various parental transference figures utterly ignored her) and it is an exciting dream! The squeeze in the last scene of the dream is associated with chest pain — perhaps I am having a heart attack and then I could be nursed in the intensive care unit."

My first interpretation of this dream was rather traditional in which I suggested that Dan's taking a roommate reminded her of the (to her unwelcome) birth of one of her siblings and therefore produced an increase of narcissistic rage fueled by both the past and present situation. This was followed by the search for an idealized parent to help her to restore narcissistic equilibrium, but it did not work because she remembers that her parents were too disappointing — garbage and tin cans. The patient then reaches to me but is frightened of this and must reverse the situation so in the dream I reached to her. That is to say, she must defend against the temptation to reach out to me. Since she can't make the reach due to her fear of loss of autonomy, anxiety about impending fragmentation manifested by hypochondria and strange body sensations develops. Thus I interpreted the "defense" — her fear of loss of autonomy — before the content, which is technically correct, although I used self psychology rather than a traditional conflict interpretation, which eventually would be based on oedipal strivings, the primal scene, and pregnancy wishes involving father.

The patient's response was to feel great rage at me while I was making the interpretation because, she said, I missed the step forward! The dream, although it represented only a small step, regardless of the prevalent defenses, she insisted, "the point is that it was not an unpleasant dream, it was hopeful." The patient said, "You are like my mother, who was always efficient, driving for performance, and missed the little accomplishments I did make as a child; I viewed this dream as a gift that would make you happy as a response to my reaching out for contact to you as with my sister, and I was pleased when I awoke and remembered it."

After thinking it over I agreed with her comment, feeling that I had made an empathic lapse (probably based on the typical countertransference frustration in the slow and frequently disrupted work with such difficult patients); she calmed down immediately and relaxed. When I asked her about the stomach bloating in the dream, she related it to the wish to be pregnant. This step would give her control over the problem of physical merger, for the baby would need her, even be inside of her, and depend on her. I saw this as a possible incipient withdrawal into the grandiose self out of disappointment in the idealization attempts with the parents; when this, too, fails one gets fragmentation, manifested by hypochondria, and the wish for nursing care.

If the reader does not attempt to interpret and reinterpret the incomplete clinical data, the reader will notice how different this approach is from the standard oedipal interpretations that might easily be made from this dream material. The therapist, says Kohut, must make a judgment about what predominates. This particular patient performed the same function for me in a minor way that Miss F. performed for Kohut (1971). My patient was an unusually brilliant and exquisitely sensitive individual with very serious pathology who raged severely whenever I lost attunement with her; at the time I was beginning to investigate the psychology of the self and I found, as did the analysts in the casebook (Goldberg 1978), that I began listening more carefully to the patient's complaints about where I was experienced by her as a selfobject that was failing her. It was here that I dimly began to recognize that the notions of self psychology had a genuine clinical validity. I started to listen to the patient in a new way, letting her guide me to a better understanding of her current selfobject needs and so tolerating these more easily in the psychotherapy.

When this happened the patient transformed gradually from an individual that would clearly be diagnosed as a borderline personality to an individual who formed a stable selfobject transference and would be diagnosed as a narcissistic personality, and who could at least tolerate a traditional psychoanalytic approach. I regarded this as an important step in my own sense of conviction that there was something legitimate about the self-psychological approach.

Above all, it caused me to hear material that I previously would have regarded as either defensive or not very relevant or important. Here, again, is the crucial argument regarding the two analyses of Mr. Z. Would a properly trained traditional analyst without the self-psychological approach still hear this material? If not, the self-psychological approach has validity because it opens up new orientations toward clinical data and leads to significant new understanding of difficult patients. Traditional psychoanalysts might reply that they would hear this material, and failure to do so simply represents a countertransference problem.

## The Case of Ms. Y.:
### An Alternative Perspective on Patient Material

Another deeply disturbed patient of mine dreamed that she was at a dance with a minister. She reported, "When he smiled at me I felt really pretty and glowing and beautiful and very feminine." The patient's associations dealt with the possibility that I might be the minister in the dream, which she found "ridiculous," and she claimed that she certainly did not want such a response to me. From the point of view of self psychology, the dream is important because it shows the formation of an idealizing transference or an archaic merger transference. The emphasis is on the paternal figure whose smile pulls together the self of this patient and gives the little girl the sense of being pretty, glowing, beautiful, and feminine. This is an illustration of Kohut's idea of a phase-appropriate response by a parent to the oedipal strivings of the little girl. A more traditional interpretation would concentrate on the falling in love, the sexual aspects, and the minister as a relatively untouchable parent figure. Rather than seeing this as a self-state dream which occurs during the formation of a selfobject transference, the more traditional approach would emphasize hidden incestuous wishes in the dream.

This was a stormy patient who already had four years of traditional psychoanalysis with a graduate analyst; the analysis ended in a failure. At one point she became overwhelmed with sexual desires for the analyst and functionally collapsed. This was regarded as a transference neurosis and was so interpreted, but the analysis had to be stopped temporarily and supportive psychotherapeutic measures instituted by the analyst. When the analysis was resumed after the patient had pulled herself together in a few months, the affect was less intense and the material was very intellectual and shallow; soon the patient began to notice that the analyst was repeatedly falling asleep and snoring in the sessions. After several such instances the patient took the initiative and stopped the treatment.

In her second psychoanalytic treatment, the patient revealed a profoundly empty and depleted self with an overwhelming need for mirroring and idealization accompanied by a terrified defense against the formation of selfobject transferences. At same time she formed a spectacular merger transference with her infant in which she regarded herself and the infant as the perfect mother–child couple, akin to the blissful Madonna-and-Child paintings of Leonardo da Vinci.

If her child fell down and suffered even a minor bruise, the patient became fragmented, suffered from overwhelming anxiety and fear, insomnia, and the various other symptoms that have been described earlier as clinical manifestations of the fragmented self. These responded relatively rapidly to interpretations based on self psychology and the treatment was able to proceed smoothly with disruptions kept to a minimum.

At this writing the patient remains one of those patients "with fragmented selves who apparently never find sufficient inner tranquility to let themselves settle into a reliable selfobject transference" (Wolf, in Stepansky and Goldberg 1984, p. 153). Thus the patient presented with compliance — which Kohut (1984) recognized as the most profound and difficult resistance of all — but defends with vigor against forming a meaningful, consciously experienced selfobject transference, for which at the same time she yearns. The case is hopeful, however, and I believe that underneath all of this a silent merger transference (Kohut 1971, p. 251) is forming.*

It appeared that the first analysis represented compliance with the analyst. The self-psychological explanation of the formation of an intensely eroticized and disruptive transference — as has been described in work with borderline patients (Chessick 1977) — helps us to understand the collapse of the first analysis as a phenomenon which represented fragmentation or disintegration products of a disappointed self which had again been failed in its expectations from the self-object analyst.

I fully recognize that numerous counterarguments are possible. One could even argue that the patient's report of her first analysis may be unreliable, but in this case I have reason, both from the nature of the patient's perceptive abilities and her general reliability, to believe that she was presenting an honest report of her first analysis. There is no implication here that traditional analysts commonly carry out their treatment in this fashion. However traditional psychoanalysis with these difficult patients carries an increased danger of frustration, disruption, and countertransference.

This vignette illustrates the way in which self psychology offers an alternative way of looking at patient material which might otherwise be ignored or thought of as irrelevant. It also presents an anti-

---

*A year later, the patient had indeed formed such a stable transference with a remarkable concomitant improvement in ego functioning.

dote to the danger coming from the traditional psychoanalytic outlook being applied too rigidly, as reported by Malcolm (1981). Here an unidentified and perhaps partly fictitious traditional New York analyst seeks repeated reanalysis from analysts with a traditional orientation as a solution to unyielding narcissistic personality difficulties. Would there not have been some value, in proceeding with a third or fourth analysis, for this analyst to have chosen someone with a self-psychological approach?

## LITERARY CASE EXAMPLE: JUDITH ROSSNER'S *AUGUST*

A provocative modern novel which has been generally praised for its clinical veracity presents a case study that lends itself to a discussion of the difference in the ambience of treatment between traditional psychoanalytic psychotherapy and self-psychology oriented psychotherapy. In *August*, Judith Rossner (1983) presents a vivid description of a borderline suicidal adolescent girl in treatment with a Ph.D. psychotherapist who herself suffers from a core depression and an empty depleted self. The therapist required two psychoanalyses of unspecified type to be able to accept a public compliment about her attractiveness, an indicator of an unintegrated repressed archaic grandiose self as depicted in Kohut's "horizontal split." Because of early disillusionment with her alcoholic father and depressed mother who commits suicide, the therapist is unable to form mature male attachments free of her narcissistic self-pathology.

The story line of the book is a pseudodramatic search by both patient and "doctor" to provide for themselves an empathic selfobject matrix. The therapist fails and remains, in her forties, essentially alone; the future of the patient, as she graduates college in her early twenties, is more hopeful. The book is also a commentary on the transitional status and genuinely tormenting social problems of modern women from two generations. One dramatic line sums up the therapist's attitude: "Women looked at a gray-haired man and saw father; men looked at a gray-haired woman and ran from death" (p. 36). Rossner indulges in a common defense in my clinical experience — she blames the therapist's inability to successfully relate to men on the pathology of the men in our culture.

The therapist carried out an intuitive mixture in the treatment that led to substantial improvement, a treatment that was allegedly a psychoanalysis but certainly not a traditional form of it. It remains unclear what the therapeutic convictions of the therapist are. What makes the story ring true is the ambience of the therapy, which illustrates what Kohut believed to be essential in firming cohesion of the self in psychotherapy.

*August* is convincing as a treatment report of a borderline patient and is a worthwhile illustration of how an intuitive therapist can apply self psychology with favorable results, even in the absence of any theoretical understanding. It was Kohut's goal to transform this intuitive expertise into a craft with theoretical underpinnings that could be taught and methodically practiced.

The title of the book refers to the traditional vacation time of psychoanalysts, and the unavoidable disruption of selfobject transferences by this and other absences. The entire drama of the book revolves around these vacation disruptions in a remarkable literary portrayal of Kohut's (1971, p. 91) emphasis on such vacations as typical of the inevitable failures in empathy that must occur in every treatment!

## A TRADITIONAL COUNTEREXAMPLE

Searles' (1985) discussion of the borderline patient is an example of how the object-relations approach differs from that of the psychology of the self. He notes the tendency of the borderline patient to "regard all his subjectively good, healthy aspects as having been created by himself, and all his psychopathology as being attributable to interactions with, and identifications with, the warped, hurtful, neglectful (and so forth) aspects of his parent figures" (p. 21). According to Searles, therapists tend to share this orientation and even come to believe that they are "the first good person, or potentially good person, whom the patient has ever encountered" (p. 10). His explanation, based on mechanisms of splitting, introjection, and projection, is diametrically opposed to that of Kohut.

When Searles is caught "semidozing" behind the couch and the patient, after a silence, remarks, "I don't know whether you're really here" (p. 14), he responds by connecting the patient's silence and remark with her early experiences of an emotionally detached mother (p. 14). A self psychologist would approach this incident differently, stressing the here-and-now failure of the selfobject therapist, and taking the patient's comment literally, as a communication of current disappointment. Searles notes that the silence and comment were preceeded by a period during which the patient appeared not to notice his "semidozing." On this basis, he interprets the silence and comment as an identification with "the more detached components of the therapist's personality" (p. 14).

# Chapter 16

~~~~~~

# Narcissistic Psychosomatic
# Disorders

The psychosomatic approach may be defined as the study of the influence of emotional factors in any disease and the investigation of the coordination of somatic and psychological factors with each other. In the chain of causal events leading to certain illnesses, some of the links can only be described in psychological terms, and these are what we look for in psychosomatic studies. There are three types of influence of psychological processes on body functions, which constitute the three areas commonly studied in psychosomatic medicine: coordinated voluntary behavior, the motivational background of which can be described only in psychological terms; Darwin's (1965) "expressive innervations," the purpose of which are to bring about a discharge of emotional tension; and possibly adaptive responses which take place in the visceral organs, involving neither direct goals, conscious motivations, nor the immediate discharge of emotional tension. Cannon (1953) explained these responses as changes in the body economy under the influence of emotions and introduced the idea of an adaptive preparation for fight or flight.

For example, the wish to receive food, if sustained, has certain typical physiologic responses associated with it, such as the secretion of gastric juices. These responses become pathological only in situations of stored tension over a long period of time. Thus when no relief of the wish or from the emotional problem or conflict by voluntary activity is possible, the organic difficulty begins to occur. When the voluntary behavior that would relieve the emotional tension never takes place — due, for example, to conflicts about this behavior — the perpetuation of the wish leads to organic pathology. This approach stresses the chronicity of the situation.

It is not necessary, however, to also postulate specific complex psychological drive-conflict constellations (Alexander 1950) in explaining each of the psychosomatic disorders. For example, narcissistic psychosomatic disorders may be defined as pathological, altered body conditions secondary to certain chronic narcissistic personality and behavior patterns. These patterns, like narcissistic personality and narcissistic behavior disorders, arise out of basic defects in the structure of the self which produce a state of chronic narcissistic disequilibrium superimposed on a faulty self-soothing apparatus. The patterns represent failed efforts at restoring narcissistic equilibrium, repetitive and chronic in nature, and accompanied by narcissistic rage secondary to the failures — which imposes an additional chronic burden on the already faulty drive-channeling and drive-controlling capacities and increases the disequilibrium, leading to a vicious pathological spiral and possible self-destruction.

## Coronary Artery Disease

If we consider coronary artery disease as one example of a narcissistic psychosomatic disorder, we find a great deal of speculation in the literature but few hard facts. In reviewing a standard textbook such as Hurst et al. (1974), the consensus is that the arterial wall of the coronary artery reacts to a variety of stimuli and pathogenic influences; there are reversible elements in the atherosclerotic process. Thus the early fatty streaks and even the early uncomplicated atheromatous lesions have been shown to be reversible in animals and human beings. Coronary artery disease is a multifactorial disease involving genetic, environmental, and other factors, only some of which have been identified. The emotional factors at present are poorly identified and described in the standard textbooks as "minor risk factors." Factors such as genetic familial history of premature coronary artery disease; elevated serum lipid levels; a diet rich in total calories, saturated fats, cholesterol, sugar, and salt; hypertension; diabetes mellitus; and cigarette smoking, are major risk factors which have been established by research. Obesity, sedentary living, personality type, and psychosocial tensions, are suggested but not established as risk factors.

The opposite point of view has been repeatedly expressed by Friedman and his co-workers in a series of publications. In the course of writing these works, Friedman et al. moved toward believing that personality type is the most important risk factor in coronary heart disease. In Friedman's (1969) *Pathogenesis of Coronary Artery Disease*, a competitive behavior pattern is seriously considered to be an additional risk factor: those individuals who have a highly competitive, aggressive, and hostile behavior pattern show a much greater incidence of coronary artery disease than less competitive individuals. Such theories were presented even by Osler in 1897, whom Friedman quotes on the worry and strain of modern life as a cause of early arterial degeneration. This view began to crystalize in Friedman's mind about 1955 when he began to observe the presence of certain traits in "almost every one" of our middle-aged and younger coronary patients.

The most salient description by Friedman (1969) of the "pattern A" is as follows: "a relatively *chronic struggle* to obtain an *unlimited* number of *poorly defined* things from their environment in *the shortest period of time* and, if necessary, against the opposing efforts of other things or persons in this same environment" (p. 84). This struggle is encouraged by the contemporary Western culture of narcissism; Friedman's emblem of such a person is "a clenched fist holding a stopwatch" (p. 85). It is important to differentiate this behavior type from the chronic or acute anxiety neurotic presenting with overt worry, fear, hysteria, or anxiety. The latter group of patients do not have an increased incidence of coronary artery disease, even though they perpetually worry about it.

This now named Type-A personality has been described so frequently (Hoffman 1984) that it is unnecessary to go into detail; furthermore, there is no agreement — despite Friedman's prodigious efforts — that Type-A personality is associated with increased coronary disease. For example, E. Friedman and Hellerstein (1973) disagree with the Type-A association and description and argue that their studies show that Type-A persons had a low incidence of coronary risk. Their coronary candidate is a phlegmatic or Type-B individual with low self-esteem! The subject is still surrounded by controversy, and more research is necessary (Moldofsky 1984).

The debate was brought to a fever pitch by Friedman and Rosenman (1974) and Friedman and Ulmer (1984), in which the theory is given as established fact: Type-A behavior is presented as the critical cause of coronary artery disease. The Friedman theory is not regarded by cardiologists as scientifically established.

Currently, there are *two* major approaches to the psychological aspects of the etiology of coronary artery disease. One approach stresses the nonspecific effects of intense psychosocial tensions, while the other claims there is statistical correlation between a certain type of personality and an increased incidence of coronary artery disease. A thorough review of the subject by Jenkins (1971) leads to some promising ideas. Jenkins hypothesizes that life dissatisfaction is a risk factor for coronary disease. Long-term struggle with persisting life problems, especially in a setting of fatigue, depression, emotional drain, is an equally suggestive etiologic factor; the conceptual separation of "stress" and "dissatisfaction" is artificial. Jenkins regards the coronary-prone behavior pattern as an unsettled issue. He mentions that infarcts are often preceded by the loss of prestige (narcissistic wounding) which is reacted to by harder work. Angina patients are described as bursting with repressed resentment; Appels et al. (1979) stress that this aggression is turned inward when the narcissistically perceived environment cannot be controlled. Rimé and Bonami (1979) document a similar phenomenon, along with the disavowed exhibitionism of coronary patients.

The coronary-prone individual has been described by various investigators as a person who not only meets a challenge by putting out extra effort, but who takes little satisfaction from accomplishments. This young precoronary patient is restless during leisure hours and even somewhat guilty about relaxation. This individual rarely takes vacations and regiments leisure time with obligatory participation in assorted social, civic, or educational activities. Traditional psychoanalytic authors (Alexander 1950, pp. 72–75, Weiss and English 1957, p. 217) have viewed this pattern as a defense against deep regressive passivity. Their conception differs from Friedman's concept of the Type-A personality. Alexander and Weiss and English stress unconscious guilt and counterphobic mechanisms in defining the coronary-prone individual.

Current studies emphasize the importance of hostility and point to the stress of American-style contemporary urban life as major contributing factors in heart disease (Williams et al. 1980). Similar studies (Dembroski et al. 1985) suggest a somewhat more psychogenic rather than environmental etiology by documenting the depression, anxiety, tension, and repressed anger that coronary-prone individuals develop under stress. This is often associated with insomnia and a sense of being tired on awakening; we have here a person vulnerable to stress who is exhausted but not necessarily a Type-A personality.

Perhaps these two basic psychological points of view — nonspecific stress and personality type — could be combined by emphasizing the role of chronic stress. For a Type-A person, whose life is characterized by emotions of aggression, anger, and ambition, the usual stresses and strains of everyday life become highly magnified. A person who views these stresses from a narcissistic stance as constituting a never-ending flow of dissatisfactions and control battles to be won with a constant eye on the competition, will be coronary prone. At the same time, a person who is under tremendous chronic emotional stress for realistic reasons is similarly coronary prone. Both situations produce the state of emotional depletion in an overburdened self; exacerbate the tendency to drink excessive amounts of coffee and use other stimulants; and prompt the individual to use tension-relieving devices such as eating, smoking, and drinking with a corresponding inability to relax and enjoy unscheduled time, rest, and sleep. In all cases I am assuming that genetic, dietary, and other etiologic factors are also implicated in this complex multifactorial disease.

## A Self-Psychological Interpretation

The Type-A personality concept, utilizing conscious psychology, can be contrasted with a more psychoanalytic point of view based on the work of Kohut. Many of the characteristics of the coronary-prone individual are similar to Kohut's description of the narcissistic personality disorder. The lack of sense of satisfaction in accomplishments, vague and poorly defined goals, the sense of time urgency, and fierce competitiveness are typical of the individual with unresolved narcissistic problems and are explained by Kohut's formulations.

Friedman and Ulmer (1984) assert that, "insecurity of status (primarily arising from an inadequate or diminished sense of self-esteem), or hyperaggressiveness, or both, almost always serve as the initiating core causes for the development of Type A personality" (p. 43). This comes, they report, from "the failure of the Type A person in his infancy and very early childhood to receive *unconditional* love, affection, and encouragement from one or both of his parents" (p. 45). The lack of sense of satisfaction in accomplishments and the vague and poorly defined goals point in self psychology to an unintegrated grandiose self and idealized parent imago with resulting serious defects in the bipolar self. In such narcissistically damaged individuals, achievements can never match expectations — exactly as described by these authors (p. 78) for the Type-A personality.

Such individuals may suffer from profound narcissistic rage (Kohut 1978), which may become chronic. The demand for absolute control over a narcissistically experienced archaic environment and an unconscious boundless ambitious exhibitionism bring the individual into constant collision with the outside world and other people. Furthermore, since the aims and grandiose goals of the narcissistic personality are relentlessly motivated by the split-off grandiose self, there can never be any lasting satisfaction of these vague, endless, and boundless needs. (We all meet such individuals in clinical practice.)

The ego increasingly cedes its reasoning, modifying, and organizing capacity to the task of rationalizing the persistent insistence on exhibitionistic success. In extreme cases, failures and weaknesses are attributed to the malevolence and corruption of uncooperative individuals outside of the self, instead of acknowledging the inherent limitations of the individual. At worst this becomes a chronic quasi-paranoid condition. In most instances reality testing is preserved, but when narcissistic rage is blocked, Kohut suggests it may shift its focus and become directed either at the self, with the consequence of a self-destructive way of life and depression, or at the soma, in which a psychosomatic disease can develop, or both.

Given the appropriate risk factors such as genetic predisposition, cigarette smoking, a high fat diet, and elevated blood pressure, which commonly accompany such ambitious driving activity, the life characterized by chronic narcissistic rage can produce coronary artery disease in the way that has been described in all the previous studies. The difference in the self-psychological point of view is that it contradicts the implied hopefulness of the outcome of the behavioral change methods suggested by Friedman and his co-workers (1974, 1984). If a person has a narcissistic personality disorder and is unconsciously fixed on unceasing efforts to achieve grandiose ambitions, attain omnipotence, and act out boundless exhibitionism, it is not possible to hold all this in check by common sense reasoning, self-control, and conscious mental exercises. Even if one deliberately curtails one's behavior, the chronic narcissistic rage continues unabated at an unconscious level. The conflict is driven underground by inhibiting the acting-out of the rage and the narcissistic aims that have produced the surface diagnostic manifestations labelled Type-A. Only the secondary effect on the body physiology, such as that from too much work and not enough rest could be eliminated in this conscious deliberate way, but the underlying narcissistic rage continues unabated with powerful unrelieved narcissistic tensions. Because it is important to eliminate the secondary effects also, nothing can be said *against* the behavioral approach of Friedman or of Carruthers (1974). It remains questionable how effective this approach would be in the prevention of coronary artery disease.

Long-term life dissatisfaction and the inability to receive refreshment from social and leisure activities, as well as the frequent finding that coronary artery disease is preceded by a setback in work involving a loss of prestige (narcissistic wounding) and reacted to by even harder work, is explained by positing an underlying narcissistic personality disorder. This offers a much sharper dynamic explanation; chronic loss or failure of narcissistically perceived archaic self-objects has occurred, with the concomitant production of profound narcissistic rage. The rage also explains the obvious disregard of the Type-A individual for a self-destructive way of life. In reviewing a study comparing small samples of patients with angina and rheumatic heart disease, Jenkins (1971) reports that the authors judged the patients with angina to be profoundly angry but attempting to repress it or to use compulsive defenses; other authors also found "well-controlled aggression" to be correlated with coronary disease risk factors (Jenkins 1976).

The narcissistic personality disorder and subsequent narcissistic rage is common to a variety of ways of living that have been described as highly correlated with coronary artery disease. I (1976) have expanded and tried to dramatize this view in a recent book. Conscious efforts to change these ways of living and behaving will be most useful in reducing the secondary effects on an unhealthy life style, but the basic disorder remains. The effect of chronic narcissistic rage, even if it is not acted out, on the development of coronary artery disease reduces our hopefulness that conscious change of life-style could somehow be a major factor in the prevention of this disorder or in the reduction of morbidity.

Further evidence corroborates this point of view, since it is common for victims of heart attacks to return to their previous way of life, gain weight, and often resume cigarette smoking. This is true despite efforts by the physician and the patient's family to prevent it, and indicates an unbearable underlying unconscious narcissistic disequilibrium, driving the patient to death.

Patients who go back to a self-destructive life-style after a myocardial infarction are urgently in need of intensive psychotherapy, just as much as patients with a severe narcissistic personality disorder. The internist or general physician who watches a postmyocardial infarction patient gain weight, resume smoking, and go on with the previous behavior has an obligation to confront the patient with the fact that the emotional disorder is life threatening, and to recommend intensive psychotherapy.

## Adult Eating Disorders

I will now examine adult eating disorders as a second example of narcissistic psychosomatic disorders. Goodsitt (1985) similarly has applied self psychology to a study of classical anorexia nervosa. Narcissistic rage which stems from the failure of early selfobjects produces a variety of the features of adult eating disorders, including migraine (Friedman and Ulmer 1984), adult temper tantrums, self-destructive activity, paranoid proclivities, body-image disturbances, and compulsive rituals. Such rage floods a defective self-soothing apparatus, and the patient regresses to eating disorders in order to gain temporary relief and to counteract threatened fragmentation of the self (Chessick 1985b). Psychoanalytic psychotherapy of these disorders requires a combination of modalities, but insight into what has happened and into the unconscious narcissistic fantasies, which differ in each individual case and determine the particular disorder pattern, is required consistently for lasting changes in the patient's life-style.

For example, a patient dreams that she, her husband, and her little girl plant a garden. The patient's parents visit and the garden grows nicely, but the mother will not go out to look at it. Father is a depressed man who after much coaxing does go out to the garden and take a look, and says rather indifferently, "That's nice." Then, however, father becomes happy and cheerful because the patient gets her little girl to eat a pizza. This is from the dream of an obese woman with a psychotic mother, who was saved from a totally depleted self by her usually depressed father who would brighten up substantially when the patient would eat. Neither the father nor the mother had much interest in any of the natural developmental or growth experiences of the patient.

Weiss and English (1957) remind us that some families are quite "oral" in their orientation to life. A treat for such a family will be a good meal rather than creative work or play. Everything about the offering and receiving of food is endowed with a high emotional value.

Kolb and Brodie (1982) and Shainess (1979) point out that the development of obesity often occurs in a family setting in which the parents compensate for their own life frustrations and disappointments through the child; the mother is the dominant family member and holds the obese child by anxious overprotection, including pushing food. She frequently has high expectations for the child's achievement in order to compensate for the failures of the parents. The obese child is one who has passively accepted the indulged role without rebellion, and has been taught to substitute food for love and satisfaction. This also produces the psychological situation Kohut (1971) labels the "vertical split" in the narcissistic personality disorder, as diagrammed by Kohut (1971, p. 185); openly displayed infantile grandiosity is related to mother's narcissistic use of the child's performance.

Hamburger (1951) described four different but closely related types of hyperphagia. One group of his patients overate in response to nonspecific emotional tensions such as loneliness, anxiety, or boredom. Another group overate in chronic states of tension and frustration, using food as substitute gratification in unpleasant life situations over long periods. In a third group, overeating represented a symptom of underlying psychopathology, most frequently, an empty depression. The final group, in which overeating took on the proportions of an addiction, was characterized by a compulsive food craving unrelated to external events, and thus was driven by an unconscious chronic narcissistic disequilibrium.

Numerous descriptive typological reports on emotional disturbances among the obese have flooded the literature. The better the study, the less the evidence for distinctive psychological features.

Stunkard (1980) described the negative body image in obese persons, who characteristically complain in psychotherapy that their bodies are grotesque and loathsome and that others view them with hostility and contempt. The obesity of persons who were obese in childhood (so-called "hyperplastic obesity," "juvenile-onset obesity," or "developmental obesity") differs from that of persons who became obese as adults ("hypertrophic obesity"). The juvenile types tend to be more severe, more resistant to treatment, and more likely to be associated with emotional disturbances. However, Stunkard (1975) and others disagree with the common notion that "middle age obesity" develops slowly and gradually; actually it occurs in a series of weight spurts, as each stressful period in middle age is accompanied in predisposed persons by excess eating.

Although many obese persons report that they overeat and gain weight when they are emotionally upset, Stunkard (1975) explains that it has "proved singularly difficult to proceed from this provocative observation to an understanding of the precise relationship between emotional factors and obesity" (p. 777). Obesity at a later stage often becomes a rationalization for failure and the attitudes of overweight persons toward themselves are complicated by the current Western cultural distaste for obesity, especially in women (Wooley and Wooley 1980).

Numerous authors have reported that the obese child becomes filled with grandiose daydreams as daily defeats in major aspirations are suffered. These fantasies are either conscious or disavowed and they differ from the psychotic because the obese person is aware that they are unreasonable. In the psychoanalytic treatment of adult obese patients, Ingram (1976) reports how these expansive and narcissistic features emerge coincident with weight reduction. In some cases, overeating appears protective against an incipient psychosis; such patients may develop a psychosis when they undertake to lose weight by vigorous dieting.

OBESITY AS AN ADDICTION

Stunkard (1975, 1980) describes about 10 percent of obese persons, most commonly women, as manifesting a "night-eating syndrome," characterized by morning anorexia and evening hyperphagia with insomnia. A "binge-eating syndrome" he says is found in about 5 percent of obese persons, characterized by sudden compulsive ingestion of large amounts of food in a short time, usually with great subsequent agitation and self-condemnation. In these two syndromes, a mere 15 percent of obese cases, it is allegedly easier to outline psychodynamics involving orality and ambivalence. Yet Bruch (1973) claims that in her experience such night-eaters are rare and binge-eaters are more common.

This leaves a large majority of obese persons in whom the disorder seems to be more subtle. In this large group that is described as "food addicts," patients have used food as a substitute for defects in psychic structure. Overeating has become an indispensable part of their life pattern and vigorous weight reduction exposes them to unbearable tensions. Vigorous treatment aimed at weight reduction alone seldom is successful and even if successful is seldom maintained for very long. Frosch (1977) places these patients among the "character impulse disorders," emphasizing their intolerance of tension or frustration based on developmental interference with their capacity for "anticipation" and confidence.

Psychoanalytic recognition of food addiction goes back to Rado (1926), who also coined the important concept of "alimentary orgasm"; the arguments for obesity as representing an addiction to food are updated and reviewed by Leon (1982). Common observations and reports of obese patients about eating show that Rado's notion of the relatively slower and longer lasting "alimentary orgasm," a diffuse feeling of well being that extends throughout the organism, complete with a sense of repose and a faraway look in the eyes, can indeed serve as a short circuit for avoiding sexual and more complex adult interpersonal intimacies. Clinical experience also confirms his contention that "a long series of foods and delicacies can be worked out, forming a regular gradation from ordinary foods up to pure intoxicants" (Rado 1926, p. 37n). I (1960) have investigated the drug end of this gradation and the "pharmacogenic orgasm". Woollcott (1981) presents a more recent discussion of this, emphasizing the "basic fault" which leads to a "fusion-individuation conflict," in some ways similar to the pathology of the borderline patient.

## A SELF-PSYCHOLOGICAL EXPLANATION

In discussing the addict Kohut (1971) writes:

His psyche remains fixated on an archaic self-object, and the personality will throughout life be dependent on certain objects in what seems to be an intense form of object hunger. The intensity of the search for and of the dependency on these objects is due to the fact that they are striven for as a substitute for the missing segments for the psychic structure. . . . [The mother of the addict] because of her defective empathy with the child's needs . . . did not appropriately fulfill the functions . . . which the mature psychic apparatus should later be able to perform (or initiate) predominantly on its own. Traumatic disappointments suffered during these archaic stages . . . deprive the child of the gradual internalization of early experiences of being optimally soothed, or being aided in going to sleep. (pp. 45–46)

In his last book, Kohut (1984) called attention to the obese Bismarck, who was enabled to reduce his "cravings" for food, wine, and tobacco by a Dr. Schweniger, who for 15 years functioned as a substitute selfobject. Kohut bases this on a report by Pflanze (1972); this report does not indicate whether Bismarck actually lost weight after Schweniger entered his life. At any rate, Schweniger was at the same time an intuitive therapist and a medical charlatan who had been dismissed on a morals charge from the medical faculty at Munich — but as a therapist he did know what to do for Bismarck.

In the language of the psychology of the self, selfobject failures of a traumatic degree during the day lead to increasing disintegration of certain sections of the self, which were experienced by Bismarck especially at bedtime as "oral cravings" that took on the character of a drive. Kohut argues that such an individual, giving up on selfobjects, turns to stimulation of body zones for inner cohesion and a sense of being alive. The addictionlike intensity however is not due to a drive, says Kohut, but due to the intense need to fill a structural defect. It only succeeds for a moment and builds no structure, so it is like eating with a gastric fistula. Schweniger was able to replace the food, wine, and cigars, and to function as a sustaining selfobject for Bismarck, sitting with him as Bismarck went to sleep, much in the manner a parent sits with a child. When he had succeeded in achieving this selfobject transference, Schweniger found himself indispensable to the Bismarck household for 15 years.

Bruch (1973) described "reactive obesity," in which overeating serves as a defense against deeper depression. A variety of authors such as Cantwell et al. (1977) have linked the eating disorders to depression; some hopeful reports (Pope et al. 1983) on the treatment of these disorders with antidepressant medication have recently appeared. Overeating in these patients represents a self-soothing effort to prevent disintegration to more profound archaic experiences that are repressed and associated with the current depressive affectual situation.

In Krystal's (1982) view these archaic experiences were often actual infantile disasters such as "colic, eczema, feeding, or sleeping difficulties" which are "covered over by a conspiracy of silence, related to the shared wish to undo the common misfortune" (p. 598). Thus overeating protects the patient against basic, disintegrating, massive affect states of a primitive archaic nature that threaten to develop if the current stress situation continues unabated. In self psychology, overeating would be said to protect against fragmentation of the sense of self.

## BULIMAREXIA

The syndrome of bulimarexia, a binge-purge cycle, has become popular (Casper 1983) among patients mostly in the teens and twenties. The syndrome can appear at any age and approximately 5 percent of those who suffer from it are male. During the binge there is a sense of loss of control and guilt; during the purge, a restitution, catharsis, and reinforcement of the sense of control. Underneath all of these eating disorders there lies, in the language of self psychology, a nameless preverbal depression, apathy, a sense of deadness in an empty depleted self, and diffuse chronic narcissistic rage. In my clinical experience the massive rage generates either paranoid fears or self-hatred with a distorted hateful self-image, migraine, temper tantrums, or any combination of these, similar to the pattern in the borderline patient. It may also appear as a curious relentless compulsive ritual, devoid of pleasure, in which the patient eats up everything in sight.

In all these patients, Bruch (1973, p. 100) points out, the fatness is only an externalization of the conviction of ugliness on the inside. A patient reported:

> I eat to feel, to get some sensation as opposed to no sensation. When you have done you are uncomfortable, but that is a feeling. Also I make myself fat, I think, to mirror how I feel inside about myself — it broadcasts a message that says, "Love this ugly person as I am." It fits with my lack of trust in people and says, "I'll make it hard for you if you want to be nice to me."

We may regard this quotation in the light of Laing's comment (Chapter 6) about how projection represents an attempt at self-mirroring. From the psychology of the self point of view, projection in these cases, whether in fantasy or actualized, can be understood as giving up on the selfobject and attempting to achieve the desperately needed mirroring, attention, and soothing. In our culture a fat person is indeed noticed, albeit in an unflattering manner. Becoming fat and thus making oneself the object of derogatory notice could be thought of as the actualization of a projective fantasy where individuals imagine that everyone is looking at them with hostile intent.

The dramatic eating disorder, whether through "alimentary orgasms," masochistic infliction of self-starvation or unpleasant compulsive stuffing, or the binge-purge guilt and restitution cycle, drains off the rage and paranoia and focuses the patient's attention from the empty depleted self and onto preoccupation with gastrointestinal tract sensations. In this manner some sort of sense of being alive is maintained. On top of the depleted and fragmented nuclear core, the patient has built various protective rituals and self-soothing activities which sometimes permit the patient to function in society.


NARCISSISTIC RAGE


At the same time, the patient must deal with the massive narcissistic rage or (as it is traditionally called) the unconscious sadism. For example, Offenkrantz and Tobin (1974) discuss these patients as "depressive characters" and emphasize the great unconscious rage at important objects who are not providing the patient with what is unconsciously felt to be needed. Rage often is turned on the therapist. Under this lies an "anaclitic depression" characterized by depletion and a hopelessness that sufficient gratification will ever be possible.

Glover (1956) in a landmark study in 1932 also placed less emphasis on fixation in the oral stage and viewed addiction as a transition state between psychotic and neurotic phases, serving the function of controlling sadism and preventing a regression to psychosis, or fragmentation. Labelling the addictions "circumscribed narcissistic neuroses," he writes that the patient's rage together with identifications with objects towards whom he is ambivalent, constitute a dangerous psychic state . . . symbolized as an internal concrete substance. The drug is then . . . an external counter-substance which cures by destruction. In this sense drug-addiction might be considered an improvement on paranoia; the paranoidal element is limited to the drug-substance which is then used as a therapeutic agent to deal with intrapsychic conflict of a melancholic pattern. (p. 208)

In this form of "*localizing* paranoid anxiety" as Glover calls it, adaptation is enabled to proceed, and the differences in choice of substance from the more benign, like food, to dangerous chemicals are postulated by Glover to be related to the degree of archaic sadism.

There is no reason for this postulate about choice of substance, because food can certainly be conceived of by the patient as destructive and totally noxious. This is best illustrated in a play by Innaurato (1977), *The Transfiguration of Benno Blimpie*, a nightmarish account of a grotesquely fat and lonely 25-year-old man, who relives the humiliating events of his life while preparing to end it by eating himself to death. Benno, who spent his childhood eating, daydreaming, and drawing, says, "Paintings, you see, aren't enough. When loneliness and emptiness and longing congeal like a jelly, nothing assuages the ache. Nothing, nothing, nothing." As the narcissistic rage erupts in the drama he depersonalizes and plans, "When I become so fat I cannot get into his clothes, and can barely move, I will nail the door shut. I will put his eyes out with a long nail and I will bite at himself until he dies" (Scene 8, pp. 16–17). At the end of the play, Benno prepares to mutilate his body with a meat cleaver.

## ADULT ANOREXIA AND ANOREXIA NERVOSA

Patients suffering from anorexia have been separated by Dally (1969) into three subgroups; various authors (Wilson 1983) have stressed the heterogeneity of this syndrome as a "final common pathway" for many disorders. Anorexia, like obesity, can appear in clinical practice in a large variety of ways. One group purges and induces vomiting; another group shows impulsive self-destructive behavior including suicide attempts, self-mutilation, and alcoholism; still another group achieves the desired end of thinness by dieting alone.

The psychodynamics of anorexia in young women have long been thought to include the impairment of development arising from an early unsuccessful mother–daughter relationship. The adolescent girl, faced with feminine individuation and threatened by the loss of dependency on the family, responds to the conflict in these cases by regression to an infantile maternal relationship with unconscious craving for blissful eating experiences. This is denied in the subsequent perpetual drama of an oscillation between eating and severe dieting; the pursuit of thinness usually represents an act of hostile and defiant compliance by the patient against the mother.

Bruch (1975) has repeatedly stated that anorexia nervosa is more akin to schizophrenic development or borderline states than to neuroses. She admits that depressive features deserve special evaluation and may indicate a true depression as the primary illness, but maintains that the disorder expresses "the underlying despair of a schizophrenic reaction" (p. 802) and recognition of the underlying potentially schizophrenic core is essential for effective treatment. In my clinical experience, an important difference between classical anorexia nervosa, which appears suddenly in early adolescence, and the usually less lethal anorexia developing in adult patients is that in the latter, the core is depressive rather than schizophrenic and the clinical material points to Kohut's descriptions of the empty depleted self and narcissistic rage.

Most traditional psychodynamic formulations concerning the cause of anorexia have centered around the phobic response to food resulting from the sexual and social tensions generated by the physical changes associated with early puberty. But even in 1945 Fenichel (1945) stated that anorexias developing in adult life "may have a very different dynamic significance." He explained that anorexia may represent a simple hysterical conversion symptom expressing the fear of an orally perceived pregnancy, or of unconscious sadistic wishes. It may also be part of an ascetic reaction formation in a compulsion neurosis, may be an affect-equivalent in a depression (in which the symptom of refusal of food makes its appearance before other signs of the depression are developed), or may be a refusal of any contact with the objective world and thus point to an incipient schizophrenia.

Fenichel comes a long way from any simplistic formulation of anorexia, at least in adults. He mentions a case reported by Eissler which illustrates that anorexia is thought of as "only one symptom of a general disturbance of all object relationships." Fenichel writes that Eissler's patient "had not gone beyond an extremely archaic stage of ego development. The mother 'remained the most important part of the patient's ego.' The refusal of food represented the longing for the primary, still undifferentiated gratification by the mother and its sadistic distortion after frustration" (p. 177). The conceptualization here is closer to that of Kohut, but 25 years earlier.

## A Self-Psychological Approach to Adult Eating Disorders

There are two general kinds of functional disturbances in the third area of psychosomatic medicine mentioned at the beginning of this chapter. One of them consists of unwanted physiological changes caused by the inappropriate use of the function in question, which Fenichel labels an organ neurosis. The other kind of disturbance has a specific unconscious meaning, is an expression of a fantasy in "body language," and is directly accessible to psychoanalysis in the same way as a dream. The term "conversion neurosis" is usually reserved for this category. A certain percentage of organ neuroses actually are affect-equivalents; they represent the specific physical expression of a given affect without the corresponding conscious mental experience. For example, anorexia in some cases is an affect-equivalent of depression as recent studies (Cantwell et al. 1977, Casper and Davis 1977) demonstrate.

In most cases of adult eating disorders a pathological discomfort — narcissistic disequilibrium — rooted in unconscious problems generates a certain behavior, which in turn causes somatic changes in the tissues. The person's behavior of dieting, overeating, or oscillation between the two was initially intended to relieve internal pressure stemming from this narcissistic disequilibrium; the somatic symptom forming the consequence of this effort usually was not originally sought by the person either consciously or unconsciously. Later, these body changes of fatness or thinness may be worked into the solution and become a central preoccupation.

Fenichel (1945) also mentions a paper by Wulff written in 1932, describing a "psychoneurosis" seen more in women and related "to hysteria, cyclothymia and addiction" and characterized by a fight against pregenital sexuality. Sexual satisfaction is conceived of as a "dirty meal." Periods of depression in which the patients stuff themselves and feel "fat, bloated, dirty, untidy, or pregnant" alternate with "good" periods in which they behave ascetically, feel slim, and conduct themselves either normally or with some elation. The alternating feelings of ugliness and beauty and the oscillation in the body feelings seem to be similar to the feelings before and after menstrual periods, and also may have an exhibitionistic component. But Fenichel, like many traditional psychoanalytic authors, vacillates between conflict interpretations using traditional psychodynamics and his intuitive clinical knowledge that such interpretations are not sufficient to explain the compulsively addictive aspects of these cases.

Following Rado, Fenichel describes "an oral-erotic excitement" involved in eating; the food addictions are unsuccessful attempts to master guilt, depression, or anxiety by activity, but no explanation is given as to how this works. Eating disorders for Fenichel become what he calls "character defenses against anxiety," in which certain basic infantile conflicts are mastered by working them out over and over again in terms of food.

Bruch (1973, 1974, 1975, 1979, 1982) developed her own therapeutic approach to eating disorders, but her concepts have the same sense of generalization about them as the old classical psychoanalytic formulations. She recognizes a problem involving self-esteem, narcissistic rage, depletion, and depression in these patients as well as a narcissistic power struggle with the parents, but she depends on interpersonal theory, using a Sullivanian approach.

Bruch (1979), in discussing anorexia nervosa, admits, "Relatively little is known how this changeover takes place, from what looks like ordinary dieting to this inflexible self-destructive but hotly defended fixation on weight and food" (p. 76). But Kohut (1971) described stages of fragmentation of the self in severe borderline and schizophrenic patients where there is a reconstitution of the self with certain parts of the body decathected and viewed as useless; such patients may indeed even cut off part of the body at this point. It is not hard to see how a fragmentation of the self in adolescents and adults can lead to a similar reconstitution where the useless part of the body self is the body fat. Bruch (1979) points out from her vast clinical experience how many anorexics spend time looking in the mirror over and over again "taking pride in every pound they lose and every bone that shows. The more pride they take in it, the stronger the assertion that they look just fine" (p. 82).

Severe anorexia can be thought of as a pathological reconstitution of the fragmented self where a part of the self becomes split off and utterly divested of libido in order to permit a shallow reconstitution of the rest; this decathected part is represented by the body fat which is then viewed as useless, unwanted, and in need of being severed. Indeed, maintaining reconstitution of the self may require a continuing and dangerous severing of this useless body fat representing the unwanted part of the self, which would explain the persistence with which these patients starve themselves as well as their rigid negativism toward treatment. If they are force-fed, they may commit suicide.

Severe pathological anorexia represents, as Bruch says, a grotesque mirror image of obesity. She maintains also that both are related to faulty hunger awareness. This leads to Bruch's claim that the lack of awareness of living one's own life is of fundamental significance to the development of severe eating disturbances. In my clinical experience, this curious sense of being ineffective or being a child in an adult world is characteristic of patients with eating disorders.

A clinical feature I emphasize, as in the "case" of Benno Blimpie, is not given so much prominence by Bruch: that of the deep inner emptiness, chronic narcissistic rage, and consequent paranoid proclivities in such patients. Yet Bruch (1973) reports a case of a fat student nurse who was hospitalized for an acute schizophrenic episode and was observed to eat ravenously whenever she had an argument or felt threatened. Her explanation was that she was afraid that the hostility of others and their angry words would rattle around inside her and keep on wounding her. "By stuffing herself with food she would cover her sore inside, like with a poultice, and she would not feel the hurt so much" (p. 92). The deep intrapsychic dynamics involving cycles of introjection and projection or alternatively Kohut's concept of the depleted nuclear self and its disintegration products are omitted in Bruch's formulations.

The eating disorders protect the patient from unbearable affects which then appear if the eating disorder is stopped. The extremely negative self-image and self-hatred — or in Kohut's terms the depleted self with the disintegration product of narcissistic rage — precede the development of obesity, as emphasized by Stunkard and Burt (1967), Powers (1980), and many others. This intrapsychic psychopathology forms the foundation of the various adult eating disorders, which then develop when the narcissistic tension becomes unbearable and the faulty preoedipal self-soothing system becomes overwhelmed. The self then threatens to fragment or actually does so, as in *The Trans-figuration of Benno Blimpie*.

As a clinical illustration, we may take Bruch's (1973) description of "thin fat people," borrowed from Heckel — who warned us already in 1911 that the loss of weight by a fat person does not represent a cure by itself. Indeed the patient may show much more serious psychopathology when the weight is lost, and the battle may shift to an attempt to keep from gaining weight by an obsessive preoccupation with maintaining a semistarved appearance that is so popular among fashion models in our culture. These dissatisfied people are still representatives of an eating disorder. Their compulsion with staying excessively slim is a common clinical sequel in cases of obesity treated with various forms of behavior modification or other symptom-focused therapies. These therapies have converted a miserable fat person into an even more miserable thin person, and in both cases the person is compulsively preoccupied with eating. Usually these adult patients do not progress to a malignant state of anorexia nervosa, but reach a certain miserable stability in their thinness.

The narcissistic aspects of adult compulsive eaters or dieters are especially striking along with their very low sense of self-esteem, conviction of inadequacy, and compensatory fantasies and daydreams of "astounding grandiosity" (Bruch 1973). Obese patients often show a curious "all or nothing" attitude, so that when confronted with the fact that their unlimited aspirations are not obtainable, they are apt to give up, lay around at home, and grow fatter! In clinical work with such patients it is dangerous to allow the patient to assume that, if psychotherapy is successful and they achieve thinness, it will somehow lead to the realization of their grandiose expectations. This sort of attitude is greatly reinforced by advertising.

The inability of such patients to follow a diet acts as a safeguard against putting their narcissistic fantasies to the test of reality. As long as they are fat, they feel that they have it in their power now or in the future to set everything right by losing weight. Their basic psychological problems do not come into full awareness until they have lost weight. Remaining fat is an important defense against facing their own narcissistic psychopathology. Rigid dieting may precipitate a psychotic reaction or a profound depression. During the psychoanalytic treatment of schizophrenics, Federn (1947) observed that the psychosis was sometimes precipitated by intentional weight reduction.

In my clinical experience no patient has substantially reduced weight and maintained weight reduction without experiencing an extremely difficult and painful process. The inhibition of activity in obese persons is a more fundamental aspect of the disorder than the overeating. Lack of activity expresses a disturbance in the total approach to life and manifests, as Bruch (1973) puts it, "a real lack of enjoyment in using one's body, or a deep-seated mistrust of one's ability of mastery" (pp. 314–315); in Kohut's terms it is a representation of the empty depleted nuclear self. Thus the known value of exercise in weight reduction has to do with the reversal of a lifelong pattern of passivity, emptiness, daydreaming, and inactivity.

## "COMPULSIVE" EATERS

The group of fat people who are compulsive eaters represent, as Hamburger (1951) pointed out, an important subgroup of eating disorders. These patients seem unable to let unfinished food alone; they must compulsively finish everything. They are acting out a ritual of pleasing somebody else, a ritual which hides a deep, narcissistic rage. Either the anxious, overcontrolling parent insists that food is precious and sadistically demands the consumption of every bit of food that the parent provides, or the spouse — on whom the patient is pathologically dependent — has a deeply neurotic need to see the patient eat everything in sight. These patients are compulsively repeating a pattern that brought them mirroring approval from the vital selfobject in the past in order to maintain a false self, which is less unbearable than fragmentation and rage. The role of compulsive rituals in controlling aggression is predominant. Other patients compulsively eat only selected foods such as sweet rolls or ice cream, etc. In these patients there seems to be a combination of an organ neurosis and a conversion disorder; I have been able in some cases to trace the specific food to a vital association with the longed-for parental selfobject.

## *Psychotherapy of Eating Disorders*

Pernicious familial interference with reducing regimens can be expected. In the case of children and adolescents it is the parents who undermine the dietary regime, and in the case of married people it is frequently the spouse who has an unconscious vested interest in keeping the patient fat. This may come to the point where the therapist has to insist that other members of the family go into treatment if the case is to be successful. Every kind of ancillary support group such as Weight Watchers or TOPS, as well as medical supervision of diet and exercise, should be encouraged (Ingram 1976).

It does not follow from any of this however, that the eventual understanding of the unconscious meaning of the disorganized eating patterns through traditional methods is a mistake. But a traditional psychoanalysis based on drive psychology runs the risk of ignoring all that has been learned about such disorders. Self-psychology oriented psychotherapy, in an approach with which even Bruch (1974, 1979, 1982) would agree, concentrates first on the building of structures: "an attempt to repair the conceptual defects and distortions, the deep-seated sense of dissatisfaction and isolation, and the conviction of incompetence" (Bruch 1979, p. 143). This type of therapy focuses secondarily on interpretation and is consistent with Fenichel's characterization of most eating disorders as organ neuroses rather than conversion neuroses.

The most serious problem in intensive psychotherapy of the eating disorders is not that of a schizophrenic loss of reality testing, but of a deep empty depression in a defective nuclear self, often with core paranoid fragments, manifested clinically by a derogatory self image, cynicism, and hopelessness. Profound narcissistic rage also begins to show itself as the eating disorder is corrected. Thus, a long and difficult intensive psychotherapy is to be expected because we are dealing with a deep preoedipal disorder characterized by severe early structural defects in the nuclear self. The best clinical measure of basic change in these patients is in the reduction of their derogatory body image distortion (Garner et al. 1976, Casper et al. 1979, 1981).

Paranoid distortions and fuzzy reality testing need to be corrected by careful attention to the current realistic situation. As Bruch (1973) writes, "They suffer from an abiding sense of loneliness, or the feeling of not being respected by others, or of being insulted or abused, though the realistic situation may not contain these elements. The anticipation or recall of real or imagined insults may lead to withdrawal from the actual situation and flight into an eating binge" (p. 337). Even their confusion of body image is complicated (Powers 1980), combining inaccurate perception of actual size or shape with an unrealistic negative self-appraisal often consolidated in adolescence.

Such patients tolerate a silent psychoanalytic therapist poorly. The therapist, as Basch (1980) points out, must, at least at the beginning of treatment, be willing to participate with the patient in discussion of the details of the patient's current situation. At the beginning of therapy the patient must experience the therapist as practically useful and helpful in getting the patient to explore the details of and the solutions to the problems of everyday living. Krystal and Raskin (1970) call this "facilitating the establishment of a benign introject," in which the therapist is used "to create an object-representation which they can utilize for inspiration and achieving a major change in their identity and function" (p. 106). In other words, an idealizing transference must be allowed to form. If this early phase of psychotherapy is properly traversed, an addictive transference to the therapist forms, resembling the narcissistic selfobject transferences described by Kohut, and the intensive psychotherapy shifts increasingly into an interpretive psychoanalytic mode.

## COUNTERTRANSFERENCE PROBLEMS

The most serious countertransference problem encountered in the intensive psychotherapy of eating disorders is also understandable in self-psychological terms as described by Gunther (1976). The deep, empty depression in these patients produces a painful sensation of disequilibrium in the therapist, as the latter's normal liveliness, enthusiasm, and human investment in the patient are met repeatedly by a silent and depleted response or narcissistic self-preoccupation. This constitutes repeated narcissistic disappointment for the therapist over years; any therapist who works with eating disorders must have ample independent sources of emotional supply and empathy and be free of the temptation to turn to patients for gratification, soothing, or narcissistic massage. As the weight problem begins to correct itself patients become "worse" as the anger, despair, projective proclivities, and intolerance of any frustration or humiliation shows itself more and more in the interactions with the therapist (Ingram 1976).

Therapists may deal with their narcissistic disequilibrium and consequent narcissistic rage at these patients by a reaction formation, becoming a replica of the overanxious parent and shifting to a so-called supportive treatment due to excessive projective concerns about the patient's fragility. The patient thus gains control of the therapy and leads the therapist on a merry chase by threats of suicide, psychosis, or extreme fluctuations in weight. Because of the typical projection fantasy of these patients, as reported by Offenkrantz and Tobin (1974), that "the therapist needs the patient to become abstinent in order to alleviate the therapist's own sense of inner emptiness, lack of pleasure, and craving for relief," careful, continuing self-analysis is required to prevent externalization (Chessick 1972a) of this fantasy. Consultation with colleagues is often helpful.

The therapist in the intensive psychotherapy of these disorders is often called upon to decide when recommendations of outside medical help, groups, and even anxiolytic drugs are necessary. Danger arises when these aids are advocated due to countertransference disappointment, anger, and frustration, rather than in the service of the patient's need. If this occurs, the patient reexperiences empathic failure with the "food-stuffing mother." Conversely, withholding these when they would be appropriate is also a destructive manifestation of countertransference; careful self-analytic investigation on each occasion is required.

When the patient must take realistic steps to change her or his life-style, the previously compliant and cooperative patient begins to show a tough capacity to engage the therapist in a bitter struggle. The willingness of the therapist to enter into this struggle and still maintain an empathic and analytic interpretive stance is probably the crucial factor that determines whether the treatment will succeed. As Nacht (Chessick 1974) said, analogous to Kohut's (1984, pp. 15–16) statements about early parental selfobjects, the therapist's comments are not as important as what kind of person the therapist actually is.

It is extremely difficult for the therapist to maintain empathic contact with and a deep inner sense of commitment to an extremely disturbed patient who is only very slowly responding to the treatment, and whose eating disorder seems fixed. At the same time, the therapist must resist the temptation to soothe himself or herself by adopting a supportive or messianic role. A test is made of the therapist's skills, capacities, training, and personal analysis, as demonstrated in the case of severe anorexia treated by Mintz (Wilson 1983).

In the narcissistic psychosomatic disorders, the defective self-soothing mechanisms must be repaired by appropriate selfobject transferences and transmuting internalizations. The patient must be enlisted as a partner in order to develop better reality testing and a new life-style based on a stronger functioning ego, developed both through appropriate interpretations and the establishment of a more cohesive sense of self (Chessick 1985b).

# Section IV

# CLINICAL EVALUATION

# Chapter 17

―――

# Kohut and Continental Psychiatry and Psychoanalysis

K ohut's self psychology is sometimes erroneously claimed to be just another version of "existentialism" or of "continental psycho-analysis," the implication being that it is not science and not authentic psychoanalysis. But Kohut's description of clinical material and his experience-distant conception of the bipolar self as a supraordinate concept has little in common with the self as agent of Sartre and Laing or with the emphasis on an authentic self in the writing of Kierk-egaard. The latter notion is essentially moral and philosophical, and not derived from empathy or vicarious introspection with patients.

The deepest or at least the most original thinkers in recent continental psychiatry and psychoanalysis as represented, for example, by Lacan and Foucault, wish to decenter the self altogether, either as a psychological or psychoanalytic or even philosophical concept. Although Sartre paradoxically borrowed much from Heidegger, his notion of the self as an agent that chooses is really closer to Husserl's (1913) "transcendental ego" (which Sartre paradoxically specifically rejects) than to Heidegger, Lacan, or Foucault. The reason for this lies in the belief, held in common by Heidegger, Lacan, and Foucault, that the self is formed by background social practices which wholly determine its nature. If this is correct, introspective self-reflection (Descartes' *Cogito*), in which the individual conceives of the self as an independent thinking subject, is really a "misrecognition," as Lacan calls it.

All this is vastly different from Kohut's notion of the self, and in no way can Kohut's thought be labelled "existential," "structural," or "poststructural" in nature. There are similarities between Heidegger, Lacan, Foucault, and Kohut, but the basic position of Heidegger, Lacan, and Foucault rests on the decentering of the self and places them in direct opposition to the psychology of the self. Heidegger also, like Sartre, does not accept Freud's notion of the unconscious. I (1986a) have discussed his work relevant to psychotherapists elsewhere. For Kohut, the sense of self is defined differently and is thought of as arising from within, while for structuralist and poststructuralist thinkers the introspective sense of self is an illusion formed by inherent neurophysiological structures or by forces of culture.

The psychology of the self runs counter to modern French structuralist and poststructuralist psychoanalysis and philosophy. The work of Barthes, Levi-Strauss, Foucault, Lacan, and Derrida, along with the texts of Nietzsche, Freud, and Saussure which they use in their own special way, has called into question the notion of the self as subject or consciousness which might serve as a source of meaning and a principle of explanation for our apparently free choices. Foucault (1972) tells us in *The Archaeology of Knowledge* that the "researches" of psychoanalysis, linguistics, and anthropology have "decentered" the subject in relation to setting the shape of its desires, the forms of its language, the rules of its actions, or the play of its mythical and imaginative creations. That is to say, the arguments of these authors have made the self something constituted by or resulting from the accidental influences of external or internal independent conditions rather than viewing the self as a controlling consciousness which is the master and ultimate origin of culture.

These continental thinkers focus only on derivatives of child development that accompany or follow the acquisition of language or symbolic systems. Preverbal issues are ignored for the most part, as are the biological forces of aggression and even Freud's death instinct. In self-psychological terms, the structuralists and Lacan ignore the experiential or archaic selfobject aspect of development and of the therapeutic relationship, and emphasize exclusively linguistic and symbolic expressions, almost as if the biological and preverbal did not exist, and all communication between humans is capable of verbal or symbolic delineation.

These philosophers are the "existentialist" precursors of Kohut, because they stress a hermeneutic approach that resembles empathy or vicarious introspection instead of observation and experiment; they belong, along with those who are described in Kaplan, Freedman, and Sadock's (1980) *Comprehensive Textbook of Psychiatry*, to "a small but vocal group of psychiatrist-philosophers" (p. 1283). For example, Ricoeur (1974) in his essay on "Consciousness and the Unconscious" asks the crucial question of what world view and vision of man will make possible a unique science of man. What must man be in order to assume the responsibility of sound thought and yet be susceptible of falling into insanity; to be obligated to strive for greater intellectual understanding and still remain a product of Freud's deterministic topographic or structural models insofar as (in the words of Lacan) the id speaks through him? All of these thinkers emphasize the experience of human living; they deemphasize the biological aspects of man.

It is a superficial resemblance of certain aspects of self psychology to early existential psychiatry that accounts for the confusion of these quite different approaches. For example, in 1913 Jaspers (1972), in his textbook of phenomenological psychiatry so often cited by existential psychiatrists, distinguished between "rational" and "empathic" understanding. In phenomenological psychiatry, "we sink ourselves into the psychic situation and *understand genetically by empathy* how one psychic event emerges from another" (p. 301). However, Jaspers was firmly opposed to Freud's psychoanalysis.

In psychiatry and psychoanalysis on the European continent today, there are many opposing viewpoints ranging from traditional psychoanalysts akin to the American Psychoanalytic Association, to existential psychoanalysts (discussed in Chessick 1977a), to the radical contemporary followers of Lacanian psychoanalysis and Foucault's views on psychiatry. I (1986b) have discussed Lacan and Foucault in detail elsewhere and will focus here on comparing Lacanian psychoanalysis with self psychology.

## Lacan On Psychopathology

For Lacan (Lemaire 1981), the "I" of discourse is formed in the "mirror stage" of development, around 6 to 18 months of age, when the infant first looks at its reflection in the mirror and achieves a false sense of the unity of itself. This is an imaginary, quasihallucinatory phase of development; a false I.

The second stage of development is "the-name-of-the-father," in which the child, acquiring speech, enters the symbolic order of language and culture. This curious phrase (a Lacanian pun on the French words *nom* [name] and *non* [no]) is a metaphor that Lacan uses for the social order, the mapping of all human relationships and interchanges which the child enters into via the acquisition of speech. The consequences of this kind of theory held great appeal for French Marxists; the theory united the views of Freud and Marx. It implied that, if you change the culture, a different person will emerge when the infant completes "the name-of-the-father" stage.

In delineating the essential psychopathology of neuroses and psychoses, Lacan describes the "paternal metaphor": the father has to be accepted by the mother or the child will remain subjected to her and cannot fit into the symbolic order. This disaster Lacan calls "foreclosure." Thus the mother's attitude to both the father and the child is critical to the genesis of mental illness. In the normal state, identification with the father liberates the child and provides the child with a secure place in the family and the culture. If foreclosure occurs, the child fails to enter into the symbolic order. The person so constituted remains in nondistinction between the self and the external world, dwelling in the realm of the imaginary — that is, psychosis. In the neuroses there is a disturbed relationship between the imaginary and the symbolic worlds, so that speech and behavior become deformed, represented by neurotic symptoms. In contrast to the psychotic, who lives in an imaginary world, the neurotic displays what Lacan calls a wish fulfilled but mutilated.

LACAN'S METHOD

Muller and Richardson (1982), in their guide to Lacan's (1977) *Écrits*, explain how Lacan translates the topographic theory of the early Freud into linguistics. Free association is thought of as the flow of "Signifiers," a term borrowed from the linguistic theory of Saussure. Each Signifier refers not to an individual "signified" mental concept of desire, but to another Signifier in the chain of free associations. The subject, as he develops and becomes articulated with language, alienates his primary unconscious desire in the Signifier chain. As Lacan puts it, we have the wanderings of true desire caught in the net of Signifiers.

Freud's "condensation" aspect of primary process is actually metaphor, a linguistic process in which one phrase stands for a set of others suggesting a likeness, for example, "a volley of oaths." "Condensation" of Freud's theory is therefore a series of Signifiers connected through metaphor. Freud's "displacement" is metonomy, a linguistic process in which one contiguous element stands for another, for example, "a good table" for good food. When Lacan makes his most famous statement that the unconscious is structured like a language, he means that the unconscious consists of repressed early Signifiers of desire connected by the rules of metonomy and metaphor. The unconscious consists entirely of early Signifiers, which had to be further disguised due to the demands of fitting into the cultural order. There are no drives and no instincts; no biology is involved.

## Lacan's Theory of Human Development

The phase of inaugural primary narcissism ("unbounded phase") occurs first in human development. Next comes the imaginary or mirror stage which is preverbal, presymbolic, and forms a false ego. This is described at length in Lacan's (1968) famous 1953 speech delivered in Rome, and forms the basis of his disagreement with traditional psychoanalytic structural theory. Then, in a brief transitory stage, the child comes up against the "forbidden." This results in the symbolic stage as the child acquires language; there is a split between the inner and outer world, between a false "I," (a false ego) and the outer world. In order to resolve this, the child must identify with the father's laws and cultural order and enter the quest for objects in a manner ever further removed from its original desire.

The child originally desires to be a phallus in union with the mother. It is the desire to be the desired of the mother, to be the mother's phallus. Lacan uses the world "phallus" here as a symbol; he is not using it only specifically to mean the penis. It is also what the mother wants the most, that which would bring her fulfillment. This is a Hegelian concept; in order to understand Lacan, one must be familiar with Hegel, who said that "desire" is to be the desired of the other person. As one develops toward adulthood, the chain of Signifiers moves further from the originally signified desire and from one's true self and, consequently, from understanding the meaning of one's own speech. The adult individual knows less about what is really meant by his or her linguistic expressions when speaking to another person.

There are three fundamental ideas in Lacan. First, the individual is constituted by language. The individual has no essence, center, or instincts. The unconscious consists only of the earliest Signifiers which are structured like a language. Second, discourse embodies society; a politics is embedded in our language and we are all caught up in it, since the human being is only an individual subject because of language and membership in society. Third, there is no such thing as an autonomous ego. This is a false notion, an *ex post facto* explanation says Lacan. For instance, if one wants to explain why stocks went down today, one might say, "The market is nervous about interest rates." This gives the stock market a sort of anthropomorphized personality. Lacan, in a form of psychoanalytic heresy, an anathema to the United States "ego psychology" school which he detested, says the concept of ego is false and misleading. It leads to the incorrect false centering of the human subject, just as the stock market is anthropomorphized in the example above. It may help to compare Lacan's views on the ego with those of R. D. Laing. Laing moves from an early view of recognizing the value of the ego in adaptation to a later radical position of advocating a smashing of the ego in order to release one's transcendental self (Collier 1977). Lacan says the ego is always false and stands in the way of knowledge of our true desires.

For Lacan, *desire* is the driving human force, not libido. It comes from animal demand, the demand of the brute, as he calls it. Until the human enters the mirror stage, the human is like a brute and has demand — the raw demand that an animal would have. The infant begins in a dual symbiosis with the mother, the realm of primary narcissism. As this ruptures, the infant realizes that it is not the mother. At this point human want begins to appear, the human form of desire. The human desires the paradise of fusion with the mother, to be what the mother desires most and in a fusion with her. Lacan uses for this the symbol "phallus" which is the Signifier of this desire for perfect union with the mother.

For Lacan, a primordial castration has occurred when this fusion is inevitably disrupted by the vicissitudes of development. Following Heidegger, he says the first experience of human limit occurs when this union is ruptured. Lacan does not distinguish between female and male earliest development. The dialectic of desire, based on Hegel's theory, occurs next. The ultimate quest is to be recognized and desired by the desired. This is closely related to the "gleam in the mother's eye" that Kohut mentions. Indeed, for Kohut (1971) there is also a "mirror stage" (p. 124) of preverbal beginnings, but there the similarity ends, for Kohut's mirror stage involves the mirroring and confirming response of the archaic selfobject to the emerging self of the infant and does not involve either mirrors or imaginings. Kohut is referring to an experience, not an image. For Lacan, the child wants to be the desired of the mother, her fullness, her phallus, but must end up expressing only culturally legitimate desires through endless derivative Signifier chains, multiple displacements in language.

It is impossible to become the desired of the mother because the father, who has the phallus, is there. When Lacan uses the term "father," he means three things: the real father, the imaginary father, and the law of the father. For Lacan the father is a "spoil-sport." He says to the infant, you cannot sleep with your mother. He says to the mother, you cannot reappropriate your product. So the oedipal struggle is in having to forego the original desire and channel it through the symbolic cultural order, expressing it in some way through words. It is interesting to compare this with the traditional drive-conflict psychoanalytic view of the resolution of the oedipal struggle. For example, Loewald (1980) describes the father as representing "castrating reality." He explains, "The longing for the father, seeking his help and protection, is a defensive compromise in order to come to terms with his superior, hostile power" (p. 9). For Lacan, to identify with the father is to find legitimate Signifiers which means accepting the culture, the facts of life, and human finitude. This is a process that Lacan calls *oedipization*, by means of which one enters the social order. When one has accomplished this, the oedipal struggle is resolved; from then on in one's language, a chain of Signifiers occurs in which the signified desire becomes hidden, sliding incessantly under the chain of Signifiers.

## Lacan On Psychoanalytic Therapy

This concept of the signified "sliding" under a chain of Signifiers is central to Lacan's theory of treatment. He (Turkle 1978) opposed all alleged authoritarianism and bureaucratic attitudes of psychoanalytic leaders, institutes, and hierarchies. He also opposed the structural theory of Freud and the ego psychology school of the United States and its goal of adaptation. Lacan argued that the psychoanalytic "establishment" represents the middle-class values of the culture, which psychoanalytic therapy must dissect in order to clarify and reveal the demand of the analysand: pure desire hidden in the very symbolic or cultural order.

Lacan's attack poses a paradox for institutionalized psychiatry and psychoanalysis. Surely there have to be some rules; if we eliminate them all, we end up with a cult. Lacan also recognized the great danger in institutionalized psychiatry and psychoanalysis, the danger of a collusion to hide the truth if the goal of treatment is to adjust to and adapt to a culture to which one should not adjust and adapt.

Lacan flaunts all the rules for diagnoses and standard nomenclatures. His notorious "five minute hour," the idea of self-proclaimed readiness to be an analyst, the famous "pass" in his institute (where your fellow students decide whether you should be an analyst or not), his own frequent change of institutes, his teaching of psychoanalysis to university students, his "happenings" or surrealistic seminars, his confrontations and his many broken allegiances, and his esoteric and punning style of communication — all constituted an effort to jolt us from established middle-class hierarchies and values. The details of Lacan's behavior and flamboyant activities are given by Clément (1983) and Schneiderman (1983).

For Lacan psychoanalysis is hermeneutics. It brings out underlying contexts and structures from the unconscious. It reveals a personal code. The past is hidden by linguistic transformations which occur because the individual must fit into the symbolic order. Historical reconstruction in psychoanalysis is not important, for psychoanalysis is a discourse with the "other." It brings to light the desires that are hidden in the metaphors and tropes, for the human subject is endlessly displaced and reconstituted by the symbolic order of desire through which language passes. This study of the patient's language then, says Lacan, can guide the patient back to insatiable, unconscious desires.

"Repression" for Lacan is simply a set of linguistic transformations using metaphor and metonomy that the child must use in order to fit into the symbolic order during oedipalization. In this sense, for Lacan, "Man is a marionette of his culture." The enemy is the ego which is born in the mirror phase, a false notion that the individual has of the self as an entity.

In summary, Lacan decenters the self. Everyone has a divided self, says Lacan, in contrast to Laing; from the mirror stage on we are all alienated from our true self. There is no autonomous ego or center to a person. He changes the focus of theory from biology or instincts to language, and from mechanisms to tropes. It is clear that Lacan and Kohut differ entirely in their notions of the self and human development.

Kohut and Lacan also differ entirely in their methodology. Lacan never offers a case history. There is no original instinctual unconscious for Lacan, only chains of Signifiers in the unconscious. His theory is a surrealist theory that cannot be established by clinical evidence or research. In psychopathology the person loses his or her grip on the chain of Signifiers, and the analyst must restore discourse to its owner. Psychiatric labels are useless, for each person's unique narrative is crucial.

For Lacan (1978), psychoanalysis or psychoanalytic psychotherapy is a reversal due to the "dummy" (*le mort*) analyst. The silence of the analyst causes a two-fold regression: backward among the chains of Signifiers "undoing the secret knots," as Lacan puts it, toward the unconscious primal Signifiers of desire which constitute the unconscious; and to the loss of false narcissistic images by which the ego is constituted in the mirror stage. This regression is caused by the frustration of the patient's desire in the psychoanalytic situation. The dummy of the analyst frustrates the patient's demand. Through transference, the chain of Signifiers retrogresses until it reaches the truth of the patient's desires and restores full speech to the patient.

Leavy (1980) attempts to provide a clinical example in which a patient is constantly complaining of the intrusiveness of the analyst. Leavy tries to demonstrate that underneath this patient's constant complaint about the intrusiveness of the analyst is the patient's desire to be intruded upon by the analyst-father: "Why do you ignore my attractiveness?" It is a demand on the part of the patient to be recognized and it is similar to Kohut's conception of the patient's demand for mirroring from the selfobject analyst. Leavy's case material illustrates what is meant by the incessant sliding of the signified under the Signifiers; there is a continual chain of Signifiers in the various complaints of the patient that are quoted by Leavy, under which is sliding the desire to be recognized. The patient wishes to have her attractiveness confirmed by the analyst; perhaps at a deeper Lacanian level, to be the desired of the analyst.

The main advantage of Lacan's approach is his stress on the informed doctor who relates to patients as people and pays attention to what each patient is uniquely saying. Lacan emphasizes the transaction between the individual and society and, like Foucault, points toward the study of society to explain the individual. A politics is embedded in our language, language embodies society, and we enter society when we develop language, says Lacan. This emphasis on language as constituting the self of the individual is quite different than Kohut's focus on preverbal selfobject experiences.

## Foucault and Kohut

Michel Foucault (Dreyfus and Rabinow 1982) says that the key question of philosophy is the one of what we ourselves are. Since for Foucault we have only cultural practices which made us what we are, contemporary philosophy must be political, historical, and interpretive. But the human sciences are always to some extent pseudosciences because, while claiming to advance under the banner of science, they have remained intimately involved with micropractices of power. One of Foucault's most important concepts is that of the repressive hypothesis. It insists that the truth is intrinsically opposed to power and can play a liberating role both personally and politically. The latest representative of this hypothesis is the philosopher Jurgen Habermas of the Frankfurt School, who views self-reflection as a way of liberating man from oppressive societies.

When Kohut (1984) describes Freud's idea that knowledge will cure as a cognitive ideal of the nineteenth century, he is attributing to Freud the repressive hypothesis. However Kohut would not agree with Foucault's (1973a) argument that the human sciences are always inherently unstable, derived, epistemologically complex, precarious, and full of disagreement due to the double nature of man. For Foucault, they are dubious, and they can never be considered to be like the natural sciences; because, for example, the psychiatrist as an investigator embodied in a given culture (Foucault 1973), and the objects he studies, have both been produced by the prevailing paradigms ("epistemes") or, as Foucault later (1980, 1980a) calls it, the biopower of their culture, its manipulations and interactions. Therefore "knowledge" in the human sciences depends on discursive practices (epistemes) or nondiscursive practices (biopower) in any given culture at the time. There are no context-free, value-free, objective human sciences similar to the natural sciences. Kohut, on the other hand, insists that psychoanalysis can be a science, with empathy as its own special method of gathering data, so his view is much less radical and pessimistic.

CONCLUSION

The history of the human sciences leads to an unveiling of the nonconscious as constitutive both of the individual and the scientist who investigates the individual. Danger is inherent in the use of the human sciences to serve micropower practices, normalization, and oppression by the investigator who is also so constituted in that service.

This is true regardless of the model psychiatry employs. The biological model views man as an organic "thing" or groups as "bodies," leading to sociobiology and ethology. Marx's economic model views the individual as the simple expression of class and other economic conflicts. The philological model, hermeneutics, began in the field of psychiatry with Freud; hidden meanings are discovered by interpretation, leading to what is called by Ricoeur (1970) the history of desire. The linguistic model claims that there are hidden universal structures in the signifying system of language and myth, from which the discipline of semiotics arises. Hybrid systems such as that of Freud combine the natural science notions of "apparatus" and "energetics" with hermeneutics. That of Kohut combines clinical data gathered by the method of empathy with forces such as those postulated by the Zeigarnik phenomenon. Laing's political model views diagnosis as a repressive political act. Foucault's two models (Dreyfus and Rabinow 1982, Chessick 1986b) are "archaeology," which reveals that hidden epistemes determine knowledge, and "genealogy," which reveals that hidden micropower practices determine knowledge. Finally, the nihilistic models of Nietzsche and Derrida (Sturrock 1979) seek to prove that there is a paradox inherent in all systems revealed by deconstruction of their texts.

The psychiatrist can never be merely another medical specialist. If the psychiatrist understands the history of the discipline, the psychiatrist must be aware of all these other models and of the dangers involved in claiming possession of the scientific truth about any person. Jaspers (1972) already in 1913 emphasized this repeatedly.

The psychology of the self, like the work of Foucault, has much to say about social problems. Kohut is not just another psychoanalytic theorist. Like Freud, he had a strong social conscience and attempted repeatedly to understand and discuss contemporary social problems, utilizing his psychoanalytic discoveries for that purpose. The test of the moral worth of a society is the way in which it treats the poor, the sick, and the mad. As Foucault (1973) says, the history of madness, of the poor, or of the deviants in a given culture is the means by which a culture defines itself. Is this not similar to the proposal of Kohut for an extension of empathy as crucial to averting the erasure of the individual, who might suffocate in the world of runaway technology and dehumanization?

# Chapter 18

## Empathy

Does empathy have a healing power or is it simply a mode of observation? If a person feels understood empathically by another person, does this exert a healing effect? If so, how are we to describe this healing effect metapsychologically?

### Approaches to Empathy before Kohut

In a preliminary and experimental approach I (1965) likened empathy to what Nacht (1962) called "a certain deep inner attitude" in the therapist. When we take the position of another person, our imagination moves from ourselves into the other person. We may experience certain changes in our own muscles and actual physical posture. To empathize does not mean that the individual must experience physical sensations; empathy can be physical, imaginative, or both. Fenichel (1945), quotes Reik, who maintained that empathy consists of two acts, "a) an identification with the other person, and b) an awareness of one's own feelings after the identification, and in this way an awareness of the object's feelings" (p. 511).

Regardless of identifiable organic sensations, empathy connotes a form of personal involvement and an evocation of feeling. Our empathy is no less real if our bodies undergo no physical change and if we move into the situation of the other person only in our fantasies.

I (1965) refer to the work of Katz (1963) who, along with Reik (1949), presented some metapsychologically imprecise and intuitive definitions and discussions of empathy. Katz discusses the fielding of signals through a "kind of inner radar" which works from cues in the conversation or impressions we receive. Reik (1949) explains that "in order to comprehend the unconscious of another person, we must, at least for a moment, change ourselves into and become that person. We only comprehend the spirit whom we resemble" (p. 361).

Perhaps no other author before Kohut emphasized the importance of empathy as much as Harry Stack Sullivan. He never really defined the term but spoke of empathy developing through "induction" and postulated that the tension of anxiety present in the mothering one "induces" anxiety in the infant. The process by which this induction takes place is referred to as a manifestation of an interpersonal process that Sullivan called empathy. He (1953) also introduced the term "empathic linkage," meaning a situation in which two people are linked in such a way that one induces a feeling in the other. Anticipating the objections to the concept of empathy, Sullivan wrote:

> I have had a good deal of trouble at times with people of a certain type of educational history; since they cannot refer empathy to vision, hearing, or some other special sensory receptor, and since they do not know whether it is transmitted by the ether waves or air waves or whatnot, they find it hard to accept the idea of empathy. (p. 41)

Later, in a passage characteristic of his famous incisive irony, he continues, "So although empathy may sound mysterious, remember that there is much that sounds mysterious in the universe, only you have gotten used to it; and perhaps you will get used to empathy" (pp. 41–42).

Fromm-Reichmann (1950) offered a dramatic clinical example of the empathic process. She explained how "some empathic notion for which I cannot give any account" made her turn back toward a patient with consequences that later marked the beginning of successful therapy of that patient. This example, like Sullivan's definition, leaves empathy as a rather mysterious intuitive process and demonstrates empathy by the presence of a response in the therapist that can be observed by the patient or by an observer. Fromm-

Reichmann (1950) insisted that empathy between the patient and therapist is crucial to psychotherapy. Therapy, she says, should be offered in the spirit of collaborative guidance, aimed at the solution of difficulties in living and the cure of symptoms. She concludes, "The success or failure of psychoanalytic psychotherapy is, in addition, greatly dependent upon the question of whether or not there is actually an empathic quality between the psychiatrist and the patient" (p. 62).

All seem to agree that the use of empathy in psychotherapy calls for a pendulumlike action alternating between subjective involvement and objective detachment. Traditional analysts refer to this as a regression in the service of the ego when it is used toward specific goals. When the good empathizer regresses in the service of the ego, that person engages in a playful kind of activity, inwardly imitating events in the life of the patient. The activity is regressive only in the sense that it calls for a relaxed and unstructured experience associated with the fantasy of the child or the poetic license of the artist. The therapist must then be able to swing back to an objective and detached relationship in order to make clinical use of the information gained through the empathic process.

Long before Kohut, Fliess (1942) explained that the skill of the therapist depends on the ability "to step into [the patient's] shoes, and to obtain in this way an inside knowledge that is almost first-hand. The common name for such a procedure is empathy" (pp. 212–213). Levine (1961) claimed that empathy, if handled correctly, leads to a type of immediate comprehension of the patient's problems, a comprehension superior to the intellectual variety of understanding.

French and Fromm (1964) discussed "empathic thinking" in dream interpretation, stressing "empathic understanding" as a direct intuitive communication between the unconscious of the patient and that of the therapist. The patient evokes in the therapist "an empathic sense of what is going on" in the unconscious of the patient. Freud (1912), in his comparison of the therapist's unconscious as a telephone receiver adjusted to the patient's "transmitting unconscious" implied a sort of resonance between the therapist's unconscious and that of the patient. This resonance enables the therapist to understand the language of the patient's unconscious:

> Just as the receiver converts back into sound-waves the electric oscillations in the telephone line which were set up by the sound waves, so the

doctor's unconscious is able, from the derivatives of the unconscious which are communicated to him, to reconstruct that unconscious, which has determined the patient's free associations. (p. 116)

French and Fromm (1964) point out that there must then occur a translation from this empathic understanding into a language suitable for scientific analysis. This translation is called "conceptual analysis" by these authors, and thus we have again the pendulumlike action described above.

## FACTORS INTERFERING WITH EMPATHY

Empathy calls for flexibility and willingness to enter into new, unprotected, and unexplored areas. Each patient has some unique quality which calls for a personal and unprecedented appreciation. The therapist must venture alone into the inner experience of another person and can neither apply a label nor feel complacent about this new understanding.

On a clinical basis it is the anxiety of the individual therapist, so often disguised and unrecognized, which interferes with empathy most of all. Greenson (1960) discusses the pathology that interferes with empathy and the metapsychology of empathy. As Kohut (1971) pointed out, an especially great characterological barrier to empathy is formed by unanalyzed narcissism in the therapist, since the tendency to experience others as selfobjects precludes the recognition of their individual personalities and points of view.

This interference may manifest itself in subtle forms, as in the tendency of therapists to identify themselves with the fixed routines and traditions of their profession. I have noted in consultations with colleagues in practice years after their residency training a tendency to become inflexible in their clinical approaches and procedures. The therapist can become so absorbed in professional skills and techniques that relationships with patients become depersonalized. Often, the gestures of empathic communication are made, but the reality and the freshness of the meeting are lost and in their place an almost inevitable artificiality intrudes. When this occurs, it reflects a lack of vigilance on the part of the therapist; he slips into a comfortable and apparently efficient routine (Chessick 1985c).

ANTICIPATION OF KOHUT'S VIEWS

In my (1965, Chessick and Bassan 1968) early experimental work on empathy it was already demonstrably clear that empathy had a crucial role in understanding the patient. Those therapists who stress insight use empathy primarily as a means of gaining knowledge of the inner experiences and the unconscious processes of the patient. For them, empathy involves an internal imaginative activity necessary in interpreting the dynamics of the patient. Although such therapists participate in the patient's experience, what they share with the patient is only the result of their own empathic activity translated into interpretations. They believe that the patient's self-insight cures the patient.

Positive emotions spontaneously develop in the patient as a response to empathy of the therapist, a universal and well-known human phenomenon. Empathy is communicated to the patient either by an intuitive behavior on the part of the therapist or by the communication of insight which has been gained through the empathic process. This is consistent with Kohut's (1971) view that many therapists in the past practiced as effectively as self-psychologists because they utilized their intuitive empathic skills. The purpose of self psychology is to specify these techniques and make them teachable as a craft to all therapists. For example, Greenberg and Mitchell (1983), in reviewing some case presentations by Jacobson, point out that in spite of her different theoretical orientation, "some of her technical procedures in fact sound remarkably like Kohut's" (p. 324).

When the therapist engages in an empathic process with the patient, a certain gratification is felt by the patient as she or he becomes aware of the active empathizing going on in the therapist. This is an especially important aspect in the therapy of borderline patients since the empathic relationship can be a new experience in the patient's life, particularly in treating patients who have experienced a great deal of emotional coldness in childhood.

Menninger (1958), anticipating Kohut's later advocacy of accepting the idealization of the patient, said that when there is consistent empathy coming from the therapist it sometimes calls forth in the patient a natural and realistic feeling of love or affection for the therapist. He implied that acceptance of this love by the therapist, without trying to defend by ascribing it all to transference, may be an important experience in the patient's life.

A common clinical experience shows itself in patients who as babies had a mother who tended to respond with panic to their anxiety rather than with empathic calming. This sets off a "deleterious chain of events" (Kohut 1984, p. 83) in which the mother may chronically wall herself off from the baby, depriving the baby of the beneficial effect of merging with her as she returns from experiencing mild anxiety to calmness. She may continue to respond with panic which causes either "a lifelong propensity toward the uncurbed spreading of anxiety or other emotions" or forces the child to wall itself off "from such an overly intense and thus traumatizing" response, leading to an impoverished psyche and an inability to be fully human.

## Kohut on Empathy

Kohut (1984) posits three functions for empathy: it is the indispensable tool of psychoanalytic fact finding; it expands the self to include the other, constituting a powerful psychological bond between individuals in order to counteract man's destructiveness against his fellows; and it arises out of the selfobject matrix, becoming the accepting, confirming, and understanding human echo evoked by and needed by the self as a psychological nutriment without which human life could not be sustained. In this shift from his primary definition of empathy as a mode of observation or psychoanalytic fact-finding to the other functions of empathy Kohut caused the greatest controversy.

Kohut (1971) presents a discussion of the misuse of empathy. The use of empathy in the observation of a nonpsychological field "leads to a faulty, prerational, animistic perception of reality and is, in general, the manifestation of a perceptual and cognitive infantilism" (p. 300). Kohut distinguishes between empathy and intuition. He defines intuitions as simply the same as any other reactions and judgments of a rational sort except that they occur much faster. What appears to be an intuitive grasp of a situation is really a speeded-up series of rational decisions such as those one may observe when a master chess player glances at the board and quickly sees the right move. This process fundamentally differs from vicarious introspection as a mode of observation.

Kohut (1971) claims that potential for empathic perception is acquired early in life; empathic talent may arise paradoxically in the same situation that can present a danger to the formation of the nuclear self due to fear of archaic enmeshment with the parent. For example, if the narcissistic parent considers the child as an extension of the parent beyond the period in which such an attitude is appropriate "or more intensively than is optimal, or with a distorted selectivity of her relevant responses, then the child's immature psychic organization will become excessively attuned to the mother's (or father's) psychological organization" (pp. 277–278). This may lead to a sensitive psychological apparatus with unusually great ability for the perception and elaboration of others' psychological processes. This skill may be employed later in a psychotherapeutic career, especially if it is combined with a need to master "the threatening influx of stimuli with an unusual growth of secondary processes aimed at understanding the psychological data and bringing order to the psychological material" (p. 280).

In his first book Kohut is aware that he will be compared with the philosopher Dilthey (1833–1911). He objects to Dilthey's view because he claims that Dilthey changed empathy from limiting its role to a data collecting process to using it to replace the explanatory phases of scientific psychology. Kohut condemns this as "a deterioration of scientific standards and a sentimentalizing regression to subjectivity, i.e., a cognitive infantilism in the realm of man's scientific activities" (1971, p. 301).


EMPATHY AND SCIENCE

However, Dilthey's name arises frequently in discussions of Kohut. The project of formulating a methodology appropriate to the human sciences was seen by Dilthey "in the context of a need to get away from the reductionist and mechanistic perspective of the natural sciences and to find an approach adequate to the fullness of the phenomena," writes Palmer (1969, p. 100). Philosophers such as Nietzsche, Dilthey, and Bergson, according to Palmer (and I would add the psychiatrist-philosopher Jaspers), were attempting to reach "the experiential fullness of human existence in the world" (p. 101). Dilthey saw a fundamental distinction between all human studies and the natural sciences. This does not mean he attempted a return to some mystical ground or source for all life, but he hoped to achieve fullness of life through empathy, getting in touch with another's human experience from within ourselves. This constituted a methodology for Dilthey fairly similar to Kohut's insistence that empathy or vicarious introspection was the indispensable method of psychoanalytic fact finding. Of course for Dilthey it was described in a more philosophical and poetic fashion. Subsequent philosophers have pointed out that his sharp distinction between the natural and the human sciences is a nineteenth-century notion that can no longer be defended, because the basic premises of the natural sciences also rest on human foundations that can only be grasped empathically (Chessick 1980b).

A brief discussion of the current scientific status of empathy is presented by Goldberg (1983a). He points out that there is a division in the psychoanalytic literature on the role of empathy in psychoanalysis. One view, although agreeing that empathy may be desirable, sees it as a relatively rare and unreliable phenomenon, fraught with the dangers of error due to countertransference. The other sharply contrasting view sees empathy as a common and universal mode of communication between people. It distinguishes between two ways of knowing: "direct, outward, public observation or extraception, and inward, private observation or introspection. The combination of introspection and putting oneself in another's place is empathy" (p. 156). Even in this brief review Goldberg mentions Dilthey and his concept of a sympathic insight into another person, allowing one to build up a picture of that person's life and to understand that individual's experience.

Hartmann (1927) at an early date objected strongly to this approach in psychoanalytic work and claimed that it was unscientific and unreliable. The situation was improved by Kohut's (1978) definition in 1959 of empathy as vicarious introspection, which gave us a working definition for empathy as a method for finding out about another person's inner life and made it possible to guard against the abuse of empathy. Like any scientific investigation, vicarious introspection must not be unnecessarily biased, and it must be subject to verifiability by further uses of the method, remaining alert to the effects of our own observations and interventions. Goldberg (1983a) concludes that "empathy seems to have a therapeutic effect when it is sustained" (p. 168) and he concurs with Kohut's placing of empathy into a central position in psychoanalysis.

The entire subject of the role of empathy within the psychoanalytic situation as conceived by various authors is reviewed by Levy

(1985). He complains of the "multiple and different meanings" (p. 369) Kohut gave to empathy. He warns of the transference gratifications involved in Kohut's positing a therapeutic factor of major import besides the analyst's interpretations, as was also suggested in Loewald's (1980, chap. 14) paper, part of which was published in 1960, describing the analyst as a potentially new object for the patient in addition to his or her interpretive function. Loewald's paper also bears a remarkable resemblance to some of Kohut's concepts but is in the language of traditional psychoanalysis.

## Criticism of Self Psychology's Emphasis on Empathy

The increasing emphasis by self psychologists on empathy has been subject to stormy criticism from traditional psychoanalysts. Shapiro (1974, 1981, Leider 1984) claims that he does not even know what empathy is and views it as a form of animism which would destroy psychoanalysis as a science. Lichtenberg, Bornstein, and Silver (1984, 1984a) have collected two volumes of reprints and some new papers on the subject of empathy, indicating its difficulty and controversiality. Their collection offers Buie's (ibid. 1984, pp. 129–136) support of Shapiro's attack, in which both authors criticize the vagueness and unreliability of the concept. They note the "confusion" among self psychologists, who began by defining empathy as a mode of observation that implies only "in-tuneness" (Kohut 1977, pp. 115, 304; Goldberg 1980, p. 458), which they contrast with Goldberg's (1978) summary of Kohut's later work. Here, the emphasis shifts from the analyst as observer to the analyst as a person who responds in an empathic fashion, now defining empathy as "the proper feeling for and fitting together of the patient's needs and the analyst's response" (Goldberg 1978, p. 8). Shapiro and Buie both prefer Kohut's early version of empathy as strictly a mode of observation. They sharply disagree with self-psychologists on whether empathy provides anything more than what is provided by accurate psychological understanding. They stress the dangers of mysticism in regarding empathy as a special psychic function which utilizes, for example, Reik's (1949) "third ear." Buie (1981) explains three limitations in the accuracy and scope of empathy: "Patients may limit or distort the expression of behavioral cues about their state of mind; referents available in the mind of the empathizer may be inadequate; and the inferential process is inherently uncertain" (p. 305).

The German word *Einfühlung* was used in the late nineteenth century to describe esthetic perception and was translated into English as "empathy." It was defined as "a tendency to merge the activities of the perceiving subject with the qualities of the perceived object," as quoted from Paget in 1913 by Reed (Lichtenberg, Bornstein, and Silver 1984, p. 7). Reed gives seven definitions of empathy (pp. 12–13) on the basis of carefully cited quotations. Empathy is:

1. Both knowledge and communication.
2. Simultaneously a capacity, a process, and an expression.
3. An ability to sample others' affects and to be able to respond in resonance to them.
4. A method of data gathering.
5. An inner experience of sharing in and comprehending the psychological state of another person.
6. A special method of perceiving.
7. A means of communication and of nonrational understanding.

Pao (1983) offers still another definition from a Sullivanian viewpoint:

> To make use of one's empathic capacity to understand another person's needs and wants is not a solo activity. It is a process in which the two participants — the one who desires to understand and the one who desires to be understood — must both participate actively. Together, these two participants will gradually set up a more and more intricate "network" of connected communication. (pp. 152–153)

Olinick (Lichtenberg, Bornstein, and Silver 1984) regards Kohut's definition of empathy as vicarious introspection to be "facile and answers none of our questions" (p. 145). He is especially concerned about the differentiation between sympathy and empathy since they are often confused in the literature. An even more important differentiation must be made between empathy and paranoiac sensitivity as pointed out by Noy who explains, "We may be impressed by the keen sensitivity to others that a candidate displays in supervision or in seminar discussions, only to discover later that it is a paranoiac sensitivity, grounded in a general attitude that perceives the patient as a potential enemy" (Lichtenberg, Bornstein, and Silver 1984, p. 175n).

Post and Miller summarize the various objections to the emphasis on empathy and pay special attention to those which regard empathy as imprecise or minimally accessible to objective measurement, and to those which maintain that emphasis on empathy encourages deviations from traditional psychoanalysis, reintroducing the issue of a corrective emotional experience at the expense of the curative power of insight. However, they claim that such objections have been treated by various authors whom they cite, and they ask why the same objections continue to be made in the literature. Post and Miller maintain that most of the criticisms of the empathic approach "do not seem judicious; sometimes they are based on a gross misreading of the relevant literature; at other times this literature does not seem to have been read at all; at still others, the empathic position is accurately represented and then dismissed by fiat, without argumentation," and try to explain this on the ground that the empathic stance "may evoke profound apprehensiveness in some analysts, leading sooner or later to disavowal" (Lichtenberg, Bornstein, and Silver 1984, p. 232).

Lichtenberg (Lichtenberg, Bornstein, and Silver 1984a) tries to answer criticism by quoting from the work of Kohut. There is a highly personal issue here, involving the character style of the analyst. Can the therapist accept a central emphasis on the notion of empathy? It is a conception different qualitatively from the usual methods of scientific observation, and lends itself much more to subjective interpretation and use, as well as misuse.

## Empathy and the Analytic Ambience

The central emphasis on empathy by self-psychologists has brought with it considerable discussion of the issue of abstinence and the general ambience of psychoanalysis and psychoanalytic psychotherapy. Self-psychologists such as Wolf (1976) emphasize the danger of carrying Freud's rule of abstinence to an extreme, leading to a cold and unnatural ambience. Freud, as reviewed by Fox (1984), regarded the frustration of the desires coming from transference love necessary to the prevention of a transference cure. Wolf (1976) points out that, carried to an extreme, this distance produces an ambience in the treatment which was not the ambience provided for his patients by Freud. He argues that a warm ambience does not interfere with the development of a negative transference; providing an average, expectable environment for the patient cannot be seen as a collusion between the patient and the therapist to avoid the emergence of patient hostility and criticism. Poland (1984) warns, however, that a deliberate attempt to provide "empathic response" could lead to such collusion, and represents "an excess of therapeutic activity [based] too often [on a] failure of empathic perceptive accuracy" (pp. 288–290).

Kohut (1984) does not object to claims that the provision of an empathic ambience for his patients constitutes a corrective emotional experience for his patients. Myerson (1981) studied Guntrip's (1975) report of his analysis with Winnicott, and Kohut's (1979) two analyses of Mr. Z., and concluded that a corrective experience is involved in both Kohut's and Winnicott's clinical work. This is probably more extreme in Winnicott's analysis of Guntrip, where he tells Guntrip, "You are good for me," allegedly drawing Guntrip out of his schizoid shell to discover that there is no retaliation and that nothing happens to the analyst.

Fox (1984) writes that through the influence of Eissler's (1953) paper on parameters, the principle of abstinence of Freud has become the misapplied rule of abstinence. Fox concludes that there still seem to be "deprivers" and "gratifiers" among psychoanalytic therapists, and he reminds us that too much deprivation can be experienced by the patient as a narcissistic wounding, while too much gratification (as he says Kohut offers) leads to the lack of formation of an oedipal transference. He would turn Kohut's theory upside down and claim that Kohut sees such a dearth of "instinctual" oedipal lust and aggression because he is offering the patient too much gratification in his attempt to provide an empathic ambience.

Poland has contributed to a better delineation of the psychoanalytic ambience. He (1975) distinguishes tact as a "circumscribed analytic technical function dealing with *how* a statement is made, based on an understanding of the patient" (p. 155). He points out that when tact is working properly, it is invisible and comes into view mainly at times when it fails or threatens to fail; "when we notice a mistake on our part or when we become concerned with how to pose a statement to a patient" (p. 155). Poland (1975) believes that "highly developed tact is central to the art of analysis" and that it is related to, but not the same as, empathy. Tact follows empathy and is founded on a combination of that which is learned about the patient's inner workings through both cognitive understanding and empathy. He claims, "We learn with empathy and understanding, and we interpret with tact" (p. 156).

Poland offers the clinical concept of "pseudotact," which represents the resistance of a patient who wants to avoid giving offense. The patient carefully delays mentioning something nasty about the therapist or avoids provocative comments, especially in areas felt to be "sensitive" for the analyst, such as race, religion, physical appearance, and so on, in order to be "tactful and polite." Conversely, pseudotact may be a countertransference manifestation in which the analyst avoids making an interpretation because, out of reaction formation to sadism, the therapist does not wish to impose pain on the patient.

Poland (1974) tries to view empathic and cognitive sources of information in the therapy process "as facets of an essential unitary experience" (p. 292). He (1984) differentiates empathy from tact and neutrality. He also repeats his earlier (1975) distinction between tact and empathy and points out that tact is subordinate to the requirement for neutrality, which is the requirement of impartiality and the avoidance of imposing oneself or one's values in trying to dominate the other person. Gitelson's (1952) comment is also valuable: "It is of primary importance for the analyst to conduct himself so that the analytic process proceeds on the basis of what the patient brings to it" (p. 7).

In conclusion, let us review a clinical vignette offered by Poland (1984). A "young analyst" is treating a young woman who cannot afford a baby sitter. The patient tells the analyst that each day she locks her 5-year-old son in a small room, unattended, for the two hours needed for her analytic sessions. When colleagues responded with horror, "the analyst explained that his task was not to feel guilty but rather to analyze the material as it arose. In fact, he had never questioned or commented to the patient on the peculiar arrangements" (p. 295). We all would agree with Poland's comment that "such dramatic pseudo-neutrality is, one hopes, rare" (p. 295). But Poland leaves unanswered a crucial question raised by this example. How could this person become a psychoanalyst? Does this example not provide support for Kohut's (1984) argument about the defect commonly found in the analysis of psychoanalytic candidates? Does it not tend to send us back to a study of Kohut's (1977, 1984) discussion of the whole problem of how a psychoanalyst should be trained and what sort of a person he or she ought to be, as well as to review his scattered comments (1978) on the selection of training analysts?

The emphasis by self psychologists on empathy is one of the most acrimonious issues separating self psychologists and traditional analysts. On this issue we have reached an irreconcilable disagreement between the orientations of self psychologists and traditional psychoanalysts. Personal preferences seem to rest on personal factors and clinical experience. Yet, each camp sometimes suggests that a faulty training analysis or a misunderstanding of psychoanalysis may explain or at least influence the choice or orientation of the other group. Some better method of studying, understanding, and perhaps resolving these differences must be found.

# Chapter 19

---

# Criticism

In this chapter I present 18 categories of debate about the psychology of the self. The reader may use these categories as indicators and guides for evaluating the psychology of the self and for studying the psychiatric literature critical of the subject.

## NOSOLOGY

The definition of narcissism remains controversial, both as applied to the individual and as applied to the culture as a whole. Freud expanded this concept in at least four ways (Satow 1983); since Freud, the term has been applied in many ways to both individuals and groups. Freudians, Kleinians, ego psychologists, object relations theorists, and self psychologists all present different theoretical systems for understanding narcissistic phenomena. The confusion is compounded by the use of "schizoid" diagnostically "by adherents of relational models (Fairbairn, Guntrip), who are interested in articulating their break with drive theory" (Greenberg and Mitchell 1983, p. 385), for patients labelled "narcissistic" by North American authors.

No agreement exists on the differentiation of narcissistic personalities from borderline personalities, or on the choice of treatment. Many of Kernberg's patients who are narcissistic but characterized as functioning on a borderline level would not be considered narcissistic personality disorders by Kohut. For self psychologists, the term "borderline" seems to apply mainly to patients who show an irreversible fragmentation of the self in a trial of psychotherapy; most other authors use the DSM-III diagnostic signs and symptoms which overlap with other DSM-III personality disorders.

Stein (1979) complains that Kohut's (1977, Kohut and Wolf 1978) categories of disorders of the self actually "swallow up" the various neurotic disorders as these have been previously described in the literature. He continues, "[Kohut's] categorization is not much help in establishing useful criteria for those who could benefit from 'traditional' [his term] psychoanalysis, as against a presumably far greater number who require the application of his method" (p. 676). More generally London (1985) places the weakness of self psychology in the "reductionism of its theories" (p. 105).

## THE DEFICIENCY THEORY OF ETIOLOGY

Stein (1979) states that the simple principle which holds disorders of the self to be the result of lack of parental empathy is too easy a solution for the extraordinarily complex problems of the etiology of psychopathology: "Blaming one's parents, whether they deserve it or not, is simple and satisfying; it reflects, at best, only part of the truth of the origins of human character" (p. 677). More technically, Rothstein (1980) claims that Kohut reduced the genesis of narcissistic personality disorders to a "unifactorial disappointment in the mirroring self-object" (p. 451). He considers this to be a "reductionistic construction."

Several authors, such as Schafer (1985), point out that in Kohut's system the patient is seen mainly as a victim of the failures of early selfobjects. This "seems to discourage adequate scrutiny of the analysand's unconscious, highly ambivalent, powerful, active, and early part in experiencing and even arranging a life of inhibition, suffering, and mistreatment" (p. 292). Silverman (1985) suggests that countertransference factors may cause Kohut's followers to accept "their patients' projective attribution of total responsibility for their neurotic disturbances to parental abuse and failure" (p. 181). However, a case he presents could easily be described as having formed a selfobject transference, if one follows Kohut.

Treurniet (1983) argues that what self psychologists call "deficit" is actually a "reversible phenomenon originating in insufficient help to overcome conflicts experienced by the preoedipal child" (p. 77). He believes therefore that self psychology "corrodes some of the most central explanatory concepts of psychoanalysis — conflict, transference, and resistance" (p. 98). Basch (Stepansky and Goldberg 1984), on the other hand, claims that Kohut's etiological approach began with Ferenczi and follows the psychoanalytic tradition, centering on the facilitating interplay between the infant and its environment.

PROGNOSIS

Kohut's self psychology views the narcissistic personality disorder in a relatively benign fashion as representing developmental arrest. Kernberg (1972–1982a) views the narcissistic personality disorder as severely pathological, and the treatment of it as difficult, characterized by periods of explosion and great discomfort for both the patient and the therapist. On the whole there is an often criticized tendency for self psychologists to present the treatment of narcissistic personalities and (among some followers of Kohut) borderline personalities in a more hopeful way than is found in the presentations of such patients in psychoanalytic literature. Kohut, as discussed, was not optimistic about the psychoanalytic treatment of borderline patients. More studies of the application of self psychology to the treatment of borderline patients will help resolve this question of prognosis and lead to better understanding of the conflicting diagnostic approaches, theories, and therapeutic recommendations.

THE SELF AS A SUPRAORDINATE CONCEPT

Schwartz (1973) reviewed a panel on technique and prognosis in the treatment of narcissistic personality disorders held at the 1972 fall meeting of the American Psychoanalytic Association. During the meeting, Spruiell argued that the supraordinate concept of "self" has been allowed to encroach on the structural model concepts of the ego and its functions. He (1974) suggests that originally "the ego *was* the self" (p. 277). Later, as it became defined more abstractly in terms of its functions, the ego came to mean more "but at the same time less — to those to whom it no longer represented the self" (p. 277). Spruiell suggests that there is a correlation between those psycho-analysts who emphasize the importance of preoedipal conflicts over the traditional Oedipus complex in psychopathology and those who have relegated the ego to a lesser position and attempted to empha-size the overriding importance of the self.

*Pari passu* with this according to Slap and Levine (1978), Kohut "minimizes the importance of the contents of the patient's fantasies and downgrades the significance of intrapsychic conflict" (p. 504). He emphasizes structural deficits over conflicts and defenses. Kohut's (1977) claim that one need not deal with all aspects of the personality once the maintenance of the self is assured strikes Stein (1979) as a reversal of Freud's (1937) approach in "Analysis Terminable and In-terminable." Freud warns us not to leave drives and conflicts alone: "The warning that we should let sleeping dogs lie, which we have so often heard in connection with our efforts to explore the psychical underworld, is particularly inapposite when applied to the conditions of mental life" (p. 231).

Rangell (1981a) sees no need for Kohut's paradigm since "The self has always been incorporated into structural theory" (p. 685). A panel on the relationship between the theory of the ego and the concept of the self is reviewed by Richards (1982, pp. 718–720) and he con-cludes (1982a) that use of the self as a "superordinate [sic] concept in psychoanalytic theory" is unwise: "[George] Klein, Gedo, and Kohut all offer the self as a kind of conceptual tranquilizer for the philosophical, theoretical, and clinical dualities that are inherent in psychoanalytic work" (p. 956).

This problem is compounded by various conflicting definitions of the self and Kohut's (1977) earlier statement that the self "in its essence" cannot be defined. Kohut himself shifted from an early (1971, p. xv) concept of the self as existing side by side with but not as one of the mental agencies (id, ego, superego), to his later concept of the bipolar self as a supraordinate organizing principle, a "supraordinated configuration whose significance transcends that of the sum of its parts" (1977, p. 97). This issue of whether the self should be viewed as supraordinate or as a content of the mental apparatus remains one of the strongest areas of disagreement among psychoanalysts (Meyers 1981).

## DIFFICULTIES WITH TERMINOLOGY

Giovacchini (1977, 1978) questions Kohut's use of terms such as horizontal splitting rather than repression, vertical splitting rather than dissociation, and transmuting internalization: "The novel combination of an adjective and a noun does not mean that we have a new and creative idea" (1978, p. 619). Similarly, the term "fragmentation" has come under considerable question by, for example, Rothstein (1980), who considers it a "jump toward abstraction embodied in the concept of 'fragmentation'" (p. 436) and by Kernberg (1982a) who questions the whole notion of "disintegration" products of the "'fragmentation' of a feeble self" (p. 375). London (1985) claims that fragmentation of the self is "simply another term for structural regression" (p. 97).

Ticho (1982) reports that "a considerable part of Heinz Kohut's theory of the psychology of the self is not as new as many seem to think" (p. 849); although the definitions of the self vary considerably among schools such as those of Adler, Jung, Horney, and Sullivan, concepts of the self played a central role in their theories. Indeed, Stepansky (1983) believes there is a close relationship between the work of Adler and Kohut, especially in their position as dissenters from the prevailing psychoanalytic tradition. Imber (1984) tries to delineate what she calls "some very striking similarities" as well as "some important differences" between the ideas of Sullivan and Kohut. Arguments for and against the similarities of Kohut's self psychology to theories of his earlier psychoanalytic predecessors rest on the assessment of the terminology used by Kohut's predecessors. Self-psychologists complain that this similarity is only superficial and that careful study of Kohut's use of the concept of self clearly differentiates him from his predecessors.

## THE DOUBLE-AXIS THEORY

Kohut's (1971) early concept of separate lines of development for libido and narcissism, often referred to as the "double-axis theory," quickly came under attack. Kernberg (1974, 1974a, 1975) repeatedly questions this theory. Hanly and Masson (1976) argue that it is untenable. Goldberg (1976) answers their attack by stating that when one says "narcissism is not a separate line of development," one is really saying, "I choose not to look at narcissism as a separate line of development" (p. 69). Lichtenberg (1978) regards the matter as unsettled and states that a fully assembled line of development for narcissism has not yet been delineated even in the self-psychological literature.

## INFANT CAPACITIES

Many authors such as Giovacchini (1982) argue that Melanie Klein, Kohut, and even Freud assume certain capacities in the infant that have not been demonstrated to exist; examples are the clear recognition of external objects and the capacity for introjection. These arguments often group Kohut's concept of the virtual self with Klein's complicated assumptions about the knowledge and fantasy life of the infantile ego. The "virtual" self of Kohut (1977, p. 101) is described in terms of increase or decrease in tension, not in terms of specific fantasies and perceptions, in contrast to Klein.

On the other hand, Kohut's theory is open to the question of whether the infant has sufficient self- and object-cognitive discrimination to form an idealized parent imago. Critics argue that the infant would need to be somewhat cognitively aware of the parent and the external world; a similar problem exists regarding Kohut's notion of the grandiose self.

## THE GRANDIOSE SELF

An even more important controversy revolves around whether the grandiose self is a normal developmental formation found in all children or whether it represents a pathological formation. Kernberg, influenced by the work of Klein, regards the grandiose self as a pathological structure. He attempts to describe the differential qualities of normal infantile narcissism and pathological narcissism, with special emphasis on the difference between the grandiosity of normal small children and the grandiosity expressed in pathologically narcissistic adult patients (1974a, p. 219). Kohut (1984) has answered this argument and Gedo (1977), although he offers an orientation different from both Kohut and Kernberg, disagrees with Kernberg's view that the grandiosity primarily defends against rage and aggression.

## THE ZEIGARNIK PHENOMENON

This postulate of self psychology (Kohut 1977) assumes that an inner motivation prompts undeveloped structures to resume their development when given the opportunity; the energy behind this motivation has nothing to do with Freud's concept of instinctual drives, and the origin of it is not explained. It rests on the Zeigarnik (1927) effect which, in Kohut's interpretation, refers to the finding that the interruption of any task leads to tension and to the tendency to resume that task at the earliest opportunity, relieving the tension. Self psychologists utilize the phenomenon to explain why selfobject transferences develop. They are believed to result from the Zeigarnik effect-based need to complete unfinished developmental tasks. It is necessary to appeal to such a concept if one eliminates the notion of drives as motivational in the formation of selfobject transferences; this leaves self psychology open to criticism from academic psychologists and metapsychologists. Slap and Levine (1978) write:

> We see no reason why the person would somehow sense a need for the structure he or she never had (and which is, in any case, a theoretical construct). Instead it is more economical to assume that a person that repetitively seeks objects similar to lost infantile objects is doing just that, for some combination of drive-gratifying and defensive reasons. (p. 509)

An important clinical derivative of this debate appears in the choice of interpretations of patient material and transference phenomena. The therapist must decide whether the data, even when manifestly sexual in nature, should be interpreted as representing issues concerning the formation of and defenses against selfobject transferences or object-instinctual transferences.

## AGGRESSION

The conceptualization of aggression is one of the most controversial aspects of self psychology. Kohut regards it as a disintegration product of normal assertiveness secondary to phase-inappropriate disappointment in selfobjects, and suggests that assertiveness may enter yet another line of development with transformations of its own. For early Kernberg, Melanie Klein, and traditional psychoanalysts, aggression arises from a primary drive of some kind. There are substantial differences between the later views of Kernberg and traditional psychoanalysts as to the genesis of aggression (Goldberg 1985). For later Kernberg (1982) it is intertwined with the earliest projected and then introjectively internalized object relations. In the later theories of Freud aggression is a manifestation of the death instinct, and Melanie Klein accepts this view.

It is difficult, considering the extreme primitive aggression that has been unleashed all over the world in the twentieth century, not to view aggression as a primary drive. It is also difficult (Tuttman 1978) to agree with self psychologists, who view aggression as a disintegration product, a manifestation of reactions to defective maternal empathy. Thus, Rothstein (1980) writes that self-psychology de-emphasizes a wellspring of basic rage that is part of every human being. It "de-emphasizes the instinctual biological underpinnings of the aggressive drive" (p. 432) as described by Freud. For Freud we are creatures beset by lustful and aggressive drives, confined by the superego and the demands of reality, attempting reluctantly to tame the drives and reach a compromise that would preserve as much drive satisfaction as possible. This leads to a basically pessimistic view of humanity not found in Kohut (Chessick 1984c).

Gedo (1979) reminds us that the rejection of the death instinct by most analysts leaves the important phenomena of the repetition compulsion without motivational explanation. Those traditional analysts who disagree with Kohut's description of aggression as a breakdown product of normal assertiveness will have to either embrace the death instinct as an explanatory concept, move on to various object relations theories, or develop conceptualizations of their own.

The question of whether there are primary drives, or whether all "drives" are disintegration products due to the failure of the selfobject matrix of the child, offers a clearer choice of solutions than the various conflicting theories of aggression. The study of the disintegration of normal assertiveness into aggression secondary to selfobject failure has experimental potential, and preliminary work has appeared (Lichtenberg, Bornstein, and Silver 1984a). The complete denial of any drives in the Freudian sense by self psychologists is one of the major differences in these two approaches.

## IDEALIZATION

The idealizing transference or idealization, especially when it arises in narcissistic or borderline personality disorders, is believed by Kernberg (1974, 1974a, 1975a) to represent a defense against oral rage, envy, and paranoid fears related to the projection of sadistic trends that would appear in the treatment as intense envy and deval-uation of the therapist. For Kernberg, such a transference needs to be interpreted so that the underlying sadism may emerge and be worked through in the treatment. For Kohut, the idealizing trans-ference is an important and desirable development in the treatment of narcissistic personalities and should be allowed to appear undis-turbed. It represents not a defense, but an attempt to take up once more the task of building the structure of the self, motivated by the Zeigarnik phenomenon. This "reluctant compliance" with the ideal-izing transference is a point of criticism of self psychology, since, if Kernberg is right, the effect would be collusion (Langs 1981) to hide the appearance of intense rage. This issue is not merely theoretical since every therapist is forced to choose between these approaches when deciding whether and how to interpret an idealizing trans-ference.

## TRANSMUTING INTERNALIZATION

Gedo (1980, 1984) complains about Kohut's concept of trans-muting internalization. He argues that it is essentially undefined, and that there is no evidence that it represents the curative process in the psychoanalysis of narcissistic disorders. Patton and Sullivan (1980) presented a detailed description of Kohut's concept of transmuting internalization and, although they regard it as a "difficult" concept, they attempt to place it in psychoanalytic perspective. A related, un-resolved issue arises from an examination of the similarities and dif-ferences in the traditional concepts of introjection, incorporation, and identification on the one hand, and transmuting internalization on the other. Much of the confusion in the literature arises from ignoring the crucial differences in orientation between Kohut's self psychology and traditional psychoanalysis. Transmuting internalization describes the building of the bipolar self, whereas the other concepts — introjection, incorporation, identification — assume the traditional drive theory and are related to the building of the ego and the superego.

We can watch the results attributed to transmuting internalization develop with patients if we are willing (at least temporarily) to accept the orientation of Kohut and think of the material as related to the vicissitudes of the state of the patient's self, a state we "observe" by vicarious introspection. The issue of whether transmuting internalization is a basic curative element in psychoanalytic treatment is related to the argument about whether there is a separate developmental line for narcissism. It rests on whether the therapist is willing to view the clinical data from Kohut's orientation.

## DREAM INTERPRETATION

A number of authors, such as Schafer (1985) and Stein (1979), insist that Kohut's so-called self-state dreams are interpreted on the basis of manifest content and therefore, Stein writes, "Kohut's view of dream interpretation is widely at variance with that established by Freud in 1900 and elaborated by analysts since then" (pp. 673–674). Stein believes that Kohut indulges in "anagogic interpretation" (Stein 1984), reviving a pre-Freudian view of dreaming. The example Stein (1979) gives is Kohut's (1977) analysis of the daydream of Mr. X. (pp. 203–211). To this argument Goldberg (1976) has already replied, "It should be unnecessary to explain that many dreams in our literature are presented for brevity's sake without all the associations; without thus condemning the writer for laxity" (p. 69).

Kohut (Lichtenberg and Kaplan 1983) denies that self-state dreams are interpreted from their manifest contents and points out that associations to such dreams, although they must be carefully noted, lead nowhere. This constitutes a clinical clue that we are dealing with a self-state dream! The argument over dream interpretation arises from the question of whether any clinical phenomena can be understood without reference to drives, defenses, and conflicts. To a traditional psychoanalyst who has been properly trained to investigate all clinical phenomena for the existence of drives, defenses, and conflicts, the notion of a self-state dream surely would appear to be a reversion to pre-Freudian mysticism.

## THE OEDIPAL PHASE AND THE OEDIPUS COMPLEX

Self psychology challenges the central postulate of Freud's psychoanalysis which maintains that the Oedipus complex is at the core of all adult psychoneuroses. Kohut (1977, 1984) accepts the existence of an oedipal phase in development, but he claims that in the normal situation it does not lead to an Oedipus complex. Only if the oedipal phase occurs in the presence of an enfeebled or fragmented self, or is responded to with phase inappropriate manifestations on the part of the parenting selfobjects, will there be the appearance of disintegration products from the normal oedipal phase (the lust and aggression that manifests itself as the Oedipus complex).

Wallerstein (1981) takes the position that although Kohut may be correct in his assertion that pathology of the oedipal phase is not as ubiquitous and basic to human psychic functioning as many have thought, "This to me in no way diminishes the basic nature and the ubiquity of the oedipal *conflict* as central to the vicissitudes of normal human development" (p. 388). A more typical view is Waldron's (1983) question as to whether Kohut's approach, which Waldron conceives of as "avoiding a full analysis of the elements of oedipal conflicts as they manifest themselves in the current life of the patient" (p. 628), can be claimed to lead to better therapeutic results. Waldron is skeptical of such a claim and argues that it has not been substantiated and that "it would appear to be at variance with accumulated clinical experience" (pp. 628–629).

The assumption that Kohut's approach avoids oedipal issues appears repeatedly in the literature. Glenn (1984) writes, "When an interpretation implicitly or explicitly excludes the sexual, the analyst encourages an incomplete and inexact analysis" (p. 320); he speaks here of material that has manifest sexual content. Rangell states (Richards 1984) that "the oedipal phase and castration anxiety are most often defended against and avoided in new theories. Etiologic foci are fixed conveniently on either side of the oedipal conflicts, avoiding them from above and from below" (p. 590). A similar complaint has less frequently been made by traditional psychoanalysts about Kernberg's work and about the contentions of other object relations theorists.

The interpretation of patient material regarding sexual activities and fantasies in terms of primarily nonsexual or narcissistic and structural deficit difficulties raises one of the most important disagreements between self psychologists and traditional analysts. It is hard to imagine how such a central disagreement could ever be resolved, and the literature is replete with criticism of this nature, pertaining especially to published case material of self psychologists.

Here is where Grünbaum's (1983, 1984) criticism of Freud's "tally" argument is well demonstrated, because both sides invoke this kind of argument to "prove" their claims. However, in the area of severe pathology, such as narcissistic and borderline personality disorders, the disagreement could arise out of the nature of the clinical data in itself, rather than from a shortcoming in psychoanalytic scientific method. In these cases, where the distinction between self and object is at a vanishing point, regardless of what theoretical conceptions are employed, other considerations besides the Oedipus complex become paramount. Furthermore, as Loewald (1980) points out, "as we become more aware of and better acquainted with these forms of mental functioning, we have also come to recognize that problems in the classical neuroses, which had been seen mainly in the light of psychosexual conflicts rooted in the oedipal phase, are often importantly codetermined by disruptive, distorting and inhibiting influences occurring during earlier phases" (p. 377).

CASE MATERIAL

In Chapter 13, I described criticisms of Kohut's (1979) "two analyses of Mr. Z." Two other paradigmatic cases of self psychology have been singled out for criticism. Stein (1979) challenged the case of Mr. M. presented by Kohut (1977), questioning Kohut's understanding of the dynamics of the case, his conception of the etiology of the patient's difficulties, and his actual psychoanalytic treatment procedure. Stein, like a number of other authors, remains unconvinced by the self-psychological explanations, interpretations, and techniques that are employed in the case.

Just as the case of Mr. M. is central to Kohut's (1977) presentation of the "psychology of the self in the broader sense," the case of Miss F. is central to Kohut's (1971) presentation of the "psychology of the self in the narrow sense." Kernberg (1974a) suggests that Kohut's interpretation of this case implicitly blamed "the patient's mother for having caused the patient's anger" and functions as "protecting the patient from full examination of the complex origins of her own rage" (p. 232). For Kernberg, Kohut's interpretation was inexact and supported the patient's defenses. Gedo (1984), working from his own point of view, also disagreed with Kohut's characterization of Miss F. — who responded with fury whenever his interventions went beyond whatever the analysand could have stated — as a patient that showed an aspect of a mirror transference requiring "echoing." As in the case of Mr. Z., self psychologists reply that case presentations are meant to be illustrations rather than "proofs" of points of view and are thus open to varying interpretations. Grünbaum (1983, 1984) would ask: What *are* proofs of points of view in psychoanalysis? Edelson (1984) answers that it *is* possible to obtain scientific proof in this field, provided that hypotheses are posed and clinically tested with proper regard for methodology.

### AMBIENCE

Self psychologists claim that the ambience of their treatment is more benevolent and to some extent different and perhaps even more curative than in the traditional practice of psychoanalysis (Wolf 1976). This is primarily a function of their increased emphasis on the empathic understanding of the patient at any given time and a recognition of the importance of responses to the patient based on empathic understanding. Traditional psychoanalysts find this claim difficult to accept, since they maintain it contains an underlying implication that they are not as empathic with their patients as self psychologists. This is a mistake in understanding the claim of the self psychologists involved, because it is a matter of emphasis and conviction regarding the importance of remaining closely attuned by vicarious introspection to the self-state of the patient at any given time. Therapists profoundly influenced by self psychology have kept their sensitivity to the reactions of their patients more in the foreground of their concentration; it is the common observation of this change in a therapist brought about by prolonged immersion in self psychology that lends credence to the claim of self-psychologists that they provide a more curative milieu. Traditional psychoanalysts reply that the issue here is one of countertransference and a properly analyzed analyst, and requires no new theoretical orientation.

## CORRECTIVE EXPERIENCE OR PSYCHOANALYSIS?

The statement that Kohut's form of psychoanalysis is not psychoanalysis runs through the critical literature on self psychology. This is a variant of the more general question of whether nurturing psychotherapies can be considered part of psychoanalysis or whether psychoanalysis should be restricted to cure solely through the interpretation of the transference neurosis. Kernberg (1974a) says Kohut's techniques "have re-educative elements in them which foster a more adaptive use of the patient's grandiosity" (p. 238). Friedman (1978) considers the controversy between Kohut and Kernberg as a reenactment of a long-standing debate about the importance of interpretation; he feels that interpretation has become increasingly central to psychoanalysis due to competition from many other psychotherapies which threaten the distinct identity of psychoanalysis.

Giovacchini (1978) writes, "This distillation of Kohut's technical orientation causes me to wonder what relevance any of his ideas have to analysis and how they differ from any supportive manipulation" (p. 619). Slap and Levine (1978) claim that Kohut's "therapeutic method depends on suggestion and learning, but not insight, conflict resolution, or making the unconscious conscious" (p. 507). If this is true, it is hard to see how Kohut's self psychology could be included under psychoanalysis.

Rothstein (1980) writes, "Kohut's work has evolved to the point where he is advocating a reparative object relationship to transmute a developmental interference" (p. 447). He regards the "psychology of the self in the broader sense" as a "radical departure" from Kohut's earlier work, and he points out that Kohut's (1971) first book was entitled *Analysis (of the Self)* and Kohut's (1977) second book was entitled *Restoration (of the Self)*. Rothstein continues, "It seems reasonable to conclude that if an analyst chooses to see himself primarily as a reparative object, a supportive psychotherapy has been conducted" (p. 448).

Basch (1981) would disagree with this formulation. As stated before, he judges a treatment to be a psychoanalysis if the pathology is

being brought into the transference to the analyst, interpreted so as to enhance the patient's understanding of himself and worked through to the point where the formerly malfunctioning structures have been restored or the defective structures strengthened to such an extent that the patient is capable of leading a productive life. (p. 345)

Based on this criterion Basch feels that Kohut's contribution "is in complete harmony with classical Freudian analysis" (p. 345).

Treurniet (Lichtenberg and Kaplan 1983) considers self psychology in the broader sense "a grave and serious loss" to psychoanalysis, "especially from the viewpoint of technique" (p. 194). He is worried about the impression that the self psychologist "rescues" the patient from an unempathic traditional analyst and he feels that the "psychology of the self in the broader sense," "is threatening to rob psychoanalysis of some of its most valuable technical conceptual tools, the dynamic and economic points of view" (p. 194).

Richards (1984) questions the emphasis on empathy in self psychology. Although it is an important and implicit premise of successful clinical work, it does not constitute the clinical work: "The theoretical and technical primacy accorded empathy by self psychology can serve at best to sensitize us to a single precondition for the successful application of a technique still properly rooted in classical conflict theory" (p. 600).

## SELF PSYCHOLOGY AND FREUD'S PSYCHOANALYSIS

The views of Kohut and Kernberg are irreconcilable and there are areas in which no substantive agreement can be found (Ornstein 1974). According to Greene (1984), self psychology is "best considered a psychology separate and distinct from psychoanalysis" (p. 52) because the concepts of self psychology differ significantly from those of psychoanalysis and conflict with psychoanalysis on many important theoretical issues. For Friedman (1980) Kohut's theory "is actually a different *kind* of theory from Freud's" (p. 409). I (1980a) have suggested that although the "psychology of the self in the narrow sense" is compatible with Freud's theories, the "psychology of the self in the broader sense" is not, and is based on a somewhat different, more holistic, and less Freudian notion of the self than the narrow sense theory. The employment of the concept of self in the narrow and broader sense theories is different and not entirely consistent between the theories.

Rothstein (1980a) maintains that Kohut moved from an original attempt to work within ego psychology to creating a new paradigm. After a brief review of Kuhn's (1962) theory about the evolution of scientific paradigms, Rothstein addresses the narcissistic investment in psychoanalytic paradigms and their creators in general, which he thinks contributes to "irrational polemical aspects of paradigm competition" (p. 394). The question of whether Kohut has offered a new paradigm or a complementary theory remains partly semantic, since Kuhn himself has regretted his use of the term because it is unfortunately vague. He attempted to replace it with terms such as "exemplars" and "models" (Kuhn 1977). I have maintained that Freud would probably accept the "psychology of the self in the narrow sense" as a complementary theory but would reject the "psychology of the self in the broader sense" as indeed representing a different paradigm — but Freud did not design his psychoanalysis for the treatment of narcissistic and borderline personality disorders.

Kohut's distinction between Guilty Man and Tragic Man has brought him close to some existentialist concepts, but there is a fundamental difference between self psychology and existential psychoanalysis; the former retains the unconscious as a central concept. Still, Kohut's emphasis on lack of maternal empathy has been accused of reductionism in a fashion similar to existential psychoanalysis, and has avoided the complexities of postulated intrapsychic phenomena such as those of Klein and Kernberg. Kohut is not in the tradition of existential or continental psychiatry or psychoanalysis, because his work emphasizes the self of the patient as "observed" by vicarious introspection, rather than concentrating on the self as a consciously choosing agent, on the phenomenology of self-awareness, or on the decentering of the self.

# Chapter 20

---

# Final Considerations

In their review of psychoanalytic theory, Greenberg and Mitchell (1983) contend that "each theorist declares his allegiance, explicitly or implicitly, to either the drive/structure model or the relational/structure model. This allegiance determines his theoretical strategy" (p. 380). Although psychoanalysts such as Kohut or Sandler have attempted to present what Greenberg and Mitchell call "mixed model strategies," they believe that "the evaluation of psychoanalytic theories is a matter of personal choice" (p. 407), and that all psychoanalytic theories are predicated upon certain philosophical presuppositions concerning the nature of man (Chessick 1980b).

## Noninterpretive Elements in Psychoanalytic Cure

Dorpat (1974) reviews the concept of the internalization of the patient-analyst relationship as it has appeared in traditional discussions of patients with narcissistic disorders. The tradition began with Freud (1940a), who states that psychoanalysis provides an opportunity for "after-education" for the patient: "It can correct mistakes for which his parents were responsible in educating him" (p. 175).

Strachey (1934), in his description of the central role of "mutative interpretations," pointed out that such interpretations effect an internalization of the analyst and the formation of new superego structures by a process he calls "infiltration" (p. 290). Dorpat (1974) proposes that "the reparative internalization process evolves from a stage of a fantasy relationship involving imitative identifications with the analyst, to a later stage of selective identifications with the analyst" (p. 183). He argues that the internalization of patient-transactions, described by Loewald (1962) as characteristic of all psychoanalytic treatment, is most obvious and crucial in the analysis of patients with developmental defects as compared to the analysis of patients with traditional neurotic disorders. Even in the standard psychoanalytic literature there continues an important debate about the role of noninterpretive elements in psychoanalytic cure.

Kohut (1984) recognizes that this issue is unresolved in self psychology and recommends a further study of his notion of transmuting internalization. He raises many significant questions. How does this take place? "Can enduring psychic functions be acquired with the aid of selfobjects" that are not identical with "an intermediate gross borrowing of the selfobject's functions?" (p. 100). What is the role of frustration in the psychology of the self? How is optimum frustration related to the laying down of psychic structure; how does optimum frustration lead to the building of this structure by transmuting internalization? What is the relationship between gross identifications with the selfobject analyst, and the process of transmuting internalization? "Is there a decisive difference . . . between the acquisition of psychic structure in adult life . . . in the course of psychoanalytic treatment, and the acquisition of psychic structure in childhood" (p. 101), and if so, what is this difference? As Kohut points out, the problem of the formation of psychic structure in the psychoanalytic process remains a critical, unresolved issue in both traditional psychoanalysis and self psychology.

Stone (1981) presents a review of the noninterpretive elements in psychoanalytic treatment as seen from beyond the vantage point of self psychology; his description of the psychoanalytic situation shows that the ambience of the treatment advocated by self psychology can emerge from traditional psychoanalytic considerations. Factors which determine a desirable ambience are:

1. The analyst's attitude, which should be reasonable, sensible, and not "equated with coldness, aloofness, arbitrary withholding,

callousness, detachment, ritualization, or panicky adherence to rules for their own sake" (p. 100).

2. The tone and rhetorical quality of the analyst's verbal interventions; Stone advocates "an affirmative affective tone" and warns us against the potential sadistic gratification that may dominate an analytic attitude as characterized in the quotation above.

3. Elasticity, which is best characterized by Freud's case presentations, in which "Freud's common sense is never excluded from his reservations and exceptions regarding the application of the more severe 'deprivations'" (p. 102). Stone believes it is implicit in Freud's method that "empathy is an integral part of analytic technique in any case" (p. 103) although he distinguishes this from Ferenczi's attempt to give patients the sort of demonstrative love of which they had been deprived in early childhood.

4. A climate, as demonstrated in Freud's case histories by Lipton (1977, 1979), in which can be established "a living personal relationship with each patient that was natural, friendly, and appropriate" (Stone 1981, p. 106n). When patients reacted to the personal relationship, Freud was ready to interpret such reactions but did not allow this to inhibit his naturalness.

5. Empathy. Stone does not believe that the analyst's mirroring empathy can make up for defects in the archaic selfobjects, but he does argue that it can make for a much better analysis. He sees no need for self psychology as a special system of therapy in which the treatment of the disorders of the self can be contrasted with the treatment of the neuroses of structural conflict.

6. Nuances of technical method: the atmosphere in which details such as fees, scheduling, and handling of the end of each hour, are treated by the therapist, as well as reactions to absences, intercurrent life crises, and other events. Atmosphere represents a critical noninterpretive element in psychoanalytic therapy.

7. The "indestructibility" of the analyst, as described by Winnicott (1969), when exposed to the intense hostility of patients is an important noninterpretive factor. Stone explains, "It must not be ignored that it is between the two adults that it all begins and ends. 'What sort of person is this to whom I am entrusting my entire mental and emotional being?'" (p. 113).

Beyond Freud's common sense, "there is no specific mode of communication for such attitudes" (p. 115), but there is an increasing body of opinion even in traditional psychoanalytic literature that the therapist who ignores these factors imperils the success of an expensive, arduous, and long-term treatment. Failure may mean the difference between psychological life and psychological death for a patient.

## Self Psychology's Impact on Psychoanalytic Therapy and Psychoanalysis

Important advances in the conceptualization of the process of listening to a patient in psychoanalytic psychotherapy have been made since Freud. The existential point of view stresses the encounter and assessment of the state of the patient's being-in-the-world, listening to the material without preconceptions, and following closely the phenomena of the encounter in order to react spontaneously. Kohut and his followers have elaborated our understanding and search for transferencelike structures — the mirror and idealizing transferences — as they manifest themselves in the patient's material, and have advocated a continuing assessment of the patient's sense of self, ranging from a firmed-up state to a fragmentation. Kernberg and other moderate neo-Kleinians have called our attention to projective identification and manifestations of split-off "all bad" self and object representations as they are projected onto the therapist, stressing the search for these in the material and behavior of the patient.

Langs (1981, 1982) presents a controversial view which stresses therapist pathology, the need of the patient to cure the therapist, and the spiraling communicative interaction (see Chessick 1982a). Blanck and Blanck (1973, 1979) have called attention to the reliving of early phases of ego development in the transference and patient-therapist interaction. These views are also controversial and lead to some directly conflicting clinical and theoretical approaches when compared to Langs. Blanck and Blanck require the therapist to be flexible, and they offer alternative ways of evaluating the patient's material which they say can lead to a considerable increase in opportunities for understanding and subsequent effective and correct interpretation.

There is a tendency for arguments on this topic to degenerate into emotional, wild analysis of the opponent, fostering the polarization of those who are "for" and "against" various positions. At this point we must treat different views as alternative possibilities which can enhance our skill at listening to patients in psychotherapy. Sometimes it is most valuable to try to shift from one view to the other, for example, from the traditional Freudian listening to the Bion style of listening without memory, desire, or understanding, especially in those cases where the therapy is not going well. This may provide new insights or hypotheses to be validated although the therapist must shift between inconsistent and irreconcilable positions.

I (1971, 1985c) have offered a series of suggestions for the teaching of psychoanalytic listening to psychotherapists in training. The special stance required, which must be learned painstakingly under careful supervision in order to tune in effectively to communications coming from the unconscious of the patient, is the hardest task to master in becoming empathic and sensitive in dyadic relationships.

In some instances, empathy is confused with specific technical interventions, as described by Schwaber (1981). She explains that "patients with more serious pathology seem to require some more active responsiveness on our part . . . we may feel we ought to say or do something more immediate . . . Such an intervention has often been taken as synonymous with an empathic response" (p. 128). However it is not direct interventions by the analyst that utilize the work of empathy — and indeed such interventions may demonstrate a lack of empathy — but the unrelenting search for the meaning of the patient's communications. The success or failure of this procedure is demonstrated by the interventions, or lack thereof, decided upon by the analyst. To try to think of patients simply as bearers of symptoms can be done in psychopharmacology; but in trying to enter into a person's life in order to make effective lasting interventions, the understanding of a novelist or the sensitivity of an artist are required. Schwaber (1983) reminds us that for a long time the scientific outlook obscured "the impact of the analyst-observer as *intrinsic* to the field of observation" (p. 386).

Schwaber (1979) believes that Kohut's (1971) monograph "can be singled out as having made a unique impact as a turning point in clinical theory development and in stimulating further creative endeavour" (p. 468). Transference, according to her version of self psychology, "shifts our perspective and deepens our focus on the interwoven matrix of the patient-analyst as a contextual unit" (p. 476). The self-psychological perspective in psychoanalysis for Schwaber involves listening from the orientation of empathy and vicarious introspection in order to discover how one is experienced and responded to as part of the other person; this opens up new avenues to psychoanalytic understanding of the patient. She (1983) emphasizes repeatedly the importance of this shift in perspective through which even our understanding of the phenomenon of resistance changes. We move from viewing resistance as a product of internal pressures within the patient to viewing it as a phenomenon "in which the specificity of the analyst's contribution was seen as intrinsic to its very nature" (p. 381). The old view, according to Schwaber, of assuming the analyst to be the silent arbiter of whether or not distortion has taken place, implies a hierarchy in the therapeutic relationship in which the one who knows the truth incurs "the risk thereby of subtly, if not overtly, guiding the patient in accord with this view" (p. 391). When analysts claim to be a blank screen, arbiters of reality and distortion, they ignore their own participation in their patients' distortions, as well as the possibility of countertransference affecting their decisions.

A noxious experience of the analyst in the transference may be intrinsic to the way in which the patient experiences the analyst, but the analyst may resist seeing this due to a wish to deny unwitting participation in the patient's experience. In this situation the analyst retreats to a position of assumed scientific independence and neutrality; the therapist becomes the judge of reality and distortion. This is an old problem in psychoanalysis: it is always possible that the attribution of patient material to "transference" can protect the analyst from recognizing his or her countertransference contribution to stimulating patient material. Gill (1982), working from an orientation outside self psychology, considers *all* transference material to be based on some stimulation from the analyst in the clinical situation, a view which is diametrically opposed to the "blank screen" orientation. I (1986) review this problem elsewhere, followed by a discussion from Gill.

Ornstein and Ornstein (1980) emphasize the impact of self-psychology on the formulation of interpretations in clinical psychoanalysis. Interpretations of transference and resistance have been based on the notion that the patient confuses the old and the new object in a distortion of reality. In transference interpretations or reconstructions, the analyst traditionally (explicitly or implicitly) "pointed to the anachronistic nature of the wish for satisfaction or reassurance and thereby aimed at correcting the distortion directly" (p. 208). According to Ornstein and Ornstein (1980), "Such attempts unnecessarily increase the unavoidable resistances, often create an excessively frustrating ambience, and foster those surface adaptations that preclude deep, intrapsychic structural change or the acquisition of new psychic structures" (p. 208).

These authors advocate what they call empathic reconstructive-interpretations, which focus on picking out the immediate precipitant of the patient's behavior, on trying to understand its transference meaning, and "acknowledging its appropriateness in the context of the regressive revival of the childhood constellation" (p. 208). The interpretation no longer tries to correct distortions in terms of adult reality but focuses on trying to understand and to explain the patient's childhood experiences "as the precursor of his present-day regressive response in the analysis, including the analyst's role in precipitating it" (p. 208). Ornstein and Ornstein believe that, if the process is based on correct empathic perception, understanding, and accurate reconstructions, the patient will feel understood and will take the initiative to explore these transference distortions. This, they contend, represents the felicitous road to structural change in psychoanalytic treatment.

## IS THERE A "TRADITIONAL PSYCHOANALYST"?

Many traditional psychoanalysts believe that views such as those of Schwaber and of Ornstein and Ornstein set up the traditional psychoanalyst as a straw man, a kind of caricature of an unempathic, aloof, arrogant, arbitrary authority figure who pressures the patient to accept his or her version of reality. There are many well analyzed and well trained psychoanalytic therapists, and since it is impossible to be in their consulting rooms and observe the details of their work with patients, the evidence that there is such an individual as a "traditional psychoanalyst" — caricature or not — is unconvincing.

Although a basic explanation of patient material by drive and conflict theory — emended by the followers of Freud (described by Greenberg and Mitchell [1983]) to extend the drive/structure orientation — may characterize the analyst's metapsychological or scientific convictions, adherence to the drive/structure model does not necessarily produce a "traditional psychoanalyst." Traditional or orthodox psychoanalysts who adhere to the drive/structure theory vary in their clinical practice, from those who studiously avoid noninterpretive interventions to those who emphasize the important curative factors involved in noninterpretive interventions.

Loewald (1980), once a student of Heidegger, wrote, "I suspect that there is no psychoanalytic understanding worthy of the name that leaves that which is to be understood altogether untouched and unchanged" (p. 381). Although he follows the traditional view that understanding is communicated to the patient by interpretation, he also adds that understanding represents an act to which the patient must be open and lend himself or herself. He concludes, "Understanding would seem to be an act that involves some sort of mutual engagement, a particular form of the meeting of minds" (p. 382).

The problem is made even more complicated because, as Schwaber (1983) points out:

> One of the most difficult challenges one encounters in reviewing the literature is to find clinical material which relates the specific details of the analyst's participation. More often, the patient's material is described in an already dynamically formulated fashion, with the reader deprived of the opportunity to learn what the analyst did or did not say. (p. 381)

Even if we had detailed transcripts and could assume that the recording of such transcripts did not have a profound effect on the psychoanalytic treatment itself, we would still have only a secondhand version of the noninterpretive interventions. This makes the problem of how to evaluate such interventions difficult to resolve.

CONCLUSION

It is general clinical knowledge that threats to previously traumatized patients can often provoke panic and impulsive self-destructive violence in their attempt to avoid the worst psychic catastrophe of all — fragmentation of the nuclear self. The psychotherapy of preoedipal patients, if based on an empathic understanding of their disappointment in archaic selfobjects and the catastrophic abuse from their early selfobjects, may well avert devastating self-fragmentation and self-destruction.

Generalizing on a universal scale, Kohut (1978) recommends intensification, elaboration, and expansion of man's inner life in order to reduce worldwide aggression and the threat of self-destruction of the species. Kohut's vision that individuals, families, and nations must relate through empathic understanding rests on his hope for the ex-

pansion of the inner life of the individual and for the higher development of the aesthetic and civilization potential of society at large.

This vision links Kohut's thought to the urbane nineteenth-century
tradition of the British man of letters, perhaps nowhere better and
more brilliantly expressed than in Matthew Arnold's (1869) essay on
"Culture and Anarchy." With Kohut we have come full circle, back
to the British tradition of the urbane, reasonable, tolerant, empathic
man who wants "a fuller harmonious development of our humanity, a free play of thought upon our routine notions, spontaneity of
consciousness, sweetness and light" (p. 191) that Arnold considers to
be "some lasting truth to minister to the diseased spirit of our time."

# References

———

ABEND, S., PORDER, M., AND WILLICK, M. (1983). *Borderline Patients: Psychoanalytic Perspectives.* New York: International Universities Press.

ABRAHAM, K. (1919). A particular form of neurotic resistance against the psychoanalytic method. In *Selected Papers on Psychoanalysis.* London: Hogarth Press, 1949.

ADLER, G. (1981). The borderline-narcissistic personality disorder continuum. *American Journal of Psychiatry* 138:1–50.

AICHORN, A. (1955). *Wayward Youth.* New York: Meridian Books.

AKHTAR, S., AND THOMSON, J. (1982). Overview: Narcissistic personality disorder. *American Journal of Psychiatry* 139:1–20.

ALEXANDER, F. (1950). *Psychosomatic Medicine.* New York: Norton.

AMIS, M. (1985). *Money: A Suicide Note.* New York: Viking.

APPELS, A., POOL, J., AND VAN DER DOES, E. (1979). Psychological prodromata of myocardial infarction. *Journal of Psychosomatic Research* 23: 405–421.

ARLOW, J., AND BRENNER, C. (1984). *Psychoanalytic Concepts and the Structural Theory.* New York: International Universities Press.

ARNOLD, M. (1869). *Culture and Anarchy,* ed. R. Super. Ann Arbor: University of Michigan Press, 1980.

BACH, S. (1975). Narcissism, continuity and the uncanny. *International Journal of Psycho-Analysis* 56:77–86.

_____ (1977). On the narcissistic state of consciousness. *International Journal of Psycho-Analysis* 58:209–233.

_____ (1977a). On narcissistic fantasies. *International Review of Psycho-Analysis* 4:281–293.

BAK, R. (1973). Being in love and object loss. *International Journal of Psycho-Analysis* 54:1–8.

BALINT, M. (1953). *Primary Love and Psycho-Analytic Technique*. New York: Liveright.

_____ (1968). *The Basic Fault: Therapeutic Aspects of Regression*. London: Tavistock.

BARNES, H. (1980–1981). Sartre's concept of the self. *Review of Existential Psychology and Psychiatry* 17:41–66.

BASCH, M. (1980). *Doing Psychotherapy*. New York: Basic Books.

_____ (1981). Selfobject disorders and psychoanalytic theory: A historical perspective. *Journal of the American Psychoanalytic Association* 29:337–351.

_____ (1983). Empathic understanding: A review of the concept and some theoretical considerations. *Journal of the American Psychoanalytic Association* 31:101–126.

BETTELHEIM, B. (1982). *Freud and Man's Soul*. New York: Knopf.

BICK, E. (1968). The experience of the skin in early object-relations. *International Journal of Psycho-Analysis* 49:484–486.

BION, W. (1963). *Elements of Psycho-Analysis*. New York: Basic Books.

_____ (1967). *Second Thoughts: Selected Papers on Psycho-Analysis*. London: Heinemann.

BLANCK, G., AND BLANCK, R. (1973). *Ego Psychology*. New York: Columbia University Press.

_____ (1979). *Ego Psychology*, vol. II. New York: Columbia University Press.

BORNSTEIN, M. (1984). Commentaries on Merton Gills's *Analysis of Transference*. *Psychoanalytic Inquiry* 4:391–392, 446.

BREU, G. (1979). Medics: Heinz Kohut. *People Weekly* 11:60–63.

BREUER, J., AND FREUD, S. (1893–1895). Studies on Hysteria. *Standard Edition* 2:1–305.

BROAD, C. (1978). *Kant: An Introduction*. Cambridge: Cambridge University Press.

BROWN, L., AND HAUSMAN, A. (1981). Intentionality and the unconscious: A comparison of Sartre and Freud. In *The Philosophy of Jean-Paul Sartre*, ed. P. Schilpp. La Salle, Ill.: Open Court.

BRUCH, H. (1973). *Eating Disorders*. New York: Basic Books.

_____ (1974). *Learning Psychotherapy*. Cambridge: Harvard University Press.

_____ (1975). Anorexia nervosa. In *American Handbook oj Psychiatry*, 2nd ed., vol. IV, ed. S. Arieti. New York: Basic Books.

_____ (1979). *The Golden Cage*. New York: Vintage Books.

_____ (1982). Anorexia nervosa: Therapy and theory. *American Journal of Psychiatry* 139:1531–1538.

BUIE, D. (1981). Empathy: Its nature and limitations. *Journal of the American Psychoanalytic Association* 29:281–308.

BUTLER, C. (1984). Commentary. In *Hegel: The Letters*, trans. C. Butler and C. Seiler. Bloomington: Indiana University Press.

CALDER, K. (1980). An analyst's self-analysis. *Journal of the American Psychoanalytic Association* 28:5–20.

CALEF, V., AND WEINSHEL, E. (1979). The new psychoanalysis and psychoanalytic revisionism. *Psychoanalytic Quarterly* 48:470–491.

CANNON, W. (1953). *Bodily Changes in Pain, Hunger, Fear and Rage*. Boston: Branford.

CANTWELL, D., STURZENBERGER, S., BURROUGHS, J., SALKIN, B., AND BREEN, J. (1977). Anorexia nervosa: An affective disorder. *Archives of General Psychiatry* 34:1087–1096.

CARRUTHERS, M. (1974). *The Western Way of Death*. New York: Pantheon Books.

CASPER, R. (1983). On the emergence of bulimia nervosa as a syndrome. *International Journal of Eating Disorders* 2:3–16.

_____, AND DAVIS, J. (1977). On the course of anorexia nervosa. *American Journal of Psychiatry* 134:974–978.

_____, HALMI, K., GOLDBERG, S., ECKART, E., AND DAVIS, J. (1979). Disturbances in body image estimation as related to other characteristics and outcome in anorexia nervosa. *British Journal of Psychiatry* 134:60–66.

_____, OFFER, D., AND OSTROV, J. (1981). The self-image of adolescents with acute anorexia nervosa. *Journal of Pediatrics* 98:656–661.

CASSIMATIS, E. (1984). The "false self": Existential and therapeutic issues. *International Review of Psychoanalysis* 11:69–77.

CHESSICK, R. (1960). The "pharmacogenic orgasm" in the drug addict. *Archives of General Psychiatry* 3:545–556.

_____ (1965). Empathy and love in psychotherapy. *American Journal of Psychotherapy* 19:205–219.

_____ (1966). Office psychotherapy of borderline patients. *American Journal of Psychotherapy* 20:600–614.

_____ (1968). The "crucial dilemma" of the therapist in the psychotherapy of borderline patients. *American Journal of Psychotherapy* 22:655–666.

_____ (1969). *How Psychotherapy Heals*. New York: Science House.

_____ (1971). *Why Psychotherapists Fail*. New York: Science House.

_____ (1971a). The use of the couch in psychotherapy of borderline patients. *Archives of General Psychiatry* 26:306–313.

_____ (1972). The development of angiospastic retinopathy during the intensive psychotherapy of a borderline patient. *Archives of General Psychiatry* 27:241–244.

_____ (1972a). Externalization and existential anguish. *Archives of General Psychiatry* 27:764–770.

_____ (1973). Contributions to ego psychology from the treatment of borderline patients. *Medikon* 2:20–21.

_____ (1974). *The Technique and Practice of Intensive Psychotherapy*. New York: Jason Aronson.

_____ (1974a). Defective ego feeling and the quest for Being in the borderline patient. *International Journal of Psychoanalytic Psychotherapy* 3:73–89.

_____ (1974b). The borderline patient. In *American Handbook of Psychiatry*, 2nd ed., vol. 3, ed. S. Arieti. New York: Basic Books.

_____ (1976). *Agonie: Diary of a Twentieth Century Man*. Ghent, Belgium: European Press.

_____ (1977). *Intensive Psychotherapy of the Borderline Patient*. New York: Jason Aronson.

_____ (1977a). *Great Ideas in Psychotherapy*. New York: Jason Aronson.

_____ (1978). Countertransference crises with borderline patients. *Current Concepts in Psychiatry* 4:20–24.

_____ (1979). A practical approach to the psychotherapy of the borderline patient. *American Journal of Psychotherapy* 33:531–546.

_____ (1980). *Freud Teaches Psychotherapy*. Indianapolis: Hackett.

_____ (1980a). The problematical self in Kant and Kohut. *Psychoanalytic Quarterly* 49:456–473.

_____ (1980b). Some philosophical assumptions of intensive psychotherapy. *American Journal of Psychotherapy* 34:496–509.

_____ (1982). Intensive psychotherapy of a borderline patient. *Archives of General Psychiatry* 39:413–422.

_____ (1982a). Psychoanalytic listening: With special reference to the views of Langs. *Contemporary Psychoanalysis* 18:613–634.

_____ (1983). *A Brief Introduction to the Genius of Nietzsche*. Washington, D.C.: University Press of America.

_____ (1983a). Problems in the intensive psychotherapy of the borderline patient. *Dynamic Psychotherapy* 1:20–32.

_____ (1983b). Marilyn Monroe: Psychoanalytic pathography of a preoedipal disorder. *Dynamic Psychotherapy* 1:161–176.

_____ (1983c). *The Ring*: Richard Wagner's dream of preoedipal destruction. *American Journal of Psychoanalysis* 43:361–374.

_____ (1984). Sartre and Freud. *American Journal of Psychotherapy* 38: 229–238.

_____ (1984a). Was Freud wrong about feminine psychology? *American Journal of Psychoanalysis* 44:355–368.

_____ (1984b). A failure in psychoanalytic psychotherapy of a schizophrenic patient. *Dynamic Psychotherapy* 2:136–156.

_____ (1984c). Matthew Arnold, the death instinct, and the future of man. *Cogito* 2:31–48.

_____ (1985). Prolegomena to the study of Paul Ricoeur's "Freud and Philosophy." In press.

_____ (1985a). The search for the authentic self in Bergson and Proust. In. *Psychoanalytic Perspectives in Literature and Film*, eds. J. Reppen and M. Charney. Madison, N.J.: Farleigh Dickinson University Press.

_____ (1985b). Clinical notes towards the understanding and intensive psychotherapy of adult eating disorders. *Annual of Psychoanalysis* 13:301–322.

_____ (1985c). Psychoanalytic listening II. *American Journal of Psychotherapy* 39:30–48.

_____ (1986). Transference and countertransference revisited. *Dynamic Psychotherapy*. In press.

_____ (1986a). Heidegger for psychotherapists. *American Journal of Psychotherapy*. In press.

_____ (1986b). Kohut and the contemporary continental tradition: A comparison of Kohut with Lacan and Foucault. *Dynamic Psychotherapy: Theoretical and Clinical Contributions*, ed. P. Buirski. New York: Brunner/Mazel. In press.

_____, AND BASSAN, M. (1968). Experimental approaches to the concept of empathy in psychotherapy. In *An Evaluation of the Results of Psychotherapy*, ed. S. Lesse. Springfield, Ill.: Charles C Thomas.

CLÉMENT, C. (1983). *The Lives and Legends of Jacques Lacan*, trans. A. Goldhammer, New York: Columbia University Press.

CLEMENTS, C. (1982). Misusing psychiatric models: The culture of narcissism. *Psychoanalytic Review* 69:283–295.

COLLIER, A. (1977). *R. D. Laing: The Philosophy and Politics of Psychotherapy*. Hassocks, England: Harvester Press.

CREASE, R., AND MANN, C. (1984). How the universe works. *Atlantic Monthly*, 254:66–93.

CREWS, F. (1980). Analysis terminable. *Commentary* 70:25–34.

DALLY, P. (1969). *Anorexia Nervosa*. New York: Grune & Stratton.

Darwin, C. (1965). *The Expression of Emotion in Man and Animals*. Chicago: University of Chicago Press.

Davis, G. (1976). Depression: Some updated thoughts. *Journal of the Academy of Psychoanalysis* 4:411–424.

De Beauvoir, S. (1984). *Adieux: A Farewell to Sartre*. New York: Pantheon Books.

Dembroski, T., MacDougall, J., Williams, R., Haney, T., and Blumenthal, J. (1985). Components of Type A, hostility, and anger-in: Relationship to angiographic findings. *Psychosomatic Medicine* 47:219–233.

De Wald, P. (1964). *Psychotherapy*. New York: Basic Books.

Dorpat, T. (1974). Internalization of the patient-analyst relationship in patients with narcissistic disorders. *International Journal of Psycho-Analysis* 55:183–188.

Dreyfus, H., and Rabinow, P. (1982). *Michel Foucault: Beyond Structuralism and Hermeneutics*. Chicago: University of Chicago Press.

Dryud, J. (1984). Sartre and psychoanalysis: What can we learn from a lover's quarrel?. *Contemporary Psychoanalysis* 20:230–244.

Eagle, M. (1984). *Recent Developments in Psychoanalysis*. New York: McGraw-Hill.

Edel, L. (1969). *Henry James: The Treacherous Years: 1895–1901*. Philadelphia: Lippincott.

Edelson, M. (1984). *Hypothesis and Evidence in Psychoanalysis*. Chicago: University of Chicago Press.

Eissler, K. (1953). The effect of the structure of the ego on psychoanalytic technique. *Journal of the American Psychoanalytic Association* 1:104–143.

———— (1971). Death drive, ambivalence, and narcissism. *Psychoanalytic Study of the Child* 26:25–78.

———— (1975). The fall of man. *Psychoanalytic Study of the Child* 30:589–646.

Ellenberger, H. (1970). *The Discovery of the Unconscious: The History and Evolution of Dynamic Psychiatry*. New York: Basic Books.

Ellis, H. (1898). Auto-erotism: A psychological study. *Alienist and Neurologist* 19:260–299.

Ewing, A. (1967). *A Short Commentary on Kant's "Critique of Pure Reason."* Chicago: University of Chicago Press.

Fairbairn, W. (1963). Synopsis of an object-relations theory of the personality. *International Journal of Psycho-Analysis* 44:224–225.

Fairlie, H. (1977). Sloth or acedia. *New Republic*, October 29, 1977, pp. 20–33.

FEDERN, P. (1947). Principles of psychotherapy in latent schizophrenia. *American Journal of Psychotherapy* 2:129–147.

FENICHEL, O. (1945). *The Psychoanalytic Theory of Neurosis.* New York: Norton.

FERENCZI, S. (1955). *Selected Papers. Volume III: Final Contributions to the Problems and Methods of Psychoanalysis.* New York: Basic Books.

FERGUSON, M. (1981). Progress and theory change: The two analyses of Mr. Z. *Annual of Psychoanalysis* 9:133–160.

FINLAY-JONES, R. (1983). Disgust with life in general. *Australian New Zealand Journal of Psychiatry* 17:149–162.

FLIESS, R. (1942). The metapsychology of the analyst. *Psychoanalytic Quarterly* 2:211–227.

FOUCAULT, M. (1972). *The Archaeology of Knowledge,* trans. A. Smith. New York: Pantheon Books.

——— (1973). *Madness and Civilization,* trans. A. Smith. New York: Vintage.

——— (1973a). *The Order of Things.* New York: Vintage.

——— (1980). *Power/Knowledge: Selected Interviews and Other Writings,* ed. C. Gordon. New York: Pantheon Books.

——— (1980a). *The History of Sexuality,* vol. I, trans. R. Hurley. New York: Vintage.

FOX, R. (1984). The principle of abstinence reconsidered. *International Review of Psychoanalysis* 11:227–236.

FRENCH, T., AND FROMM, E. (1964). *Dream Interpretation.* New York: Basic Books.

FREUD, A. (1971). Difficulties in the path of psychoanalysis: A confrontation of past with present viewpoints. In *The Writings of Anna Freud,* vol. VII. New York: International Universities Press.

FREUD, S. (1905). Three essays on the theory of sexuality. *Standard Edition* 7:125–248.

——— (1905a). Fragment of an analysis of a case of hysteria. *Standard Edition* 7:3–124.

——— (1911). Psycho-analytic notes on an autobiographical account of a case of paranoia (dementia paranoides). *Standard Edition* 12:3–84.

——— (1912). Recommendations to physicians practising psycho-analysis. *Standard Edition* 12:109–120.

——— (1914). On narcissism: An introduction. *Standard Edition* 14:67–104.

——— (1914a). On the history of the psycho-analytic movement. *Standard Edition* 14:1–66.

——— (1917). Mourning and melancholia. *Standard Edition* 14:237–258.

——— (1920). Beyond the pleasure principle. *Standard Edition* 18:3–66.

_____ (1921). Group psychology and the analysis of the ego. *Standard Edition* 18:67–144.

_____ (1923). The ego and the id. *Standard Edition* 19:3–68.

_____ (1926). Inhibitions, symptoms and anxiety. *Standard Edition* 20: 77–178.

_____ (1930). Civilization and its discontents. *Standard Edition* 21:59–148.

_____ (1933). New introductory lectures on psychoanalysis. *Standard Edition* 22:3–184.

_____ (1937). Analysis terminable and interminable. *Standard Edition* 23:209–254.

_____ (1940). Splitting of the ego in the process of defense. *Standard Edition* 23:273–278.

_____ (1940a). An outline of psycho-analysis. *Standard Edition* 23:141–208.

Friedman, E., and Hellerstein, H. (1973). Influence of psychosocial factors on coronary risk and adaptation to a physical fitness evaluation program. In *Exercise Testing and Exercise Training in Coronary Heart Disease*, ed. J. Naughton and H. Hellerstein. New York: Academic Press.

Friedman, L. (1978). Trends in the psychoanalytic theory of treatment. *Psychoanalytic Quarterly* 47:524–567.

_____ (1980). Kohut: A book review essay. *Psychoanalytic Quarterly* 49: 393–422.

Friedman, M. (1969). *Pathogenesis of Coronary Artery Disease*. New York: McGraw-Hill.

_____, and Rosenman, R. (1974). *Type-A Behavior and Your Heart*. New York: Knopf.

_____, and Ulmer, D. (1984). *Treating Type-A Behavior and Your Heart*. New York: Knopf.

Fromm-Reichmann, F. (1950). *Principles of Intensive Psychotherapy*. Chicago: University of Chicago Press.

Frosch, J. (1977). The relation between acting out and disorders of impulse control. *Psychiatry* 40:295–314.

Garner, D., Garfinkel, P., Stancer, H., and Moldofsky, H. (1976). Body image disturbances in anorexia nervosa and obesity. *Psychosomatic Medicine* 38:327–336.

Gediman, H. (1975). Reflection on romanticism, narcissism, and creativity. *Journal of the American Psychoanalytic Association* 23:407–423.

Gedo, J. (1977). Notes on the psychoanalytic management of archaic transferences. *Journal of the American Psychoanalytic Association* 25:787–803.

_____ (1979). Theories of object relations: A metapsychological assessment. *Journal of the American Psychoanalytic Association* 27:361–374.

_____ (1980). Reflections on some current controversies in psychoanalysis. *Journal of the American Psychoanalytic Association* 28:363–384.

_____ (1984). *Psychoanalysis And Its Discontents*. New York: Guilford Press.

_____, AND GOLDBERG, A. (1973). *Models of the Mind: A Psychoanalytic Theory*. Chicago: University of Chicago Press.

GILL, M. (1982). *Analysis of Transference*, vol. I. New York: International Universities Press.

GIOVACCHINI, P. (1977). A critique of Kohut's theory of narcissism. *Adolescent Psychiatry* 5:213-239.

_____ (1978). Discussion in symposium on Kohut's "Restoration of the Self." *Psychoanalytic Review* 65:617-620.

_____ (1979). *Treatment of Primitive Mental States*. New York: Jason Aronson.

_____ (1982). *A Clinician's Guide to Reading Freud*. New York: Jason Aronson.

GITELSON, M. (1952). The emotional position of the analyst in the psychoanalytic situation. *International Journal of Psycho-Analysis* 33:1-10.

GLENN, J. (1984). Review of "Practice And Precept In Psychoanalytic Technique: Selected Papers of Rudolph M. Loewenstein." *Psychoanalytic Quarterly* 53:315-322.

GLOVER, E. (1956). *On the Early Development of Mind*. New York: International Universities Press.

GOETHE, J. VON (1774). *The Sufferings of Young Werther*, trans. B. Morgan. New York: Ungar, 1954.

GOLDBERG, A. (1975). The evolution of psychoanalytic concepts of depression. In *Depression and Human Existence*, ed. E. Anthony and T. Benedek. Boston: Little, Brown.

_____ (1976). A discussion of the paper by C. Hanly and J. Masson. *International Journal of Psycho-Analysis* 57:67-70.

_____ (ed.) (1978). *The Psychology of the Self: A Casebook*. New York: International Universities Press.

_____ (ed.) (1980). *Advances in Self Psychology*. New York: International Universities Press.

_____ (1980a). Letter to the editor. *International Journal of Psycho-Analysis* 61:91-92.

_____ (1982). Obituary: Heinz Kohut. *International Journal of Psycho-Analysis* 63:257-258.

_____ (ed.) (1983). *The Future of Psychoanalysis*. New York: International Universities Press.

_____ (1983a). On the scientific status of empathy. *Annual of Psychoanalysis* 11:155-159.

GOLDBERG, D. (1985). Panel: On the concept "object" in psychoanalysis. *Journal of the American Psychoanalytic Association* 33:167-186.

GOODSITT, A. (1985). Self psychology and the treatment of anorexia nervosa.

In *Handbook of Psychotherapy for Anorexia Nervosa and Bulemia*, ed. D. Garner and P. Garfinkel. New York: Guilford Press.

GRAVES, R. (1955). *The Greek Myths*, vol. I. Baltimore: Penguin.

GREENBERG, J., AND MITCHELL, S. (1983). *Object Relations in Psychoanalytic Theory*. Cambridge: Harvard University Press.

GREENE, M. (1984). The self psychology of Heinz Kohut. *Bulletin of the Menninger Clinic* 48:37–53.

GREENSON, R. (1960). Empathy and its vicissitudes. *International Journal of Psychoanalysis* 41:418–424.

GRINKER, R., AND WERBLE, B. (1975). *The Borderline Patient*. New York: Jason Aronson.

GRÜNBAUM, A. (1983). Freud's theory: the perspective of a philosopher of science. *Proceedings of the American Philosophical Association* 57:5–31.

_____ (1984). *The Foundations of Psychoanalysis*. Berkeley: University of California Press.

GUNTHER, M. (1976). The endangered self: A contribution to the understanding of narcissistic determinants of countertransference. *Annual of Psychoanalysis* 4:201–224.

GUNTRIP, H. (1974). Psychoanalytic object relations theory: The Fairbairn-Guntrip approach. In *American Handbook of Psychiatry*, 2nd ed., vol. 1, ed. S. Arieti. New York: Basic Books.

_____ (1975). My experience of analysis with Fairbairn and Winnicott. *International Review of Psychoanalysis* 2:145–156.

HAMBURGER, W. (1951). Emotional aspects of obesity. *Medical Clinics of North America* 35:483–499.

HANLY, C. (1979). *Existentialism and Psychoanalysis*. New York: International Universities Press.

_____, AND MASSON, J. (1976). A critical examination of the new narcissism. *International Journal of Psycho-Analysis* 57:49–66.

HARTMANN, H. (1927). Understanding and explanation. In *Essays on Ego Psychology*. New York: International Universities Press, 1964.

_____ (1950). Comments on the psychoanalytic theory of the ego. In *Essays on Ego Psychology*. New York: International Universities Press, 1964.

HEIMANN, P. (1966). Comment on Dr. Kernberg's paper. *International Journal of Psycho-Analysis* 47:254–260.

HOFFMAN, N. (1984). Meyer Friedman: Type A behavior cardiovascular research continues. *Journal of the American Medical Association* 252:1385–1393.

HOLZMAN, P. (1976). The future of psychoanalysis and its institutes. *Psychoanalytic Quarterly* 45:250–273.

HUNTER, P. (1977). Sartre's existential humanism and Freud's existential naturalism. *Psychoanalytic Review* 64:289–298.

HURST, J., LOGUE, R., SCHLANT, R., AND WENGER, N., eds. (1974). *The Heart: Arteries and Veins*. New York: McGraw-Hill.

HUSSERL, E. (1913). *Ideas: General Introduction to Pure Phenomenology*, trans. W. Gibson. New York: Macmillan, 1952.

IMBER, R. (1984). Reflections on Kohut and Sullivan. *Contemporary Psychoanalysis* 20:363–380.

INGRAM, D. (1976). Psychoanalytic treatment of the obese person. *American Journal of Psychoanalysis* 36:227–235.

INNAURATO, A. (1977). *The Transfiguration of Benno Blimpie*. London: T. Q. Publications.

JACOBSON, E. (1964). *The Self and the Object World*. New York: International Universities Press.

JAMES, M. (1973). Review of *The Analysis of the Self*. *International Journal of Psycho-Analysis* 54:363–368.

JANIK, A., AND TOULMIN, S. (1973). *Wittgenstein's Vienna*. New York: Simon and Schuster.

JASPERS, K. (1972). *General Psychopathology*. Chicago: University of Chicago Press.

JENKINS, C. (1971). Psychological and social precursors of coronary disease. *New England Journal of Medicine* 28:244–255, 307–317.

_____ (1976). Recent evidence supporting psychological and social risk factors for coronary disease. *New England Journal of Medicine* 294:987–994, 1033–1038.

JONES, E. (1955). *The Life and Work of Sigmund Freud*, vol. 2. New York: Basic Books.

JOSEPH, E., AND WALLERSTEIN, R., eds. (1982). *Psychotherapy: Impact on Psychoanalytic Training*. New York: International Universities Press.

JUNG, C. (1933). *Modern Man in Search of a Soul*. New York: Harcourt Brace.

KAINER, R. (1984). From "evenly-hovering attention" to "vicarious introspection": Issues of listening in Freud and Kohut. *American Journal of Psychoanalysis* 44:103–114.

KANT, E. (1781). *Critique of Pure Reason*, trans. N. Smith. New York: St. Martin's Press, 1965.

KAPLAN, H., FREEDMAN, A., AND SADOCK, B. (1980). *Comprehensive Textbook of Psychiatry*, 3rd ed. Baltimore: Williams and Wilkins.

KATZ, R. (1963). *Empathy, Its Nature and Uses*. New York: Glencoe Free Press.

KAUFMANN, W. (1980). *Discovering the Mind*. New York: McGraw-Hill.

KERNBERG, O. (1972). Critique of the Kleinian school. In *Tactics and Tech-*

*niques in Psychoanalytic Therapy*, ed. P. Giovacchini. New York: Science House.

_____ (1974). Contrasting viewpoints regarding the nature and psychoanalytic treatment of narcissistic personalities: a preliminary communication. *Journal of the American Psychoanalytic Association* 22:255–267.

_____ (1974a). Further contributions to the treatment of narcissistic personalities. *International Journal of Psycho-Analysis* 55:215–240.

_____ (1975). *Borderline Conditions and Pathological Narcissism*. New York: Jason Aronson.

_____ (1975a). Further contributions to the treatment of narcissistic personalities: A reply to the discussion by Paul H. Ornstein. *International Journal of Psycho-Analysis* 56:245–248.

_____ (1976). *Object Relations Theory and Clinical Psychoanalysis*. New York: Jason Aronson.

_____ (1980). *Internal World and External Reality*. New York: Jason Aronson.

_____ (1980a). Melanie Klein. In *Comprehensive Textbook of Psychiatry*, 3rd ed., ed. H. Kaplan, A. Freedman, and B. Sadock. Baltimore: Williams and Wilkins.

_____ (1982). Self, ego, affects and drives. *Journal of the American Psychoanalytic Association* 30:893–917.

_____ (1982a). Review of *Advances In Self Psychology*. *American Journal of Psychiatry* 139:374–375.

Kierkegaard, S. (1859). *The Point of View for My Work as an Author: A Report to History*, trans. W. Lowrie. New York: Harper and Row, 1962.

Klein, M. (1975). *Envy and Gratitude and Other Works 1946–1963*. New York: Delta.

Klein, M., and Tribich, D. (1981). Kernberg's object-relations theory: A critical evaluation. *International Journal of Psycho-Analysis* 62:27–43.

Kleist, H. (1976). *The Marquise of O — and Other Stories*, trans. M. Greenberg. New York: Ungar.

Kohut, H. (1966). Forms and transformations of narcissism. *Journal of the American Psychoanalytic Association* 14:243–272.

_____ (1968). The psychoanalytic treatment of narcissistic personality disorders. *Psychoanalytic Study of the Child* 23:86–113.

_____ (1971). *The Analysis of the Self*. New York: International Universities Press.

_____ (1977). *The Restoration of the Self*. New York: International Universities Press.

_____ (1978). *The Search for the Self*, ed., P. Ornstein. New York: International Universities Press.

_____ (1979). The two analyses of Mr. Z. *International Journal of Psycho-Analysis* 60:3–27.

———— (1982). Introspection, empathy, and the semi-circle of mental health. *International Journal of Psycho-Analysis* 63:395–407.

———— (1984). *How Does Analysis Cure?* Chicago: University of Chicago Press.

————, AND WOLF, E. (1978) The disorders of the self and their treatment: An outline. *International Journal of Psycho-Analysis* 59:413–425.

KOLB, L., AND BRODIE, H. (1982). *Modern Clinical Psychiatry*. Philadelphia: Saunders.

KRYSTAL, H. (1982). Adolescence and the tendencies to develop substance dependence. *Psychoanalytic Inquiry* 2:581–618.

————, AND RASKIN, H. (1970). *Drug Dependence: Aspects of Ego Function*. Detroit: Wayne State University Press.

KUHN, T. (1962). *The Structure of Scientific Revolutions*. Chicago: University of Chicago Press.

———— (1977). *The Essential Tension: Selected Studies in Scientific Tradition and Change*. Chicago: University of Chicago Press.


LACAN, J. (1968). *Speech and Language in Psychoanalysis*, trans. A. Wilden. Baltimore: Johns Hopkins University Press.

———— (1977). *Écrits: A Selection*, trans. A. Sheridan. New York: Norton.

———— (1978). *The Four Fundamental Concepts of Psycho-Analysis*, trans. A. Sheridan. New York: Norton.

LAING, R. (1960). *The Divided Self*. New York: Pantheon Books.

LANGS, R. (1981). *Resistances and Interventions*. New York. Jason Aronson.

———— (1982). *Psychotherapy: A Basic Text*. New York: Jason Aronson.

LASCH, C. (1978). *The Culture of Narcissism*. New York: Norton.

LEAVY, S. (1980). *The Psychoanalytic Dialogue*. New Haven: Yale University Press.

LEIDER, R. (1983). Analytic neutrality: A historical review. *Psychoanalytic Inquiry* 3:655–674.

———— (1984). Panel report on the neutrality of the analyst in the analytic situation. *Journal of the American Psychoanalytic Association* 32:573–586.

LEMAIRE, A. (1981). *Jacques Lacan*. London: Routledge and Kegan Paul.

LEON, G. (1982). Personality and behavioral correlates of obesity. In *Psychological Aspects of Obesity*, ed. B. Wolman. New York: Van Nostrand and Reinhold.

LEVINE, M. (1961). Principles of psychiatric treatment. In *The Impact of Freudian Psychiatry*, ed. F. Alexander and H. Ross. Chicago: University of Chicago Press.

LEVY, S. (1985). Empathy and psychoanalytic technique. *Journal of the American Psychoanalytic Association* 33:353–378.

LICHTENBERG, J. (1973). Review of *The Analysis of the Self. Bulletin of the Philadelphia Association of Psychoanalysis* 23:58–66.

_____ (1978). Is there a line of development of narcissism?. *International Review of Psychoanalysis* 5:435–447.

_____, AND KAPLAN, S., eds. (1983). *Reflections on Self Psychology.* Hillsdale, N.J.: Analytic Press.

_____, BORNSTEIN, M., AND SILVER, D. (1984). *Empathy*, vol. I. Hillsdale, N.J.: The Analytic Press.

_____, BORNSTEIN, M., AND SILVER D. (1984a). *Empathy*, vol. II. Hillsdale, N.J.: The Analytic Press.

LIPTON, S. (1977). The advantages of Freud's technique as shown in his analysis of the Rat Man. *International Journal of Psycho-Analysis* 58: 255–273.

_____ (1979). An addendum to "The advantages of Freud's technique as shown in his analysis of the Rat Man." *International Journal of Psycho-Analysis* 60:215–216.

LITTLE, M. (1981). *Transference Neurosis and Transference Psychosis.* New York: Jason Aronson.

LOEWALD, H. (1962). Internalization, separation, mourning, and the superego. *Psychoanalytic Quarterly* 31:483–504.

_____ (1973). Review of *The Analysis of the Self. Psychoanalytic Quarterly* 42:441–451.

_____ (1980). *Papers on Psychoanalysis.* New Haven: Yale University Press.

LOEWENSTEIN, R., NEWMAN, L., SCHUR, M., AND SOLNIT, A., eds. (1966). *Psychoanalysis — A General Psychology.* New York: International Universities Press.

LONDON, N. (1985). An appraisal of self psychology. *International Journal of Psycho-Analysis* 66:95–108.

MAASS, J. (1983). *Kleist: A Biography.* Trans. A. Manheim. New York: Farrar, Straus and Giroux.

MACCOBY, M. (1976). *The Gamesman: The New Corporate Leader.* New York: Simon and Schuster.

MAHLER, M., PINE, F., AND BERGMAN, A. (1975). *The Psychological Birth of the Human Infant.* New York: Basic Books.

MALCOLM, J. (1981). *Psychoanalysis: The Impossible Profession.* New York: Knopf.

MASSON, J. ed. (1985). *The Complete Letters of Sigmund Freud to Wilhelm Fliess: 1877–1904.* Cambridge, MA: Harvard University Press.

MASTERSON, J. (1976). *Psychotherapy of the Borderline Adult: A Developmental Approach.* New York: Brunner/Mazel.

MEAD, G. (1962). *Mind, Self, and Society.* Chicago: University of Chicago Press.

MEISSNER, W. (1978). Notes on some conceptual aspects of borderline personality organization. *International Review of Psychoanalysis* 5:297–311.

———— (1978a). Theoretical assumptions of concepts of the borderline personality. *Journal of the American Psychoanalytic Association* 26:559–598.

———— (1978b). *The Paranoid Process*. New York: Jason Aronson.

———— (1980). Classical psychoanalysis. In *Comprehensive Textbook of Psychiatry*, 3rd ed., ed. H. Kaplan, A. Freedman, and B. Sadock. Baltimore: Williams and Wilkins.

———— (1980a). The problem of internalization and structure formation. *International Journal of Psycho-Analysis* 61:237–248.

———— (1984). *The Borderline Spectrum*. New York: Jason Aronson.

MENNINGER, R. (1958). *Theory of Psychoanalytic Technique*. New York: Basic Books.

MEYERS, S. (1981). Panel on the bipolar self. *Journal of the American Psychoanalytic Association* 29:143–160.

MISCHEL, T. (1977). *The Self: Psychological and Philosophical Issues*. Oxford: Blackwell.

MITCHELL, S. (1981). Heinz Kohut's theory of narcissism. *American Journal of Psychoanalysis* 41:317–326.

———— (1984). The problem of the will. *Contemporary Psychoanalysis* 20: 257–265.

MODELL, A. (1963). Primitive object relations and the predisposition to schizophrenia. *International Journal of Psycho-Analysis* 44:282–292.

———— (1968). *Object Love and Reality*. New York: International Universities Press.

———— (1976). The holding environment and the therapeutic action of psychoanalysis. *Journal of the American Psychoanalytic Association* 24:255–307.

MOLDOFSKY, H. (1984). Clinical research at the interface of medicine and psychiatry. In *Psychiatry Update*, vol. III, ed. L. Grinspoon. Washington, D.C.: American Psychiatric Press.

MONEY-KRYLE, R. (1974). The Kleinian school. In *American Handbook of Psychiatry*, 2nd ed., vol. I, ed. S. Arieti. New York: Basic Books.

MONTGOMERY, P. (1981). Obituary—Heinz Kohut. *New York Times*, October 10, 1981, p. 17.

MOORE, B., AND FINE, D., eds. (1967). *A Glossary of Psychoanalytic Terms and Concepts*. New York: American Psychoanalytic Association.

MULLER, J., AND RICHARDSON, W. (1982). *Lacan and Language: A Reader's Guide to Écrits*. New York: International Universities Press.

MURDOCH, I. (1980). *Sartre: Romantic Realist*. New York: Barnes and Nobel.

MURPHY, W. (1973). Narcissistic problems in patients and therapists. *International Journal of Psychoanalytic Psychotherapy* 2:113–124.

MYERSON, P. (1981). The nature of the transactions that occur in other than classical analysis. *International Review of Psychoanalysis* 8:173–189.

NACHT, S. (1962). The curative factors in psychoanalysis. *International Journal of Psychoanalysis* 43:206–211.

ODIER, C. (1956). *Anxiety and Magic Thinking*. New York: International Universities Press.

OFFENKRANTZ, W., AND TOBIN, A. (1974). Psychoanalytic psychotherapy. *Archives of General Psychiatry* 30:593–606.

ORNSTEIN, P. (1974). A discussion of the paper by Otto F. Kernberg on "Further contributions to the treatment of narcissistic personalities." *International Journal of Psychoanalysis* 55:241–247.

_____ (1981). The bipolar self in the psychoanalytic treatment process: Clinical-theoretical considerations. *Journal of the American Psychoanalytic Association* 29:353–376.

_____, AND ORNSTEIN, A. (1980). Formulating interpretations in clinical psychoanalysis. *International Journal of Psychoanalysis* 61:203–212.

ORNSTON, D. (1985). Freud's conception is different from Strachey's. *Journal of the American Psychoanalytic Association* 33:379–412.

OSTOW, M. (1979). Letter to the editor. *International Journal of Psycho-Analysis* 60:531–532.

OXFORD (1970). *English Dictionary*. Oxford: Oxford University Press.

PALMER, R. (1969). *Hermeneutics: Interpretation Theory in Schleiermacher, Dilthey, Heidegger, and Gadamer*. Evanston, Ill.: Northwestern University Press.

PAO, P. (1983). Therapeutic empathy and the treatment of schizophrenics. *Psychoanalytic Inquiry* 3:145–167.

PATTON, M., AND SULLIVAN, J. (1980). Heinz Kohut and the classical psychoanalytic tradition: An analysis in terms of levels of explanation. *Psychoanalytic Review* 67:365–388.

PETERFREUND, E. (1971). *Information, Systems, and Psychoanalysis: An Evolutionary Biological Approach to Psychoanalytic Theory*. New York: International Universities Press.

PFLANZE, O. (1972). Toward a psychoanalytic interpretation of Bismark. *American Historical Review* 77:419–444.

POLAND, W. (1974). On empathy in analytic practice. *Journal of the Philadelphia Association for Psychoanalysis* 1:284–297.

_____ (1975). Tact as a psychoanalytic function. *International Journal of Psycho-Analysis* 56:155–162.

_____ (1984). On the analyst's neutrality. *Journal of the American Psychoanalytic Association* 32:283–299.

Pope, H., Hudson, J., Jonas, J., and Yurgelun-Tood, D. (1983). Bulemia treated with imipramine. *American Journal of Psychiatry* 140:554–558.

Powers, P. (1980). *Obesity: The Regulation of Weight*. Baltimore: Williams and Wilkins.

Proust, M. (1981). *Remembrance of Things Past*, trans. C. Moncreiff, R. Kilmartin, and A. Mayor. New York: Random House.

Pruyser, P. (1975). What splits in "splitting"? *Bulletin of the Menninger Clinic* 39:1–46.

Quinn, S. (1980). Oedipus vs. Narcissus. *New York Times Magazine* November 9, 1980, pp. 120–131.

Rado, S. (1926). The psychic effects of intoxication. In *Psychoanalysis of Behavior: Collected Papers of Sandor Rado*. New York: Grune and Stratton, 1956.

Rangell, L. (1981). From insight to change. *Journal of the American Psychoanalytic Association* 29:119–142.

────── (1981a). Psychoanalysis and dynamic psychotherapy: Similarities and differences twenty-five years later. *Psychoanalytic Quarterly* 50:665–693.

────── (1985). The object in psychoanalytic theory. *Journal of the American Psychoanalytic Association* 33:301–334.

Reich, A. (1960). Pathological forms of self-esteem regulation. *Psychoanalytic Study of the Child* 15:215–232.

Reik, T. (1949). *Listening with the Third Ear*. New York: Farrar, Straus.

Richards, A. (1982). Panel Report on psychoanalytic theories of the self. *Journal of the American Psychoanalytic Association* 30:717–734.

────── (1982a). The supraordinate self in psychoanalytic theory and in the self psychologies. *Journal of the American Psychoanalytic Association* 30:939–958.

────── (1984). Panel report on the relation between psychoanalytic theory and psychoanalytic technique. *Journal of the American Psychoanalytic Association* 32:587–602.

Ricoeur, P. (1970). *Freud and Philosophy: An Essay on Interpretation*. New Haven: Yale University Press.

────── (1974). *The Conflict of Interpretations*. Evanston, Ill.: Northwestern University Press.

Riesman, D., Glazer, N., and Denney, R. (1950). *The Lonely Crowd: A Study of the Changing American Character*. New York: Doubleday.

Rimé, E., and Bonami, M. (1979). Overt and covert personality traits associated with coronary heart disease. *British Journal of Medical Psychology* 52:77–84.

Roazen, P. (1975). *Freud and His Followers*. New York: Knopf.

ROBBINS, M. (1980). Current controversy in object relations theory as an outgrowth of a schism between Klein and Fairbairn. *International Journal of Psycho-Analysis* 61:477–492.

———— (1982). Narcissistic personality as a symbiotic character disorder. *International Journal of Psycho-Analysis* 63:457–473.

ROSENFELD, H. (1964). On the psychopathology of narcissism: A clinical approach. *International Journal of Psycho-Analysis* 45:332–337.

———— (1971). A clinical approach to the psychoanalytic theory of the life and death instincts: An investigation into the aggressive aspects of narcissism. *International Journal of Psycho-Analysis* 52:169–178.

ROSSNER, J. (1983). *August*. Boston: Houghton Mifflin.

ROTENBERG, C. (1983). A contribution to the theory of treatment of personality disorders. *Journal of the American Academy of Psychoanalysis* 11:227–249.

ROTHSTEIN, A. (1980). Toward a critique of the psychology of the self. *Psychoanalytic Quarterly* 49:423–455.

———— (1980a). Psychoanalytic paradigms and their narcissistic investment. *Journal of the American Psychoanalytic Association* 28:385–396.

SACHS, D. (1979). On the relationship between psychoanalysis and psychoanalytic psychotherapy. *Journal of the Philadelphia Association for Psychoanalysis* 6:119–145.

SADOW, L. (1969). Ego axis in psychopathology. *Archives of General Psychiatry* 21:15–24.

SARTRE, J. (1964). *Nausea*. New York: New Directions.

———— (1973). *Being and Nothingness*, trans. H. Barnes. New York: Washington Square Press.

———— (1976). *Critique of Dialectical Reason*. London: New Left Books.

———— (1984). *War Diaries*. New York: Pantheon Books.

SATOW, R. (1983). Response to Colleen Clements's "Misusing psychiatric models: The culture of narcissism." *Psychoanalytic Review* 69:296–302.

SCHAFER, R. (1968). *Aspects of Internalization*. New York: International Universities Press.

———— (1985). Wild analysis. *Journal of the American Psychoanalytic Association* 33:275–300.

SCHNEIDERMAN, S. (1983). *Jacques Lacan: The Death of an Intellectual Hero*. Cambridge: Harvard University Press.

SCHUR, M. (1972). *Freud: Living and Dying*. New York: International Universities Press.

SCHWABER, E. (1979). On the "self" within the matrix of analytic theory. Some clinical reflections and reconsiderations. *International Journal of Psycho-Analysis* 60:467–479.

_____ (1981). Narcissism, self psychology, and the listening perspective. *Annual of Psychoanalysis* 9:115–131.

_____ (1983). Psychoanalytic listening and psychic reality. *International Review of Psychoanalysis* 10:379–392.

SCHWARTZ, L. (1973). Panel report on technique and prognosis in the treatment of narcissistic personality disorders. *Journal of the American Psychoanalytic Association* 21:617–632.

_____ (1978). Review of *The Restoration of the Self. Psychoanalytic Quarterly* 47:436–443.

SCRUTON, R. (1982). *Kant.* Oxford: Oxford University Press.

SEARLES, H. (1985). Separation and loss in psychoanalytic therapy with borderline patients: Further remarks. *American Journal of Psychoanalysis* 45:9–27.

SEGAL, H. (1974). *Introduction to the Work of Melanie Klein.* New York: Basic Books.

_____ (1980). *Melanie Klein.* New York: Viking.

_____ (1983). Some clinical implications of Melanie Klein's work: Emergence from narcissism. *International Journal of Psycho-Analysis* 64: 269–276.

SENNETT, R. (1984). *An Evening of Brahms.* New York: Knopf.

SHAINESS, N. (1979). The swing of the pendulum — from anorexia to obesity. *American Journal of Psychoanalysis* 39:225–235.

SHAPIRO, E. (1978). The psychodynamics and developmental psychology of the borderline patient: A review of the literature. *American Journal of Psychiatry* 135:1305–1315.

SHAPIRO, T. (1974). The development and distortions of empathy. *Psychoanalytic Quarterly* 43:4–25.

_____ (1981). Empathy: A critical evaluation. *Psychoanalytic Inquiry* 1: 423–448.

SILVERMAN, M. (1985). Countertransference and the myth of the perfectly analyzed analyst. *Psychoanalytic Quarterly* 54:175–199.

SLAP, J., AND LEVINE, F. (1978). On hybrid concepts in psychoanalysis. *Psychoanalytic Quarterly* 47:499–523.

SMITH, N. (1962). *A Commentary to Kant's Critique of Pure Reason.* New York: Humanities Press.

SOLBERG, L. (1984). Lassitude: A primary care evaluation. *Journal of the American Medical Association* 251:3272–3276.

SOLL, I. (1981). Sartre's rejection of the Freudian unconscious. In *The Philosophy of Jean-Paul Sartre,* ed. P. Schilpp. La Salle, Ill.: Open Court.

SPEER, A. (1970). *Inside the Third Reich: Memoirs.* New York: Macmillan.

SPILLIUS, E. (1983). Some developments from the work of Melanie Klein. *International Journal of Psycho-Analysis* 674:321–332.

SPITZER, R., Chairperson (1980). Diagnostic and Statistical Manual of Mental Disorders, 3rd ed. Washington, D.C.: American Psychiatric Association.

SPRUIELL, V. (1974). Theories of the treatment of narcissistic personalities. *Journal of the American Psychoanalytic Association* 22:268–278.

STEIN, M. (1979). Review of *The Restoration of the Self. Journal of the American Psychoanalytic Association* 27:665–680.

_____ (1984). Rational versus anagogic interpretation: Xenophon's dream and others. *Journal of the American Psychoanalytic Association* 32: 529–556.

STEPANSKY, P. (1983). Perspectives on dissent: Adler, Kohut, and the idea of a psychoanalytic research tradition. *Annual of Psychoanalysis* 9:51–74.

STEPANSKY, P., AND GOLDBERG, A., eds. (1984). *Kohut's Legacy: Contributions to Self Psychology*. Hillsdale, N.J.: Analytic Press.

STERBA, R. (1982). *Reminiscences of a Viennese Psychoanalyst*. Detroit: Wayne State University Press.

STONE, L. (1961). *The Psychoanalytic Situation*. New York: International Universities Press.

_____ (1981). Notes on the noninterpretive elements in the psychoanalytic situation and process. *Journal of the American Psychoanalytic Association* 29:89–118.

STRACHEY, J. (1934). The nature of the therapeutic action of psychoanalysis. *International Journal of Psycho-Analysis* 15:127–159.

STUNKARD, A., AND BURT, V. (1967). Obesity and the body image II. *American Journal of Psychiatry* 123:1443–1447.

_____ (1975). Obesity. In *American Handbook of Psychiatry*, 2nd ed., vol. IV, ed. S. Arieti. New York: Basic Books.

_____ (1980). Obesity. In *Comprehensive Textbook of Psychiatry*, 3rd. ed., vol. II, ed. H. Kaplan, A. Freedman, and B. Sadock. Baltimore: Williams and Wilkins.

STURROCK, J., ed. (1979). *Structuralism and Since: From Lévi Strauss to Derrida*. New York: Oxford University Press.

SULLIVAN, H. (1953). *The Interpersonal Theory of Psychiatry*. New York: Norton.


TARACHOW, S. (1963). *An Introduction to Psychotherapy*. New York: International Universities Press.

TARTAKOFF, H. (1966). The normal personality in our culture and the Nobel Prize complex. In *Psychoanalysis: A General Psychology*, ed. R. Loewenstein, L. Newman, M. Schur, and A. Solnit. New York: International Universities Press.

TAYLOR, C. (1975). *Hegel*. New York: Cambridge University Press.

TEICHOLZ, J. (1978). A selective review of the psychoanalytic literature on theoretical conceptualizations of narcissism. *Journal of the American Psychoanalytic Association* 26:831–862.

TICHO, E. (1982). The alternate schools and the self. *Journal of the American Psychoanalytic Association* 30:849–862.

TOLPIN, P. (1983). A change in the self: The development and transformation of an idealizing transference. *International Journal of Psycho-Analysis* 64:461–483.

TREURNIET, N. (1983). Psychoanalysis and self psychology: A metapsychological essay with a clinical illustration. *Journal of the American Psychoanalytic Association* 31:59–100.

TRILLING, L. (1971). *Sincerity and Authenticity: Six Lectures*. Cambridge: Harvard University Press.

TUCHMAN, B. (1984). *The March of Folly*. New York: Knopf.

TURKLE, S. (1978). *Psychoanalytic Politics*. New York: Basic Books.

TUTTMAN, S. (1978). Discussion in symposium on Kohut's *Restoration of the Self*. *Psychoanalytic Review* 65:624–629.

VOLKAN, V. (1976). *Primitive Internalized Object Relations*. New York: International Universities Press.

WAELDER, R. (1930). The principle of multiple function: Observations on overdetermination. *Psychoanalytic Quarterly* 5:45–62.

WALDRON, S. (1983). Review of *Doing Psychotherapy* by Michael Franz Basch. *Psychoanalytic Quarterly* 52:624–629.

WALLERSTEIN, R. (1981). The bipolar self: Discussion of alternative perspectives. *Journal of the American Psychoanalytic Association* 29:377–394.

WEBSTER (1961). *New International Dictionary of the English Language*. Springfield: Merriam.

WEISS, E., AND ENGLISH, O. (1957). *Psychosomatic Medicine: A Clinical Study of Psychophysiologic Reactions*. Philadelphia: Saunders.

WILLIAMS, R., HANEY, T., LEE, K., KONG, Y., BLUMENTHAL, J., AND WHALEN, R. (1980). Type-A behavior, hostility, and coronary artherosclerosis. *Psychosomatic Medicine* 42:539–549.

WILLIAMSON, A. (1984). *Introspection and Contemporary Poetry*. Cambridge: Harvard University Press.

WILSON, C., ed. (1983). *Fear of Being Fat*. New York: Jason Aronson.

WINNICOTT, D. (1953). Transitional objects and transitional phenomena: A study of the first not-me possession. *International Journal of Psycho-Analysis* 34:89–97.

——— (1958). *Collected Papers: Through Paediatrics to Psycho-Analysis*. New York: Basic Books.

_____ (1965). *The Maturational Process and the Facilitating Environment.* New York: International Universities Press.

_____ (1969). The use of an object. *International Journal of Psycho-Analysis* 50:711–716.

_____ (1971). Letter to Mme. Jeannine Kalmanovitch. *Nouvelle Revue de Psychoanalyse*, vol. 3. Quoted by M. Kahn in the Introduction to *Winnicott's Collected Papers*, 2nd ed. Toronto: Clarke, Irwin, 1975.

WOLF, E. (1976). Ambience and abstinence. *Annual of Psychoanalysis* 4: 101–115.

_____ (1979). Transference and countertransference in analysis of disorders of the self. *Contemporary Psychoanalysis* 15:577–594.

_____ (1980). Tomorrow's self: Heinz Kohut's contribution to adolescent psychiatry. *Adolescent Psychiatry* 8:41–50.

_____, GEDO, J., AND TERMAN, D. (1972). On the adolescent process as a transformation of the self. *Journal of Youth and Adolescence* 1:257–272.

WOLLHEIM, R. (1984). *The Thread of Life.* Cambridge: Harvard University Press.

WOOD, A. (1981). *Karl Marx.* London: Routledge and Kegan Paul.

WOOLCOTT, P. (1981). Addiction: Clinical and theoretical considerations. *Annual of Psychoanalysis* 9:189–206.

WOOLEY, S., AND WOOLEY, O. (1980). Eating disorders: Obesity and anorexia. In *Women and Psychotherapy*, ed. A. Brodsky and R. Hare-Muslin. New York: Guilford Press.

ZEIGARNIK, B. (1927). Über das Behalten von erledigten und unerlodigten Handlungen. *Psychologische Forschung* 9:1–85.

# Index